HOPE AND FEAR

HOPE AND FEAR

Modern Myths, Conspiracy Theories and Pseudo-History

RONALD H. FRITZE

REAKTION BOOKS

For Twylia
My love, friend, wife, adventuress and dog whisperer

Published by
REAKTION BOOKS LTD
Unit 32, Waterside
44–48 Wharf Road
London N1 7UX, UK

www.reaktionbooks.co.uk

First published 2022
Copyright © Ronald H. Fritze 2022

Printed and bound in Great Britain
by Bell & Bain, Glasgow

A catalogue record for this book is available from the British Library

ISBN 978 1 78914 539 7

Contents

If men were always able to regulate their affairs with sure judgment, or if fortune always smiled upon them, they would not get caught up in any superstition. But since people are often reduced to such desperate straits that they cannot arrive at any solid judgment and as the good things of fortune for which they have a boundless desire are quite uncertain, they fluctuate wretchedly between hope and fear. This is why most people are quite ready to believe anything. When the mind is in a state of doubt, the slightest impulse can easily steer it in any direction, and all the more readily when it is hovering between hope and fear, though it may be confident, pompous, and proud enough at other times.

Benedict de Spinoza, *Theological-Political Treatise* (1670)

INTRODUCTION

The hardest things to understand about much of the past are its errors and delusions.

J. M. ROBERTS[1]

A great deal of intelligence can be invested in ignorance when the need for illusion is deep.

SAUL BELLOW[2]

People will believe the strangest things. In the early decades of the twenty-first century, that seems to be distinctly true. Myth, pseudo-history, pseudoscience and conspiracy theories appear to be swelling up at a bewildering rate. Or maybe it just seems that way to the people living through it. The fact is that myths, meaning tales that people believe to be true but are not, have been around from the beginning of human history. Technology like the Internet has simply made it easier to create and to spread strange beliefs and modern myths.

Queen Elizabeth II of the United Kingdom is a victim of a variety of weird beliefs and conspiracy theories. The American right-wing extremist and conspiracist Lyndon LaRouche had long been anti-British and accused British financiers of all sorts of nefarious tricks and plots to manipulate the global economy. In 1980, he added the queen to his cast of villains and accused her of being a world-class drug dealer. It became a rant that LaRouche and his acolytes continued to repeat throughout the rest of the decade. Eventually LaRouche lost interest, but the queen's problems with conspiracy theories were not over.[3] New Age guru and evolving conspiracist David Icke decided that Elizabeth II was a shape-shifting reptilian alien.

Icke is a former football player, sportscaster and Green Party politician. In 1994, his focus shifted from environmental issues to include conspiracy theories. His initial ideas followed the standard New World Order conspiracy script of a secret and corrupt elite trying to dominate the world. Within a few years, however, Icke took his conspiracy theory to a new level with his book *The Biggest Secret* (1999), which claimed that the New World Order conspiracies were actually being controlled by a super-elite of reptilian aliens whom he called the Archons. They most appropriately came to Earth from the constellation Draco and they have thoroughly infiltrated the leadership of human society. The reptilians are shape-shifters and can take on the appearance of humans. Many world leaders, such as George H. W. Bush, were reptilians. The ranks of the Archons, of course, included Elizabeth II. One has to marvel at the tight-lipped discretion of the palace staff, who have ensured that this astonishing information has remained a secret. Maybe they are reptilians as well?[4]

The death of Princess Diana in 1997 resulted in a new flurry of conspiracy theories, some of which included the royal family. LaRouche and his people quickly became involved. They accused the royals of having Diana killed to prevent her marrying Dodi Fayed because he was a Muslim. Predictably, Icke also developed in great detail his own conspiracy theory about Diana's death in *The Biggest Secret*. According to Icke, the reptilian royal family need periodic infusions of human DNA from approved bloodlines in order to maintain their ability to conceal themselves among humans. In Princess Diana's case, her family, the Spencers, were descendants of the Merovingian dynasty made famous in popular culture by the books *The Holy Blood and the Holy Grail* and *The Da Vinci Code*. That royal pedigree made Princess Diana a perfect mate for Prince Charles. What she discovered was that she had married into a clan of humanoid lizards and her only purpose was to be a royal brood mare. Otherwise, her marriage was a sham. After the two little princes were born, Princess Diana became superfluous. Once she started to create problems, she needed to be eliminated. That set of circumstances led to her death, which was also a sort of ritualistic sacrifice.[5]

Obviously to most people these conspiracy theories postulating drug-dealing monarchs and covert reptilian elites are absurd. The implausibility and preposterousness of this speculation does not stop people from believing it. LaRouche had a following and Icke's is larger and more international. Starting out as a sage of the New Age, Icke went on to fuse it with a version of New World Order conspiracism spiced up by the addition of a nasty reptilian elite. This combination allowed Icke to appeal to both generally leftist New Agers and normally right-wing conspiracists. Although the right-wing conspiracist Alex Jones initially disparaged Icke's reptilian thesis, eventually he came to warmly embrace it. Icke became a popular guest on Jones's radio show *InfoWars*.[6] Icke's conception of the reptilians shifted after a few years. They became more spiritual interdimensional beings than physical interstellar travellers. The spiritual reptilians were also more benign than the malevolent physical reptilians.[7]

Queen Elizabeth II is not the only head of state to become personally entangled with conspiracy theories. Barack Obama, the 44th President of the United States, suffered through several conspiracy theories that questioned just who he truly was. One version claimed that he was the Antichrist and another that he was a secret Muslim agent. One more claimed that Obama had not been born in the United States and so was not eligible to serve as president. The second and third conspiracy theories fitted together quite nicely and mutually reinforce each other. Devotees of the one call Obama 'the Muslim' while supporters of the other call him 'the Kenyan'.[8]

The birther theory, which claims that Obama was not born in the United States, has never faded away, unlike the Antichrist or Muslim theories. It goes back to 2004 when the fringe conspiracist Andy Martin began questioning the origins of the rapidly rising young politician. Martin's initial focus, however, was on Obama being a secret Muslim. It was not until 1 March 2008 that someone going by the handle FARS published a post on the Webforum Free Republic that claimed Obama had taken his oath as a senator using the Koran. In addition, it asserted that Obama was not born in the United States and that his mother had flown him to Hawaii and registered his birth there. No evidence was offered to support these claims, but they were now loose on the Internet, where evidence is optional and indeed not preferred. FARS's claims quickly gained attention and a growing following. The Republican leadership was more responsible at that time and worried that such ludicrous claims could backfire on their party. Reflecting this concern, the mainstream conservative *National Review Online* published a column on birtherism by James Geraghty on 9 June 2008. It was titled 'Obama Could Debunk Some Rumors by Releasing His Birth Certificate'. Geraghty was a birther sceptic and his column pointed out the trivial and implausible nature of the birther claim, urging the Obama campaign to spike it by releasing his birth certificate. The next day a second article appeared pointing out that there was little information on a birth certificate that could hurt Obama's presidential campaign. In response, Obama's campaign released his short-form birth certificate and Geraghty pronounced it to be valid proof of Obama's birth in Hawaii.[9]

Unfortunately, the *National Review*'s debunking provided birtherism with much greater exposure and even a degree of legitimacy in the minds of people looking for reasons to dislike and to discredit Obama. Some supporters of Hillary Clinton aggravated the situation by going rogue and sending out an anonymous email stating that Obama was born in Kenya and had been flown to Hawaii, where his mother registered his birth. Fringe Obama-haters proceeded to make a fairly clear situation murkier by filing multiple frivolous lawsuits seeking proof of Obama's foreign birth, forging supposed Kenyan birth certificates or questioning the authenticity of his Hawaiian birth certificate. The situation became so ridiculous that judges began fining or threatening to fine people bringing these nuisance lawsuits to court. By 2009, mainstream Republicans began repudiating birtherism, with Michael Medved being the first conservative commentator to break with it publicly. Not being totally immune to the lure of conspiracy theories, Medved speculated that birtherism might be a conspiracy to make conservatives look crazy.[10]

Birtherism subsided for a time but never went away. It revived in 2011 as Obama's first term as president was coming to an end and the presidential election of 2012 was looming on the horizon. During February 2011, Donald Trump, known as a reality TV star and a flamboyant and controversial businessman, spoke to a meeting of the Conservative Political Action Committee (CPAC) and raised the birther issue. It was a good choice of talking point for an audience with a large component of Obama-haters. When Trump took his birther theories to Fox News on the conservative commentator Bill O'Reilly's show, O'Reilly scoffed at the idea. Fox's viewers, also a group with a significant proportion of Obama-haters, loved Trump's promotion of birtherism. Other hosts of Fox News shows invited Trump to appear and promote it. One show even made him a weekly guest. At that time, Trump was attempting to gain the Republican Party's nomination for the presidency. The time was not ripe for Trump, however. He had no chance of winning the nomination and dropped out so he could continue to make money with his reality television show *The Apprentice*. Birtherism, however, did get Trump a wider following.[11]

Trump revived birtherism. As Chuck Todd put it, 'no one did more to vault the false issue to the cable news echo chamber than Donald Trump.' Trump and his people continued to put out a lot of dubious information about Obama's origins, as did others such as Sheriff Joe Arpaio of Maricopa County, Arizona, and the author Jerome Corsi.[12] Time after time, their claims were debunked thoroughly but to no avail. The result was that birtherism went mainstream, with majorities of seemingly rational Republicans starting to believe the birthers' claims. Chuck Todd mocked the senseless gullibility of people believing that Obama was a plant to get a Muslim foreigner in the White House. As he put it, 'Maybe if the infant had been named "George Lincoln Washington," the whole "planting" theory might have attracted more believers.' Still, Trump proved to be a master of the rhetorical strategy of 'I was just raising a question.' It is the strategy favoured by conspiracy theorists, pseudo-historians and modern fabulist mythographers when they push their challenges to established mainstream knowledge. They question the unquestionable and by repetition seek to undermine the credibility of long-proven facts and theories. Ever since his debut as a birther in 2011, Trump has seesawed between promoting birtherism and claiming he no longer believes it. So, what does Trump really think? That depends on what day it is. As his biographer Michael D'Antonio has pointed out, Trump sees no downside in his birtherism. It gets him a solid, loyal audience and committed supporters. Prior to the election of Senator Kamala Harris as the Democratic Party's candidate for the vice-presidency in 2020, a new version of birtherism arose. It was claimed that Harris was not born in the United States. Like the Obama birther theory, the Kamala Harris theory is a complete fiction that has been thoroughly debunked. Also like the Obama birther theory, it is not going away.[13]

On a higher note in the annals of conspiracism and pseudo-history, 2019 witnessed the Storm Area 51 event. In the mythology of the UFO movement, Area 51 is the secret base where crashed flying saucers from Roswell and other places and their alien crews, both dead and alive, are stored and studied. After all, didn't the 1996 film *Independence Day* show that was exactly what was going on there? But that movie was science fiction. The popular lore about Area 51 is voluminous, although mostly false or fabricated and highly repetitive, but it remains an object of fascination nonetheless.

On 20 June 2019, Matty Roberts watched a video podcast of the *Joe Rogan Experience* that featured Bob Lazar, a long-time conspiracy theorist of Area 51. What he saw inspired Roberts to concoct a little joke. He set up a Facebook page on 27 June 2019 announcing an event. It invited people to gather at Area 51 on 20 September and rush the base demanding to see and free the alien prisoners. Roberts never intended or imagined that any such thing would actually take place. Much to his surprise, and to the annoyance of the United States Air Force, the announcement went viral only three days later. Eventually over 2 million people said they would attend while another 1.5 million stated that they were interested. The event attracted an inordinate amount of media attention, as wild and silly news items frequently do. Soon two music festivals were planned and local merchants began to prepare for an influx of visitors. One big concern was just how many people would actually show up for the event. Area 51 is located in an inhospitable desert with only a few tiny towns, some with fewer than a hundred residents. It was not capable of accommodating a few thousand visitors, let alone hundreds or even tens of thousands. There were only 184 motel rooms in the whole region around Area 51 while camping facilities were meagre and primitive. Even more potentially serious, the Air Force was not about to allow a crowd of wacky civilians to storm a super-secret military base on a lark. In the end, Storm Area 51 proved to be a tempest in a thimble rather than a teacup. The music festival attracted only about 1,500 attendees while a mere 150 people appeared at the main gate of the base at Area 51. The gate was not stormed, no aliens were freed and the mystique of Area 51 remained intact. Meanwhile, the Oklahoma City Animal Shelter used the event to encourage the adoption of rescue animals by asking people to 'storm our shelter', where they would find dogs wearing tinfoil hats to ward off aliens. The cats, apparently, refused to participate in the tinfoil hat business. Storm Area 51 is a wonderful case study of the power and limitations of myth in the popular culture of the Internet age.[14]

On a less happy note, the outbreak of the COVID-19 pandemic at the beginning of 2020 brought sickness, death and economic disruption on a global scale. The pandemic also proved to be a prodigious generator of conspiracy theories. Although epidemiologists had been warning for years that the outbreak of a global pandemic was inevitable, when it did occur some people reacted with denial. The pandemic was called a hoax, a conspiracy to discredit President Donald Trump, which if true would have to have been a global conspiracy of immense international proportions. Claims arose that the pandemic was not a natural occurrence; rather, it was caused by a virus that accidentally got out of a laboratory in Wuhan, China. A variant of this scenario claimed that the virus was a Chinese bioweapon. Yet another version asserted that the virus definitely was a bioweapon but that China had intentionally released it into the hapless world. Clearly some people simply found a conspiratorial human enemy to be a more comforting explanation for the calamity than a mindless fragment of genetic material – a virus.[15]

Existing conspiracy theories merged with or were grafted on to the pandemic. Viewers of national and international news have been treated to videos broadcast on television or posted on the Internet which showed people promoting some outlandish conspiracy theories. As the pandemic worsened in Florida, on 23 June 2020 the West Palm Beach County Commissioners held a meeting to decide whether to make the wearing of masks in public areas mandatory. It took over six hours. There was time scheduled for public comments. One woman remarked, 'I don't wear a mask for the same reason I don't wear underwear; things gotta breathe.' Apparently, according to her, the female nether regions are part of the respiratory system. Needless to say, her comment demonstrated a profound misconception about human anatomy. While this raises some questions about the quality of high-school health classes in that part of Florida, perhaps she simply slept through them. In case you are wondering, she was wearing blue jeans, which are apparently more breathable than masks or underwear. Another woman in a red T-shirt did a fair amount of ranting at the commissioners, during which she called them insane and threatened them with arrest and divine retribution. After the meeting, the same woman was interviewed by a local television station's reporter. She proceeded to insist that the pandemic was part of a plot by the New World Order, a conspiracy theory that posits that a secret super-elite really rules the world. In the case of the pandemic, the conspirators' horrendous goal was to reduce the human population by 95 per cent. If she is correct, the conspirators must be very disappointed, since the death rate for COVID-19 is not nearly high enough.[16]

A few weeks later, on 27 July, a group of doctors calling themselves America's Frontline Doctors held a press conference by the Supreme Court building in Washington, DC. They were COVID-19 deniers or minimizers, and the summit conference was organized by the Tea Party Patriots. One of the doctors stole the show. Stella Immanuel, a Nigerian-educated physician, proceeded to declare that the real threat was demon sperm (presumably a reference to the incubi or succubae who supposedly tormented the dreams of people in the medieval past). She also mentioned the danger of alien DNA and warned that humanity was threatened by reptilian conspiracies. The video of the press conference was quickly taken down by Facebook and Twitter due to the grossly false and potentially dangerous claims that had been made. While social media companies do need to engage in more gatekeeping and fact-checking of claims that are palpably false and potentially harmful, the news conference of this fringe group of doctors contained enough ludicrous claims that it probably did its cause far more harm than good. The conference did, however, attract the favourable attention of President Donald Trump, never one to let science get in the way of what he wished reality to be. What do these outbreaks of manifestly delusional ideas show us? Clearly the claims of the West Palm Beach anti-maskers and the demon sperm doctor are echoes of the ideas of David Icke and other conspiracists. Some significantly irrational ideas that threaten public health and safety are circulating among otherwise apparently normal people.[17]

Icke's theories, along with those of other conspiracists, pseudoscientists and pseudo-historians, have deep and twisted roots in the past. Tracing some of those roots is what this book tries to do. It is neither an exhaustive overview of the subject; nor is it even comprehensive. Either approach would require several long volumes. Instead, this book is a selective look at what I will call junk knowledge: pseudo-history, pseudoscience, conspiracy theories and modern myths. The first chapter discusses the concepts and terminology associated with junk knowledge. The second chapter, 'Why Do People Believe Strange Things?', looks at the diverse reasons why people believe things that are patently untrue, often ridiculous and sometimes even hurtful and dangerous. Evolutionary psychology, cognitive psychology, social psychology, socialization, culture and religion all play a role in enabling people to believe the unbelievable. The Ten Lost Tribes of Israel are the subject of the third chapter. It traces how the myth of the Ten Lost Tribes developed over almost 3,000 years. If people could travel back in time to the centuries after the fall of Samaria and the northern kingdom of Israel, they would discover that if they asked about the Ten Lost Tribes, they would be met by incomprehension. Still the myth developed and came to be used by Jews and Gentiles and for both philosemitic and antisemitic purposes. Chapter Four looks at the deep historical roots of modern conspiracy theories. David Icke's theories are largely based on a confabulation of modern elements that have roots stretching back to the French Revolution, the Knights Templar, the building of Solomon's Temple and the lost wisdom of ancient Egypt. The Illuminati arose out of this milieu and have had an amazing longevity in the thinking of conspiracists. Such longevity is especially remarkable given that the ruthless and relentless Illuminati have so far failed to achieve world domination. They are, however, persistent. The occultist and supernatural beliefs which were so popular among many Germans in the first half of the twentieth century and that were embraced by the Nazis are examined in Chapter Five. Nazism as an ideology was far more than its occult and supernatural aspects. What Nazism's conglomeration of pseudo-history, pseudoscience and racism did was make the ideology more plausible and more acceptable by giving it a veneer of science and history. It helped to justify tyranny and genocide. Finally, Chapter Six looks at the myth of Roswell, which is the belief that an extraterrestrial flying saucer or saucers crashed at Roswell, New Mexico, in July 1947. It consists of tales of government cover-ups, acquisition and incorporation of alien technologies, secret government treaties and alliances with aliens, alien contact and alien abductions, along with other related aspects of the post-1947 UFO movement.

At this point, I want to describe the methodology and philosophy of this book. My methodology is a combination of the genealogical and the evolutionary approaches to the history of the ideas being studied. It is necessary to locate the origin of the pseudo-history, the myth or the conspiracy theory. What is the event or the events on which the story is based? After that, the reconstruction of how these stories grew or developed over time reveals contradictions and inconsistencies that raise doubts about their credibility. In the case of the Ten Lost Tribes, we discover several troublesome facts. First, the Assyrians only deported a small percentage of the inhabitants of the ancient northern kingdom of Israel. Most of the Ten Tribes continued to live in the conquered northern kingdom or moved into Judah, the surviving southern kingdom. Although the apocryphal book of 2 Esdras told how the oppressed Ten Tribes in exile took refuge in the land of Arzareth, the historical record says differently. In the Hellenistic era, representatives of all twelve tribes of Israel helped to create the translation of the Hebrew Bible into the Greek translation known as the Septuagint. St Paul and other New Testament writings also record that all twelve tribes were living in Palestine during the era of the Julio-Claudian emperors. The Ten Tribes were not lost. The family tree of super-conspiracies about a New World Order supposedly lead back to the Illuminati or the Knights Templar, but it is a family tree with blank spots and large gaps. It is the type of record that does not inspire confidence in the credibility of the conspiracy narrative. The general lack of documentary and archaeological evidence for the theories and speculations of junk knowledge also undercuts the credibility of such ideas. Promoting narratives that are incompatible with anything known from physics, chemistry and other sciences also raises doubts.

In researching this book, I have read about, and sometimes studied in detail, many theories and beliefs that were outlandish, eccentric or surreal. One is taken aback that seemingly reasonable people could actually believe such things. That said, these beliefs and ideas are a source of fascination and wonder because people do find them credible. The process by which these ideas originated, developed and evolved is a tribute to human imagination, even if it bears little or no resemblance to scientific or historical reality. Many people who tune into the television show *Ancient Aliens* are simply curious about what its creators will get up to next. Otherwise, they have no commitment to the various theories presented by the series. Countless thriller novels or films are based on such pseudo-historical or pseudoscientific theories. James Rollins's 'Sigma Force' novels are based on a series of pseudo-historical and pseudoscientific theories that provide the premises of his plots. Dan Brown struck gold when he based the plot of his bestseller *The Da Vinci Code* (2003) on the purported nonfiction book *The Holy Blood and the Holy Grail* (1982) by Michael Baigent, Richard Leigh and Henry Lincoln. The filmmaker Roland Emmerich has based the plots of a number of his films on pseudo-historical and pseudo-scientific premises. *Stargate* (1994) was based on the ancient astronaut theory; *Independence Day* connected an alien invasion of the Earth to flying saucer crashes at Roswell, New Mexico, and marooned aliens held at Area 51. Catastrophic climate change due to global warming was the theme of *The Day After Tomorrow* (2004) while *10,000 BC* (2008) used the concept of an advanced Ice Age civilization that was Atlantis. Returning to catastrophism, *2012* (2009) combined Charles H. Hapgood's discredited theories about crustal displacement and pole shifts with the Maya prophecies about the end of the world to good effect. Twenty years later, he returned to the alien invasion plot with the sequel *Independence Day: Resurgence* (2016). *Stargate* inspired a television series, *Stargate SG1* (1997–2007), which itself inspired six spin-off television series and TV movies.

It's all good fun so long as you remember they are all only novels, films or television shows. Not everyone, however, makes that distinction. The popular television series *The X-Files* (1993–2002) focused on plots involving UFOs or other unexplained mysteries. Its creator Chris Carter always said it was fiction. That did not stop some viewers from regarding it as a sort of docudrama based on actual events. That is what is called fact/fiction reversal.

When people start believing things and ideas that are not true, it can become a problem for any society. Nazi Germany is a good example of a nation where too many citizens came to believe pseudoscientific claims about the racial superiority of Germans and the degeneracy and malevolence of Jews, Slavs and Gypsies. Devastating wars of aggression and genocide followed. In 2020, 75 years after end of the Second World War, the world of the Internet had made it easier to spread lies about how the Holocaust never happened and is a hoax. People have become radicalized by falsehoods they see and read on the Internet. The lone wolf terrorist Dylann S. Roof became radicalized by white supremacist propaganda that he saw there. As a result he gunned down nine Black people doing Bible study in the Emanuel African Methodist Episcopal Church in Charleston, South Carolina, on 17 June 2015. He is not a tragic exception. People in the United States and other countries have been similarly radicalized by white supremacists' and conspiracy theorists' Internet rantings. The Internet is also a favourite tool of radical jihadi Islamists for recruiting new members to their terrorist ranks.[18]

When faced with so many myths, pseudo-historical narratives, pseudoscientific theories and conspiracy theories, there is a need to re-assert common sense and intellectual integrity. In these days of relativism, some scholars of religion and cultural studies tell us that it is not good academic practice to make value judgements about people's beliefs, which is fine for most beliefs and opinions circulating in society. Does that mean human sacrifice or child sacrifice is okay if it is part of somebody's religion? Thousands of people claim to have been abducted by aliens and some of them are rather obsessive about it. Does that mean we should politely refrain from judging those claims as utterly implausible? At some point, a line is crossed in terms of human decency, preposterousness or just plain silliness. Some conspiracy theories have helped to undermine public trust in governments to a degree that is unhealthy and even dysfunctional. Democratic republics depend on a degree of trust to function properly. Too much distrust causes people to disengage from the democratic process. There has to be a balance between trust and scepticism in how citizens interact with their governments in democratic societies. There also needs to be a balance in how societies should respond to the types of junk knowledge circulating in contemporary society. A Disneyfied version of the myth of Atlantis is relatively benign. A German of the 1930s believing that a *Herrenvolk* (master race) lived on the lost Atlantis and that he is one of their descendants is a completely different and malign story. So, I agree with W.E.B. Du Bois: he criticized the racist Dunning School of Reconstruction historiography that dominated the writing of Southern history during the 1920s and '30s. His criticism applies to the ideas of junk knowledge as well. As he put it in 1935, 'If history is going to be scientific, if the record of human action is going to be set down with that accuracy and faithfulness of detail which will allow its use as a measuring rod and guidepost for the future of nations, there must be some standards of ethics in research and interpretation.'[19]

My study of fringe beliefs has led me to conclude that a lot of them are socially unhealthy and some are potentially hazardous to civil society. In fact, some of them are already dangerous. If I appear at times to be disapproving and judgemental about some of these fringe ideas and beliefs, I am. But I have quoted Mark Twain on this issue in the past and I will quote him again with continued and wholehearted agreement: 'It may be thought that I am prejudiced. Perhaps I am. I would be ashamed of myself if I were not.'[20]

Finally, readers will have noted that the title of this book is derived from the Spinoza epigraph that appears at its start. Spinoza attributed belief in superstition to hope and fear. As you will see, Spinoza was an astute observer. In every manifestation of junk knowledge discussed in this book, hope and fear play a big role.

ONE

Thinking about Pseudoscience, Pseudo-History, Modern Myths and Conspiracy Theories

A procession of the damned.
By the damned I mean the excluded.
We shall have a procession of the data that Science has excluded.
. . .
The power that has said to all these things that they are damned is
  Dogmatic Science.

CHARLES FORT[1]

H umans are curious. While some people are reluctant learners or even seemingly impervious to learning, most of us enjoy it. We also recognize that 'knowledge is power', as Sir Francis Bacon succinctly stated in 1587. It is a truism that the fictional Tyrion Lannister exemplified in the television series *Game of Thrones* with his T-shirt-worthy aphorism, 'I drink and I know things.' Unlike Sir Francis and Tyrion, modern society is blessed with access to a universe of knowledge that is just a few clicks away on the computer. The problem is that modern society is also cursed by that same access, since it is entangled with an even more massive amount of purported knowledge that is actually false, fake, distorted, obsolete, corrosively propagandistic and/or taken out of context. Sometimes it can be hard to separate accurate and objective knowledge from the inaccurate and tendentious. The Internet is only one source of knowledge and is relatively recent in its impact on society, although that impact is prodigious. False knowledge, however, has been around for a long time and has been conveyed by books, newspapers, magazines, radio, films and television. And, of course, there were the perennial old-school conveyers – rumours, whispers, gossip and tall tales.

Besides being curious, humans like a good story. It has been that way from time out of mind: just think of Homer and the tales of Gilgamesh and Sinuhe. These ancient stories were fiction but they also had some basis in reality. Humans also like to experience wonder. We enjoy the exotic and the mysterious along with secrets and fantasy. Quite often fantasy and fiction can be more fun and enjoyable than reality and fact. The problem comes when people fail to distinguish between fact and fiction, or truth and falsehood, or reality and fantasy.

We live in a world where conspiracy theories proliferate. Accusations of fake news are common but are usually directed against truth-telling journalists. Pseudoscientific malarkey has sometimes adversely affected how AIDS/HIV has been treated, misleads people into becoming anti-vaxxers and hinders efforts to control the COVID-19 pandemic.[2] Calling the pandemic a hoax is particularly problematic: one of the minimizers, Boris Johnson, prime minister of the United Kingdom, contracted the disease and ended up in intensive care for a number of days before finally recovering. Later, a COVID-19 denialist, Jair Bolsonaro, president of Brazil, tested positive for the virus while the greatest COVID-19 repudiator, Donald Trump, president of the United States, became infected. Throughout the pandemic, some people seem to miss the incongruity of U.S. president Donald Trump downplaying the pandemic while getting himself and many of his staff tested frequently, and while he was ill, he received cutting-edge medical treatment (privileges not enjoyed by the vast majority of Americans). The situation was not helped when Trump recommended that people use unapproved, inadequately tested and potentially dangerous treatments such hydroxychloroquine as a preventative. Obviously there is a lot of bad information circulating, which many people do not recognize for what it is. Unfortunately, it is causing all sorts of bad decisions and actions. An appropriate name for this misinformation phenomenon is 'junk thought' or 'junk knowledge', a term coined by Susan Jacoby in 2008.[3] It has also been called 'fringe' or 'border' knowledge, 'counter-knowledge' and 'mumbo jumbo'. It has taken and continues to take many forms: myth, the paranormal, the supernatural, the occult, pseudoscience, pseudo-history and conspiracy theories.

'Myth' is a word with many different meanings. In everyday speech, one commonly used definition of myth, according to the *New Oxford American Dictionary*, is 'a widely held but false belief or idea'. The *Shorter Oxford English Dictionary* provides a similar but more detailed definition: 'A widely held (esp. untrue or discredited popular) story or belief; a misconception or misrepresentation of the truth; an exaggerated or idealized conception of a person, institution, etc.; a person, institution, etc., widely idealized or misrepresented.' Furthermore, in popular discourse, the terms 'myth' and 'legend' are commonly used interchangeably. Scholars, however, view myth and legend as distinct concepts. For them, a myth is an invented story which is used allegorically or tropologically to explain some natural event or phenomenon, or some aspect of the human condition or psyche. The story of Persephone's abduction by Hades was a myth used to explain the changing of the seasons. A legend, on the other hand, is a story about the past that has some basis in real historical events, although the story has often been distorted with the passage of time.[4] Heinrich Schliemann's discovery of the ruins of Troy transformed the Trojan War from being a myth created by Homer to a legend. In a recent overview of the concept of myth, Robert Segal defined it as a story but he qualifies his definition by proposing 'that to qualify as a myth, a story, which can of course express a conviction, must have a powerful hold on its adherents. But the story can be true or false.' By conviction, Segal means that the adherents strongly believe what the myth proposes to claim or mean.[5] The myths that this book will address are largely of the type that matches Segal's definition, except that none of them will be true. So, they will also conform to the *Oxford American Dictionary*'s definition.

The paranormal, the supernatural and the occult are closely related to each other and are used to describe events or phenomena that are beyond the scope of normal scientific understanding and the laws of nature. 'Paranormal' is used more in scientific settings, like the study of phenomena such as remote viewing or telekinesis. In contrast, 'supernatural' tends to be used mostly in a magical context. The term 'occult' is used to describe mystical and magical powers and phenomena, but includes the idea that the occult is a body of knowledge and practices that has accumulated over the ages. The word comes from the Latin *occultus*, which means hidden, concealed or private. As the historian Eric Kurlander has pointed out, the occult also has a connotation of elitism. In his view, the occult did not encompass the border knowledge or pseudoscience and racial mythologies that were part of the popular culture of Nazism.[6]

Junk, pseudo- or fringe knowledge consists of knowledge that is non-standard and not considered part of mainstream scholarship, basically because it is seen as taking fallacious ideas as serious and valid. The German word for this phenomenon is *Grenzwissenschaft*, which means border knowledge or fringe knowledge. The two biggest components of junk knowledge in modern society are pseudoscience and pseudo-history (including the subset of pseudo-archaeology). To understand fully what pseudoscience and pseudo-history are, we need to understand what science and history are. Science is the methodical study of the natural world that is empirically based on observation and experimentation. History (including archaeology) is the methodical study of the human past that is based on evidence from the surviving records and artefacts. Both disciplines strive for conclusions that are drawn from evidence and data. Scientists and historians try to maintain objectivity and avoid cherry-picking their data or evidence to reach a predetermined conclusion. Furthermore, knowledge and conclusions in science and history are always tentative and subject to change based on new research findings. So, while science and history are bodies of knowledge, that knowledge is not written in stone.

Practitioners of science and history are only human. They can make mistakes and a few are even unethical or dishonest. Fortunately, science and history are also self-correcting and they engage in peer review. Scholars constructively criticize each other's work. Making a new discovery or convincingly revising an existing interpretation or theory are the most dramatic ways to get ahead in the scholarly professions. On the other hand, sloppy work can attract derision while dishonest work can make one a pariah and unemployed. Scholarly works include footnotes, endnotes, charts, tables, graphs and bibliographies, all based on research. These types of scholarly apparatus provide a guide to how the research was done, what evidence was found and how the conclusions were reached. As a result, a consensus reality emerges among the great majority of scientists and historians. This consensus reality can shift to a greater or lesser degree as new research and new methods appear. For the most part, however, there is broad or consensus agreement among scholars. Needless to say, some extreme relativists and postmodernists do not want to concede that facts and reality exist or that open-mindedness and objectivity can be even partially achievable. For them, the discourses and narratives of science and history are just constructs, like pseudoscience and pseudohistory. Considerations of truth and accuracy are not relevant or valid. This, however, is not a work of postmodernism, so let's move on.

Conspiracy theories are another component of junk knowledge or thought – and a big one at that. First, however, conspiracy theory needs to be defined. A conspiracy is a plan or agreement by two or more people to commit a crime or some other illegal or unethical act. The assassination of Abraham Lincoln was a conspiracy, as was the attempt to blow up the English Parliament by the Gunpowder Plotters in 1605. The Watergate scandal was all about conspiracies attempted by u.s. president Richard Nixon and his inner circle. All of these involved small groups of people involved in acts of violence or other criminal acts. More recently, there have been similar conspiracies, like Timothy McVeigh blowing up the Murrah Federal Building in Oklahoma City or the 9/11 destruction of the World Trade Center in New York by Al-Qaeda operatives. Both of these events also attracted the attention of conspiracy theorists. McVeigh claimed to be a lone patriot (actually he had a couple of accomplices) seeking to inflict retribution on the tyrannical U.S. government for the atrocity it committed at the siege of the Branch-Davidian compound at Waco, Texas. Some conspiracy theorists have labelled McVeigh's heinous act as a false flag operation by the government to discredit the anti-government militia movement. Although Osama bin Laden and Al-Qaeda took credit for the 9/11 attacks and there is solid evidence that confirms their claim, conspiracy theorists have concocted various alternatives. These range from the attacks being the responsibility of the Israeli intelligence agency Mossad to bolster anti-Islamic or anti-Arab feelings among Americans to the U.S. government plotting the attacks to justify the invasions of Afghanistan and Iraq. Even more recently, the COVID-19 pandemic has brought out a host of conspiracy theories, as discussed earlier in the Introduction.

These later conspiracy theories are a manifestation of conspiracism. Conspiracism is a belief in or a tendency to see conspiracies everywhere and to formulate conspiracy theories to explain why things happened the way they did. People who write about conspiracism tend to follow one of two schools of thought. One group takes a negative view. They see conspiracism as a tendency to explain events through a conspiracy theory even when there are more plausible explanations available. As a result, society suffers from unnecessary anxieties and confusion.[7] In contrast, the other group takes a positive view of conspiracism. They argue that conspiracy theories are often true and so their revelations of conspiracies benefit society. A good example of this positive approach is Kathryn Olmsted's *Real Enemies: Conspiracy Theories and American Democracy, World War I to 9/11*. She traces how the U.S. government conspired to get the country involved in both world wars and engaged in other plots and deceits such as the Watergate scandal and the Iran-Contra affair, among others. As she points out, during the twentieth century, American conspiracy theories were no longer primarily about external and/or internal groups conspiring against the United States and its government. Instead, the U.S. government was now conspiring against its own citizens. The growth in the size of the federal government that began with the First World War and has continued ever since is responsible for this shift. For her, 'A conspiracy theory is a proposal about a conspiracy that may or may not be true; it has not yet been proven.' That said, Olmsted does not regard conspiracism and conspiracy theories ultimately to be all that constructive.[8]

Other scholars of conspiracism and conspiracy theories limit their definition to beliefs that are not true and also tend to be unfalsifiable. This point of view began with the philosopher Karl Popper in 1934 with his book *Logik der Forschung*, which appeared in a revised English translation as *The Logic of Scientific Discovery* in 1959. As the political scientist Michael

Barkun has put it, 'The more sweeping a conspiracy theory's claims, the less relevant evidence becomes ... because conspiracy theories are non-falsifiable.' Every piece of evidence against the existence of a conspiracy is simply dismissed as being a part or a product of the vast conspiracy. Therefore, conspiracy theories in this more restrictive definition are inherently untrue. However, the journalist and student of conspiracy theories Anna Merlan cautions, 'Anyone who tells you we can always easily distinguish fictitious plots from real ones probably hasn't read much history.'[9] The focus of this book is on the type of conspiracy theories studied by Barkun, Merlan and Thomas Konda, so it is probably a pretty safe bet that they are fiction, not fact. After all, so far nobody has captured a genuine reptilian or a verifiable agent of the Illuminati, and a lot of people have been looking for a long time.

What are the traits of a conspiracy theory? Kathryn Olmsted observes, 'Conspiracy theories are easy ways of telling complicated stories.'[10] The story is reduced to a battle between good and evil in many conspiracies but not all. As Anna Merlan points out, the narratives of conspiracies are sometimes not simple; rather, they can be complicated and confusing even to the point of incoherence in their ambiguities and contradictions. The conspiracy theories in Milton William Cooper's underground classic *Behold a Pale Horse* (1991), along with his other writings and radio talks, are good examples of muddle and messy thinking. Merlan accurately observes, 'The point is more often to identify an enemy than outline precisely what they've done.'[11]

How does one go about evaluating the various conspiracies and conspiracy theories that make it into the news, social media and popular culture? One of the first principles is to apply Occam's Razor – also known as the rule of parsimony. It suggests that the simple or simpler explanation of any event or phenomenon is always to be the preferred choice in the absence of evidence to the contrary. This is the principle followed by good mechanics and repairers as well as scholars. In other words, when the car or the computer is not working, first check if there is fuel in the tank or if the computer is plugged in.

Another important principle is to distinguish clearly between something being possible and something being probable. Ultimately, just about anything is possible. When someone states that we are in for an *Independence Day*-type alien invasion at some point in the future, it really cannot be said that that is impossible. It has never happened before (sorry, *Ancient Aliens* and *Roswell* fans) but that does not make it impossible. It does, however, make it highly improbable. So, it is important to assess the probability of something being true or false, not just whether it is theoretically possible.

The sceptic Michael Shermer has composed a list of characteristics of a conspiracy theory that are generally reliable indicators that it is not true. The first thing to evaluate is whether the dots supposedly connecting the parts of a conspiracy theory are really connected in a causal way or are simply random coincidences. Following the principle of Occam's Razor, the simplest explanation is usually random coincidence. Another common component of conspiracy theories is to attribute almost limitless power and abilities to the conspirators. In real life, however, people make mistakes, plans or plots go awry, and there are definite limitations on the actual power of the conspirators or ruthless dictators. George Orwell's Big Brother may have been invincible, omnipotent and omniscient, but Hitler and Stalin were not. Nor, apparently, are the Illuminati, since their two-centuries-old plot has not yet succeeded. The more complicated a conspiracy theory is, the more difficult it is to execute and the less likely it is to be true. Furthermore, the more people involved in a conspiracy, the harder it is to keep it a secret. So, the idea that the moon landing in 1969 was faked is ludicrous. Between 20 July 1969 and 11 December 1972, there were a total of six moon landings. It would have taken thousands of people to have pulled off such a deception. Yet in the course of over fifty years, no one has revealed the hoax or made a deathbed confession about it. The common-sense implausibility of all these people remaining silent about this conspiracy or any other large-scale conspiracy has been analysed quantitatively. The conclusion is that no conspiracy could exist for more than four years without somebody alerting society to its existence. And the Illuminati and the New World Order have been around for how long?[12]

Conspiracy theories that pursue bold goals of epic and global proportions are unlikely to be true. The average conspirator is too practical-minded to consider world domination a realistic goal. Conspiracy theories link themselves implausibly to big events while at the same time assigning threatening or malevolent meanings to harmless and unimportant events. Facts and speculation are frequently mixed together in the presentation of a conspiracy theory. This characteristic makes it hard to determine the plausibility and probability of the claims that are being made. It is also a red flag that the conspiracy theory is not true. Conspiracy theorists often display indiscriminate antagonism and distrust towards government agencies and private organizations that do not appear to have any apparent factual basis. Finally, conspiracy theorists often persist in promoting a conspiracy theory and refuse to contemplate other possible explanations. They ignore any evidence that does not confirm their theories and only recognize evidence that supports what they already believe. Such behaviour is the mark of a conspiracy theory that is wrong or false.[13]

Michael Barkun points out that conspiracism views human events as the products of a plan or design rather than coincidence or random chance. This worldview is reflected in three propositions found in almost all conspiracy theories: (1) nothing happens by accident; (2) nothing is as it seems; and (3) everything is connected. The evil conspirators in such theories are very powerful and for that reason are very frightening. On the positive side, it makes the world meaningful. There is a struggle between good and evil that needs to be fought and that gives life a purpose and an order rather than simply being random and chaotic.[14] Barkun also identifies three types of conspiracy based on the scope of the individual conspiracy: (1) event conspiracies; (2) systemic conspiracies; and (3) super-conspiracies. An event conspiracy is focused on a single event or single group of related actions. The conspiracy to conceal Obama's alleged birth in Kenya and the claim that China released the COVID-19 virus from a bioweapons laboratory in Wuhan to create the pandemic are both event conspiracy theories. Systemic conspiracy theories have a much wider scope. These types of conspiracies strive to take control of a country, a region or even the world. The conspiracy theories based on the forged 'Protocols of the Elders of Zion' are a good examples of systemic conspiracy theories. According to these theories, a group of elite Jews are continuously plotting to take over various nations and ultimately the world. The most monstrous of the conspiracy theories in both quantitative and qualitative terms are the super-conspiracy theories. These theories involve a network of event and systemic conspiracies that are being orchestrated by an invisible and unknown body of evil and seemingly omnipotent plotters to achieve a paramount goal. The idea that extraterrestrial invaders are engaged in various conspiracies with earthly leaders to create a hybrid alien-human race to take over the Earth and enslave or exterminate humanity is an existentially threatening super-conspiracy. When conspiracy theories get so big that whole governments or a secret global government are behind them, they attract both left-wing and right-wing anti-government believers. It is a phenomenon that has been called fusion paranoia.[15] Some super-conspiracy theories take on a definite religious focus. Barkun calls this shift of focus 'improvisational millennialism', which he defines as a conspiracy leading to a good-versus-evil struggle that results in the destruction of the existing world followed by a new world where good reigns victorious. The religious aspects of improvisational millennialism are derived from various components of the New Age belief systems. The process of syncretization of pieces from various beliefs – Christian, Islamic, Buddhist, theosophist and neopagan, among many other possibilities – creates the various versions of improvisational millennialism. New Age traditions serve as a cultic milieu for improvisational millennialism that is continually being reshuffled into new versions.[16]

Conspiracists claim to base their claims on evidence and facts which make their theories true and correct. Elaborate arrays of footnotes, charts, tables, graphs and bibliographies are presented as proof. They have the outward appearance of the epitome of scholarly apparatus. As the historian Richard Hofstadter insightfully pointed out in 1964, the conspiracist scholar provides the

> appearance of the most careful, conscientious and seemingly coherent application to detail, the laborious accumulation of what can be taken as convincing evidence for the most fantastical conclusions, the careful preparation for the big leap from the undeniable to the unbelievable ... He has little hope that his evidence will convince a hostile world. His effort to amass it has rather the quality of a defensive act which shuts off his reception apparatus and protects him from having to attend to disturbing considerations that do not fortify his ideas.[17]

Anyone who has attempted to plough their way through the blizzard of highly technical but disingenuously and dubiously relevant evidence presented to discredit the existence of gas chambers in Nazi extermination camps or to explain the real conspiratorial reasons why the World Trade Center towers collapsed or why Obama's birth certificate is bogus will recognize what Hofstadter is talking about. Even more of a problem is that the vaster and more all-encompassing a conspiracy theory, the more impossible it is to falsify. Evidence becomes meaningless. Any evidence that discredits a conspiracy theory can be explained away as fabrications created by the all-powerful conspirators. As a result, to believe in such super-conspiracies becomes an act of faith, not the result of investigation and research that lead to a logical conclusion. Instead, belief in a conspiracy theory comes first and is followed by attempts to find evidence, no matter how tendentious, irrelevant or taken out of context, that reinforces the original belief. Such conspiracy theories are virtually invulnerable to refutation if true believers are the target audience.[18]

In the world of junk thought and knowledge, pseudoscience and pseudo-history are fellow travellers with conspiracy theories. Barkun has classified these forms of junk knowledge as stigmatized knowledge.[19] While these forms of knowledge are labelled as false and mistaken by mainstream scholars at universities and other scientific institutions, their supporters consider the ideas to be true. Barkun divides stigmatized knowledge into five categories. First, there is forgotten knowledge. It is the lost wisdom of the ancient past from mythological places like Atlantis or the largely forgotten lore of some ancient sage like Hermes Trismegistus. Superseded knowledge is the second category and refers to the forms of knowledge that were once regarded as valid and authentic but are now considered untrue and suspect. In the past, there were the so-called occult sciences such as alchemy, astrology, white magic and hermeticism. From the Renaissance to well after the beginning of the Scientific Revolution in the seventeenth century, respectable scholars dabbled in the occult sciences. The astronomer Johannes Kepler and the proto-psychiatrist Simon Forman derived some of their income from casting horoscopes. They were not unique or outliers in engaging in such practices. The occult sciences were widely regarded as science and respect-able forms of scholarship. Superseded knowledge includes discredited scientific theories – such as the geocentric concept of the universe, phren-ology and Lamarckian evolutionary theory – that were once considered to be authentic knowledge but are no longer. A third category is ignored knowledge; examples include the practices of folk medicine found among groups of low social status such as isolated and poor people living in the countryside.

Another big category is rejected knowledge, which consists of know-ledge claims that have been spurned by mainstream society from the time they first appeared and have continued to be rejected ever since. Barkun used the example of alien abduction, which has been rejected by main-stream authorities from its very beginning but still manages to attract millions of believers, including many who claim to have been abducted personally. Barkun also points out that the use of the term and concept of 'rejected knowledge' was pioneered by the English scholar James Webb in 1974. Webb equated the occult with rejected knowledge, but his conception of the occult focused on the 'hidden' aspect of the word rather than the magical. As Webb described it:

> The occult is *rejected knowledge*. It may be knowledge that is actively rejected by an Establishment, or knowledge which voluntarily exiles itself from the courts of favor because of its recognized incompatibility with prevailing wisdom ... [it is] an Underground whose basic unity is that of Opposition to an Establishment of Powers that Are.

His concept of 'rejected knowledge' encompasses aspects of Barkun's five types of stigmatized knowledge.[20]

Barkun's fifth category is suppressed knowledge. It is knowledge that the authorities know is true but which has been hushed or covered up. The reasons for the suppression of this knowledge vary. In some cases, the authorities may want to prevent a public panic or a dangerous outburst of public outrage. We know that U.S. authorities worried about the flying saucer flaps and manias provoking the type of hysteria sparked by Orson Welles's radio broadcast of H. G. Wells's *War of the Worlds* in 1938. In other cases, the motive might be self-serving or malevolent. Technical facts about why the World Trade Center's towers collapsed on 9/11 might be suppressed to protect the real culprits behind the attack such as the CIA or Mossad. Information about the origins of AIDS or COVID-19 might be suppressed to conceal that they were somebody's bioweapon. Many people may suspect the existence of the suppressed knowledge but only a select few are privy to the real facts and proof, and they are not about to share. Barkun points out that the category of suppressed knowledge subsumes aspects of the other forms of stigmatized knowledge. As a result, the adherents of stigmatized knowledge can claim that the stigmatization is part of a conspiracy to keep the public ignorant of the truth. Therefore, to be stigmatized becomes a sign that the knowledge really is true and so bypasses the need for validation by empirical evidence.[21]

Another cultural phenomenon that provides a continuing foundation for pseudoscience, pseudo-history and conspiracy theories is the cultic milieu. The concept of the cultic milieu came into scholarly prominence in 1972 with the publication of a now classic article, 'The Cult, the Cultic Milieu and Secularization', by the British sociologist Colin Campbell.[22] As the title declares, Campbell was seeking to explain something about the nature of cults, which are often mystical, loosely organized, ephemeral and follow a belief system that is seen as deviant by mainstream society. He rightly viewed cults as a form of religion that also includes various aspects of pseudo-history, pseudoscience and conspiracism. What Campbell noted was that cults arose and would later decay and cease to exist. At the same time, as older cults died out, new cults would appear. It was the existence of a cultic milieu that made the persistence of cults possible. The cultic milieu was a subculture. It consisted of the magazines, pamphlets, books, lectures, radio programmes and meetings that promoted various deviant or unorthodox beliefs and ideas. Since Campbell wrote in 1972, the Internet and niche networks on cable television have also presented the heterodox ideas and beliefs of the cultic milieu to an ever-larger public. Chain bookstores usually have a New Age section, while works of pseudo-history and pseudoscience jostle for space with mainstream books in the history and science sections. *Ancient Aliens* and *The Curse of Oak*

Island along with *Pawn Stars, American Pickers, Swamp People* and similar quality programming have crowded traditional history programmes into the margins of the History Channel. Other, once promising networks like Discovery, the Learning Channel and Arts and Entertainment have also largely abandoned their original focus on educational programming about science, history and related fields. They do, however, cater to what Campbell regarded as the essence of cultists – that they are seekers. What they seek is a way to find spiritual truth and personal fulfilment outside the traditional belief systems of mainstream religion.

The cultic milieu provides a vast repository of heterodox ideas and beliefs – the rejected knowledge of Webb and the stigmatized knowledge of Barkun. The diversity of the cultic milieu and its ability to reshuffle its components into an infinite kaleidoscope of beliefs and ideologies are what make the creation of new groups of seekers and the persistence of the cultic phenomenon possible. In addition, the cultic milieu also attracts substantial support from what Campbell called 'passive consumers'.

These passive consumers have an interest in and a curiosity about the deviant beliefs and ideas of the cultic milieu. That means they will buy the books and magazines, listen to the radio programmes, watch the television shows, attend the lectures and conferences, click on the websites and occasionally use cultic services like fortune-telling and palm reading. They might even organize a seance (despite it being a sure path to disaster in many horror films). Events like AlienCon are the embodiment of the cultic milieu. The focus might ostensibly be on the show *Ancient Aliens*, but in the vendors' area an attendee can find a lot more than just *Ancient Aliens* T-shirts. There is aromatherapy, herbal cures and other alternative medicinal lore and goods along with various New Age products. A stop at the booth of the Inner Traditions publishing company offers an assortment of books dealing with all aspects of the cultic milieu from *Awakening Your Crystals* and *Soul Dog* to *Dark Fleet: The Secret Nazi Space Program and the Battle for the Solar System* and *The Murder of Moses*. Many attendees of these events are seekers and true believers, but more are passive consumers who attend out of curiosity rather than commitment.

In 2012 Colin Campbell gave a lecture, 'The Cultic Milieu Revisited', at Leipzig University. In it, he discussed how the orthodox mainstream that had prevailed into the 1960s has broken down since 1972. Society in general is now more heterodox, pluralistic and tolerant. Part of that new culture is the mainstreaming of the New Age movement which evolved out of the cultic milieu. As a result, much of the cultic milieu is no longer cultic: that is, deviant and marginalized.[23] A milieu still exists. It is a milieu of the occult, the supernatural, pseudoscience, pseudo-history and conspiracism which stands apart from traditional learning, higher education and the world of science. It is the junk knowledge milieu. This milieu has existed for a long time. It is a reaction against the disenchantment of the world by the Enlightenment, secularization and modernism that is now a part of Western culture.[24] And it is not necessarily a positive part of Western culture either, as the grim experience of Nazism testifies. The cultic milieu or junk knowledge is antagonistic towards what it views as mainstream authorities such as university-based academics, intellectuals, scientists and government experts along with the knowledge that they represent.[25] It is what James Webb called the occult, both underground and establishment. Recent scholarship has dubbed this version of the cultic milieu an oppositional subculture. Certainly, conspiracy theorists and ufologists take an oppositional attitude towards any information coming from government agencies or universities (unless it happens to agree with them, of course). Such are the foundations of conspiracy theories, pseudoscience and pseudo-history today.

What are the differences and contrasts between pseudo-scholarship or junk knowledge and methodologically sound and empirically based scholarship? Mainstream scholars base their conclusions on evidence and data. First comes the research and fact-finding; these then inform the conclusions and interpretations. Scholars also accept that the discovery of new evidence can oblige them to revise conclusions that previously seemed to be solid. Valid interpretations of evidence require an understanding of the context that produced the historical documents and artefacts. In contrast, pseudo-scholars start with their conclusions and theories and proceed to cherry-pick the evidence for items that seem to support their preconceived conclusions. If the evidence is not a good fit, they shoehorn it into place anyway. This approach often involves ignoring the historical context of the evidence.

Mainstream scholars form a research community that shares ideas and engages in debate. They evaluate and criticize each other through peer review. There are numerous occasions in which mainstream scholarship has ultimately been proved to be wrong. When mainstream scholarship is confronted with the error and sufficient evidence to the contrary, it adjusts the theory or interpretation accordingly. Alfred Wegener's theory of continental drift was derided by other scientists when he first proposed it, but over time evidence accumulated to show he was substantially correct. Subsequently, the concept of plate tectonics appeared and revised Wegener's original concept in a way that better explained the process of continental drift.[26] Scholarly bodies have self-correcting mechanisms built into their methods and institutions. It is what helps science, history and similar disciplines to advance human knowledge.

Pseudo-scholarship does not follow or adhere to empirical methods and self-correcting procedures. It is almost unheard of for fringe scholars to criticize each other publicly, even though their individual theories are as much or more at variance with each other as they are with mainstream theories and interpretations. Criticism of another fringe scholar never occurs in print media or when the television cameras are recording. An observer occasionally sees glimpses of professional rivalries and disagreements at meetings like AlienCon and even more so at small meetings.[27] Pseudo-scholars do not engage in peer review or other self-correcting procedures.

How can pseudo-scholarship and junk knowledge in science, history and other disciplines be recognized by the general public? That is a difficult task. Pseudo-scholars use a number of techniques to bolster their credibility or to distract away from any questions that might arise about their credibility. They use outdated and superseded scholarship and theories and portray them as cutting-edge research to support their ideas and theories. For example, they might cite Ignatius Donnelly's *Atlantis: The Antediluvian World*, which was published in 1882, to support their ideas about Atlantis and other lost continents. Now Donnelly's book is a classic of Atlantology but that does not mean it is credible scholarship. In its day, its claims were not as far-fetched as they appear now. They were, however, still very much on the fringe. Since then, scientific advances have rendered the contents utterly implausible.[28] The same applies to theories about the hollow Earth, civilized life on Mars, or hyper-diffusion of the culture of Atlantis or ancient Egypt.

Pseudo-scholars also spend a lot of time denigrating mainstream academics and scientists. They accuse academics and scientists of being the ones using and protecting outmoded or just plain false theories and interpretations that constitute orthodox knowledge. They portray mainstream scholars as being focused on irrelevancies and trivialities rather than the big picture and the big truth. They continually attack the reliability and credibility of experts. If anything, these types of attacks on experts and the concept of expertise are greater and more sustained than ever today, as the obfuscating denialism about the COVID-19 pandemic demonstrates.[29] The possession of academic credentials in terms of university degrees, academic positions and scholarly publications has been turned into a cause for suspicion and a reason to reject anything that mainstream scholars might have to say in their field of expertise.

However, if an opportunity arises for getting support for pseudo-knowledge from a mainstream scholar, suddenly academic credentials become valid and credible. A good example of this phenomenon is Barry

Fell, the author of *America BC: Ancient Settlers in the New World* (1976) and other similar subsequent books. Fell claimed that ancient Celtic, Celtiberian, Irish and even Egyptian people regularly visited North America and mined copper during the centuries prior to 500 BC and the rise of Classical civilization. These visits continued for centuries into the early Christian era. Some of the evidence cited for these contacts included stone structures at Mystery Hill, New Hampshire. Another piece of evidence is alleged inscriptions using Irish Ogham writing that Fell claimed to be able to decipher. The authenticity of many of these inscriptions and Fell's expertise to translate them were and continue to be rejected by the overwhelming majority of archaeologists. That said, Fell was a professor at Harvard University, an impressive academic credential. It was one that his supporters exploited whenever possible. The fact is that Fell was a highly regarded professor – of invertebrate zoology. That part was always left out when he was identified in some documentary about pre-Columbian visitors to the Americas. That omission of an accurate portrayal of his expertise and credentials must strike a reflective person as at best rather disingenuous.

Another tactic used by purveyors of junk knowledge is to bury the reader in details, which archaeologist Garrett Fagan has dubbed the 'kitchen-sink' mode of argument.[30] Jerome R. Corsi's *Where's the Birth Certificate? The Case that Barack Obama Is Not Eligible to Be President* (2011) contains a mountain of detail. The result is confusion for the readers, who are left wondering if there is actually something to the birther claims since there appears to be so much evidence. It obscures the fact that the paper trail for Obama's birth in the state of Hawaii is unimpeachable to objective observers.

Pseudo-scholars often rely heavily on using anomalies as evidence and proof for their contentions. An anomaly is something strange, unexpected, abnormal or peculiar. In others words, it does not have an explanation. UFOs are unidentified flying objects; that is what the anacronym means. The great majority of unidentified flying objects end up being explained as something quite normal. Ufologists, however, have little hesitation about claiming the remaining unexplained UFO reports as evidence of extraterrestrial visitations. In fact, these unexplained sightings of a UFO are anomalies. Is it in the realm of possibility that these anomalous sightings are alien spacecraft? Yes, it is, just as a future alien invasion is possible. For now, though, there is no credible proof that the anomalous UFO sightings are some sort of flying saucer. An anomaly cannot be used as proof or disproof of anything other than we do not have all the answers. Michael Shermer has pointed out that valid beliefs and theories 'are not built on single facts alone [that anomalies can disprove], but on a convergence of evidence from multiple lines of inquiry'. This use of a convergence of evidence and comparative method when applied empirically is what makes the social sciences and history scientific. Furthermore, just because something cannot be explained scientifically does not mean it will never be explained. Over the years, science has cleared up many mysteries and seemingly inexplicable phenomena. The proper approach is to take a wait-and-see attitude rather than defaulting to a supernatural or paranormal explanation.[31]

Pseudo-scholars also employ a tactic of reversing the burden of proof. In other words, they get to throw out a sensationalistic claim and it should be allowed to stand until mainstream scholars disprove it. In reality, it is up to the pseudo-scholar to prove their contentions. As the sceptical scientist Carl Sagan put it, 'Extraordinary claims require extraordinary evidence.' He did not originate this dictum. In the mid-eighteenth century, the philosopher David Hume wrote, 'A wise man ... proportions his belief to the evidence.'[32] Purveyors of junk knowledge instead will often retreat and claim they are just asking questions, which is true, but they are tendentious and leading questions designed to reverse the burden of proof regarding their offbeat claims.

Junk knowledge also engages in fact–fiction reversal. Fictional events and concepts become part of real history for adherents of pseudo-history, pseudoscience and conspiracy theory. Edward Bulwer-Lytton's *The Coming Race* (1871) is an early utopian science fiction novel about the discovery of a human society living in the hollow Earth. Its people have developed incredible creative and destructive powers called *vril* which they have used to expand and conquer much of their underground world. If they ever emerge, it would inevitably bring about the extinction of the people living on the Earth's surface. Vague stories of a Vril society or societies have been in circulation since the Nazi era thanks to the scientist and refugee Willy Ley's initial mention of it in an article published in 1947. It set up all sorts of wild speculations about a Nazi Vril society and the Third Reich's attempts to harness *vril* as a wonder weapon. Nicholas Goodrick-Clarke's researches brought the Vril society into a more prosaic perspective, but the fact–fiction reversal had already become embedded in the cultic milieu.[33]

Mainstream scholars have made the accurate observation that junk knowledge – unlike mainstream science, history and other disciplines – does not advance through continuing research that reveals new facts and evidence which make new and improved theories and interpretations possible. The truth about empirical scholarship and science is that their findings and theories are always provisional. Interpretations and theories change as new research prompts new ways of thinking about a subject. How much have Erich von Däniken's ideas about ancient astronauts changed since his *Chariots of the Gods?* first appeared in 1968? What new evidence and insights has he unveiled and developed? Based on his subsequent books and his appearances on *Ancient Aliens*, there have been no significant new findings in over fifty years. Adherents of Charles Hapgood's ideas about crustal displacement or the related idea of a lost ancient super-civilization lying under the Antarctic icecap have uncovered no new evidence to support his theories. Advances in mainstream science have resulted in new tests and measurements that could have proven Hapgood's hypothesis about pole shifts if they had occurred. In fact, they indicate the opposite. Hapgood was wrong, unless you are a true believer that ignores the science. The failures of pseudoscientific hypotheses to become established theories is a rather large epistemological red flag.

One question that has been around since the 1930s has been the line of demarcation between genuine science and pseudoscience, which can be expanded to the demarcation between empirical knowledge and junk knowledge. The philosopher Karl Popper asserted that the boundary separating science from pseudoscience was that the claims of pseudoscience were unfalsifiable by experiment or observation. The evolutionary biologist and sceptic Massimo Pigliucci has pointed out that this line of demarcation leaves much of the fields of biology and geology, along with psychology, the social sciences and history, in the realm of pseudoscience. Practitioners of these disciplines may not always or ever conduct experiments, but they do systematically gather evidence, facts and data in a forensic manner as detectives do. This process allows all scholars and researchers to make inferences about what they are studying. The more evidence they accumulate, the stronger the inference. It is important to remember that science functions more by proving a hypothesis or theory to be incorrect or false rather than proving a theory is correct or true. As has been mentioned already, truth in science is always provisional and never absolute. The same applies to other disciplines that use a more comparative and evidential approach such as history. Historians seek to reconstruct the events of the past as best they can, given the surviving historical evidence. Since the amount of historical evidence for some eras is sparse to the point of non-existent while, for more recent times, it can be overwhelming in its abundance, historical knowledge cannot be permanent. Historians also interpret what they have assembled in their researches and give it context and meaning. Professional ethics require that all of these things should be done with a spirit of fairness that tries as much as possible to avoid bias and subjectivity. If history, as well as science, is done according to rigorous scholarly standards and methods, it will go a long way towards exposing the myths, misconceptions and outright frauds of pseudo-history and pseudoscience along with making the world and the past more comprehensible.

So where does that leave the demarcation between mainstream academic knowledge and junk or pseudo-knowledge? There are degrees of junk knowledge. Some works and presentations are pure bunk, but others are combinations, with varying degrees of mainstream academic knowledge mixed with junk knowledge. That is where the demarcation line becomes fuzzy. For scholars, especially those with a direct speciality in the subject at hand, it is fairly easy to identify a work of junk knowledge, just as a jeweller can easily discern when a diamond is of the highest quality, an inferior gem or just a fake. It is a different matter for the non-specialist general public. They do not know the scholarly literature, they are not familiar with the historical documents, they are not aware of the proper methodology and they may not have been taught the critical thinking skills needed to recognize the various red flags discussed in this chapter. That is why mainstream scholars, scientists and experts need to engage with the challenge posed by junk knowledge. As we shall see in the next chapter, there are also some aspects of human nature as revealed by cognitive and social psychology that make junk knowledge attractive and believable.

TWO

Why Do People Believe
Strange Things?

The inferior man's reasons for hating knowledge are not hard to discern. He hates it because it is complex – because it puts an unbearable burden on his meager capacity for taking in ideas. Thus, his search is always for short cuts. All superstitions are short cuts. Their aim is to make the unintelligible simple, and even obvious.

H. L. MENCKEN[1]

In circumstances of anxiety and uncertainty, superstition is likely to make a prominent showing. This is seen as perhaps a regression to infantile attitudes, or to beliefs acquired early in life and afterwards suppressed; or perhaps as a means of obtaining some sort of illusory control over a frightening situation.

JAMES WEBB[2]

How can the question posed by the title of this chapter be answered? Some might say that people believe strange things because they are stupid. While that might be true in some cases, it is obvious that many intelligent people believe in some rather quirky and irrational ideas. Others suggest that believers in strange things are uneducated or ill-educated. As a result, they are ignorant and more prone to fall for fallacious opinions. There is plenty of evidence that scientific illiteracy does leave people open to pseudoscientific concepts and theories. None of this, however, explains why people stubbornly persist in error when they are confronted with indisputable facts that are manifestly to the contrary of what they believe. Many people find this phenomenon of stubborn persistence in error to be perplexing and even quite troubling. We ask, how can they continue to do that? The answer apparently is that there is a complex combination of causes for such behaviour that involves evolutionary biology, cognitive psychology, social psychology, socialization, culture and religion.

The best place to start to gain an understanding of why people believe strange things is evolutionary biology and its impact on the cognitive psychology of human beings. We humans like to view ourselves as rational beings. The scientific name of our species is *Homo sapiens*, meaning wise man. Of course, even a superficial knowledge of history and current affairs shows that as a species, in groups and as individuals humans often engage in unwise and even self-destructive behaviour. Humans do think but their thinking is often not rational or coherent or consistent. According to the prominent sceptic and historian of science Michael Shermer, 'Beliefs come first, explanations follow. I call this process belief-dependent realism.'[3] Acquiring a repertoire of beliefs is part of the process of socialization that everyone experiences in their interactions with parents, other family members, friends, schools, religion and general culture. The socialization process has a deep impact on the things that people believe. At the same time, individuals formulate some beliefs, at least partially, on their own. As Shermer asserts, 'The brain is a belief engine.' Human brains are genetically hard-wired to take the sensory information they receive and identify patterns. An example that Shermer uses is the scenario in which an early human is on the ground foraging for food. The human notices sounds, sights and smells coming from a nearby clump of vegetation, indicating that a large predator may be lying in wait to pounce on an unsuspecting victim. So, the cautious human prey climbs into the safety of the closest tree. If there really is a lion hiding in the bush, it was a life-saving decision. If the rustling of the bushes was caused by a breeze, the interruption of foraging causes no real harm. The brain is programmed to look for these types of sensory patterns as a survival mechanism. Some of the patterns are meaningful and lead to accurate and useful assessments. Often, however, the brain discerns a pattern that is not really there and is not meaningful. A common example from everyday life is when people see images in the clouds.

Human brains strive to connect the dots. Shermer calls this process 'patternicity'. Furthermore, humans try to invest these patterns with a significance, a purpose and an agency. He calls this process 'agenticity'. Sometimes the pattern is not real. A good example of connecting dots in an ultimately meaningless way is ley lines. New Age believers claim that the Earth is sprinkled with places that possess a mystical energy, such as the Great Pyramid of Giza, Stonehenge and Uluru, along with a host of similar places. These sites are not randomly distributed. They actually form a pattern or grid that reflects some unexplained or otherwise undetectable supernatural phenomenon, or some sort of ancient alien mapping or energy-generating system that connected flying saucer landing bases together in prehistoric times. The problem with this idea is that equally compelling patterns could be discovered and have been discovered based on the distribution of pizza restaurants and churches. All it takes is patience and the time to play around with straight lines on a map.[4] Patternicity and agenticity are especially potent generators of false alarms and ridiculous plots when it comes to conspiracy theories.

All of us have our own belief-dependent reality, which is based on our personal experiences, our cultural environment and our access to information. For much of the twentieth century, there was a relatively solid consensus reality that grounded the societies of industrialized democratic nations such as the United Kingdom, the United States, Canada and Western Europe along with many of the countries of Latin America. Within each country, people read the same or similar books, magazines and newspapers. They listened to the radio and saw the same films. By the 1950s, televisions quickly became a mainstay for news, entertainment and documentaries. There were only three major networks in the United States while in the UK the British Broadcasting Corporation (BBC) had a monopoly of television broadcasting from 1932 to 1955. At that point the Independent Television Network (ITN) came into being. Most American and British viewers had a choice of three or four channels. Large urban areas such as New York and Chicago offered a few more choices in the United States as independent television stations appeared. All of these channels were broadly similar and they sought to attract a wide general audience. Other industrialized nations had about the same number of choices. To a very great extent, the information cultures of these societies were fairly homogeneous. It was that homogeneity that helped to create and sustain a consensus reality. This situation remained stable until the advent of cable television and the Internet made hundreds of television channels and billions of websites available.

All of these information outlets also served as gatekeepers in terms of the nature and type of information that was presented to the public. The primary goal was to attract a mass audience; therefore, the tastes and interests of niche groups were not given much attention and went largely unserved. Things were less monolithic in the realm of print media. Special interest magazines, newspapers and books were readily available even though their audience was relatively small. The decisions about who was published or broadcast were predominantly economic in nature. Would the item sell or attract an audience and so turn a profit? Some decisions were based on concerns about morality and public decency, and led to the creation of standards which inhibited or prevented certain topics from being published, made into a film or broadcast on radio or television.

Gatekeepers were also concerned to block what was viewed as bad science, bad history or bad scholarship from being disseminated to a mainstream readership or audience. An outstanding example of a gatekeeping failure was the attempt by astronomers to prevent the publication of Immanuel Velikovsky's *Worlds in Collision* in 1950. Velikovsky's maverick and ultimately untenable ideas had such an attraction for the reading public that publishers were willing to put profit above intellectual integrity.[5] About the same time, the right-wing John Birch Society struggled and failed to become a mainstream movement. Their problem was that the Birchers had a worldview that was incompatible with mainstream consensus reality, not to mention just plain reality. When the movement's leader wrote a book accusing a president, the respected and even beloved Dwight Eisenhower, of being a communist agent, that was simply too preposterous for an overwhelming majority of Americans, even in the fearful era of the 1950s.

Certainly, strange ideas have always been present in human societies; our innate behaviours of patternicity and agenticity ensure that connecting the dots of perception and experience will continue unabated. These also mean that sometimes those dots will be connected incorrectly and falsely incorporated into some people's belief-dependent realities. When that type of connection occurs, another aspect of human cognition appears – confirmation bias. Once humans develop and accept a belief or opinion, they immediately go to work proving their idea is correct and true. The bias comes in when they concentrate only on finding evidence that supports their belief. Contrary facts or evidence are ignored or given the slightest attention. Another term for this is 'motivated reasoning'. As the journalist Anna Merlan explains, 'We tend to give more weight to studies, news articles, and any other form of information that confirms our preexisting beliefs and values, and find ways to reject things that don't line up with what we *feel* to be true.' Colloquially this behaviour is called cherry-picking the evidence. It is a method that undermines any scientific or empirical effort to determine and to provide a valid and science-dependent belief system.[6]

Michael Shermer describes a wide variety of subsets of confirmation bias. There is hindsight bias, which is a tendency to make the past fit with present knowledge or situations. In the field of historical scholarship another name for this is a Whig interpretation of history. This bias ignores the contingency of past events and makes them inevitable. Another confirmation bias is the status quo bias. At its most basic, it argues that we have always done it this way and it has worked, so why change? Researchers often struggle with expectation bias, which is when an observer or a researcher pays more attention to data and evidence that confirm their expectation about what the outcome or conclusions of their study or experiment will produce. Expectation bias is closely related to the tendency of the self-fulfilling prophecy, in which a certain outcome is desired so extraordinary measures and manipulations are taken to make that outcome occur. Confirmation bias is a universal trait of human nature, so individuals and societies need to be aware of it and guard against it if they want to live in a world of reality rather than one of fantasy.[7]

When people become adherents of a dubious belief, they frequently run into a problem. Events in the world of reality do not continually confirm their belief system and they suffer from cognitive dissonance. This occurs when a person's or a group's beliefs come into conflict with evidence, facts, reality or even other beliefs. This state of conflict and contradiction creates stress and anxiety for the believer; that is the dissonance. The stress or dissonance needs to be relieved. The psychologist Leon Festinger developed his concept and theory of cognitive dissonance when he studied a UFO cult that claimed to have been informed by extraterrestrial visitors that a cataclysmic flood was going to bring about the end of the world, particularly the destruction of the greater Chicago region, where most of the cultists lived. Of course, the date for the flood came and went with no apocalyptic catastrophe. The cult did experience an initial shock and a degree of disillusionment that led to some members apostatizing. The core group, however, persisted. They explained that the failure of their prediction of the flood was not actually a failure. In the immediate aftermath, the extraterrestrials had informed the group that, thanks to the cult's prayers and faith, the world had been saved from destruction.[8]

People use the same sort of justification when they fail to quit smoking, despite all the studies showing the health risks and the evidence of their own deteriorating physical well-being. Festinger concluded that many people experiencing cognitive dissonance will do whatever it takes to reduce the stress, even if it means ignoring the conflicts between reality and their beliefs and behaviour. In the case of beliefs about UFOs and conspiracy theories, the ultimate dodge is to make their beliefs unfalsifiable. At that point, the cognitive dissonance disappears. The pandemic of the COVID-19 virus, which began in 2020, has brought out many people who claim it is a hoax or the result of a bioweapon unleashed by China, the New World Order, Bill Gates or any number of villains. Denying the reality of the pandemic or blaming it on a conspiracy of evil humans also alleviates the anxiety produced by the spectre of an unthinking, unfeeling and relentless virus ploughing its way randomly through the human population. How do you fight something like that? The answer, in fact, is with science-based medical practices and drugs, but they require patience, fortitude and forbearance. Those qualities are always in short supply. The main problem, however, is that significant segments of the population in some countries reject the expertise and authority behind any scientific solution. Instead, they fall back on magical thinking, conspiracy theories and cognitive dissonance. Blaming the Chinese, fake news or the Deep State creates a human enemy who is more comfortable to deal with than a faceless virus. A further step is to reject the reality or existence of the problem by calling it a hoax. The name for this phenomenon is denialism, and it is another method of alleviating cognitive dissonance. Unfortunately, it does so by ignoring, disputing or rejecting historical evidence and scientific findings in a fundamentally irrational manner.[9]

How is it that many people apparently feel so free to dismiss expert knowledge along with the facts and science that underpin such knowledge? Researchers have identified two personality traits that enable people to ignore experts – the Dunning-Kruger effect and narcissism. The Dunning-Kruger effect is the phenomenon when people with low competence or knowledge consistently rank themselves as much more competent or knowledgeable than they really are. According to psychologists, the Dunning-Kruger effect stems from a lack of metacognition, which is their cognition about their cognition. In layperson's terms, they lack the knowledge or awareness of the limitations of their talents or knowledge; more bluntly, they are ignorant about their ignorance. In terms of political affairs, it means many people think they know more than they really do. So, they do not feel any need to educate themselves and become better informed. This condition makes them more susceptible to conspiracy theories and junk knowledge that provide easy explanations and answers for their beliefs and prejudices. Remember, belief comes first, and confirmation bias and motivated reason do the rest with the assistance of the Dunning-Kruger effect. No assistance from rational and critical thinking is wanted or needed. The Dunning-Kruger effect even serves to make low-competence people more confident. It also provides the foundation for some of the psychological defence mechanisms that allow people to lessen or ignore the discomfort and stress from cognitive dissonance. The large number of people who reject the huge consensus among scientists that human activity is accelerating and aggravating climate change is a good example of the phenomenon. Frequent reports of widespread record high temperatures and evidence of melting polar icecaps are blithely ignored. In this way, ideas that fly against reason and reality can persist. In other words, a little knowledge really can be a dangerous thing.[10]

Narcissism is another personality trait that is common among believers in conspiracy theories and other forms of junk knowledge. It is important to keep in mind that, like most personality traits, all people have a degree of narcissism. Everyone also possesses some level of self-esteem, which varies from individual to individual. In fact, a certain level of narcissism is healthy for an individual. All of us exhibit undue selfishness on occasion. Incongruously, however, narcissists often possess a low level of self-esteem. As a result, they act in ways that conceal this shortcoming. Narcissists also display an unwarranted sense of their importance. They crave and expect admiration and have a strong sense of entitlement. In comparison with other people, narcissists view themselves as special or superior. This self-image often causes them to behave arrogantly towards other people. In addition, they lack empathy towards other people's feelings or needs. It also means that they take advantage and use other people while feeling no sense of loyalty or social obligation towards those around them. Needless to say, narcissistic people can be difficult to be around. Fortunately, only 1 per cent of the population have high enough levels of narcissistic behaviour to be classified as having narcissistic personality disorder (NPD). That also means, however, there are unfortunately a lot of people who have not reached the level of narcissism to be diagnosed with NPD but are still capable of being obnoxious and socially disruptive.[11]

Research has shown that narcissistic people tend to be attracted to and believe in ideas and concepts from the realm of junk knowledge, particularly conspiracy theories. Several studies have found a strong correlation between belief in conspiracy theories, low self-esteem and narcissism. This does not mean that all believers in conspiracy theories are narcissists; nor does it mean that all narcissists believe in conspiracy theories. How and why conspiracy theories, low self-esteem and narcissism interact is unclear, but the existence of the correlation is definite. Narcissists often exhibit paranoia due to their belief that they are special and superior compared to most of the people around them. They think people envy them and are jealous of them. As a result, they assume people are out to get them and conspire against them. Furthermore, because narcissists are supposedly superior, their belief in conspiracy theories makes them privy to secrets not available to the average and inferior people around them. People who share conspiracist beliefs belong to a special elite group that sets them apart from the rest of society. This is collective narcissism, and it is self-reinforcing by its conferral of a valued membership in a special in-group. As a group they are engaged in a collective struggle against the various conspiratorial groups that are out to destroy them and their rights to entitlement and privilege. Given such a worldview, the effort to debunk any given conspiracy theory is an existential threat to the individual and collective narcissists. It is also a threat that they can easily parry by falling back on the tactic of making their conspiracy unfalsifiable, by framing it as an all-powerful systemic or super-conspiracy or as improvisational millennialism.[12]

Another psychological theory that is used to explain why people come to accept irrational ideas and beliefs is the concept of locus of control. Locus of control is another personality trait. If a person believes they have control over their life through their own actions and abilities, they exhibit an internal locus of control. If a person believes that outside forces such as chance, coincidence or the social structure among other things control their life, they exhibit an external locus of control. Humans, however, do not simply possess either an internal or an external locus of control. There is a continuum that goes from an extreme internal to an extreme external locus of control, with most people operating in the fuzzy middle areas. One's locus of control fluctuates with age and personal circumstances. Within an individual, it can vary with different settings and issues. As people get older, they tend to develop more of an internal locus, which is understandable since most people become more economically secure with age. But among the elderly, growing physical infirmity will tend to increase a person's external locus of control. An individual's internal locus of control suffers a serious blow if that person was economically secure and loses a good job and then cannot find another similar position. At the global level, the external threat of climate change or a pandemic can cause a significant increase in some people's stress levels and their external locus of control. An interesting question for psychological researchers would be: where do anti-maskers and people who go to crowded beaches, bars or pubs, and political rallies during a pandemic rank on the continuum from internal to external locus of control?[13]

What psychologists have discovered is that when it comes to conspiracy theorists and believers in the supernatural or magical thinking, they tend to rank high in terms of an external locus of control. Studies have demonstrated a strong relationship between external locus of control and belief in conspiracy theories time and time again. Therefore, given people's innate trait of patternicity and agenticity, when it is combined with some people's tendency to an external locus of control that believes they are subject to vague but powerful external forces they have no control over, it is quite easy for them to connect the dots and believe a conspiracy theory or some other millennialist vision.[14]

Various journalists and social critics have commented on this connection between external locus of control and conspiracy theories or occult beliefs. Francis Wheen has observed that 'the new irrationalism is an expression of despair by people who feel impotent to improve their lives and suspect that they are at the mercy of secretive, impersonal forces, whether these be the Pentagon or invaders from Mars.' Governments see weird beliefs as a useful distraction from reality. David Aaronovitch agrees that 'very often conspiracy theories take root among the casualties of political, social, or economic change.' Anna Merlan points out that 'times of tumult and social upheaval tend to lead to a parallel surge in conspiracy thinking.' She goes on to identify decreasing social mobility, feelings of political disenfranchisement, and an increasingly confusing and insecure social safety net and system of healthcare as sources of anxiety, discontent and feelings of helplessness. These are the signs of societies that are increasingly dysfunctional and consequently are potential hotbeds of people with high levels of external loci of control.[15]

Another attraction of conspiracy theories and other junk knowledge is that most people prefer a simple explanation or narrative rather than a complex and nuanced one. It has already been noted that simple but false explanations are natural companions to the Dunning-Kruger effect. Conspiracy theories and many other pseudoscientific or pseudo-historical ideas are fairly simple and uncomplicated when compared to more complex evidence-based scientific theories or historical narratives. Bad things happen like deindustrialization eliminating once well-paid and secure manufacturing jobs. Scholarly explanations of the problem talk about the globalization of the economy, new technologies, factories moving to areas where labour costs are low, and a reluctance by conservative governments to regulate huge companies when aspects of capitalism become dysfunctional. They are all part of a set of processes that are not always clearly understood by the experts. As explanations, they just do not satisfy ordinary people. They seem amorphous and confusing. So, monocausal explanations are much preferred. It is far easier to blame greedy Jewish bankers or a faceless and malevolent New World Order. That reduces the unhappy situation to a conflict between good and evil, and gives the victims an enemy to fight or at least to hate. The same problem applies to explaining the origins of humanity and civilization in the primordial past. An empirical explanation will talk about human evolution, environmental challenges, human innovation, cultural diffusions, migrations of people, the development of government and bureaucracy, and the role of religion all working in tandem in the history of human civilization. A much simpler and apparently more attractive explanation for some people is that it was aliens!

The narrative of good versus evil makes conspiracy theories, pseudo-science and pseudo-history even more attractive to their adherents. Believers are the good guys. They are the heroes of their own lives, especially the fantasyland aspects of their lives, as they battle the Deep State, reptilian alien infiltrators, or satanic Jews and their Mud People minions. In this view of the world and its travails, the adherents of strange beliefs are not just good – they are the chosen, either by God or by destiny. It is just the place that a narcissist might want to be. The Christian Identity movement claims that the white people of the British Isles and North America are actually the descendants of the Ten Lost Tribes of Israel, in particular the tribes of Ephraim and Manasseh. Now that is a formidable pedigree of chosenness. As for the Jews, they are actually frauds and the evil spawn of Satan. Many Germans during the first half of the twentieth century increasingly believed they were a special people with a destiny. In this belief, they exemplified the answer to the rhetorical question posed by David Aaronovitch, 'Who . . . wouldn't want to be on the side of the gifted and insightful?'[16] In the primeval age of lost continents such as Atlantis and Hyperborea, the ancient Germans had supposedly possessed superpowers and technologies, but over time they degenerated through interbreeding with lesser humans. Nazism was all about restoring the German people to their destiny as the master race or *Herrenvolk*. That was the identity promoted by Nazi and *völkisch* ideology. It made the Germans feel special and gave them hope, albeit a false and ultimately catastrophic hope. For a time, though, this Aryan identity was very seductive, as pseudoscience and pseudo-history often are.

The attractions of believing in conspiracy theories come down to three basic desires. First, there is a desire for certainty and understanding regarding the world. The simple or simplistic explanations of conspiracies easily fulfil that expectation, at least superficially. Second, believing in a conspiracy theory provides a feeling of control and security even if the conspiracy itself threatens the survival of humanity. Just knowing there is a threat means the potential victims can resist or even defeat it. Third, being in the know and one of the good and elite people engaged in a cosmic struggle gives a positive self-image. Such psychological benefits provide a big incentive for many people to believe conspiracy theories, no matter how implausible.[17]

The strange ideas of junk knowledge are largely a product of modernism and mass society. The invention of the printing press made it possible to mass produce information. All the other technological innovations in knowledge and information distribution are enhancements of that monumental change. During the nineteenth century, further innovations in printing made books, newspapers and magazines cheaper, which mass consumption made possible. The invention of the telegraph in the 1840s made the instantaneous transmission of news and information over great distances possible for the first time. The first films appeared during the last years of the nineteenth century, and by the beginning of the 1920s they were a major entertainment industry. Inventors were experimenting with radio during the 1890s, and by the 1920s it had become another medium for instantaneous communication as well as the broadcast of news and entertainment. As the twentieth century progressed, television, computers and the Internet provided further venues for instantaneous communication and the dissemination of information. As costs declined and access widened through the Internet, information went democratic and mass market at the same time. The trajectory of information availability did not stop with mainstream knowledge. It also moved into the chaotic, the anarchic and the nihilistic. It was technological change that has allowed the junk knowledge that inhabited the margins of societies to seep into the mainstream of culture more than was ever before possible. The success of the television series *Ancient Aliens* is a case in point. For many of its viewers, it is a guilty pleasure or an idle curiosity. For others, however, it is their religion and their view of reality and human history. It is a place where fact and fiction reverse and a supermarket of weird theories that replenishes the mental shelves of its true believers. It is the cultic milieu in hyper-drive. Still, as David Aaronovitch has noted, the primary creators and consumers of junk knowledge are both educated and members of the middle class. They are the ones with the leisure time and the disposable income to spend on events like AlienCon, subscribing to outré websites or paying membership dues to one or more societies focusing on weird things like hollow Earth theories and ufology.[18]

Some scholars suggest that the rise of postmodernism and relativism among academics has exacerbated this proliferation of junk knowledge. Since the 1970s, culture wars have been fought and continue to be fought.[19] Meanwhile, the public is told by hyperbolic far-right talking heads on the television that most university professors are teaching that truth does not exist and everything is relative, so anything goes. Now, it is important to keep in mind that such hardcore postmodernists are a tiny minority on most campuses, and they are definitely not to be found in colleges of engineering or the natural sciences. In departments of the humanities and social sciences, there is a postmodernist presence and it can have an impact. What it does is create a safe zone for academics such as Leonard Jeffries, Ward Churchill and Martin Bernal. Their dubious narratives promulgate theories about the widespread use of smallpox blankets as bioweapons against Native Americans, unscientific claims that more melanin in one's skin results in higher intelligence, or a tendentious history of alleged racism in Classical scholarship. Very few academics actually engage in that sort of thing. But if they do, they suffer the same fate that befalls most faculty: the students are not listening. So, no learning occurs, and in the case of the extreme postmodernists, no harm is done. Still, some harm is actually done by excessive postmodernism. As the journalist David Aaronovitch warns, 'If all narratives are relative, then we are lost.' Extreme relativism promotes an 'anything goes' toleration that dulls critical thinking. As the journalist and social critic Francis Wheen asserts, 'This is the enfeebling legacy of post-modernism – a paralysis of reason, a refusal to observe any qualitative differences between reasonable hypotheses and swirling hogwash.' It is impossible to accurately measure the impact of postmodernism, but it is somewhere between paltry and extensive.[20] Certainly the postmodernist bogeyman is a tool used by right-wing pundits to undermine the credibility of academics as experts in their areas of specialization. That is why Aaronovitch insists that scholars and researchers need to engage in a 'dogmatic insistence' on getting the relevant facts and events depicted accurately, truthfully and with intellectual integrity.[21]

Kathryn Olmsted, a historian of conspiracy theories, takes a different approach to the problem. She suggests that the best way to reduce the surge in conspiracy theories impacting modern societies, particularly the United States, is for the government to be more transparent. In the context of government secrecy, this appears to be sound advice. It is also advice that arises from how Olmsted studied conspiracy theories. Her research focused on conspiracies related to government wrongdoing and attempts to cover it up. That is why she puts an emphasis on the government behaving itself. A more transparent government would help to reduce the proliferation of conspiracy theories.[22] It would not, however, stop them. The history of the UFO movement demonstrates that transparency does not necessarily allay suspicions and conspiracy theories about the government. Although the U.S. government was initially secretive for many years about what it knew about UFOs, when the government adopted a more transparent stance, it was a failure. Later government reports and revelations explaining UFOs were rejected by ufologists. Accusations of the U.S. government engaging in cover-ups have continued unabated because the credibility of the government on that issue is non-existent as far as the UFO movement is concerned. Furthermore, as was discussed earlier, if there is a systemic conspiracy or a super-conspiracy involving flying saucers, the suspicious ufologists would simply claim that the government conspirators had the power to conceal or fake evidence at every turn. Unfalsifiable conspiracy theories are immune to debunking by evidence or government transparency.

Aaronovitch is correct; junk knowledge and its accompanying con-spiracy theories need to be confronted with facts and evidence-based rebuttals. Many academics, however, have declined to engage with junk knowledge. They consider such activity a waste of their time. This can be a form of snobbish elitism. Academics are supposed to be educators, so they need to educate the public about the fallacies inherent in junk knowledge. Some scholars argue that engaging with junk knowledge will give these false beliefs and concepts attention and legitimacy. Another argument against confronting the purveyors of junk knowledge, most recently made by the professor of rhetoric Jenny Rice, is that debunking and rebuttal cannot change the true believers' minds. She counsels against engaging with them.[23] When it comes to the true believers, she is right: it is too late. The acceptance of junk knowledge has become too baked into their being and identity for any amount of debate to change that. Their core ideas have been constructed to be unfalsifiable, at least to them. Nobody is going to change Alex Jones's mind. Maybe he really believes the stuff he puts out and maybe he does not. Recent leaked videotapes indicate that Jones's public high regard for Donald Trump may not reflect his private opinions.[24] It is important to remember what Upton Sinclair said: 'It is difficult to get a man to understand something when his salary depends upon his not understanding it.'[25] The fact is, humans are prone to what is called 'belief perseverance' or 'conceptual conservatism'. They will persist in a belief even when presented with solid information and facts that contra-dict it. Even more perplexing is that when confronted with debunking, the believer is paradoxically reinforced in their debunked belief. This is called a backfire effect. Backfire effects occur when the mythic belief is made more familiar, when too much debunking is presented and/or when the believer's worldview is threatened.[26] So Rice is right about the true believers, but she is focusing on the wrong audience. As other sceptics have asserted, engag-ing in debunking, rebuttal and fact-checking and teaching the principles of critical thinking are really intended for and needed by the audience of those who are exposed to but not yet committed to weird ideas. They can and should be taught and shown how to tell the difference between the diamonds of true knowledge and the fake gems of junk knowledge.

Furthermore, this hands-off attitude of academics stopped being appropriate when technology provided the tools for spreading junk know-ledge widely and for the conscious creation of false stories and baseless conspiracy theories. Anna Merlan has pointed out this problem in her *Republic of Lies* and adds that social media 'have a way of flattening infor-mation, making every source look the same or appear equally plausible'.[27] Social media companies have been resistant to being fact-checkers and gatekeepers but that is changing. Even so, it still leaves plenty of outlets on the Internet for disseminating bogus conspiracy theories and false narratives. In a world of motivated reasoning, as Merlan has succinctly observed, 'partisan goals trump accuracy goals.' Research has shown that the prevalence of conspiracy theories and related anti-government junk knowledge generates feelings of anxiety and a sense of helplessness in many people. In other words, conspiracy theories are increasing the level of external locus of control in many people. The effect is to reduce political, civic and social engagement. Despite these problems, Merlan also maintains that the Internet remains a potent tool for free speech and combatting social and political ills.[28] It is up to civic-minded people of good will to prove that Merlan and Euripides – 'Man's most valuable trait is a judicious sense of what not to believe' – are right.[29]

THREE

The Many Journeys of the Ten Lost Tribes of Israel

In the ninth year of Hosea, the king of Assyria captured Samaria and he carried the Israelites away to Assyria and placed them in Halah and on the Habor, the river of Gozan and in the cities of the Medes.

2 KINGS 17:7

Thus says the Lord God: Behold, I will take the people of Israel from the nations among which they have gone and will gather them from all around and bring them to their own land.

EZEKIEL 37:21

In 722 BCE, Samaria, the capital of Israel, the northern kingdom of the ten Hebrew tribes, fell to the army of Assyria. It was the final blow that ended the kingdom of Israel. The Assyrians made the conquered kingdom a province of their empire. Following their usual procedures of conquest, the Assyrians deported the political elite and skilled artisans to various parts of their empire to prevent the recurrence of rebellion and to take advantage of skilled craftsmen where they were needed. The fall of Samaria also marked the beginning of the myth of the Ten Lost Tribes of Israel. Frequently, myths do not have a definite starting place in the historical record but this myth does. Over time it would grow in terms of the details of its lore, its geographical scope and its significances to various peoples. Books, articles and essays dealing with the Ten Lost Tribes could fill a library. The Ten Lost Tribes have been located anywhere from the arctic North to South Africa or from almost anywhere in the Americas to various places in East and South Asia. Various groups have been identified as or claimed to be descendants of the Ten Lost Tribes – Gypsies, the British, all or some of the Native American tribes, the Atlanteans, the Pathans of Afghanistan, the horrific peoples of Gog and Magog, the Bene Israel of western India and the Hottentots of southern Africa, among a host of others. The myth of the Ten Lost Tribes has been put to multiple uses by numerous, diverse groups. It provides a wonderful example of how the myths and legends of alternative history evolve, expand and are utilized for good or for evil.

In the Beginning

The details of the fall of Samaria and the deportation of the Israelite elite are somewhat murky although the broad historical context is quite clear. Beginning in 745 BCE, the political and military situation in the ancient Middle East changed dramatically. Various small kingdoms had flourished in what are now the modern states of Israel, Jordan, Lebanon and Syria from about 1000 BCE in the aftermath of the collapse of the great empires of the late Bronze Age. Assyria had been among those great empires, but it had survived relatively unscathed by the crisis. By 883 BCE, the era known as the Neo-Assyrian empire under Ashurnasirpal II (r. 883–859) had begun. Assyrian power grew and expanded, but despite forays into the lands of the Aramaeans in Syria, they failed to make permanent conquests. If they managed to turn some of the small kingdoms into tribute-paying vassals, they were satisfied. Often they faced stiff resistance as the Aramaean states, the Phoenician coastal cities and the kingdom of Israel formed effective defensive alliances.[1]

While the Assyrians were an exceptionally formidable military power, they experienced periodic instability at the top. Being an Assyrian king was a dangerous position to hold. Rebellious sons and usurping generals appear frequently in Assyrian history. Such unstable kingships were not just a problem for the Assyrians either, as in their tumultuous history the petty Middle Eastern kingdoms, including Israel, experienced similar instability over and over again. In the case of Assyria, the cutthroat politics occasionally brought kings to the throne who were great warriors. One of the most outstanding of these was Tiglath-Pileser III (r. 744–727 BCE). He started Assyria's rise to be the first world empire of the ancient Near East. Under him, the Neo-Assyrian empire expanded in every direction. Moreover, he was no longer content with just extorting tribute from the defeated states; he converted them into provinces of his empire.[2]

Initially many of the states in Syria, the Levant and Palestine avoided an invasion by Tiglath-Pileser through the expedient of agreeing in 738 BCE to pay tribute to Assyria. The problem was that Assyrian tribute demands were very onerous. As a result, resentment and discontent became rampant throughout the region. When Menahem, the king of Israel who negotiated the Assyrian tribute, died in 735, his son and successor Pekahiah was assassinated by the anti-Assyrian Pekah. Upon coming to the throne, Pekah stopped paying tribute. He joined with Rezin of Damascus, the leader of the western kingdoms' alliance against the Assyrian threat. Tiglath-Pileser struck back in 733 and 732 BCE. He defeated and killed Rezin and captured Damascus. Israel lost its northernmost territory, which was converted into an Assyrian province. Tiglath-Pileser went on to deport 13,500 people from the conquered part of Israel, instigated a coup that deposed and killed Pekah, and placed the supposedly loyal Hoshea on the throne of Israel.[3]

Tiglath-Pileser died in 727 BCE and was replaced by his son Shalmaneser V (r. 727–722 BCE). Initially, Hoshea continued to pay the tribute, but it remained a heavy burden for the people of Israel and a source of unremitting resentment against their king, who paid by collecting necessary but onerous taxes from his subjects. Domestic discontent forced Hoshea to stop paying tribute about 726 BCE. That triggered an invasion by Shalmaneser, which appears to have resulted in the early capture of Hoshea. Samaria, the capital of Israel, however, held out against the besieging Assyrian army for a few years, not falling until 722 BCE.[4]

Nothing is really known about the siege of Samaria. It is not clear whether the city was taken by storm or surrendered due to starvation. In fact, it is not even clear who captured Samaria. The Bible indicates that Shalmaneser V captured the rebellious city, but some scholars argue that it was actually his successor Sargon II (r. 722/1–705 BCE) who finished off Samaria. It appears that Sargon was an Assyrian general who overthrew Shalmaneser and usurped the throne. Again, the details of what happened are lacking. Conquered Israel was turned into another Assyrian province, and Sargon II claimed to have deported 27,280 people while the Bible's account credits the deportation to Shalmaneser.[5]

During the three centuries of the Assyrian empire, scholars estimate that it deported 4.5 million people. The combined deportations of the Israelites by Tiglath-Pileser and Shalmaneser or Sargon totalled almost 41,000 people, or less than 1 per cent of the total Assyrian deportations. Therefore, the Israelites were hardly alone in their tribulations. More significant to the myth of the Ten Lost Tribes, the Assyrians did not denude Israel of its Hebrew population. Estimates of the population of the kingdom of Israel vary significantly. One estimate calculated on the basis of Menahem's collections of the tribute money puts the population at 800,000. More reliable estimates based on a survey of settlements in ancient Israel from the era of the Assyrian invasion have concluded the population was at least 222,500 but more likely as high as 350,000. That means that the number of people deported by the Assyrians accounted for no more than 20 per cent of the population and was perhaps only a little over 10 per cent. If the more doubtful estimate of a population of 800,000 is correct, the proportion of deportees falls to 5 per cent. Of the Israelites left behind, archaeological evidence indicates that many moved to the southern Hebrew kingdom of Judah. In other words, no matter which estimate is used, the great majority of the Ten Tribes never left the homeland of David and Solomon and so were never lost.[6]

According to the biblical account, the deportees of the Ten Tribes were taken to Assyria and placed in 'Halah and on the Habor, the river of Gozan and the cities of the Medes' (2 Kings 17:7, a list of destinations repeated in 2 Kings 18:9–12). Archaeological evidence shows that people with Hebrew names were living in Nineveh as well. Certainly, the book of Tobit in the Apocrypha concerns Israelite exiles that Shalmaneser had deported to Nineveh and Israelite exiles living in Media. Back in Israel, the northern kingdom was gone forever. Its lands had been parcelled into the Assyrian imperial provinces of Megiddo, Gilead and Samaria. Meanwhile, the Assyrians deported people from Hamath, north of Damascus, and Cuthah, near Babylon, into Samaria. Although they brought their own gods, over time they merged with the indigenous population to become the Samaritans.

The destruction of the kingdom of Israel was a traumatic event for both the Israelites and the Hebrews of the remaining southern kingdom of Judah. The Judahites submitted to Assyria and paid the oppressive tribute. Goaded into rebellion along with other small states along the eastern coast of the Mediterranean Sea, Judah survived an abortive siege of Jerusalem by the armies of the Assyrian king Sennacherib (r. 704–681 BCE) in 701. Ultimately, the Judahites managed to outlast the Assyrians, whose empire abruptly succumbed to the Babylonians and the Medes during 614–609 BCE. But their travails with the great powers of Mesopotamia were not over. The Neo-Babylonian empire took Assyria's place as a world empire and eventually defeated Egypt in a struggle for control of the lands of the Levant. In the process, the kingdom of Judah was destroyed and Jerusalem was conquered by the armies of the Babylonian king Nebuchadnezzar in 597 and 587 BCE. The latter siege resulted in the destruction of the city and the deportation of its remaining population to Babylon. Some Judahites, taking along the prophet Jeremiah, fled to Egypt to avoid the wrath of the Babylonians. So by that time, portions of all twelve tribes had been deported or had fled to live in exile outside of the lands of Israel and Judah.[7]

The myth of the Ten Lost Tribes of Israel arose out of the eschatological, apocalyptic and messianic expectations that flourished among the exiles of the Judahites in Babylon and continued when they were allowed to return to Jerusalem and Judah. So instead of simply being forgotten like the other 99 per cent of the 4.5 million Assyrian deportees, the 41,000 Israelite deportees became the subject of numerous myths and legends. Their memory lives on in a vast amount of often contradictory lore that has accumulated over the centuries but has no basis in the biblical accounts or any convincing contacts with descendants of the Ten Tribes.

The two hundred years from 740 to 540 BCE were a difficult time for Israel and Judah and the small kingdoms that were their neighbours. They were overrun by the Assyrians and Babylonians, with Egypt periodically attempting to seize some of Palestine and the Levant for itself. Various prophets had warned the Israelites and Judahites that their sinful ways would bring on God's judgement and severe punishment. The destructive invasions and deportations were seen as the punishments that the prophets had been foretelling. But alongside the devastation that Isaiah, Jeremiah, Amos and others had predicted, they also told of God's mercy, which would include the reuniting of the twelve tribes. Israel and Judah would be one again and would be faithful to God. They also asserted that their God, Yahweh, was the only god and was the God for all humanity, not just the Children of Israel.

Part of the prediction came true fairly quickly. Led by Cyrus II the Great (r. 559–530 BCE), the Medes and the Persians destroyed the Neo-Babylonian empire in 539 BCE. A tolerant ruler, Cyrus II allowed the first group of Judahite exiles to return to the area around the ruins of Jerusalem. Over time, other groups of exiles would follow so that the two tribes of Judah and Benjamin were restored to their homeland. Many exiles, however, would remain in Babylon or other places. Would the Ten Tribes of Israel rejoin them in the Promised Land? The answer of the prophets and their rabbinic successors was yes, but they were vague as to how that second stage of the reunion would occur.[8]

According to the biblical account, God had promised Abraham, Isaac, Jacob and the Children of Israel a homeland, a promised land located largely on the territory of modern Israel. There a monarchy arose to rule the united twelve tribes. After a false start under Saul, the great King David secured the kingdom of Israel. His son Solomon ruled over that powerful kingdom and built the great temple in Jerusalem. But Solomon acquired foreign wives and tolerated foreign gods. He also placed harsh demands for taxes and forced labour on his subjects. The Ten Tribes of the north grew more and more discontented. So, when Rehoboam, the son of Solomon, came to the throne and refused to give the northerners any relief, they rebelled and proclaimed Jeroboam of the tribe of Ephraim as their king. In this way, after a brief period of greatness, the kingdom of the Children of Israel had become divided. From that point, the fortunes of the divided kingdoms declined, despite occasional upward swings. Both kingdoms dallied with false, foreign gods, which did not please Yahweh. So eventually, first Israel in 722 BCE, then Judah in 587 BCE, succumbed to powerful invaders and saw part of their population deported. In the polytheistic worldview of most of the ancient Near East, such defeats meant your god was weak and ineffectual. That was a crushing realization for an ancient society, and the Assyrians taunted their victims with that message.

The Israelites and Judahites, however, did not give in to despair. Their prophets promised and predicted restoration and reunion for them along with redemption for them and all mankind. As Jeremiah, speaking for God, told the exiles, 'For I know the plans I have for you, declares the Lord, plans for welfare and not for evil, to give you a future and a hope' (Jeremiah, 29:11). Isaiah added more detail when he predicted of the restored kingdom:

> In that day the Lord will extend his hand yet a second time to recover the remnant that remains of his people, from Assyria, from Egypt, from Pathros, from Cush, from Elam, from Hamath and from the coastlands of the sea. He will raise a signal for the nations and will assemble the banished of Israel and gather the dispersed of Judah from the four corners of the earth (Isaiah 11:11–12).

Ezekiel even presented an elaborate plan for the division of the land of Israel among the twelve tribes which he universalized to all humanity by adding, 'for the sojourners who reside among you and have had children among you. They shall be to you as native-born children among the tribes of Israel' (Ezekiel 47:22).

One of the things that the Judahite exiles in Babylon had fervidly hoped for was the restoration of the Davidic dynasty of kings that had ruled Judah and would rule the restored and reunited kingdom. Initially, they hoped that Zerubbabel, a descendent of King David chosen by the Persians to be their governor of the province of Judah, would be the restored king. When that expectation was dashed, it did not end the longing for a restored monarchy. Out of the longing arose the idea of a messiah, meaning an 'anointed one'.

Messianism developed two versions. One version was of a conquering Messiah. He would lead the Jews and establish them as an independent and powerful kingdom. The other version looked for a mostly spiritual Messiah who would peacefully and supernaturally lead the Jews and all humanity into an era that would be both prosperous and free of strife.

Most important, it would be pleasing to God. This vision of an age of harmony and order would be eternal, which gave messianism its eschatological character. The restoration of such a Davidic kingdom would mark the end of history. But messianism's vision of the last days and the end of history had variations. An apocalyptic version developed. The root of the word 'apocalypse' means 'revelation'. What an apocalypse revealed was hidden or secret knowledge about the last days of the world. Generally, the apocalyptic accounts told hair-raising and sensational stories of titanic struggles over the restoration of God's messianic kingdom between the armies of good and evil. And since the restored Davidic kingdom was to include All-Israel, meaning the twelve tribes, it also would bring back the Ten Tribes of Israel. The Ten Tribes became a component of messianism, eschatology and apocalypticism among Jews and later Christians. Over time, a lot of additional non-biblical lore about the Ten Tribes would evolve and expand. This myth would be used for various purposes by different groups.[9]

Messianism and the Ten Lost Tribes

It is important to understand that it was not until after the Second Temple Period (*c.* 515 BCE–70 CE) that the classic lore associated with the Ten Lost Tribes really started to accumulate. It has already been pointed out that the majority of the members of the Ten Tribes had remained living in the area that had been the northern kingdom of Israel or had fled to the kingdom of Judah. Note that the Gospel of Luke mentions that when Jesus was presented at the Temple of Herod, the prophetess Anna was a member of the tribe of Asher (Luke 2:36). Earlier than that, when Ptolemy II Philadelphus (r. 285–246 BCE) ordered the translation into Greek of the Jewish scriptures that is known as the Septuagint, the high priest Eleazar gathered together 72 translators, six from each of the twelve tribes. Later in 59 CE, in his testimony before Herod Agrippa II and Queen Berenice, St Paul referred to his mission to the twelve tribes (Acts 26:7). Of the portion of the Ten Tribes who had been deported, the prophets knew where they were located. The second book of Kings lists those places – 'Halah and on the Habor, the river of Gozan and in the cities of the Medes'. The book of Tobit in the Apocrypha tells the story of Tobit and his son Tobias of the tribe of Naphtali. Tobit had been deported to Nineveh by Shalmaneser V. He becomes blind and has to send his son Tobias to claim money Tobit had left with other Jews living in Ecbatana in Media. Nineveh and Ecbatana are both places where Israelite exiles would be expected to be dwelling, based on the account of 2 Kings. Keep in mind that, although set in the eighth or early seventh century, Tobit was written between 225 and 175 BCE. What this information shows is there was no secret or mystery about where the Israelite exiles were living. They had not been misplaced or lost, at least for the first five centuries of their exile.[10]

When the myth of the Ten Lost Tribes began to develop, one of their roles was to serve as protectors of oppressed Jews. They were expected to make an appearance when the oppression of the Jews became too dire. It is clear, however, that Jews during the Second Temple era did not yet think of the Ten Tribes as guardians. When the Seleucid king Antiochus IV Epiphanes (r. 175–164 BCE) persecuted the Jews, it sparked the revolt of the Maccabees (167–160 BCE). At no time during that struggle did the rebels expect help from the Ten Tribes. The same observation applied to the capture of Jerusalem in 64 BCE by the Roman general Pompey the Great. His soldiers massacred 12,000 Jews in the Temple precinct and Pompey desecrated the Holy of Holies in the Temple by entering it. No one evoked the intervention of the Ten Tribes. Finally, there was no expectation of help from the Ten Tribes during the Jewish Revolt of 66–73 CE, despite the Second Temple in Jerusalem being destroyed.

The myth of the Ten Tribes being both lost and special began developing shortly after the destruction of the Temple in Jerusalem which ended the Second Temple era. The apocryphal book of 2 Esdras or 4 Ezra documents the early features of the developing myth. The second book of Esdras was definitely composed after the destruction of the Temple in 70 CE, no later than around 100 CE and possibly as early as 83 CE based on some internal evidence in the text. Its anonymous author purports to be the Esdras or Ezra of the restoration to Judea of the Judahite exiles in Babylon. So, its supposed historical setting circa 515 BCE is centuries earlier than when the account was composed. The book presents a series of apocalyptic visions. In Chapter Thirteen, God tells Esdras how there will come a time when God's son will appear at Mount Zion and the nations will gather. The son of God will condemn the warring nations and destroy them. Then he will gather to himself the peaceful nations. Specifically, God states that the Ten Tribes of Israel will be among the peaceful survivors.

> These are the Ten Tribes that were led away from their own land into captivity in the days of King Hoshea, whom King Shalmaneser of the Assyrians led captive; he took them across the river and they were taken into another land. But they formed this plan for themselves, that they would leave the multitude of the nations and go to a more distant region, where mankind had never lived, that there at least they might keep their statutes that they had not kept in

their own land. And they went in by the narrow passages of the Euphrates river. For at that time the Most High performed signs for them and stopped the channels of the river until they passed over. Through that region there was a long way to go, a journey of a year and a half and that country is called Arzareth.

Then they dwelt there until the last times; and now, when they are about to come again, the Most High will stop the channels of the river again, so that they may be able to pass over. Therefore you saw the multitude gathered together in peace. But those who are left of your people, who are found within my holy borders, shall be saved. Therefore when he destroys the multitude of the nations that are gathered together, he will defend the people who remain. And then he will show them very many wonders (2 Esdras 13:40–50).

These verses were written in the aftermath of the defeat of the Jewish revolt against Rome and the destruction of the Second Temple with the accompanying diaspora of many Jews. Not only had they failed to gain their independence, but the Jews lost the revered centre of their religion – the Temple in Jerusalem. It was a traumatic event for Jews everywhere, including the author of 2 Esdras. In response to that situation, his purpose was to give his fellow Jews hope. At the same time, he contributed two strains to the myth of the Ten Lost Tribes. First, the exiled Israelites left the places where the Assyrians had placed them. Instead, they sought and found a never-before-inhabited land after an eighteen-month trek. It was called Arzareth, which might sound exotic but in Hebrew simply and prosaically means 'another land'. Second, the account in 2 Esdras emphasizes that the exiled members of the Ten Tribes had sought the distant land so that they could follow God's laws. They had failed to follow the divine commands while living in the kingdom of Israel and that disobedience got them conquered and exiled. Now the Ten Tribes were on the move and no one knew where they were living. At the same time, the Ten Tribes had become good Jews once more by following the divine laws. Most importantly, the Ten Lost Tribes gained a positive role in God's final judgement of humanity when the world will be set right. About the same time, the great Jewish historian Flavius Josephus (37–100 CE) mentioned in his *Antiquities of the Jews* that 'the Ten Tribes are beyond the Euphrates till now and are an immense multitude and not to be estimated by numbers.'[11]

Meanwhile, the concept of the Messiah had stopped being an abstraction who would arrive someday in the future. Judea and all of Palestine were a very discontented region within the Roman empire. Assassinations and minor insurrections were breaking out. The Romans considered most of the rebels to be just bandits or usurpers, such as Simon of Perea and Athronges. But occasionally a rebel leader would assert a religious motivation and even claim supernatural powers. In 36 CE a Samaritan prophet tried to lead his followers to Mount Gerizim as a prelude to setting up an independent kingdom. Pontius Pilate's brutal intervention stopped that movement. Theudas during the mid-40s CE led his followers to the Jordan River and claimed he would part its waters. Roman troops put a stop to Theudas by beheading him. Another prophet arrived from Egypt between 52 and 58 CE and claimed to possess the Joshua-like power to cause the walls of Jerusalem to fall down. He tried to gather an army to attack the city, but Roman forces defeated the rebels although the Egyptian prophet managed to escape. Later, a Roman tribune would ask the apostle Paul if he was the Egyptian (Acts 21:38). During the Jewish War (66–73 CE), several rebel leaders attempted to claim the kingship of Israel. One of these, Simon Bar Giora, displayed some religious actions that might indicate he had pretensions to being the Messiah. None of these people overtly claimed to be the Messiah; nor does Josephus state in his histories that they did. As a Jew, Josephus would have been alert to such a claim. The book of Acts (5:36) states that 'Theudas rose up, claiming to be somebody.' But whether Luke, the author of Acts, meant that he was a false Messiah is unclear. The fact is, Jesus never claimed to be the Messiah. His followers attributed that designation to him. Messiahs were not appearing during the late Second Temple era, despite what some writers claim. The coming of the Messiah, however, was being thought about and talked about. Jewish messianism was about to begin having a very significant impact on the myth of the Ten Lost Tribes.[12]

Another revolt broke out in Judea in 131 CE as Jews continued to be extremely aggrieved under Roman domination. In particular, the emperor Hadrian's plan to ban circumcision and plant a Roman colony on the site of Jerusalem with its own temple to Jupiter pushed the Jews to rebel. The great rabbi Akiba had been visiting various Jewish communities in the Roman empire to organize support for a revolt. Meanwhile, a man arose to lead the revolt: Simon Bar Cosida. Rabbi Akiba declared him to be the Messiah. Some accounts even claim that Akiba also bestowed the name of Bar Kochba (meaning 'son of a star') on the rebel leader. Others, however, maintain that only the Christians called him by that name. For about two years Judea was virtually an independent kingdom ruled by Bar Kochba. Coinage issued by him included the image of a star and declared 'Freedom of Israel' and 'Freedom of Jerusalem'. Bar Kochba definitely claimed to be the genuine Messiah. So if the Messiah had restored the Davidic kingdom, then All-Israel should have been gathering in Judea. Prophecy said that the Ten Tribes should have been on their way to join the revolt but they did not appear. Their absence, however, did not cause Rabbi Akiba to doubt that Bar Kochba was the Messiah. Rather, he declared that the Ten Tribes no longer existed and had been absorbed by their neighbours. Most other rabbis like Eleazar disagreed with Akiba and would go on to classify Bar Kochba as a false Messiah. In the meantime, the belief was established that when the Messiah appeared, the Ten Tribes would come to his aid. Later, Jews would extend that belief to include that the Ten Tribes might appear to help whenever Jews were suffering oppression or persecution.[13]

Another element of Ten Tribes geography that entered Jewish lore was the River Sambatyon. First, the idea arose in rabbinical literature of a river that flowed six days a week and was dry or calm on the seventh day. It was a sabbatical river. The earliest mentions of the Sambatyon simply described it as a normal river. Embellishments – such as the idea it rested on the sabbath – followed. According to the Talmud, the rabbi Akiba used the Sambatyon as one of his proofs that the sabbath is a God-ordained day of rest. Additional information claimed that the river flowed violently during the six days, making it virtually impassable. More elaborate descriptions contended that the river's current was so powerful that it picked up and carried rocks and boulders, and crossing the river was not just extremely difficult but led to certain death. The most extravagant accounts held that it was actually a river of rocks and boulders, not water. Josephus in his *Jewish War* tells that during his triumphal journey after the fall of Jerusalem, the Roman general and later emperor Titus saw a sabbatical river in southwestern Syria that was dry six days a week but flowed on the sabbath, which is the opposite of other accounts. Pliny the Elder mentioned a river in his encyclopedic *Natural History*, simply saying, 'In Judea is a stream that dries up every sabbath.'[14] Ancient geography was not an exact science.

Rabbinical literature also began connecting the Sambatyon to the Ten Tribes. The *Targum Jonathan* identified the Sambatyon as the Gozan River mentioned in 2 Kings 18:6. This text marked the beginning of the idea that some of the Ten Tribes lived in exile beyond the Sambatyon River. In some cases, the Sambatyon became the only place of exile for the Ten Tribes. Such a location linked up nicely with the account in 2 Esdras about the travelling for eighteen months to reach a river and cross into a hitherto uninhabited land. God allowed them to pass over the violent river, but once there the now faithful Ten Tribes were trapped. During the six weekdays, it was impossible to cross the Sambatyon. But when the Sambatyon rested, Jewish law required the Ten Tribes to rest as well. Only when the Messiah finally arrived would God stop the Sambatyon and allow the Ten Tribes to help establish the restored Davidic kingdom.[15]

The Roman empire had smashed two attempts to re-establish the Jewish state of Israel. Besides military defeat, the surviving Jews were massacred or dispersed within the Roman empire and beyond. Rome's fall hardly ended their problems. The Byzantine empire, centred on Constantinople, was not particularly friendly to Jews. Elsewhere the Islamic caliphate that dominated North Africa and the Middle East from the seventh and eighth centuries onwards tolerated Judaism but would not brook any attempts to establish an independent Jewish state. However, Jews faced the most virulent oppression and antisemitism during the Middle Ages in Christian Western Europe. The Church wanted Jews to convert and so show that they accepted Christ as their saviour and Messiah. Persecution and discriminatory laws limiting the economic activities of Jews were designed to secure conversions. At the same time, the Church promoted the idea that because the Jews had caused the death of Christ, they were guilty of deicide. Owing to their refusal to convert, Jews were also viewed as the children of the Devil. As such, it was believed that they plotted against Christians by poisoning wells, spreading plague and sacrificing Christian children in order to use their blood in satanic rituals.

Jews lived in a hostile world and messianism gave them hope for a better future. The Ten Tribes living in some faraway land were on standby to come to the aid of oppressed Jews and to assist with the establishment of the Davidic kingdom. Some versions of messianism suggested that particularly intense persecutions and struggles would precede the appearance of the Messiah. So, whenever Jews experienced outbreaks of intense antisemitism, they had to wonder and hope that the Messiah might be arriving soon to restore Israel and reunite the twelve tribes.

There were a number of local or regional messianic movements during the High and Late Middle Ages. When Christians decided to take the Holy Land back from the Muslims, the efforts to inspire support for the First Crusade in 1096 and the Second Crusade in 1146 and 1147 were often accompanied by a massacre of Jews in one medieval city or another. Various medieval monarchs began expelling Jews from their kingdoms. Edward I led the way in 1290 when he forced Jews to leave England. Philip IV of France followed suit in 1306 by expelling the Jews of France. When the Black Death began devastating Europe, the search for a scapegoat led straight to the Jews and more massacres during 1348 and 1349.

During the centuries of Muslim control after 711, the Iberian Peninsula had been a safe haven for Jews. The Sephardic community of Jews there was prosperous and highly cultured. But when Christian Crusaders badly defeated the forces of the fanatical Muslim Almohades at the battle of Las Navas de Tolosa in 1212, Christian domination of the Iberian Peninsula became the new reality. Antisemitism began to increase among the people and was egged on by various bigoted clergy. Bad feelings were probably aggravated by Castilian monarchs using Jews as tax collectors. Calls for forced conversions increasingly occurred and were sometimes carried out. Finally, in 1391, a series of riots, massacres and forced conversions resulted in about half the Jewish population converting to Christianity under threat of death. This episode led to the creation of a large number of *conversos* (meaning Jews who converted to Christianity), but the sincerity of their conversion was not trusted by the Church or their Christian neighbours. Conspiracy theories about Jewish and *converso* plots began to appear that were sinister anticipations of the later conspiracy theories associated with the pamphlet 'The Protocols of the Elders of Zion'. They persisted in the Iberian lands well into the eighteenth century.[16] This endemic distrust eventually led to the establishment of the nefarious Spanish Inquisition in 1478. Ultimately, the Jews of Spain were expelled in 1492, with those of Portugal following in 1497. These persecutions and expulsions also meant that many Jewish refugees moved to the Low Countries, Italy, the German-speaking lands of Central Europe, some areas of Eastern Europe and the Ottoman empire.

These expulsions were very traumatic for the Jews. Messianism once again provided a good means of coping and remaining hopeful in the face of terrible persecution. Generally, rabbis urged caution and taught that the coming of the Messiah could not be forced. Still, it was a comfort to believe that somewhere in the steppes of Tartary, the mountains of Central Asia, the depths of the Arabian Desert, or the vastness of Ethiopia the Ten Tribes stood ready to march to the rescue. The legendary kingdoms served another purpose as well. Medieval Christian clergy seeking to convert Jews often argued that God was against the Jews refusing to convert, as evidenced by the miserable position that they occupied in Christendom. Faithful Jews could riposte by pointing out that there were many large and powerful Jewish kingdoms of the Ten Tribes in Asia or Africa. So, God was not against them. Jews in the Middle Ages lived in the eschatological hope that the Messiah would come and restore the Davidic kingdom with the help of the Ten Tribes. The myth of the Ten Tribes functioned to provide hope for the Jews of Christian Europe as their potential protectors.

Although there were always sceptics, the messianic expectations of the Jews caused many of them to eagerly accept stories about encounters with the Ten Tribes or people who claimed to be their emissaries. An early account of travels among the Ten Tribes appeared in 883. A man calling himself Eldad the Danite arrived at the Jewish community at Kairouan in modern-day Tunisia. He claimed to be a representative of the tribe of Dan and told them of his travels. The Jews of Spain also heard from him. In his diary or letters, Eldad told of the fortunes of the Ten Tribes. According to him, his own tribe of Dan had completely avoided the conquest of the kingdom of Israel by Assyria and deportation. They left Israel voluntarily because they refused to join the rebellion of Jeroboam against Rehoboam which created the divided monarchy. Instead, the Danites made their way to Cush (meaning Ethiopia) and conquered a kingdom for themselves. Later on, when Sennacherib conquered Israel, he conducted two deportations. The first deportation moved the tribes of Reuben, Gad and the half-tribe of Manasseh to Halah and Habor. A second deportation removed Asher and Naphtali to Assyria. Of course, the Bible said nothing about Sennacherib deporting more Israelites. But when Sennacherib died, Gad, Naphtali and Asher made their escape and joined the Danites in Ethiopia. There they lived in the kingdom of Havilah, an important producer of gold. Nearby them, an island on the impassable Sambatyon River was the dwelling place of the reclusive tribe or children of Moses, consisting solely of Levites. Eldad mentioned visiting the tribes of Issachar, Reuben and Zebulon, which were living in the mountains of Media and Persia. There they spoke Hebrew and lived by the Jewish scriptures. He also mentioned that Ephraim and a half-tribe of Manasseh inhabited the mountains near Mecca. Incredible warriors, just one of them was a match for a thousand Arabs. Simeon and the other half-tribe of Manasseh resided in Babylonia and were the most numerous of the Ten Tribes. All in all, Eldad presented a very rosy picture of the fortunes of the Ten Tribes in the Horn of Africa and the lands of Mesopotamia and Persia.[17]

The Jews of the Mediterranean world of the ninth century readily embraced Eldad the Danite although they checked his story with the Gaon of Baghdad, the head of an important Jewish school. The Gaon vouched for Eldad and his tales of the lost Ten Tribes, which circulated among the Jews of that era and ever after. Jews were inspired to learn that powerful Jewish kingdoms living independent and religious lives existed, some of them by the Sambatyon River. The scholar Pamela Barmash has suggested that Eldad's account is really the beginning of the myth of at least some of the Ten Tribes being great warriors and living by the Sambatyon waiting for the Messiah's call.[18]

Over the following centuries, Eldad's reputation for truthfulness has had its ups and downs. Rabbi Chisdai (better known as Hasdai ibn Shaprut) was a Spanish Jew working for the caliphs of Córdoba. In his letter of about 960, he spoke highly of Eldad. The great Moses Maimonides, generally a cautious rationalist, also took Eldad's account seriously. Other medieval scholars, however, considered Eldad to be an impostor. During the nineteenth century, regard for Eldad's account reached its nadir when the great Jewish bibliographer Adolf Neubauer pronounced him a fraud in 1889. On the other hand, Elkan Nathan Adler in 1930 argued that Eldad and his account were genuine. More recently, David J. Wasserstein, Tudor Parfitt and Zvi Ben-Dor Benite have all expressed doubts about the verisimilitude of Eldad's tales of the Ten Tribes. But in his day and for long after, whether true or false, Eldad gave Jews hope.[19]

Other Jewish travellers of the Middle Ages encountered or heard about some of the lost tribes in Africa and Asia. Rabbi Benjamin of Tudela, who travelled in Asia from 1165 to 1173, is the best known. Unlike Eldad, Rabbi Benjamin's professed identity and travels were completely authentic. He lived in the kingdom of Navarre, and his extensive travels took him from Spain to Rome and Constantinople and on to Palestine, Baghdad and Persia. From there he continued to India and Ceylon and possibly made it all the way to China. While returning home, he stopped at Aden and travelled cross-country from the Red Sea's western coast to Aswan on the Nile. From there he made his way up the Nile to Cairo and Alexandria. Before arriving home in Navarre, he returned to Rome. During his journey, he encountered Jews in Kurdistan who claimed to be descendants of the Ten Tribes and were in contact with the rabbis of Baghdad. Along the way, he heard about a false Messiah named David Alroy, who tried to foment a rebellion against the king of Persia and the Muslim caliph. Rabbi Benjamin also was told that the tribes of Dan, Zebulon, Asher and Naphtali had formed a kingdom under the rule of a Levite in the mountains around Nishapur. No mention, however, is made of the Sambatyon River in Rabbi Benjamin's account. As a medieval Jewish report concerning the Ten Tribes, Rabbi Benjamin's details are rather modest. It is entirely possible that he encountered Jewish communities in Kurdistan and beyond. The Jewish travellers Elijah of Ferrara in 1434 and Obadiah Jared a Bertinoro during 1487–90 left similar accounts of Jews descended from the Ten Tribes in Ethiopia, India and Central Asia along with mentions of the Sambatyon River with its island inhabited by Levites. In both cases, however, they were repeating second-hand accounts rather than relating things they had seen in their travels. They were not alone. Italian Jews visiting Palestine during the fifteenth century regularly sent home reports of the Ten Tribes standing in readiness to march or even being on the march. Such reports periodically stirred Jewish messianic hopes while causing apprehension among Christians, including the papacy. It was a situation that made the acceptance of the enigmatic David Reuveni's claim to be an emissary of the Ten Tribes and commander of their formidable armies easier to accept.[20]

David Reuveni (also Reubeni) arrived in Venice from Egypt in 1524 with quite a tale to tell. Proceeding to the recently created Jewish ghetto, he announced that he was a son of the deceased King Solomon and the younger brother of King Joseph. Their realm of Kaibar or Habor was an independent Jewish kingdom in the mountains east of Mecca and consisted of the tribes of Reuben, Gad and a half-tribe of Manasseh. He had come seeking an alliance with the papacy and Emperor Charles v to free Israel from the rule of the Muslim Ottoman empire. The Jews of Venice and other parts of Italy readily embraced his quest and provided finance for Reuveni's travels. He had aroused their messianic ardour with his talk of the Ten Tribes getting ready to march to war, which is not to say that there were not some sceptics. From Venice, he travelled to Rome, where the recently elected pope, Clement vii, gave him an enthusiastic welcome and a receptive audience. Once more, Italian Jews were delighted as well as a little surprised by the new pope's actions. For Clement vii, Reuveni's offer of an alliance was a welcome one. The Ottoman Turks under their young Sultan Suleiman the Magnificent had gone on the offensive in the Balkans and the Mediterranean, capturing Belgrade in 1521 and Rhodes in 1522. Being given a way to strike back against the Turks was an unexpected but pleasant surprise. The problem was that the pope did not want to bring Charles v into the alliance. Instead, he sent Reuveni to see João iii of Portugal (r. 1521–57), who was already engaged in a war with the Ottomans for control of the Indian Ocean spice trade. Reuveni asked for weapons and a Portuguese ship to assist in an assault on Jidda and Mecca by the army of the Ten Tribes. Given that Afonso de Albuquerque, the highly aggressive governor of the Portuguese spice empire in India, had earlier made a raid into the Red Sea in 1513 and had his eye on Jidda, Reuveni's plan had an appeal to Portuguese interests. Certainly, he aroused the enthusiasm of the Portuguese community of conversos. One of these was Diego Pieres, who returned to the Jewish faith and took the name Shelomoh Molkho.

Unfortunately for Reuveni, he overstayed his welcome in Portugal. Evidence was mounting that Reuveni was an impostor and a charlatan. Furthermore, Shelomoh Molkho's return to Judaism was a result of Reuveni's mission. That occurrence had the potential to persuade more conversos to follow Molkho's example. It was a troubling prospect for the officials of the Portuguese government and the Church. Leaving Portugal during the summer of 1526, Reuveni reunited with Molkho in Italy during 1530 or 1531. Journeying over the Alps in August, the pair sought an audience with Charles v to persuade him to join the alliance against the Ottoman Turks. Instead, Charles v turned Reuveni and Molkho over to the Inquisition. Molkho was condemned and burned at the stake in Mantua later in 1532, while Reuveni was imprisoned for stirring up the conversos in Portugal. Details of his imprisonment have not survived, but it appears that he either died in one of the Inquisition's cells or was burned at Llerena during 1538.[21]

Jewish opinions about the authenticity of Reuveni and his story have varied from the sixteenth century to the present. Part of Reuveni's travel narrative described a journey he took prior to his arrival in Cairo to make the voyage to Venice. He claimed to have crossed the Red Sea and landed in Eritrea. From there he visited Ethiopia and the Sudan region before heading up the Nile to Cairo. Based on his description of his itinerary, Reuveni appears to have been roaming aimlessly. Also, despite his supposed travels in Ethiopia, the fact that the Ethiopians were Christians appears to have passed him by. Based on these aspects of his narrative, scholars have concluded Reuveni never went there. The existence of the desert kingdom of Reuben, Gad and the half-tribe of Manasseh has also been seriously questioned. It strains credulity to believe that a Jewish kingdom flourished for centuries in the very heartland of Islam. That said, the idea that a Jewish kingdom existed in the Arabian Desert was already a mainstay of Ten Tribes lore from Eldad the Danite through to the seventeenth century. In fact, a comparison of Eldad's account with Reuveni's indicates that some borrowing had taken place.[22]

Despite these problems with Reuveni's credibility, his narrative has been accepted as true by some people from 1524 until the present. On the other hand, Jews in Damascus and Cairo had viewed Reuveni as a fraud prior to his voyage to Venice. They were in a better position to recognize the weaknesses of his story. Once Reuveni reached Italy, he managed to charm and convince Jews and Gentiles of his genuineness, including Pope Clement vii. The readiness of the Jews of Italy and the *conversos* of Portugal to see signs of an impending arrival by the Messiah and the Ten Tribes worked in Reuveni's favour. That asset also proved to be a liability. The enthusiasm of the Portuguese *conversos* caused the initially supportive João iii to cool in his commitment to an alliance. Meanwhile, fatally for Reuveni, Emperor Charles v was both unconvinced and hostile towards him.[23]

While Reuveni was almost certainly an impostor in terms of his claim to be a prince in a kingdom of the Ten Tribes along with some of the details of his travels, he was likely very sincere in his intention to return the dispersed Jews to a restored Israel. He wanted the Messiah to come. Moti Benmelech has argued that Reuveni was a Palestinian Jew who was influenced by the messianic teachings of Abraham Halevi (also Avraham ben Eliezer Ha-Levi), a Kabbalist expelled from Spain in 1492 who made his way to Palestine in 1514. His teachings spoke of an imminent redemption and restoration of Israel, but he also advocated a passive messianism with Jews patiently waiting for miraculous events to occur. Reuveni took the imminent redemption part of Halevi's teaching but inserted the active promotion of the elements required to bring on the Messiah. Getting the Portuguese to attack Jidda and Mecca and creating an alliance of Christian Europe to defeat the Ottomans and liberate Israel were his contributions. With those events set in motion, the Ten Tribes and the Messiah were both sure to appear. When that came to pass, his imposture would no longer matter. It did not come to pass, so now is the time to turn to what Christian Europe of the medieval and Renaissance eras thought about the Ten Tribes.[24]

The Christian Millennium and the Ten Lost Tribes

Many Christians in medieval Europe believed that the Ten Tribes of Israel were somewhere out in the world. In contrast with Jewish beliefs, the popular religious culture of medieval Christians had come to view the Ten Tribes very negatively. It had not always been that way and the official teachings of the Church did not portray the Ten Tribes unsympathetically. But the official teachings of the Church did not always have much impact on the workings of popular religion. How this shift came about is a thought-provoking episode in the history of antisemitism and the myth of the Ten Lost Tribes.

Early Christians believed that the Second Coming of Christ and the end of the world were imminent, but as time went by the immediate expectations that the end was near faded. Speculation about the Second Coming, the millennial kingdom, the final battle with the Antichrist and the victory of Christ and his followers, however, continued. All sorts of ideas about what the last days and the final battle would be like developed, grew and evolved. The Jews and the Ten Tribes also had a role to play in this apocalyptic event. The Bible taught that in the last days the Jews would convert to Christianity and join Christ at his Second Coming. From a Christian point of view, that was a good thing. The Second Coming would bring with it the end of the fallen world, but after that all would be well for believers. Over time, however, a more malevolent view of the role of Jews and the Ten Tribes would evolve.[25]

Various Christian theologians of the second and third centuries asserted that the Antichrist would be born a Jew of the tribe of Dan.

About the same time, however, the chiliast Christian poet Commodianus wrote an account of the last battle between Christ and the Antichrist in which the Ten Tribes were a blessed people who formed the army of Christ while the evil nations of Gog and Magog from the book of Revelations 20 would form the army of the Antichrist. The Christian historian Paulus Orosius in his universal *Seven Books of History against the Pagans* identified the unclean nations supposedly defeated and locked up in the far mountains by Alexander the Great of legend as the Ten Tribes. One particularly influential text was the *Revelation of Pseudo-Methodius*, written after 500 in Greek or Syrian (Aramaic) and translated into Latin about 700. Its vision of the Last Days focused on the Antichrist gathering the Jews to Jerusalem where they accepted the Antichrist as their Messiah. Some accounts stated that the Antichrist would be born in Babylon but that he would move to Palestine and build a new temple for the Jews at Jerusalem. He would gather the dispersed Jews, and they would be his faithful followers who would go down to defeat and damnation at the last battle between the Antichrist and Christ. During the tenth century, Abbot Adso of Montier-en-Der produced a handbook of lore concerning the Antichrist. Adso added the details that the Antichrist's mother would be a prostitute and that Satan would enter the child in her womb. As a result, the Jewish Antichrist would be Satan incarnate and the Jews, including the Ten Tribes, would be his army.[26]

Jews had suffered from antisemitism in the pagan world of the Hellenistic kingdoms and the Roman empire. Once Christianity appeared, a new rivalry and animosity developed between Judaism and the new offshoot faith. It produced a new form of antisemitism as well. After the triumph of Christianity as the only legal religion in the Roman empire, Christian antisemitism was the only form of antisemitism to survive in Europe. Furthermore, historians recognize that from at least 1200 to the sixteenth century, Christian antisemitism was intensifying. The medieval Catholic Church's policy towards the Jews always had been and remained to convert them or, failing that, to repress them. It was not the Church's goal to annihilate Jews. Various kings, nobles, archbishops and bishops had actually taken the Jews in their territories under their protection. Often, however, these rulers were powerless to save the Jews from the rampages of virulently antisemitic lower clergy and commoners. The age of the Crusades had seen vicious pogroms against Jews in the cities of the Rhineland and along the road to Constantinople at the beginnings of both the First Crusade in 1096 and Second Crusade in 1146–7. Later as the Crusades began to fail and knowledge of the contents of the Talmud increased, apocalyptic anxieties and loathing of Jews intensified.

The mendicant friars stimulated antisemitism by preaching that Jews were servants of the Antichrist and that the Ten Tribes were standing by to attack and destroy Christendom. During the later Middle Ages, the blood libel appeared, which accused the Jews of kidnapping Christian children and using them as a human sacrifice to obtain their blood for hideous rituals.[27]

Supposed news of the Ten Tribes came to the forefront of European consciousness during the later Middle Ages. In 1145 the Crusader bishop Hugh of Jabala brought word to Rome that a mysterious and powerful Christian ruler named Prester John had appeared to turn the tide of war against the forces of Islam in their struggles with the Crusader states in the eastern Mediterranean lands. Letters purportedly from Prester John began to reach the pope and European monarchs in 1165. It turned out that the kingdom of the Ten Lost Tribes was a vassal state of that great Christian monarch. That was good news for Christendom because it meant that all was right in the world. Even in the strange and unfamiliar lands of Asia, Jews were subservient to Christians. On the other hand, Jews maintained that the kingdom or kingdoms of the Ten Tribes were powerful and independent in their own right.

Things got worse when the Mongol hordes began to threaten Europe. It had been all right in 1238 when they were only ravaging Islamic lands. By 1240 the Mongol menace was looming larger over Christian Europe. The thirteenth-century chronicler Matthew Paris described the Mongols as deformed humans who were of the race of Satan. He identified them (although with some equivocation) as the Ten Tribes that Alexander the Great had with God's help enclosed in the Caucasus. These comments made him the first English writer to mention the Ten Lost Tribes. During 1241, the year of the Mongol devastation of the Christian armies of central Europe, Matthew Paris told of a Jewish plot with the Mongols. Supposedly, the Jews of the Holy Roman Empire considered the Mongols to be fellow Jews. A secret meeting was called in which the leaders of the Jews proposed a plan to aid the Mongols: 'our brethren of the remnant of Israel, who were formerly shut up, have gone forth to bring the whole world to subjection to them and to us.' The Jews told Christian authorities that they wanted to send poisoned wine to the Mongols. Instead, they filled the wine casks with weapons. Their treachery was discovered and the perpetrators were executed or imprisoned for life. In the judgement of Matthew Paris, this incident 'openly showed forth the hidden treachery and extraordinary deceit of the Jews, who chose rather to assist these [the Mongols] open enemies of the world . . . than to aid the Christians who allowed them to live amongst them'. Whether this incident really happened is incidental to the fact that it was widely believed throughout Europe. It became a truism that the Jews were in league with the Ten Tribes in the form of the Mongols in order to destroy Christendom.

Later Sir John Mandeville, supposedly a well-travelled Englishman but actually a fictional character, also claimed to have heard that the Ten Tribes were still captives enclosed in the mountains near the Caspian Sea. It was reported

> that in the time of Antichrist those Jews will sally out and do much harm to Christian men. And so all the Jews in different parts of the world learn to speak Hebrew, for they believe that Jews who are enclosed among those hills will know they are Jews (as they are) by their speech when they arrive. And then they will lead them into Christendom to destroy Christian men. For those Jews say they know by their prophecies that the Jews enclosed among those hills will issue out and the Christians will be under their sway, just as they have been under Christian domination.

Mandeville's *Travels* first appeared in French between 1356 and 1366 and were popular and widely read during the later Middle Ages. In the German-speaking lands of Christendom, these legends of the threatening and invincible armies of the Ten Tribes waiting for the signal to crush Christianity were commonplace. They would evolve into the myth of the fearsome Red Jews that flourished in popular culture of the German laity during the fourteenth and fifteenth centuries.[28]

It has been demonstrated by several historians that apocalyptic expectations and antisemitism went hand in hand during the later Middle Ages. The Jewish belief in the coming of the Messiah with the restoration of the kingdom of All-Israel, including the wayward Ten Tribes, was mirrored by the Christian belief in the Second Coming of Christ and his battle with the Antichrist and his evil hordes, including the armies of the Ten Tribes, at the end of the world. The heroes of the Jewish Apocalypse – the Jewish Messiah and the Ten Tribes – were the villains of the Christian Apocalypse. During the early Middle Ages, Christian apocalyptic thought had the Ten Tribes and other Jews fighting for the Antichrist, but with the defeat of the Antichrist they would be converted and so saved for eternity. By the later Middle Ages, the Ten Tribes and the Jews still fought for the Antichrist, but there would be no conversion or salvation for them. It is sometimes suggested that medieval antisemitism was based on envy of the wealth that some Jews accumulated and that Jews were hated money-lenders. Social, economic and demographic research, however, has tended to reduce the importance of those motivations. Jewish moneylenders were not that common. Any seizure of Jewish wealth was more a by-product of antisemitism than its motive. Jews were despised and feared because they were different and set themselves apart. Their stubborn refusal to convert to what medieval Christians saw as the obvious truth of their faith was a source of provocation and frustration, along with the anxiety that the Jews just might be right. Medieval societies saw unity and uniformity as the greatest good. Diversity was suspect. Jews were a troubling diversity that might be planning nasty plots with their relatives, the Ten Tribes or Red Jews. As Andrew Gow has explained antisemitism in late medieval Christian apocalyptic thought, 'It is in its origin the result of deliberate intention, a hostile motivation to explain Jewish Messianism in terms of diabolical machinations.' The Jews of medieval Christendom and the Ten Tribes were the henchmen of the Antichrist. The Ten Tribes as Gog and Magog were the enemy without and the European Jews were the enemy within.[29]

These violent and antisemitic apocalyptic ideas fired up medieval Christians during the thirteenth, fourteenth and fifteenth centuries but then began to wane. Why did they start to decline? One of the most important reasons is that the Apocalypse failed to occur, even though people had been saying for a long time that the Second Coming and the millennium were imminent. People got tired of the anxious waiting. The Reformation, with its Protestant biblicism, also caused a decline in belief in the Red Jews and the Ten Lost Tribes as the army of the Antichrist masquerading as the Jewish Messiah. Luther thought the end of the world was near and saw the Turks as Gog and Magog. He also did not view the Apocalypse as a dreadful battle. For him it was a blessed end and the beginning of a new heaven and a new earth. These details, along with the myth of the enclosed and unclean nations, were not even in the Bible. The sceptical strain of Renaissance humanism also caused the educated elite to abandon the myth of the Ten Lost Tribes as the army of the Antichrist. But as one version of the myth of the Ten Tribes faded, a new setting and a new version evolved. The discovery of the Americas provided the Ten Tribes with a new place of exile.[30]

The Ten Lost Tribes in the Americas

When the European encounter with the Americas began in 1492, there occurred a growing realization of the enormity of the vast collection of strange lands and peoples that had been newly revealed. It was a shock to the worldview of the Europeans. The existence of the Native Americans or

Indians had to be explained and connected to the Old World to preserve the biblical unity of all humans. One theory for explaining these hitherto unknown people claimed they were of Jewish or Hebrew origin. But which Jews or Hebrews? Were they from the Ten Lost Tribes or refugees from the Babylonian conquest, the Jewish War, the Bar Kochba rebellion or some other group? It appears that most of the older writers about the Jewish origins of the Native Americans considered the Ten Tribes to be the ancestors. Often, however, they barely mentioned the Ten Tribes and their reader needed to be alert for scattered references. This circumstance appears to indicate that it was understood that references to Jews meant Jews of the Ten Tribes.

When Christopher Columbus landed on San Salvador Island on 12 October 1492, according to his log, he and his men saw a 'beach full of naked people'. He described them as 'the color of the Canary Islanders, neither black nor white'. Since he believed he had reached the archipelago now known as Indonesia, but in his day known as the Indies, he called the natives Indians. Although Columbus continued until his dying day to insist that he'd found a western sea route to Asia, most Europeans came to realize within a few years that a new and undiscovered land mass had been found (since the forgotten Norse discovery). The discovery that hitherto unknown people lived there also raised some serious cosmographic questions: where did these so-called Indians come from and how were they connected to existing Classical and biblical knowledge? All humans were supposed to be descended, first, from Adam and Eve and, second, from one of Noah's three sons – Shem, Ham or Japheth. So where did the American aborigines fit into this worldview?[31]

All sorts of suggestions have been put forward about the origins of the Native Americans. Just about every ancient people has been credited as their ancestors. Carthaginians, Celts, Scythians, Greeks, Romans, Chinese, Japanese and West Africans among others have been identified as the progenitors of some or all of the pre-Columbian peoples of the Americas. Even Atlanteans have featured prominently in theories about Indian ancestry. Needless to say, Jews and the Ten Lost Tribes have also been identified as the people who first settled all or at least some of the pre-Columbian Americas. The lostness and the wanderings of the Ten Tribes made them obvious candidates for being the first Americans.

Despite the high profile of Jews and the Ten Tribes in the culture of Christian Europe, the first explorers and settlers did not immediately turn to Hebrew or Ten Tribes theories to explain the aboriginal inhabitants of the Americas. They looked to the literature of Classical Greece and Rome and suggested that the Carthaginians or survivors from Atlantis had been the first settlers. In his extensive research into the history of theories about Native American origins, historian Lee Eldridge Huddleston 'was unable to locate any early explorers and historians who expressed the idea [the Ten Tribes or Hebrew theory] in writing'. The earliest known reference may be in *The Decades of the New World* by Peter Martyr de Angleria, who stated in the early sixteenth century that Columbus thought Hispaniola was the land of Ophir, where the mines of King Solomon were located. Some of its inhabitants might have been descended from Hebrew visitors. There is no other evidence that Columbus thought he had found Ophir, and his Spanish contemporaries did not support the Ophirite theory or any other version of the Hebrew/Ten Tribes theory until the last quarter of the sixteenth century.[32]

The first person definitely to advocate the Ten Tribes version of the Hebrew theory was Joannes Fredericus Lumnius of the Low Countries in his *De extremo Dei Iudicio vocatione* of 1567 and his *De vicinitate extremi judicii Dei et consummationis saeculi* of 1594. Although not widely circulated, Lumnius established the theological foundations of the Ten Lost Tribes theory. Following 2 Esdras, he claimed that they escaped the Assyrians and settled in America. The French scholar Gilbert Génébrard followed Lumnius in the same year with his *Chronographia*, which also supported the Ten Lost Tribes theory.[33]

For the first three-quarters of the sixteenth century, Spanish writers primarily advocated the Atlantean theory of Indian origins and secondarily the Carthaginian theory. Many more recent accounts wrongly credit Bartolemé de Las Casas, Diego de Landa and later Juan de Torquemada with promoting theories about the Indians being descendants of Hebrews in general and the Ten Tribes in particular. In fact, they were quite sceptical about any Hebrew contact with ancient America. Around 1580, however, another group of Spanish scholars studying the natives of Mexico found that a Ten Tribes or Hebrew theory provided a reasonable explanation of the supposed similarities between Hebrew and native Mexican customs. In their detailed studies of the aborigines of Mexico, Diego Durán, Juan Suárez de Peralta and Juan de Tovar all saw cultural parallels with the ancient Hebrews. As Durán put it in his *History of the Indies of New Spain*:

> All of these things confirm my suspicions that these natives are part of the ten tribes of Israel that Shalmaneser, king of the Assyrians, captured and took to Assyria in the time of Hoshea, king of Israel … Other evidence found in the Holy Writ can be cited to prove this idea that God, in Hoshea, chapters I, and II, and II up to XII, is said to have promised to multiply ten tribes of Israel, making

them as numerous as sand of the sea. And the fact that they have taken possession of a large part of the world clearly and manifestly shows how great was this increase.[34]

By the early seventeenth century, the Spanish chroniclers Pedro Simón and Antonio Vázquez de Espinosa concocted a narrower version of the Ten Lost Tribes theory which claimed that the Native Americans were descended solely from the Hebrew tribe of Issachar. Later, in 1681, the Jesuit scholar Diego Andrés Rocha in his *Tratado único y singular del origen de los indios occidentales de Perú, Mexico, Santa Fé y Chile* (A Unique and Singular Tract About the Origin of the West Indians of Peru, Mexico, Santa Fe and Chile) wrote that the wildness of Native Americans showed they were largely descended from Tartars and Hebrews.[35]

Other Spanish scholars strongly opposed theories that the Indians were descendants of the Ten Lost Tribes or other Jews. Despite being falsely credited with being an adherent of the Ten Lost Tribes theory, Bartolemé de Las Casas strongly rejected it. Seventeenth-century Spaniards such as José de Acosta, Juan de Torquemada, Pedro Antonio de la Calancha y Benavides and Bernabé Cobo all rejected the possibility of Native Americans being the progeny of the Ten Tribes or other Hebrews. As the often sceptical Acosta sensibly asked:

> How can it be, when the Jews have been so assiduous in preserving their language and ancient traditions, to the point that in every part of the world where they live today they differ from the rest, that in the Indies alone they have forgotten their ancestry, their law, their ceremonies, their Messiah and finally all their Jewishness?

Good-sense arguments have never stopped absurd theories from propagating, and the Ten Tribes theory of the peopling of the Americas was no exception. In fact, a new outburst of enthusiasm for it was about ready to emerge as part of the apocalyptic expectations that gripped England, the Dutch Republic and the English colonies in New England.[36]

Millennialism and messianism will never fade away as long as there are Christians and Jews, but they do have ups and downs in terms of popular enthusiasm. During the mid-seventeenth century in Europe there was an upsurge in expectations about the Last Days. Various Christian calculations placed the occurrence of the Christian millennium sometime during the mid-1650s or mid-1660s. The year 1666 had an obvious appeal since it bore the supposed Mark of the Beast, but it was by no means the stand-out among possible apocalyptic years. The English prophet and millenarian Mary Cary had proposed either 1655 or 1656. The Cambridge scholar Joseph Mede suggested that the beginning of the end would occur on or around 1660 based on a prophecy that claimed the Last Days would occur 1260 years after the fall of the Roman empire in 400. But Mede also suggested 1654 and hedged his predictions by adding that the Second Coming would occur no later than 1716. Jewish scholars were reaching similar conclusions based on calculations using their system of dating from the divine Creation. Jewish Kabbalists identified 1648 as the year the Messiah would come.[37]

The first half of the seventeenth century saw numerous events take place that would tend to cause many people to believe the end of the world was imminent. Europe was wracked by vicious wars. The Thirty Years War devastated Germany between 1618 and 1648 as well as dragging other countries into the conflict. Britain experienced a crippling series of civil wars during the 1640s and 1650s. These civil wars also caused a breakdown in social control that unleashed radical and millenarian sects like the Quakers and the Fifth Monarchy Men to agitate. Meanwhile in Eastern Europe, the Chmielnicki uprising of the Cossacks from 1648 to 1657 against the Polish-Lithuanian Commonwealth caused widespread devastation and massive and horrific massacres of Jews living in Ukraine. Persecutions and pogroms always invigorated messianic expectations among the Jews.[38]

Unlike the millennialism and messianism of the later Middle Ages, the violent aspects of the last great battle between the returning Christ and the Antichrist or the arriving Messiah and the forces of evil were significantly de-emphasized, at least among the elites and intellectuals of Christian and Jewish society. The Jewish Messiah was no longer seen as the Antichrist in Protestant circles, since they identified the pope as the Antichrist. The Ten Tribes, if they appeared, would be allies in the battle against evil rather than the shock troops of Satan. At least that would be the case for some irenical Jewish and Christian scholars such as Menasseh ben Israel and Petrus Serrarius.[39]

In 1641 a supposed encounter took place in the west-central mountains and jungles of what is now Colombia that added a new location for the Ten Tribes and contributed to the millennial and messianic ferments that had been building up during the first half of the seventeenth century. A converso named Antonio de Montezinos (formerly known as Aaron Levi) had come to the Spanish viceroyalty of New Granada. Operating out of Cartagena, Montezinos went on a trading expedition with some Indians, one of whom was named Francisco. Caught in a fierce storm while travelling in the mountains, the party feared for their lives. Francisco, however, spoke disparagingly of the Spanish. Montezinos later admonished

Francisco about his words, but the Indian reiterated his indictment of Spanish cruelties to the native peoples. He asserted that the Indians would get their revenge – adding, cryptically, with the help of an unknown people. After returning to Cartagena, the Inquisition brought Montezinos in for questioning and imprisoned him. While in prison, he made a Jewish prayer thanking God that he was not born a Gentile, which group included the Indians. But something came over him; he became angry and declared the Indians were Hebrews. He repeated this statement twice more. Having finished, he thought to himself that it could not be by chance that he had made and repeated the declaration that the Indians were Hebrews.[40]

After his release from prison, Montezinos sought out Francisco at the town of Honda on the Magdalena River. He asked Francisco to go on a journey with him. After they got out of Honda, Montezinos confessed to Francisco that he was a Jew of the tribe of Levi. At that point, Francisco agreed to take him into the wilderness, but Montezinos had to agree to do as he was commanded. The pair travelled for seven days into the wilderness until they came upon an unknown river. There Francisco made a signal and some white people appeared and started across the river in a boat. Although the cautious white people would not allow Montezinos to cross the river into their land, he learned that they were Hebrews of the tribe of Reuben. Francisco informed Montezinos that long in the past, relations between the Indians and the white people had been hostile. Several times, Indian armies had tried to invade the land of the whites and destroy them. Each time the Indian army disappeared without a trace. Making peace, the two groups became friendly and many Indians converted to Judaism. One day near the end of the world, the mysterious whites and the Indians would go forth and defeat the Spanish. After that, they would come and deliver the Jews of Europe from their oppression and together they would become the rulers of the world.[41]

This is the tale that Montezinos brought to Menasseh ben Israel, an important rabbi and messianic scholar, and to the Jewish community in Amsterdam after he arrived there on 19 September 1644. Menasseh was also a universalist who believed that all good people ultimately would be saved, whether Jewish or Christian. After some initial scepticism, the Jewish community of Amsterdam and Menasseh enthusiastically listened to Montezinos's tale. Any news of encounters with the Ten Lost Tribes was welcome to the Jews of the Diaspora. If true it was evidence that the Messiah was coming, perhaps soon. What was unique to the first half of the seventeenth century was that Jewish messianism and Christian millenarianism in northern Europe harmoniously came together in welcoming both the coming of the Messiah and the Second Coming of

Christ. Menasseh was friends with like-minded Christian millenarians such as John Dury and Petrus Serrarius, and they would correspond and collaborate on various ecumenical and millenarian projects.

At the time Montezinos arrived in Amsterdam, John Dury was serving as a chaplain in The Hague. It was there that he learned about Montezinos's encounter with the tribe of Reuben in South America. Dury passed the story to other interested parties in England, including Thomas Thorowgood and Edward Winslow. Winslow was a separatist who had come to North America on the Mayflower. When the English Civil War broke out, Winslow travelled back to England to support the cause of Parliament against King Charles I. He later became a supporter of Oliver Cromwell. After receiving Dury's news about Montezinos and the Ten Tribes in South America, he informed John Eliot back in New England during late 1648 or early 1649. Eliot is famous as the apostle to the Indians of New England. He had started his missionary work among the Native Americans in 1646. As a result of Winslow's letters about Montezinos and the Ten Tribes, Eliot began to consider that the Native Americans of New England might possibly be the descendants of the Ten Lost Tribes. Thorowgood was rector of Grimston in Norfolk and a Presbyterian moderate. His interest in the theory that Native Americans were of Jewish ancestry began in the mid-1630s when he read the books of Peter Martyr, José de Acosta and others about the Americas. He also corresponded with the New England minister Roger Williams about the theory. Undeterred by Williams's scepticism about the existence of Israelite Indians, Thorowgood had completed by 1640 a draft of what would become his *Iewes in America*. At that point, he put his manuscript away. The fact that all of Great Britain was descending into a political and religious crisis was almost certainly a major distraction for Thorowgood. He would later preach a Fast Sermon to Parliament in 1644.[42]

The Montezinos story ignited an interest or renewed an interest in Winslow, Eliot and Thorowgood concerning the possibility that the Ten Tribes had settled in the Americas and were ancestors of the various Native American tribes. Prior to Dury telling him, Thorowgood had not heard of Montezinos or Menasseh ben Israel's speculations about the Ten Lost Tribes. As a result, Thorowgood took up his *Iewes in America* manuscript again and shared it with Dury in 1648. Dury, in turn, passed the manuscript to Winslow. Both men encouraged Thorowgood to publish the work. Further enthusiasm was generated by the effort to get Parliament to establish the Society for the Promotion of the Gospel in New England. Winslow supported that effort in 1649 by publishing *The Glorious Progress of the Gospel amongst the Indians in New England*, which included letters from Thomas Mayhew and John Eliot. It included an appendix by Dury in which he speculated ecumenically about the impending start of a millennial or messianic event in 1650 that would result in 'Either we Christians shall be Mosiack, or else that themselves Jews shall be Christian.' He added in agreement with Winslow, 'I am much inclined to conjecture, that there is a sprinkling at least of Abraham's seed in these parts [of the Americas].' Meanwhile, Dury wrote to Menasseh ben Israel for more information about what Montezinos experienced in the wilds of South America. A reply arrived on 27 November 1649 which included Montezinos's narrative or relation of his adventure along with an affidavit from Menasseh. Dury shared this information with Thorowgood, who used it along with what he had learned about Menasseh's own work in his revisions of *Iewes in America*. So when *Iewes in America* finally appeared in print in 1650, its revised and expanded text also included Montezinos's relation and a sort of preface by John Dury titled *An Epistolicall Discourse of Mr. Iohn Dury to Mr Thorowgood concerning his conjecture that the Americans are descended from Israelites*. The difference was that Dury expected the Jews to play a big role in the coming millennium while Thorowgood did not. He simply thought that it was a good thing in and of itself to convert the Native Americans, descendants of the Ten Lost Tribes, to Christianity. It was a fulfilment of the Puritan goal of Christianizing and civilizing pagan and barbaric peoples. *Iewes in America* also made Thorowgood the first person to publish a full-fledged defence of the Jewish Indian theory in English.[43]

Thorowgood's *Iewes in America* was more than an attempt to prove that Native Americans were descendants of the Ten Lost Tribes. It was also a defence of the Calvinist and Puritan positions in the Church of England. In addition, it holds a place among the many works that confusingly referred to Jews when they really meant Israelites. Even in the seventeenth century, 'Jew' was used to refer to a practitioner of the Judaism of the post-exilic era. For the pre-exilic era, the term 'Israelite' referred to a person from the northern kingdom of Israel within the divided monarchy and 'Judahite' referred to a person from the southern kingdom of Judah. The Ten Lost Tribes were Israelites. Thorowgood's argument that the Native Americans had their origin in the Ten Lost Tribes was based on making comparisons and analogies between Native American and Israelite legends, domestic customs, religious beliefs and language. While it is not acceptable methodology for modern scholars of culture and anthropology, this method of comparison and analogy was commonly used during the early modern era. What Thorowgood concluded was that all of the Native Americans in both North and South America were descendants of the Ten Lost Tribes and that all of the Ten Tribes had migrated to the

Americas leaving none in Asia. Along the way from their Assyrian exile to the Americas and during their habitation there, the Ten Lost Tribes degenerated into a largely pagan and barbarous state with only vestiges of their religion and culture surviving.

Menasseh ben Israel published *The Hope of Israel; or, Esperança de Israel* in 1650 as well. He took a very different view of the Ten Lost Tribes in the Americas. The book begins with Menasseh addressing his readers: 'There are as many minds as men about the origin of the people of the Americas and of the first inhabitants of the New World and of the West Indies.' He goes on to say that of the various theories, he finds 'no opinion more probable, nor agreeable to reason, than that of our Montezinos'. Next he provides the reader with the text of Montezinos's 'Relation'. After that, Menasseh begins to work his way through the various rival origin theories, beginning with the caveat, 'It is hard to say what is certain among the so many and so uncertain, opinions concerning the origin of the Indians of the New World.' Throughout his text, Menasseh continually stresses that the Ten Lost Tribes are not gathered in one region; rather they are scattered through Asia and Africa. In section 26 of *The Hope of Israel*, he brings up the concept of the two Messiahs within Jewish messianic thought – the Messiah of Joseph and the Messiah of David. Towards the end of his book, Menasseh summarizes his views, especially that the Ten Lost Tribes had settled in many places and that some of them came to the Americas. There they continue to practise their religion and culture in hiding like Montezinos's Reubenites. The heathen and savage Native American tribes, on the other hand, are the descendants of Tartars. Menasseh further proclaims that the prophecies about the return of the Tribes to Palestine were true and would someday come to pass. The Tribes would first gather in Assyria and Egypt before their return to Palestine, where they would establish the undivided kingdom of Israel that will consist of the Twelve Tribes.[44]

Menasseh's messianic vision differed significantly from Thorowgood's theory of the Native Americans being the progeny of the Ten Lost Tribes. Menasseh thought that only a portion of the Ten Tribes were living in the Americas and they were hidden. There they continued to practise their religion and culture. According to Thorowgood, all Ten Tribes had migrated to the Americas and all the Natives Americans were their descendants, but only scraps of their religion, language and culture survived. For Dury and Winslow, both Manessah's and Thorowgood's versions of the situation of the Ten Lost Tribes in America would serve the purposes of a Christian millennialist Apocalypse. For Menasseh, the existence of groups of the Ten Lost Tribes living faithfully and inconspicuously among the Native

American savages set the stage for the Messiah's return. But Menasseh also saw stories of the Ten Lost Tribes in America as a way to get Jews readmitted into England and reverse their long-ago expulsion by Edward I in 1290. Menasseh desired this return for two reasons. One was practical. The beleaguered Jews of Europe could always use another safe haven like England for a refuge. The other was messianic: Menasseh believed that the coming of the Messiah could not proceed until Jews were present throughout the world. Their being denied entry into England presented an obstacle to the Messiah's return. The same could have been said by some Christian millennialists as well. Menasseh dedicated the second edition of *The Hope of Israel*, published in 1652, to the English Parliament. He would follow up with the pamphlets 'To His Highness the Lord Protector of the Common-Wealth of England, Scotland and Ireland' in 1655 and 'Vindiciae Judaeorum' in 1656, which further argued for the readmission of the Jews. Menasseh died in 1657. His efforts to secure readmission of the Jews had experienced only marginal success. True legal approval of Jewish residence in England eluded him.[45]

John Eliot's reaction to learning about the Montezinos story and the work of Menasseh ben Israel and Thomas Thorowgood was to cause him to reconsider his own ideas about the origins of the Native Americans. Although many theories about who and how the Americas were peopled circulated among Europeans, by the mid-seventeenth century the most widely accepted was the Tartar theory. This suggested that the Americas had been populated by the nomadic peoples of Central Asia and Siberia entering the northwestern area of North America where it was close to the northeastern region of Asia. The actual geography of this area was unknown in the seventeenth century. It was postulated that there was a narrow strait in that area which was called the Strait of Anián. Vitus Bering would later prove the speculation to be true when he explored the strait that bears his name.

Eliot had been an adherent of the Tartar theory, but the information he received from Winslow caused him to consider the possibility that the Ten Tribes were the ancestors of the Native Americans. After reading Thorowgood's *Iewes in America* in 1650, Eliot entered into correspondence with Thorowgood that began in October 1650 and lasted until October 1657. Some of Eliot's letters would later show up in Thorowgood's *Jews in America* published in 1660. Over time Eliot's support for Thorowgood's theory about the Ten Lost Tribes began to fade. One troublesome reason was that the millennium did not begin as predicted, which raised doubts with Eliot. Another reason was that Eliot had a large amount of personal experience with Native Americans through his missionary work. In contrast, Thorowgood never met any Native Americans. His conjectures did not hold up in the light of Eliot's first-hand observations. Instead, Eliot developed a theory that the Native Americans were not descendants of the Ten Tribes or the Tartars; rather they descended from Joktan, who was the younger son of Eber. Eber was a great-grandson of Noah's son Shem. He had two sons – Peleg and Joktan. It was through Peleg's line that the Hebrews of Abraham, Isaac and Jacob originated. Joktan had many sons, which included Sheba, Havilah and Ophir. These three names also represent lands located or thought to be located in the southern Arabian Peninsula or East Africa. By the sixteenth century, some people were suggesting the Ophir, the land of King Solomon's mines, was actually Peru. Eliot relates that when Nimrod, the son of Cush, led the rebellion against God's will that resulted in the building of the Tower of Babel, Eber stood against him. So when God stopped Nimrod's rebellion by the confusion of the tongues or human languages, Eber and his family got to retain the original perfect language of the Garden of Eden. And Eber's name became the name of the perfect language – Hebrew. It was the language of Eber's sons, Peleg and Jokton, and their descendants. After the confusion of languages, Eliot suggested that Eber and Joktan had headed east into the vastness of Asia and beyond. As a result of this migration, Eliot claimed 'that fruitful India are Hebrewes, that famous civil (though Idolatrous) nation of China are Hebrewes, so Japonia and these naked Americans are Hebrewes, in respect of those that planted first these parts of the world'. Later some of the Ten Lost Tribes would come to the Americas. Because both their language and the language of the Native Americans were originally Hebrew, they were able to communicate and fit in more easily. So for Eliot, the Native Americans were actually Joktanites with a scattering of some of the Ten Lost Tribes joining them much later. He shared his theory with Thorowgood in a long letter written during 1653 or 1654. Undeterred by Eliot, Thorowgood continued to promote his own theory in his new *Jews in America* (1660) while including Eliot's letter in the book.[46]

Thorowgood's theory of the Ten Lost Tribes origin of the Native Americans faced more serious and vitriolic criticism than just that posed by the alternative variant Eliot gently presented. After *Iewes in America* appeared in print, Thorowgood sent a copy to his neighbour in Norfolk, Hamon L'Estrange. Educated at Eton College and Christ's College, Cambridge, L'Estrange and his family had supported Charles 1 early in the English Civil War but retired to the country to write history and theology. Writing on 30 March 1651, L'Estrange claimed that regarding Thorowgood, 'I do much esteem and reverence for his gravity and learning.'

But as he read *Iewes in America* he 'fell upon many Sands and Rocks of reluctance to my sense'. This realization prompted him to write his rebuttal, *Americans no Iewes; or, Improbabilties that the Americans are of that race*, which was published in 1652. The first thing L'Estrange did was present his own origin theory. He suggested something similar to Eliot, but instead of Joktan's progeny settling the Americas, L'Estrange claimed it was some of Peleg's descendants. If his theory proved mistaken, L'Estrange added that 'I find argued by that learned and Iudicious [Edward] Brerewood that the Americans are the race of the Tartars, wherein (should I recede from my former argument and opinion, I should concur with his).' From there he proceeded to refute Thorowgood's evidence about the Hebrew foundations of Native American languages, religions and customs by citing counterexamples from a wide variety of ancient sources. While L'Estrange's methodology was in no way superior to Thorowgood's, what he demonstrated was that an equally valid argument could be made that many other ancient peoples showed the same similarities to the Israelites as the Native Americans. Needless to say, Thorowgood was not impressed by L'Estrange's argument and asserted that his evidence was more convincing. In his *Jews in America* published in 1660, he renewed and enhanced his claim that the Ten Lost Tribes had settled the Americas and co-opted the Tartar origin theory by identifying them as descendants of the Ten Lost Tribes. In addition, he added that he had only claimed the Israelite ancestry of the Native Americans was a probability, not a proven fact. As the 1660s progressed, the anticipated millennium did not occur, so the enthusiasm and immediacy of the theory that the Ten Lost Tribes were the progenitors of the Native American receded but never disappeared.[47]

The Mystical Messiah Sabbatai Sevi and the Ten Lost Tribes

Jewish messianism was not confined to Menasseh ben Israel's Amsterdam and Western Europe. In fact, the biggest messianic movement in Jewish history, including the hope that the Ten Lost Tribes would ride to the rescue, was taking place in the Ottoman empire at the very same time. Jews all over Europe and the Middle East were in a high state of anxiety over the massacres of Jews in the Ukraine during the Cossack uprising of Bohdan Chmielnicki that broke out in 1648. These were genocidal massacres of men, women and children by the common people, who were instigated by Chmielnicki playing on the prevailing, virulent antisemitism of the Orthodox Christian population. The rebels also hated Roman Catholicism since it was the religion of the Polish overlords of Ukraine.

The actual numbers of victims, both dead and displaced, were exaggerated at the time and for long afterwards. Still, of the Jewish population of 50,000 in the Ukraine, over 20,000 were killed. The rest fled. Such tribulations also tended to cause increased levels of messianic expectations among Jews everywhere.[48]

It was in this milieu of massacre and messianism that Sabbatai Sevi began to proclaim himself as the Messiah. Sabbatai, however, never presented himself as a divinely appointed worldly king who would re-establish the kingdom of Israel by military force and reunite the Twelve Tribes under his rule. Instead, Sabbatai claimed to have been called to be – and truly was to be – a mystical Messiah. He would become king and re-establish Israel by mystical and spiritual means without using violence. Apparently, Sabbatai and his inner circle of followers believed that when the climactic messianic moment arrived, the Turkish sultan along with his advisors and troops would recognize Sabbatai as their ruler and step aside. Then Jews of all twelve tribes would peacefully gather in Jerusalem and Palestine, and a messianic era of peace and justice would ensue.[49]

Sabbatai Sevi was born in Smyrna (now Izmir) and was a dedicated student of the Talmud and the Kabbalah. Early on he also exhibited erratic behaviour. Gershom Scholem, the great scholar of Jewish messianism, has suggested that Sabbatai Sevi probably suffered from manic-depressive psychosis. Sabbatai certainly manifested the symptoms of that psychosis on a number of occasions. Whatever his thought process might have been, during 1648 at the age of 22, he concluded that he was the Messiah. It was an insight he shared with his friends and fellow students. A number of them believed him; local Jewish leaders and rabbis did not. Undaunted, Sabbatai behaved in ways that drew disapproving attention from religious authorities, such as speaking the holy name of God, the Tetragrammaton, in public. As a result, the Jewish community of Smyrna expelled him in 1651. So he roamed the Ottoman Empire through 1654. Hostile receptions periodically forced the would-be Messiah to move. The more he wandered, the more people he met, and the more people he met, the larger his band of supporters grew. Then in 1657, millenarian Quaker missionaries began to arrive in the Ottoman empire. There were a number of times when Sabbatai and Quaker missionaries' paths crossed. Whether Sabbatai and Quakers actually met is not clear, but the enthusiasm of early Quakers would clearly have caused some degree of agitation with Ottoman officials, Muslim clerics and Jewish rabbis. Meanwhile, Sabbatai's reputation and his acceptance as the Messiah continued to increase. In April 1665, the youthful but respected Kabbalist Nathan of Gaza had a vision that Sabbatai was the Messiah. Later in June, when Sabbatai passed through

Gaza on his way to Jerusalem, the two men met and Nathan anointed Sabbatai as the Messiah. Nathan also served as a prophet and publicist for Sabbatai, which included guiding his movement in an ever more mystical direction.[50]

At this point, the Ten Lost Tribes entered the picture, not literally but as rumour. Jews had long believed that the Ten Lost Tribes would appear at the messianic moment, help the Messiah in his struggle with evil, and rescue the Jews from their suffering and oppression. Sabbatai Sevi was a different sort of Messiah. He and Nathan of Gaza preached that singing hymns would bring redemption and that his followers would be miraculously protected because any bullets fired at them by Turkish soldiers would turn around and hit the Turks. There was no need or even room for the services of the invincible soldiers of the Ten Lost Tribes in the Sabbatian movement with its mystical messianism. The only time that a Sabbatian leader mentioned the Ten Lost Tribes was a prophecy by Nathan of Gaza in late 1665. He stated that after Sabbatai became king, he would travel across the Sambation River and bring back the Ten Tribes. Yet rumours of the Ten Lost Tribes riding to the rescue, sparked by the popular imagination, began to appear. At the same time Nathan of Gaza had his vision, during April 1665 a rumour arose in Italy that Arab raiders had sacked Mecca. Stories of such a raid would have been believable since unruly and rapacious Arab tribesmen had raided Mecca in the past. But by July the story morphed into the Lost Tribes being the army that sacked Mecca, at least according to Dutch pamphlets. Word of Mecca's destruction also reached the Royal Society in London about the same time. By August, back in Italy, Venetian sources now claimed that large numbers of Jews had joined the Arabs attacking Mecca. As 1665 drew to a close, Dutch gazettes and the *London Gazette* were reporting both the pillaging of Mecca and the appearance of the Sabbatian movement. In New England, Increase Mather was telling his parishioners that the Ten Tribes were now headed to Jerusalem. By early 1666, German pamphlets were reporting the conquest of Mecca by the Ten Lost Tribes, and some named Sabbatai as their leader. Meanwhile, within the Ottoman empire, there were no stories about Mecca being laid to waste by the armies of the Ten Lost Tribes. The rumours of the Ten Tribes were a product of fevered imagination and wishful thinking among Jewish messianic enthusiasts and Christian millenarians in Western Europe not the Middle East. As was the case with David Reuveni, Christians saw the Ten Lost Tribes as allies against the Turks, rather than the henchmen of the Antichrist so dear to the hearts of late medieval Christians. This shift made sense because the Turks controlled the Holy Land, which would need liberating before the restoration of Israel could be complete. The difference in the mission of the Ten Tribes from Reuveni's time to Sabbatai's was that the Reformation had taken place. Protestant millenarians saw the Ten Tribes not just as allies against the Turks; they would also be comrades in the struggle with the papacy.[51]

While Ottoman officials did not have to fret about any imagined plundering of Mecca, they were becoming increasingly uncomfortable with the threat to the stability of their empire that Sabbatai represented. During December 1665, Sabbatai proclaimed himself both king and Messiah at Smyrna. Religious hysteria became rampant in the Jewish world, while tales of Sabbatai Sevi circulated among the Christians of Western Europe as well. The English naval official and renowned diarist Samuel Pepys recorded news of Sabbatai in Smyrna along with instances of the messianic hysteria among the Jews of London in his diary's entry for 19 February 1666. With the appearance of the Messiah, Jewish families began selling their houses in anticipation of their being miraculously returned to Jerusalem for the restoration of Israel. In February 1666, Sabbatai travelled to Istanbul and upon his arrival was promptly arrested and imprisoned. During Sabbatai's months in prison, the fervour of his followers continued unabated. So in September, the sultan and his council brought Sabbatai before them. The expectation of Sabbatai and his followers was that the sultan and the Ottoman government would simply step aside and recognize him as their ruler. Instead, they offered Sabbatai a stark choice: convert to Islam or be executed. At that point, advised by an apostate Jewish doctor, Sabbatai chose conversion to Islam. Shock, disappointment and disillusionment swept across the world of Judaism. Some hardcore Sabbatains, led by Nathan of Gaza, maintained that Sabbatai's apostasy was merely one of the trials of the messianic process. These Sabbatians held on to their beliefs for years. One group, the Dönmeh, followed Sabbatai in converting to Islam while secretly believing that Sabbatai was the Messiah and continuing to practise Judaism. They managed to survive into the twentieth century. Thus ended the last widespread and the most substantial messianic movement in Jewish history. Sabbatai's apostasy made all future messianic claims even more suspect in rabbinical circles, although in Jewish popular culture he was something of a hero along with Bar Kochba. The travails of Sabbatai were also not to be the end of the myth of the Ten Lost Tribes.[52]

The Return of the Ten Lost Tribes to North America

Back in North America, the debate over the Native Americans being the descendants of the Ten Lost Tribes or other Jews continued. John Ogilby, a geographer and Master of the Revels in Ireland, published his *America* in 1671. It was to a large degree a translation of Arnoldus Montanius's *De Nieuwe en onbekende Weereld, of, Beschryving van America en't Zuid-Land* with added material concerning British North America. Its second chapter surveyed the various theories about the origins of the Native Americans. The Ten Lost Tribes theory was discussed but ultimately refuted and rejected. Later, the Tartar origin theory was introduced and judged to be correct. Neither conclusion is surprising since a majority of European scholars always supported the Tartar origin theory. Needless to say, Ogilby's conclusions failed to convince followers of the Ten Lost Tribes theory or other Jewish Indian theories. A decade later, William Penn, the Quaker businessman and proprietor of the colony of Pennsylvania, certainly thought the Native Americans were descendants of the Ten Lost Tribes. Arriving in America to take possession of his newly granted lands in 1682, he stated, 'I am ready to believe them of the Jewish race; I mean, of the stock of the ten tribes.' He had several reasons for his opinion. First, God had guided them from northeastern Asia to northwest North America, which they proceeded to settle. Second, he observed, 'them of like countenance and their children of so lively a resemblance, that a man would think himself in Duke's-place or Bury-street in London, when he seeth them.' Finally, he found Jewish and Native American customs and rituals were very similar. Some years later in 1698, Gabriel Thomas would agree with Penn: 'The Natives, or first inhabitants of this Country in their Original, are suppos'd by most People to have been of the Ten Scattered Tribes, for they resemble the Jews very much in the Make of their Persons and the Tincture of their Complexions.' Like Penn, he added that their religious and social customs and rituals were also very similar. Nearly a century later, Daniel Gookin, in his account of the missionary efforts among the Native Americans of New England published in 1792, provided a brief overview of several theories concerning Native American origins. Evidence for and against the theories of the Ten Tribes, the Tartar/Scythians and seafaring West African tawny Moors were presented. Discussing the Ten Tribes theory, Gookin admitted that 'this opinion, that these people [the Native Americans] are of the race of the Israelites, doth not greatly obtain.' However, he adds, 'But surely it is not impossible and perhaps not so improbable, as many learned men think.' At the end of his discussion of Native American origin theories, he lamented that 'these, or any other notions, can amount to know [no] more than rational conjecture; for a certainty of their first extraction cannot be attained . . . the full determination whereof must be left until the day, wherein all secret and hidden things shall be manifested to the glory of God.' Given the current and continuing turmoil in the study of American prehistory with the collapse of the Clovis first theory that the first humans in the Americas arrived no earlier than 20,000 years ago by crossing the Bering landbridge, modern scholars are not much more certain about how and when the Native Americans first arrived than their predecessors in the eighteenth century.[53]

Gookin, in fact, expressed his uncertainty at a time when certainty about the truth of the Ten Lost Tribes origin theory was undergoing a revival. In 1775, a fur trader and practical expert on Native Americans, James Adair, published *The History of the American Indians*. Besides providing a fine anthropological study of the tribes of southeastern North America, he also presented his arguments for the theory that Israelites, Hebrews or Jews had been the ancestors of the Native Americans. Adair did not differentiate in his usage of Hebrew, Jew or Israelite, but throughout the text, it is clear, he was largely but not exclusively promoting the Ten Lost Tribes origin theory. Based on long-term, close observations, Adair followed the usual pattern of comparing social customs, rituals, religious beliefs and language to show the relation of the Native Americans with the Ten Tribes and other Jews. Adair was not a millenarian; he simply believed the Native Americans were as fully human as Europeans and that they were descended from Adam and Eve. During Adair's era, there was a big debate over monogenesis or polygenesis in terms of human origins. Was there one creation or several creations of humans? The eighteenth-century philosophers Henry Home, Lord Kames, and his cousin, David Hume, argued for several separate creations, which opened the way for declaring some people to be less human and inferior. Others, including Adair, opposed this theory. He had great respect for Native Americans based on personal experience. Connecting them to ancient Hebrews and the Ten Lost Tribes secured their place as full members of humanity. Needless to say, Adair's book had its critics and its admirers. When John Adams queried Thomas Jefferson for his opinion of Adair's book, Jefferson replied:

> Adair too had his kink . . . [but was] of as sound a mind as Don Quixote in what ever did not touch his religious chivalry. His book contains a great deal of real instruction on its subject, only requiring the reader to be constantly on his guard against the wonderful obliquities of his theory.

Other adherents of the Ten Lost Tribes or Jewish Indian origin theories, however, found Adair's scholarship to be convincing. The millenarian Elias Boudinot and the obsessive Edward King, Viscount Kingsborough, both cited and quoted Adair's book. It marked the start of a final revival of the Ten Lost Tribes and Jewish Indian theories and the start of the nineteenth century's fascination with the Ten Lost Tribes.[54]

Elias Boudinot of New Jersey was a prominent politician of the era of the Revolution and Early Republic in the United States. He was also a proto-Fundamentalist and a millenarian. As with other like-minded people, Boudinot came to see the American and the French Revolutions as millennial events. That the Native Americans were the descendants of the Ten Lost Tribes fit right into that worldview. Sometime in 1772 or shortly before, Boudinot had a visit from James Adair, who was on his way to London to arrange for the publication of *The History of the American Indians*. Boudinot was favourably impressed by Adair and his scholarship. After the book was published, he secured a copy and used it extensively in writing his own *Star in the West: or, A Humble Attempt to Discover the Long Lost Ten Tribes of Israel, Preparatory to their Return to the Beloved City, Jerusalem* (1816). Boudinot was critical of the terrible way that European settlers had treated the Native Americans. Their being remnants of the Ten Tribes certainly contributed to his sympathy. As he told his readers, it was a worthwhile endeavour to determine the current condition and location of the Ten Lost Tribes, especially since it had a direct connection to 'the second advent of the glorified Messiah, as son of God, to this our world'. Unlike Thomas Thorowgood, Boudinot thought it was possible that other peoples, besides the Ten Lost Tribes, had made their way to the Americas, either across the Bering Straits or by an oceanic voyage. In fact, that possibility helped to explain why the Native Americans had drifted so far from their Jewish roots: they had mingled with heathen Gentiles. In his presentation, Boudinot followed the well-worn path of making comparisons of beliefs, rituals, customs and language. He was followed in this effort by similar writers, such as Ethan Smith and his *View of the Hebrews; or, The Tribes of Israel in America*, which first appeared in 1823, but a second 'improved and enlarged' edition quickly came out in 1825. Some scholars have seen and continue to see this book as an inspiration or source for the Book of Mormon. But despite the appearance of such books, as Richard H. Popkin has pointed out, the Jewish Indian theory was entering a state of decline, although minor flurries occurred later in the nineteenth century over supposed discoveries of Jewish or Hebrew artefacts at Newark, Ohio, and Bat Creek, Tennessee. When he was visiting the United States in 1837, the great missionary and Ten Lost Tribes hunter Joseph Wolff was asked if he thought the Native Americans were descendants of the Lost Tribes; he said no. The exception to the crumbling of the Jewish Indian theory was the purported Jewish migration depicted in the Book of Mormon, but that did not involve the Ten Lost Tribes.[55]

The historian and philosopher Richard Popkin suggests several reasons for the demise of the Jewish Indian theory of origins. Europeans, especially the British, were either not interested in or not sympathetic to the idea of the United States being a millennial nation. The philologist Sir William Jones started a century of Lost Tribe hunting in Central Asia when he claimed the Ten Lost Tribes were living in Afghanistan. This suggestion helped take the attention of Lost Tribes hunters away from the Americas. Napoleon's invasion of Egypt caused Europeans to focus further on the Middle East. Jefferson's Indian policies viewed the Native Americans as uncivilized people needing assimilation into European-American society rather than lost Israelites who needed to be Christianized to help bring on the Second Coming of Christ and the millennium. Race scientists of 'American School' ethnography portrayed Native Americans along with Blacks as inferior beings who were products of separate, polygenetic creations. Thus Native Americans lost the distinction of being descendants of the fallen but still chosen people of the Ten Lost Tribes. One cause for the decline of the Jewish Indian theory that Popkin does not mention is the myth of the lost white race of North America that was associated with the Mound Builders. The savage ancestors of the Native Americans had supposedly destroyed the civilized Mound Builders. Therefore, they deserved no mercy from the European Americans who were pushing the frontier ever westward. It was not a pedigree suitable for descendants of the Ten Lost Tribes. Fortunately for Lost Tribe hunters in the middle of the nineteenth century, there were plenty of unexplored places left to search for them besides North America.[56]

Hunting Lost Tribes in the Wilds of Africa and Asia

From about 1840 to the 1930s, the search for the Ten Lost Tribes moved to the deserts, mountains and jungles of Africa and Asia. It was a quirky and sometimes dangerous avocation for people with more money than sense or access to the financial support of other people with more money than sense. Joseph Wolff was an indefatigable missionary and seeker of the Ten Lost Tribes. Although he was the son of a rabbi, the young Joseph converted to Roman Catholicism but quarrelled with his superiors while studying in Rome. He travelled to England where he became an Anglican and resumed his studies at Cambridge. Engaging in missionary work in

Egypt, much of the Middle East, Central Asia, India and Ethiopia from 1824 to 1836, he was also on the lookout for the Lost Tribes or evidence of them. The narratives of his travels are peppered with references to the Ten Lost Tribes, although he never managed to locate any of them. Wolff was the very model of a Lost Tribes hunter risking his life on a quixotic cause. Fortunately, his missionary work at least produced some genuine results.[57] Wolff was not alone; other seekers of the Ten Lost Tribes fruit-lessly roamed isolated regions of Africa and Asia. The medical missionary David Livingstone found their presence to be aggravating. He complained of fever-stricken travelling companions on expeditions agitating for a search to find the Lost Tribes with quotes from the scriptures and ges-tures towards the rivers of Ethiopia. During his Zambesi expedition of 1858–63, Livingstone discovered that the naval officer who was assigned to make charts of the rivers they were exploring actually 'had come to discover the "Ten lost tribes"'. The two men had not been getting along as it was, and Livingstone later scoffed at the man's true objective with the disdainful comment, 'as if, of all things in the world, we had not plenty of Jews already'.[58] Quests for the Ten Lost Tribes in Africa and Asia persisted into the 1930s. Edgar Rice Burroughs made note of it in some of his Tarzan novels from 1929 and 1933. Oddly, although in the course of his African adventures Tarzan encountered various lost civilizations and peoples from Atlantean colonists to ancient Romans to Crusaders, Burroughs never had him find descendants of the Ten Lost Tribes.[59]

The continuing phenomenon of Ten Lost Tribes hunting prompted Allen H. Godbey to write his monumental *The Lost Tribes a Myth: Suggestions towards Rewriting Hebrew History* (1930). This 802-page book actually says very little about the Ten Lost Tribes. Instead, it proceeds to demolish the erroneous foundations of the myths and legends of the Ten Tribes. Godbey points out that the bulk of the Ten Tribes of Israel were never deported. He then proceeds to survey the history and cul-ture of the various peoples identified with the Ten Tribes in Africa and Asia. These people are shown to be Jewish in religion but not biologically. Godbey went into great detail to show that Jews are not and have never been a distinct race, even in ancient times. The Middle East was a region of shifting and mixing populations practising evolving and syncretizing religions. While modern Judaism is not a proselytizing religion, during the Persian, Hellenistic and Roman periods Jews engaged in consider-able proselytizing, with many different ethnic groups adopting Judaism. As Godbey strongly asserted at the beginning of *The Lost Tribes a Myth*, 'The conception of the origin and history of the Israelites and of the later Jews, that lies back of all fanciful quests for "lost tribes" and enthusiastic discoveries of them is that the Israelites were "a peculiar people" – "after the order of Melchizedek" – that is, without ancestry or ancestral intellectual and institutional inheritances,' to which he adds: 'Is not the notion of such a segregate "pure Israelite" race a fiction from the very beginning?' Those points are exactly what Godbey strives mightily and convincingly to document in his book.[60]

The Ten Lost Tribes Go Bad:
British Israelism and Christian Identity

While various people were hunting the Ten Lost Tribes in the wilds of Africa and Asia, others had reached the conclusion that the bluebird of being the chosen people was really in their own backyard. As nationalism developed early in England and later Great Britain, the idea that they were a special people also developed. In 1558 Bishop John Aylmer had famously pronounced that 'God is English.' It was an easy step for English Protestants to see their struggles with what they considered to be popish idolatry and Catholic military threats as being comparable with the ancient Israelite struggles against the idolatries and aggressions of their neighbours. The apocalyptic events of the mid-seventeenth century saw the appearance in 1649 of John Sadler's *Rights of the Kingdom* and Gerrard Winstanley's *The True Levellers Standard Advanced*. Both books asserted a spiritual equivalency, if not a biological one, between the English and the Ten Lost Tribes. It was only a matter of time before someone would unequivocally claim a biological link between the British and the Israelites of the Ten Lost Tribes.[61]

British Israelism or Anglo-Israelism is the belief that the people of the British Isles – or at least some of them – and also some white people in North America are descendants of the Ten Lost Tribes, Ephraim and Manasseh in particular. The origins of British Israelism were not very auspicious. Richard Brothers was the first to teach and write about the British and other Europeans being a 'Hidden Israel', unaware of their biological Jewish descent. Joining the Royal Navy as a midshipman, he received a promotion to lieutenant in 1783, but a few months afterwards was put on half-pay when the war associated with the American Revolution ended. Having too little money and too much time on his hands, Brothers's mental state began to deteriorate. He came to believe God had a great purpose for him and he began to prophesy. While most of his predictions came to nothing, Brothers achieved one successful prediction. He foretold that Gustav III of Sweden and Louis XVI of France would die violently at the hands of their subjects, which came true by early 1793. In the anxious

context of the ominous unfolding of the French Revolution, such a prediction attracted much attention. Soon after, Brothers began calling himself
a 'nephew of the Almighty', apparently based on his being a descendant
of one of Jesus' brothers or sisters. In 1794 he began to publish his prophecies and claimed that hidden Jews were living throughout Europe and
that he was descended from King David. He went on to assert that he
was a Hebrew prince who would become ruler of the Earth by November
1795. He and all the Jews, both open and hidden, in 1798 would proceed to
Jerusalem to rebuild the Temple. Part of his prophecy involved George III
voluntarily surrendering his crown to Brothers. That claim irked the king,
who, beset by French revolutionaries abroad and republicans at home, was
in no mood to be tolerant of Brothers's madness. Under suspicion of treason, Brothers was incarcerated in a lunatic asylum from 1794 until 1806.
Friends secured his release and he lived on their charity while continuing
to prophesy and publish until his death in 1824. Despite his bizarre beliefs
and behaviour, Brothers still attracted a following that even included a
Member of Parliament. His proto-British Israel theories did not have any
appreciable impact on the future British Israelism movement, but they do
attest to the perennial desire of people to attach themselves the status of
being God's chosen people.[62]

The real beginning of British Israelism can be found in the writings
of John Wilson. He was an Irish weaver with an attraction for radical
politics and pseudo-historical scholarship. In 1840 he published *Lectures
on our Israelitish Origins*. He argued that the Ten Tribes had migrated
to Europe and founded the nations of the Anglo-Saxon and Germanic
peoples. It just so happened that the tribe of Ephraim settled in Britain.
That happenstance meant Britain's rise to be the most powerful imperial
power on the globe during the nineteenth century was a fulfilment of
biblical prophecy. In Genesis 48:19 the patriarch Jacob had proclaimed
in his blessing on Joseph's sons Manasseh and Ephraim: 'He [Manasseh]
also shall become a people and he shall also be great. Nevertheless, his
younger brother [Ephraim] shall be greater than he and his offspring shall
become a multitude of nations.' Needless to say, being part of the chosen
people that God had destined for greatness would have an appeal for some
members of the British upper and middle classes, as it would to almost
anyone for that matter. Wilson's British Israelism also meshed quite well
with the prevailing assumptions of racial Anglo-Saxonism and Teutonism
that dominated the mid-nineteenth century.[63]

The unification of Germany in 1870 created a new and quite serious rival for British pre-eminence politically, militarily and economically.
Teutonism that had seen Germans as partners and allies was replaced by

anti-German sentiments. That change impacted British Israelism. Edward Hine, a self-proclaimed disciple of Wilson, revised the beliefs of British Israelism accordingly. He confined the settlements of the Ten Tribes to the British Isles rather than all of northern Europe. The only exception was that the descendants of Manasseh had moved to the United States, a reflection of that country's growing power. Meanwhile, the Germans were demoted to being merely the progeny of wandering and militaristic Assyrians. From the point of view of British nationalistic prejudices, the Assyrians made very appropriate ancestors for the supposedly militaristic Germans. Hine taught that when the final days arrived, the Ephraimites and the other eight tribes in the British Isles would unite with Manasseh in the United States and the dispersed Jews to form the All-Israel that would resettle Palestine as prophesied in the Bible.

It was inevitable that British Israelism would spread to the United States and Canada. Joseph Wild, an itinerant Primitive Methodist minister from Lancashire, brought it to the United States following his emigration in 1856. Wild had been reading Wilson's writings; in 1876 he began to lecture on British Israelism himself and soon after came into contact with Hine's ideas as well. It was Hine's version of British Israelism that was reflected in Wild's *The Ten Lost Tribes* published in 1879. Wild, however, made no effort to organize a British Israel movement in the United States. That task fell to Charles Abdiel Lewis Totten.

Totten, the son of a Union general in the Civil War, was a career military man from 1873 to 1893. He left the army to pursue biblical research. His interest in British Israelism started in 1883 and he soon began to write on the subject. His writings attracted the attention of Edward Hine, who came to North America to lecture and proselytize for British Israelism during 1884–8. Part of that time was spent with Totten in New Haven, Connecticut. The proselytizing Totten joined with Hine to promote it in the United States and Canada. Later supporters of British Israelism and its offshoot of Christian Identity have extolled Totten as one of their movement's great intellectual ornaments by claiming he was a professor at Yale University. Their claim, however, is disingenuous. Totten was never a full-time faculty member of Yale; his last assignment from the army had been as an instructor in the university's military science programme from 1888 to 1892.

British Israelists in Great Britain and North America were not a large group. At its highest, the British Israel World Federation only had 5,000 members. Although they were few, they were also generally well-to-do members of the social elite. Having their already elite status bolstered by the belief that they were part of God's chosen people was pleasant in the years leading up to the First World War. Most British Israelists were book-ish people, and many of them also wrote books about British Israelism which were avidly purchased by other British Israelists. One problem was that all these books were quite repetitive. In effect, they all wrote the same book, so that if you read one of their books, you have fairly well read them all. It was a situation somewhat reminiscent of something you might find in a Jorge Luis Borges story. An even bigger problem was that the ideas presented in the British Israelists' books were based on faulty linguistics, tendentious misreadings of sources and wishful thinking. British Israelist literature looked forward to the restoration of All-Israel with the help of the descendants of the Ten Lost Tribes living in Great Britain and North America. Such ideas were perplexing and offensive to mainstream Christians and Jews. Adolf Neubauer, the great bibliographer and the cataloger of the Bodleian Library's massive collection of Hebrew manu-scripts, sometimes had visits from British Israelists seeking confirmation of their theories. Shortly before 1880, one F. W. Phillips visited Neubauer and spent over 30 minutes regaling the bibliographer with his theory that 'Cymri' (the Welsh word for Wales and Welsh people) had its origin in the name of the Israelite king Omri. Phillips asked Neubauer for his opinion on his theory, which drew the blunt reply, 'My belief is that you are more lost than the Ten Tribes.'[64]

British Israelism was not a Christian denomination. Christians from various denominations felt they could be British Israelists and suffer no conflict with their denomination's doctrines. Most British Israelists, however, tended to be Anglicans, Episcopalians or Methodists. Some denominations even formally embraced British Israelist ideas to some degree – Pentecostalism, the Church of God (Holiness) and the Worldwide Church of God. British Israelism was also philo-semitic, but that philo-semitism was based on the Christian assumption that when All-Israel was restored in Palestine, the Jews would convert. During the First World War, when the British general Edmund Allenby captured Jerusalem on 9 December 1917, it was viewed by British Israelists as the ful-filment of biblical prophecy. The army of Ephraim had delivered Jerusalem from infidels and All-Israel was about to be restored. But the Jews did not convert. As a result, philo-semitism among the British Israelists in Great Britain and North America faded. By the 1920s, antisemitism and right-wing views appeared in North American British Israelism thanks to the efforts of Reuben H. Sawyer, a Christian pastor of antisemitic opinions and an active member of the Ku Klux Klan in Oregon. He introduced British Israelism to the idea that Ashkenazic Jews were fake Jews with evil intents.

The completion of British Israelism's shift from philo-semitism to antisemitism took place during the 1930s under the leadership of Howard Rand. Ironically, Rand was not a vicious antisemite, if he was an antisemite at all. He did introduce into British Israelite thought the idea that modern Jews were not descendants of Judah; rather they were descendants of Esau. In addition, he founded the Anglo-Saxon Federation of America in 1933, which provided British Israelists in the United States with their own national organization. Rand was a pacifist who was primarily interested in studying, writing about and promoting traditional British Israelism, but he kept some bad company. In 1930 he met William J. Cameron at a British Israel convention in Detroit. Cameron was a passionate antisemite. From 1921 to 1927, he had edited the *Dearborn Independent*, owned by the equally antisemitic Henry Ford. Cameron had been closely involved in the writing and publication of the newspaper's notorious 'International Jew' series. Significant financial resources and new right-wing members were what Cameron brought to Rand's Anglo-Saxon Federation, along with his virulent antisemitism. Around the end of the Second World War, Rand lost interest in the Anglo-Saxon Federation of America and, bereft of his leadership, it soon collapsed. The remnants of British Israelism in the United States were now a solidly antisemitic and right-wing organization while still maintaining they were members of the Ten Tribes, particularly Ephraim and Manasseh. This right-wing British Israelism would morph into the venomous Christian Identity movement.[65]

After 1945 the British Israelists of southern California came under the influence of Gerald L. K. Smith, a former associate of Huey Long of Louisiana and the premier antisemite of post-Second World War America. Through the 1950s and 1960s, he transformed the right-wing segment of British Israelism in America into Christian Identity. His close associates in this effort were Wesley Swift, a Methodist pastor who became the leading Christian Identity minister prior to 1970, and William Potter Gale, a protégé of General Douglas MacArthur and a founder of the Christian Defense League and Posse Comitatus and a conspirator to assassinate Martin Luther King Jr. Christian Identity taught that the white peoples of western and northern European ancestries were God's chosen people, descendants of the Ten Lost Tribes and part of the Adamic race. On the other hand, Jews and non-whites were inferior and often inherently evil. African Blacks and Asian peoples were the descendants of pre-Adamic people created at the same time as the animals on the fifth day of creation. Lacking any connection to the creation of Adam and Eve, they were intellectually inferior and lacked souls. They were dubbed 'mud people'. Jews were worse; they were the spawn of Satan who were wickedly asserting a claim to being God's chosen people and who sought to destroy all that was great, good and godly. Adherents of Christian Identity believed that the final battle at the end of time would be a race war between Identity Christians, whites and God along with his angels on the side of righteousness and Satan, the fallen angels, the satanic Jews and the mud people on the other side. In anticipation of this eminent struggle, Identity Christians stockpiled weapons, formed paramilitary groups and adopted survivalist lifestyles. Christian Identity was quite active during the 1980s and 1990s, carrying out bank robberies and assassinations. Such antisocial crimes and terrorism prompted the FBI to investigate and infiltrate the radical Christian Identity cells. At that point support for the movement declined and it faded from the public eye. Faded – but not extinct – Identity Christianity is still out there. The story of British Israelism and Christian Identity is a case study of how the myths and legends of the Ten Lost Tribes could lead to the appearance of a quirky but benign group of believers and later evolve into a subversive organization engaged in terrorism bolstered by the belief that its members are descendants of Ephraim, Manasseh and the other Lost Tribes.

Christian Identity represents one of the most bizarre appropriations of the myth of the Ten Lost Tribes and one of the most loathsome distortions of Christianity in its 2,000 years of history. But they are not alone in asserting a claim to being part of the Ten Lost Tribes. The Karen ethnic group of Myanmar have been identified as members of the Ten Tribes. So have the Lemba of South Africa, who claim a Jewish, if not a Ten Tribes, connection. DNA testing tends to back up the Lemba's claim although the rabbis of Jerusalem disagree. Similar claims have been made for the Tutsis of Rwanda, the Maoris of New Zealand and the imperial family of Japan, among many others.[66] There are many uses for the myth of the Ten Tribes. Claiming a biological connection to the Ten Tribes has been going on for over 2,000 years and it shows no signs of going away. Why? Because it is always good to be one of God's chosen.

The myth of the Ten Lost Tribes shows us that myths can be powerful motivators for various people. Myths can be benign or malignant depending on how they are used. The Ten Lost Tribes brought hope to Jews over the centuries. They played a mixed role in the millennial visions of Christians. For antisemites, they were bogeymen who were always out there somewhere plotting the destruction of Christian society. In the following chapters, we will see how other myths, fringe history, pseudoscience and conspiracy theories can perform in the same way, confusing a society and distracting it from reality in dangerous ways.

FOUR

Templars, Secret Societies and Conspiracy Theories

There are numerous books on the Templars. The only problem is that in 90 per cent of cases (I correct myself, 99 per cent), they are pure fantasy. No other subject has ever inspired more hacks from more countries through time than the Templars.

UMBERTO ECO[1]

It will be seen then that a belief in widespread conspiracies is not always to be regarded as a sign of loss of mental balance, even when these conspiracies remain completely invisible to the general public.

NESTA WEBSTER[2]

In the annals of conspiracy theories and secret societies, 18 March 1314 is a seminal date. Jacques de Molay, the imprisoned grand master of the Knights Templar, must have awoken on that morning with a feeling of hopeful anticipation. The last few years had been catastrophic for the Knights Templar. In October 1307, Philip IV of France had the Templars in France arrested, including de Molay and other leaders. They were charged with engaging in heresy and various other deviant practices. De Molay and the other leaders had been imprisoned ever since. Shockingly, near Paris in May 1310, 54 Templars were burned at the stake as relapsed heretics. Finally, in 1312, the papacy abolished the Templar order. Despite this procession of misfortunes, de Molay and the others had reason for hope. In a secret meeting at Chinon during 1308, representatives of the pope had absolved de Molay and the other Templar leaders of wrongdoing. After languishing in prison for over six years, they expected to be freed by the ecclesiastical commission that was meeting that day. Instead, the secret absolution at Chinon was ignored. The four Templar leaders were condemned to grim imprisonment for the rest of their lives on the basis of their earlier coerced confessions. Outraged, Jacques de Molay and Geoffrey of Charney, the master of Normandy, vigorously protested and asserted their innocence. When the news of their protests reached Philip IV, he declared them to be relapsed heretics and ordered their immediate punishment. The two men were taken to the island of Javiaux on the Seine, where they were burned alive. A chronicler described the two Templars as meeting their death calmly, bravely and with assurance of their innocence. They died well and so earned the admiration of the spectators.[3]

In the aftermath of de Molay's execution, the idea of a Templar curse arose. Coincidentally, five weeks later, on 20 April, Pope Clement V died of a protracted illness. King Philip IV died the following November after falling from his horse while hunting. Some asserted that the curse was not yet finished. Four and a half centuries later, in 1793, as the French Revolution ground on, Louis XVI suffered execution on the guillotine while the power of the Roman Catholic Church in France was humbled. A claim arose that as Jacques de Molay faced his impending death, he had called down a curse on both the Capetian dynasty of French monarchs and the Church. In fact, no contemporary source records him making any such statement. Nevertheless, according to the French conservative Charles Louis Cadet de Gassicourt in his *Le Tombeau de Jacques Molay* (1796), at the death of Louis XVI, a figure in the crowd of spectators declared, 'Jacques de Molay, you are avenged.' For Gassicourt, the French Revolution was the fruit of a world-wrecking conspiracy by the Templars and their successors to bring down divine monarchy and the Church. And from that point onwards, secret societies and conspiracy theories about global plots to destroy religion and civil government have been a fixture of popular culture. In fact, they seem to be proliferating.[4]

The Nature and Background of Secret Societies and Conspiracy Theories

The occult, secret societies and conspiracy theories are fascinating topics. Some of their aspects are real and others are fictional. Novelists frequently use the occult, secret societies and conspiracies as the foundation for the plots of their thrillers, mysteries and spy novels. Films and television series use these plots as well. Countless non-fiction books, documentaries, magazine articles and news reports discuss and describe occult activities, secret societies and conspiracy theories. A lot of first-class scholarship or factual reporting mingles with even greater numbers of sensationalistic accounts and just plain fantasy. Any overview of the theories of fringe history and pseudoscience will reveal that the occult, secret societies and conspiracy theories usually provide the foundations for such beliefs.

At this point it is important to define what the terms 'occult', 'secret society' and 'conspiracy theory' mean. 'Occult' is frequently used to refer to supernatural and secret knowledge truly known to only a few people. Hence bookstores often have an occult section, although such public display tends to undercut the secret part of the definition. In fact, 'occult' technically means something that is hidden, secret, concealed or covered over. It is derived from the Latin root words *occulere* (meaning 'to conceal') and *occultus* (meaning 'having been concealed'). It has been pointed out that the hidden or concealed aspect of occult does not necessarily mean somebody concealed the knowledge or made it secret on purpose. Occult could simply mean knowledge that has not been discovered or revealed yet. So a secret of nature could be considered occult. Hence scholars studying aspects of nature and making discoveries could consider themselves to be engaged in occult activity while at the same time practising enlightened science.[5] In fact, it is the less used word 'arcane' that means something hidden or made secret on purpose. It derives from the Latin word *arcanus* (meaning 'closed' or 'shut up'). In popular usage, however, 'occult' and 'arcane' are often used interchangeably. Furthermore, modern usage associates 'occult' with the supernatural or the magical. In this case, the supernatural is some action or event that cannot be explained by the laws of natural or scientific understanding, while magic is the power to use or to influence the physical world through supernatural forces. Of course, the knowledge of magical power would be derived from secret or hidden knowledge – the occult. That knowledge would generally be the monopoly of a select few.

Supposedly, the select few possessing supernatural knowledge and powers are usually members of some secret society. However, most secret societies do not claim to possess or believe in supernatural powers. In fact, most secret societies do not lead a secret existence. The Masons, or Freemasons, are a secret society but their existence is well known throughout the world. The actual secret of most secret societies is the knowledge, lore and rituals involved in the various steps taken to initiate new members into the group. The same observation applies to the mystery religions or cults of the ancient world. The 'mystery' was those things that comprised the initiation rites of the various cults, whether it was the Eleusinian Mysteries, the cults of Cybele and Serapis, Mithraism or the worship of Isis. These are the best known and most popular of the mystery religions of late antiquity. Although the initiation rites were supposed to be kept secret, word eventually got out. A fascinating portrayal of the Isis cult is provided by Apuleius' novel *The Golden Ass*, written during the mid-second century CE. It included a detailed description of the initiation ceremony for the cult of Isis. As the goddess Isis tells the novel's hero Lucius at the beginning of his initiation, 'Those who are enlightened by the early rays of that divinity the sun, the Ethiopians, the Arii and the Egyptians who excel in antique lore, all worship me with their ancestral ceremonies and call me by my true name, Queen Isis.' The exotic rituals that followed included cultic objects covered with 'the strange hieroglyphs of the Egyptians'. Clearly, the mystery and the magic long associated with Egypt contributed significantly to the popular appeal of the Isis cult. Besides providing details of the secret ceremony, Apuleius' novel demonstrates just how pervasive was the place of the Isis cult in imperial Roman society. In its heyday, the cult of Isis towered over the religious life of the ancient world until the triumph of Christianity decisively and permanently dethroned it along with the other mystery religions. The initiation into the male-only and mostly soldiers' cult of Mithraism was particularly gruesome. It involved the ritual slaughter of a bull in a way that showered its blood on to the initiate. The lure of such secret rites even allowed them to creep into the ceremonies of early Christian baptisms.[6]

Like Christianity, the mystery religions could attract both converts and persecution. The cults of Cybele, Serapis, Mithra and Isis were all popular and spread throughout the Roman empire. As has been noted, Isis was particularly popular, which led to periodic attempts to ban the cult starting in the late Roman Republic. The first emperor Augustus also harboured grave doubts about the un-Roman nature of worshipping Isis, as did the satirist Juvenal. That attitude faded in the atmosphere of cosmopolitan tolerance that developed in the Roman empire during the late first and second centuries. Even some emperors, such as Otho, Septimius Severus and Caracalla, worshipped Isis or Serapis.[7] Mystery religions attracted followers with the lure of their secret rites, supposed magical powers and spiritual enlightenment: just the very same things that modern Rosicrucians and some oddball branches of the Masons still seek today. So secret societies are not secret, although they do have secrets. As the scholar Theodore Ziolkowski has put it, 'It is a basic human impulse to enjoy secrets; to be included in a special group that has privileged information about any subject that matters to the individual, whether the government, finance, sports, or religion.'[8]

In more recent times, secret societies have developed some shared characteristics and traits. They allow members a sense of belonging to a group based on esoteric beliefs and goals that are separate from the society around them. In other words, being a member makes them special. Members have a sense of unity with the group, and in turn they give absolute obedience to the group's leaders, who are often unknown. Within the group there is also a sense of equality which is reinforced by the wearing of masks, costumes or uniforms. Only select individuals are allowed to join the group and they have to go through an initiation. It is part of a process of progressive teaching of higher truths that leads to promotion up a series of ranks. Scholars have noted that the majority of secret societies have religious roots. Basically, the purpose of initiation is to take a normal base human being and purify them into a spiritual being – or, at least, a more spiritual human being – through occult or magical processes or ceremonies. Membership in the secret society confers benefits that are not available to non-members. Again, such benefits make them special. Not every secret society possesses all of these traits or exhibits them with the same intensity or degree. Any comparison of the Masons, the Hermetic Order of the Golden Dawn, the Nazi ss and the Ku Klux Klan shows just how diverse secret societies can be.[9]

Conspiracies are often linked to secret societies, which is only to be expected since conspiracies are by their nature secret activities. What is a conspiracy? Legally, it is an agreement between two or more persons to commit a crime through illegal actions. In the world of secret societies, a conspiracy is usually a political action or plot directed against authority, whether it be a leader, a government or an institution. As long as humans are gathered together in groups, conspiracies, whether real or imagined, arise sooner or later. As Theodore Ziolkowski has put it, 'The conspiracy phenomenon is ancient. People have believed in conspiracies as long as there have been groups of at least three people in which one is convinced that the other two are plotting against him or her.'[10]

Conspiracies have a long and bloody history. Over 3,000 years ago, the Harem Plot of 1155 BCE against Ramesses III managed to kill him, although the conspiracy failed to alter the royal succession. In its day, the northern kingdom of Israel was a hotbed of conspiracies against its kings, as the books of Kings and Chronicles abundantly show. Among the ancient Romans conspiracies abounded, with the plot of Catiline and the assassination of Julius Caesar providing prime examples. Skipping forwards to the sixteenth and seventeenth centuries, the Tudor and the Stuart dynasties of England faced numerous conspiracies to dethrone them. Plots centring on pretenders plagued the first half of Henry VII's reign. Later, Queen Elizabeth I was threatened by several conspiracies to replace her as queen with Mary, Queen of Scots. After the defeat and execution of King Charles I, both the Commonwealth and the Protectorate of Oliver Cromwell had to combat various royalist plots. Unlike most conspiracies up to that point in history, these royalist plots did involve secret societies.[11] Unlike most secret societies, however, these royalist groups arose for the sole purpose of restoring the Stuart dynasty to the throne and bringing back the Laudian Church of England. The occult played little part. The many plots to assassinate Hitler, while secret, did not involve secret societies. The one thing all these conspiracies have in common is that they were real historical events, not imagined ones.

'Conspiracies' and 'conspiracy theories' are not interchangeable terms. An overactive imagination and a desire to believe are the basis for conspiracy theories, along with fraudulent intent on occasion. Conspiracy theories assert the existence of plots that almost always involve secret societies or groups, although any real conspiracy almost never exists. The Popish Plot of seventeenth-century England is a good early example.[12] Conspiracy theories of this nature are a relatively new phenomenon in the span of history. The conspiracies associated with conspiracy theories tend to be global in nature, so the Popish Plot supposedly intended the destruction of Protestantism. Conspiracy theories often focus on big public events such as the assassination of President John F. Kennedy or the 9/11 attacks. Instead of focusing on obvious explanations based on solid evidence, conspiracy theories go for the sensational: Lyndon Johnson being behind Kennedy's assassination or the Israelis behind 9/11. And it only gets wilder over time in the realm of popular culture. According to the television series *The X-Files* (1993–2002), the sinister Cigarette Smoking Man shot Kennedy to preserve the government's secret bargain with alien invaders. Another science fiction series, *Dark Skies* (1996–7), pinned the assassination of Kennedy on bodysnatching alien invaders known as the Hives. Then there is Jeffrey Dean Morgan's character, the Comedian, in the 2009 film *Watchmen*, who shoots Kennedy. Nobody (one hopes, perhaps in vain) gives any of these examples credence as factual accounts. They do form the fringe of a conspiracy theory milieu, as do 9/11 conspiracy theorists who blame the attack on shadowy government conspirators or Israeli agents seeking to cause trouble. Accepting the obvious, that Osama bin Laden and Al-Qaeda were the admitted perpetrators, is just not seen as an option by conspiracy theorists.

Other conspiracy theories focus on covert plots that seem to erupt suddenly. The French Revolution is a good example. Instead of paying attention to the real historical context and conditions – that a corrupt and failing social and political order succumbed to the uprising of an oppressed and angry population in which even a substantial portion of the elite joined – reactionary apologists for the Old Regime concocted a conspiracy theory that absolved the failed elite of France. They claimed the French Revolution was the result of a secret but massive conspiracy by the Masons to bring down the partnership of Church and State that had sustained European civilization for centuries. Ever since, many conspiracy theories have arisen that blame society's troubles on vast, universal and hidden plots by Masons, Jews and, lately, aliens in the form of secret societies. How this phenomenon of global conspiracy theories evolved will be the subject of the remainder of this chapter.

Secret Societies and the Occult

Occult secret societies are a product of post-Reformation Europe that the Renaissance and the Reformation made possible. The recovery and revival of ancient knowledge during the Renaissance brought scholars into contact with various occult writings such as the *Corpus hermeticum*. The invention of the printing press allowed this knowledge to spread more widely and more rapidly. Meanwhile, the Reformation weakened the Roman Catholic Church's intellectual control. Exposed to this ancient occult knowledge, some scholars became enthralled by it. Keep in mind that occult writings were not reflexively dismissed as superstition and mumbo jumbo during the early modern era. The border between the occult worldview and the emerging scientific worldview was extremely hazy. Chemistry and alchemy, astronomy and astrology were difficult to differentiate. Occult studies were taken very seriously and their study was not considered disreputable. When the manuscript of the *Corpus hermeticum* arrived in Florence during 1460, the humanist scholar Marsilio Ficino was diverted by his Medici patrons from his translation of Plato's works into Latin to translating the *Corpus hermeticum* instead.[13]

It is not surprising that the scholars and educated laymen of the Renaissance took hermeticism, neo-Platonism and the occult so seriously. They did not possess a materialistic and positivist scientific worldview. They did, however, believe in the existence of the supernatural and the spiritual, and viewed life as a quest for enlightenment in this world and salvation in the next. Furthermore, there was a belief in the existence of lost ancient wisdom that, if recovered, would guide humans to enlightenment and spiritual salvation. It is important to remember that it was not until the late seventeenth century, with its debate between the ancients and moderns, that a large number of scholars came to believe that the knowledge of modern society had finally surpassed that of Classical Greece and Rome. It had been long assumed that all those indecipherable Egyptian hieroglyphs preserved all sorts of wonderful but lost knowledge. At the same time, other ancient manuscripts were being recovered, transcribed, translated, edited and published. European scholars became more and more of a community from the fifteenth to the seventeenth centuries. So it was only natural that scholars and others with enquiring and questing minds would band together in organizations like the Royal Society to coordinate their efforts. Even before that date, some people began coming together in secret societies. Their hope and goal was to take their knowledge and use it to bring about reforms of society and make the world a better place. The two earliest, enduring and most influential of these secret societies were the Rosicrucians and the Masons.

Rosicrucianism

Both the Rosicrucians and the Masons have their subgroups, and some of these make claims that their societies stretch back to the murky beginnings of human history. Reliable historical research, however, dates the origins of both secret societies to the early years of the seventeenth century. The Rosicrucians can be assigned a definite and documented set of dates. What is known for sure is that the so-called Rosicrucian manifestos, the *Fama fraternitatis* and the *Confessio fraternitatis*, were published in 1614 and 1615. The manifestos had been circulating in manuscript from as early as 1610 before they appeared in print.[14] They were followed in 1616 by the publication of *The Chemical Wedding of Christian Rosenkreutz*, which later turned out to have been written by the Lutheran pastor Johann Andreae. These works outline the beliefs and philosophy of the Rosicrucians and tell the life of the fifteenth-century German monk Christian Rosenkreutz. By his own account, Rosenkreutz went on a pilgrimage to the Holy Land. Afterwards he lived in Yemen for three years where he studied the wisdom of the Arabs. From Yemen he travelled to Fez in Morocco for two more years of studying magic and the Jewish mystical writings known as the Kabbalah. Along the way he visited Egypt, although the Rosicrucian manifestos have little to say about his brief time there. He then returned to Germany where the authorities dismissed his newfound esoteric knowledge. Undeterred, Rosenkreutz returned to his monastery and founded Rosicrucianism. Despite these claims, mainstream scholars reject Rosenkreutz as a real, historical person. Instead, they believe that he was fiction used as an allegory.[15]

A confusing aspect of Rosicrucianism is that the *Fama*, the *Confessio* and the *Chemical Wedding* were all published anonymously. They seemed to provide evidence for the existence of a Rosicrucian secret society that purported to be on the cutting edge of the occult sciences.[16] Rosicrucian ideology also seemed to provide a potentially effective counterbalance to the threat of resurgent Counter-Reformation Catholicism. At the same time, no Rosicrucians came out of the darkness of their secret society to recruit new members or thank their defenders. Why? Because there was no Rosicrucian society.

There is plausible reason to believe that the Rosicrucian manifestos were a literary fiction or even a student prank. Theodore Ziolkowski has called their publication a media event comparable to the hubbub of misinformation that resulted from the publication of Dan Brown's *The Da Vinci Code* (2003).[17] It appears that behind the scenes Andreae had written the *Chemical Wedding* shortly after 1605. Later in life, he also wrote an autobiography that remained in manuscript unknown to scholars until 1799. In it Andreae discussed the Rosicrucian manifestos. He claimed to have written the *Chemical Wedding* when he was seventeen and a student at Tübingen University. That would have placed the book's composition sometime from 1602 to 1604. Many scholars also believe that it is quite possible Andreae, perhaps with others, had written the *Fama*. So Andreae was in his late twenties or a maximum of thirty years old when the Rosicrucian manifestos were published. He would have been in his early twenties when the manifestos were being circulated in manuscript. The people doing the circulating were his coterie of friends at Tübingen. According to one scenario, the members of this group were all Lutherans interested in reigniting the fervour of Protestantism to meet the growing threat of the Catholic Counter-Reformation. Following the millennial prophecies of Joachim of Fiore, they believed a golden age was about to commence.[18] The purpose of the Rosicrucian manifestos was to stimulate others uninitiated in the ancient wisdom and Joachism to seek it out and bring on the golden age. It was a call for people to become Rosicrucians.

Another interpretation is that the manifestos were a student prank that got out of hand, just as the myths and legends that formed the basis of *The Da Vinci Code*'s plot convinced many people that the fiction was firmly historical. Evidence pointed to Andreae as the author of the *Chemical Wedding* and possibly the *Fama*. It was a charge that Andreae publicly denied throughout his life while privately admitting it in his autobiography. He had good reason to deny the manifestos. He was a Lutheran pastor with an outstanding pedigree as the nephew of Jacob Andreae, a key figure in the development of Confessional Lutheranism. In an age of intensifying Lutheran orthodoxy Andreae had a lot to lose if he became associated with the unconventional and even heretical teachings of Rosicrucianism advocated by the manifestos. Furthermore, Andreae asserted that the *Chemical Wedding* was a prank or a satire. Andreae, his mother and the rest of his family had suffered due to his father's obsession with the transformation of base metals into gold by alchemical charlatans. The *Fama* contains some passages that are very critical of the supposed alchemical production of gold.[19] When the manifestos were published, Andreae was not at all happy about it. They had been circulating in manuscript for several years before someone took it upon themselves to have them published. Whether that person or persons actually believed the doctrines of the manifestos and wanted to hasten the coming golden age or just wanted to give the joke a wider audience of the gullible is unclear. Whatever the motive, the publication caused a furore. The orthodox condemned the manifestos, while scholars seeking command of the ancient hermetic wisdom and longing for a golden age embraced them. People believed in the existence of the Rosicrucians and vainly sought to contact the people behind the manifestos. Failing in that effort, they formed their own ad hoc and informal Rosicrucian groups and new Rosicrucian societies have continued to be founded ever since.[20]

Were there true Rosicrucian societies operating during the seventeenth century? Historians' opinions are mixed. If there were such societies, they were vague and fleeting in their membership and duration. In the tense years leading up to and beyond the Thirty Years War (1618–48) and the general crisis of the seventeenth century, educated people longed for a solution to religious and intellectual turmoil and social ills. The vague ideals espoused by the Rosicrucian manifestos promised hope. As a result they attracted educated and scholarly people who wanted to become Rosicrucians. As one scholar of secret societies has put it, 'Rosicrucians created themselves out of a desire to exist.'[21] With the excitement over the manifestos, Rosicrucian societies spontaneously appeared throughout Europe, although the early enthusiasm quickly faded. The German physician and alchemist Michael Maier, writing to James I of England in 1612 when the manifestos existed only in manuscript, appears to assume that the king was already heading a Rosicrucian society in England. Maier would go on to pen two tracts defending the Rosicrucians – *Aureae mensae* (1617) and *Themis aurea* (1618). He also inserted an increased emphasis on alchemy into Rosicrucianism that has stayed with it ever since.[22]

Maier lived in England from 1611 until 1616 and had close associations with the only Rosicrucian society known to exist in seventeenth-century England. Sir Francis Bacon definitely read and used the *Fama* and the *Confessio* in his own writings. Robert Fludd, a physician and occultist, demonstrated an even greater interest in Rosicrucianism. He appears to have also been a Mason and may have been the originator of the connections between Rosicrucianism and Freemasonry. The mystic Thomas Vaughan organized a Rosicrucian group with strong alchemical interests during the 1650s. Other possible Rosicrucians in England included the astrologer William Lilly, the alchemist/chemist Sir Kenelm Digby and the polymath and founding fellow of the Royal Society Elias Ashmole. The Cambridge scholar Ezekiel Foxcroft translated the *Chemical Wedding* into English, but it did not appear in print until 1690, long after his death.[23] Fervour for Rosicrucianism faded during the late seventeenth century and the first half of the eighteenth century as the proto-Enlightenment and the Enlightenment came to dominate European thought. Still, Rosicrucianism never died out and it survived to be part of the occult revival of the mid-nineteenth century.

Freemasonry

Freemasonry has various claims to ancient origins, but for the most part it was a creation of the early Enlightenment. The murky historical origins of the Freemasons purport to lay in the associations created by medieval stonemasons: hence the masonry garb and tools that are used in its rituals and symbols. These early craftsmen were the so-called operative masons. The Scottish intellectuals who founded modern Freemasonry began to join the lodges of the operative masons during the late sixteenth and early seventeenth centuries. Over time they came to dominate the lodges, and when they founded their own lodges they used the existing craft organizations of stonemasons' lodges as their model. These intellectuals were the so-called 'gentlemen masons' or 'admitted masons' until 1757, when the term 'speculative masons' was adopted. The same process occurred in England but came later and is less well documented. Sir Robert Moray was definitely admitted into a speculative Masonic lodge located in Edinburgh in 1641, the first recorded initiation. The ceremony, however, took place in England where he was serving in the Scottish army. From the context, it is clear that speculative lodges had been in existence for some time already in Scotland. Elias Ashmole was initiated into a speculative lodge in Warrington, now in Cheshire, along with his father-in-law in October 1646. Other records show that speculative lodges were scattered throughout the English countryside during the late seventeenth century. Then, in 1717, four London lodges banded together at the Goose and Gridiron alehouse to form the Grand Lodge. From that point, Masonry spread from England to France and on to Germany; the German lodge was founded in 1737 in Hamburg by men first initiated in England.[24]

What attracted well-to-do intellectuals to join a Masonic lodge? Masonry, along with Rosicrucianism, developed during a time when royal absolutism was growing in power and the Roman Catholic Church was resurgent throughout Europe. In response, Masonry aimed to promote individual liberty and human equality, as opposed to privilege for a few and unrestrained power for the state and the Church. The secrecy of the society shielded its members from the scrutiny of the absolutist state. Masonry also promoted a simplified and non-dogmatic approach to religion that sought to make toleration and free-thinking the primary principles of society. Membership in a lodge provided people with a social life and a sense of belonging. Their common experience of initiation into the secrets of Masonry promoted a culture of equality. In this way Masonic lodges served some of the same functions as a club. Masons were also critical of what they saw as superstition. In this category they included folk magic, lore about fairies and trolls and belief in luck. But they also included many aspects of Christian beliefs, especially some that were dear to the Roman Catholic Church. As a result, the Catholic Church was hostile to Freemasonry. Given their aversion to superstition, there was officially nothing occult about Freemasonry. Mainstream Freemasonry had no need for the recovery of lost ancient wisdom or the discovery of venerable antecedents that went all the way back to ancient Egypt. At the same time, being intellectuals and free-thinkers, some Masons dabbled in magic, alchemy and the Kabbalah.[25]

Masonry had its origin myths. The predominant origin myth traced its beginning to the building of King Solomon's Temple in Jerusalem about 1000 BCE and the master mason Hiram Abiff. This myth is deeply embedded in the rituals of the basic Masonic degrees. There are other origin myths that are not part of mainstream Masonry. One credited the Knights Templar with creating Masonry. The Knights Templar comprised a crusading religious order that was headquartered in Jerusalem at the site of the Temple of Solomon, hence their name Templar. Another origin myth claimed that the Masons developed out of the medieval Rosicrucians (who did not exist, but inconvenient facts seldom deter true believers). Others suggested that the Masons had their origin in the Greek mystery cults such as the Eleusinian or Dionysian mysteries. Finally, the most ancient origin myth traced the Freemasons back to Egypt and the time of the pyramids. The Egyptians were the first master builders. In turn, they taught their building skills along with other esoteric knowledge to Moses and the Hebrews. A variant of the Egyptian origin myth reversed the transmission of knowledge and credited Joseph and his Hebrew brethren with teaching building skills to the Egyptians. That myth gave the Freemasons the most venerable pedigree possible, at least by the standards of seventeenth-, eighteenth- and nineteenth-century knowledge about ancient history. It is human nature for people to seek an ancient origin for their group, and some Freemasons have been no exception. Unfortunately, the historical record does not support them.[26]

Templarism

The most important myth of Masonic origins, in terms of the connection to conspiracy theories, was the Templar connection, which is often referred to as Templarism. It asserts that many Templars escaped the mass arrests in 1307. Supposedly, refugee Templars sought asylum in Scotland where they reconstituted themselves as Masons. Others fled west to North America with the reputedly vast Templar treasure. There they established settlements and hid their treasure, according to some, most famously on Oak Island. The Templars in Scotland were not just hiding out; they were plotting revenge against the French monarchy and the Roman Catholic Church. Their descendants, the Masons, spread Masonry into England and on the mainland of Europe with the goal of subverting and destroying the evil Church and state that had so cruelly crushed their order and killed their leaders.[27]

Templarism in Masonry actually had different and less sinister roots. Knighthood and chivalry have always had a strong attraction for many people. The early Mason and scholar Elias Ashmole was a great admirer of chivalric knighthood and especially the Templars. Masonic attraction for knightly rituals and paraphernalia became even more pronounced after the famous oration of the Jacobite exile chevalier Andrew Michael Ramsay to French Masons in 1736. Although he did not mention the Templars by name, Ramsey's speech strongly inferred their role in transmitting Masonic beliefs. He also promoted the idea that Masonry's great secret was the possession of arcane knowledge that could bring about the renewal of morality in human society. In addition, the Templars provided a seemingly plausible link between the Masonic ancestors, Hiram Abiff and the builders of Solomon's Temple, and the Masons of the eighteenth century. The crusading Templars as guardians of the Temple in Jerusalem brought the secrets of the Masons of Hiram back to Europe with them. Such origin theories involving the Templars are dismissed by modern Masonic historians, but that does not mean Templarism is extinct.[28]

Eighteenth-century Germany was the place where Templarism had its biggest impact. Germans liked the concept of Masonic lodges and gatherings of men for secret rituals and fellowship. But they wanted a society where hierarchy and social conservatism prevailed; the egalitarianism and rationalism of English Masonry were unattractive to well-to-do and noble Germans. As a result, German Masonry was more socially elitist while it was also more enthralled by the myth of Templar origins, the magical and the occult. Rituals placed particular emphasis on the hope of vengeance against those who perpetrated wrongs against the Templars.

Vengeance motifs were even inserted into the various ranks established by the German lodges.[29]

One particularly influential German Mason was Karl Gotthelf von Hund. A minor German noble, he joined the Masons in 1741 but later claimed to have received initiation into the Knights Templar in Paris during 1743. Furthermore, he asserted that the exiled prince Charles Edward Stuart, the Young Pretender, was the Grand Master of the Templars. He also maintained that 'unknown superiors' had tasked him with resurrecting the Knights Templar in Germany. During 1751 he established the Rite of the Strict Observance, which promoted Templarism in German Masonry. Some years later the German theologian Johann August von Starck began promoting a clerical version of Templarist Masonry called the Clerks Templar. Starck joined his movement with Hund's in 1768, an arrangement that was formalized in 1772. In contrast to Hund, however, Starck was far more interested in both occultism and egalitarianism. The real problem for Hund was that the 'Unknown Superiors' who had started him organizing the Strict Observance never got back to him with further instructions. Many of the Masons he recruited had joined in anticipation of the 'Unknown Superiors' reappearing and instructing them. When this failed to occur, they were disappointed. After Hund's death in 1776, disillusionment grew and the Strict Observance was dissolved in 1782. Its former members tended to drift into the more conservative Order of the Golden and Rosy Cross, which was a blend of Rosicrucianism and Masonry. Meanwhile, after 1780, Starck began a shift towards conservatism, and by his death in 1816 had come to firmly believe that an Illuminati conspiracy had instigated the French Revolution. Still, Templarist Masonry did not die out with Hund and Starck. Instead, it spread to Britain and North America but without the vengeance motif. Such Templarist Masonic groups still exist today. During the age of the French Revolution and Napoleon, however, the vengeance motif with its goal of retribution against the French monarchy and the Church caused suspicions of subversion to fall on the Masons – with dire results.[30]

Masonry and the French Revolution

The problem for Masonry was that it was not just Templarism's eccentric ideas that made it a target of suspicion. Masonry advocated equality, religious toleration, rationalism and a healthy scepticism. These ideas were anathema to absolutist monarchs and the Roman Catholic Church of the eighteenth century – not that the confessional Protestant churches were much more liberal. This type of free-thinking prompted some people to suspect the Masons of seditious intent, just as the similar ideas of the Swedenborgians in England during the 1790s had brought them under suspicion of conspiring with Revolutionary France. The mere existence of secret rituals and initiations also aroused qualms and distrust among many levels of society. Non-members tended to wonder what the secret societies were up to, and the default assumption was that it was nothing good. The factional quarrels among Masons with their competing rites and ranks also created misgivings and trepidation among many outsiders. While these circumstances brought Masonry into disrepute with some people, others did not find it at all objectionable. For many well-to-do people during the eighteenth century, the ideals of Masonry were quite attractive. By the time of the French Revolution, however, it was suffering a decline in membership. Both enthusiasm and attendance were down. Once the French Revolution got underway, many lodges suffered significant losses of membership due to people emigrating to escape danger. The Jacobin rulers during the Reign of Terror looked upon the Masons as a threat that was every bit as great as the reactionary nobility and clergy of pre-Revolutionary France.[31]

From the time of the outbreak of the French Revolution, diverse groups blamed the Masons for starting it. The supposed cabal that came to be viewed as the true instigators and leaders of the revolutionary conspiracy was the Masonic offshoot known as the Illuminati. They have been blamed for social turmoil and vast conspiracies ever since. The founder of the Illuminati was Adam Weishaupt, who was an orphan raised by Baron Johann Adam Ickstatt. Ickstatt belonged to the Bavarian ruling council and was a curator of the University of Ingolstadt. He was a staunch secularist and supporter of the Enlightenment who passed those values on to his adopted son. Weishaupt joined the Ingolstadt faculty in 1772, teaching law and philosophy. Finding the academic culture of Ingolstadt mired in conservatism and obscurantism, he joined the Masons in 1774. The Masons, with their prohibition of political and religious discussions, however, proved to be a disappointment to him. So Weishaupt and four others organized the Ancient Illuminated Seers of Bavaria, better known as the Illuminati, in 1776. Setting up a complex and demanding procedure for initiating new members into their higher ranks, Weishaupt ensured that only the Illuminati leadership would know what the organization was really up to. Growth of its membership was initially slow. By 1779 the society only had 54 members in five colonies or lodges in Bavaria. At that point another prominent Illuminati, Xavier Zwack, suggested infiltrating and taking over Masonic lodges for Illuminist purposes. It was a successful strategy, and by 1784 the Illuminati had over 650 members scattered throughout Masonic lodges in Germany, Switzerland, Austria, Bohemia, Hungary and Italy, often occupying leadership positions. The order attracted the writer Johann W. von Goethe, the scholar Johann Gottfried von Herder, the dramatist Friedrich Schiller and Ludwig II, Duke of Saxe-Gotha, as members (although Goethe and Herder quickly found the group too radical).[32]

Weishaupt despised the conservatism of the Jesuits, but he adopted their procedures of secrecy and deception for the Illuminati. Only the leaders knew how radical the goals of the Illuminati truly were. Weishaupt looked down on traditional Masonry as weak and indirectly supporting the continuation of autocratic rule and noble privilege by its apolitical policies. The problem for the Illuminati was that their secret goals for world reformation and the promotion of freedom, democracy, equality, toleration and enlightened rationalist religion were becoming known to conservative authorities. The Illuminist attempt at the Convention of Wilhelmsbad in 1782 to take over the failing Strict Observance branch of Masonry was thwarted by the conservative Jean Baptiste Willermoz, who ensured that Masons kept their traditional charitable and apolitical fraternal focus. Opposition to Illuminism mounted, and in June 1784 Elector Karl Theodor of Bavaria issued an edict banning secret societies. Then in March 1785, a second edict specifically banned the Masons and the Illuminati. Given advance warning, Weishaupt fled Bavaria but other Illuminists were arrested. In 1786 Bavarian authorities raided Xavier Zwack's home and seized his collection of Illuminati papers. These were later published to confirm the suspected plots and crimes of the Illuminati. While Weishaupt did not envision a violent revolution, internal subversion was definitely his tactic. He did envision the end of monarchy, noble privilege and the institutional Church. The conservative elite had become alerted to the danger posed by the Illuminati, and their suppression marked the beginning of a Europe-wide Counter-Enlightenment. Illuminism damaged Masonry, already in a weakened state by the 1780s, by tainting it throughout Europe with an association with efforts to destroy the traditional order and organization of Church and state. Many people came to believe that there was a grand plot and conspiracy to first undermine and then destroy the status quo of Old Regime Europe. Events after the outbreak of the French Revolution would seemingly provide confirmation of that belief for many conservatives.[33]

The French Revolution was one of the most significant events in history. Like the American Revolution, it had a profound and long-term impact. At the time, it both shocked and thrilled Europe. Many people welcomed the idea of liberty, fraternity and equality becoming the basis for civil society. But most members of the social and political elite did not like these looming changes at all. Monarchy and Church were threatened. So as the Revolution progressed, supporters of the traditional social order increasingly resisted. Meanwhile, very quickly the French Revolution turned violent and the Reign of Terror began. In September 1792 some 1,400 prisoners, most of them non-political, were massacred in Paris. Soon afterwards, the Revolutionary government put Louis XVI on trial and executed him on 21 January 1793. The execution of his wife, Marie Antoinette, followed some months later on 16 October. Both acts were a stunning repudiation of monarchy by divine right. Meanwhile, the Reign of Terror ramped up with the Revolutionary government's creation of the Committee of Public Safety. By the time the Thermidorian Reaction ended the Terror, some 300,000 people had been arrested, with 17,000 executed and another 10,000 dying in prison. Particularly horrific was the mass drowning of prisoners in the Loire at Nantes from November 1793 through February 1794. The victims numbered between 4,000 and 9,000, and consisted of priests, nuns and supporters of the royalist Vendée rebellion in western France. At the same time the Revolutionary armies of France managed to repel the invading armies of Austria and Prussia. At that point the government took the offensive and began conquering the lands surrounding France, where they proceeded to set up fellow revolutionary republics. Distraught conservatives and royalists asked themselves how this terrible series of events could have come to pass. One of the most widely accepted answers to come forth identified Masons as the culprits.

The first thing to understand is that the Masons actually did play a role in starting the French Revolution. Masonic lodges promoted tolerance, free-thinking, equality, democracy and liberty among their members. Many Masons believed that applying these values to society as a whole was a right and proper thing to do. Otherwise, most Masons were law-abiding and respectable citizens who supported the status quo (except for some modest reforms). Nevertheless, much of the elite, particularly in the Church, held them in deep suspicion. That situation, combined with the trauma and panic that the French Revolution ignited in the privileged classes of Europe, set the stage for wild speculations about the causes of the French Revolution.

The first person to blame the philosophes of the Enlightenment for causing the French Revolution was the Anglo-Irish politician and man of letters Edmund Burke. His *Reflections on the Revolution in France* appeared in 1790 and quickly became a bestseller in Great Britain and on the Continent, including France. It was very influential among German opponents of the Enlightenment. Although Burke did not bring Masons or the Illuminati into his argument, later he became a supporter of Abbé Augustin Barruel and his global conspiracy theories involving the Masons and Illuminati. As Burke wrote to Barruel on 1 May 1797, 'I cannot easily express to you how much I am instructed and delighted by the first Volume of your History of Jacobinism.' After Burke, other ever more complex and speculative theories about the origins and causes of the French Revolution began to proliferate.[34]

The first person to attack the Masons in print as the instigators of the French Revolution was Abbé Estève Bassie, a professor of theology at Montpellier. In 1790 he published in Rome *L'Esprit de la franc-maçonnerie dévoilé, relativement au danger qu'elle renferme* (The Spirit of Freemasonry Unveiled Relative to the Danger It Contains). In it, he linked the Masons' support for liberty and equality, which they shared with the philosophes, to the creation of a climate of opinion favourable to revolution, anti-monarchism and anti-clericalism. His contention is not surprising given the Roman Catholic Church's longstanding hostility to Masonry. Soon after, Abbé Jacques-François Lefranc pushed the Masonic connection with the Revolution further in his *Le Voile levé pour les curieux, ou le Secret de la Révolution révélé a l'aide de la franc-maçonnerie* (The Veil Lifted for the Curious; or, The Secret of the Revolution Revealed Using Freemasonry) published in 1791. Lefranc accused the Masons of being deeply involved in the conspiracy that caused the outbreak of the French Revolution. At the time, Lefranc was also collaborating on various literary projects with the future doyen of conspiracy theories concerning the Revolution – Abbé Augustin Barruel. The Revolutionary government did not appreciate Lefranc's opinions and imprisoned him in Paris, where he was killed during the September Massacres of 1792. Royalist newspapers began echoing the same sentiments as Bassie and Lefranc in 1792, and the savagery of the Reign of Terror only served to make later writings about Masonic conspiracies even more frenzied and expansive.[35]

The conspiracy theory expanded to include a Templar connection in 1791 with Charles-Louis Cadet de Gassicourt's *The Tomb of Jacques de Molay; or, Secret History of Ancient and Modern Initiates, Templars, Masons and the Enlightened and their Influence on the French Revolution.* Gassicourt had an interesting career. Publicly he was the son of the pharmacist Louis Claude Cadet de Gassicourt and his wife, Marie Boisselet. In reality he was the illegitimate son of Louis xv and Boisselet. Although his reputed father wanted him to study pharmacy, the young Gassicourt chose to become a lawyer while immersing himself in the writings of the Enlightenment. When the French Revolution broke out in 1789, Gassicourt supported it but later became disenchanted by the excesses of the Jacobins. He was accused of supporting the royalist uprising of the 13th Vendemaire (5 October) 1795 and was sentenced to death. Managing to avoid arrest, Gassicourt went into hiding for three years, during which time he wrote *The Tomb of Jacques de Molay*. Meanwhile, after the fall of the Jacobins, his conviction was cancelled. At that point, he finally took up pharmaceutical studies and enjoyed a successful career under Napoleon and the restored Bourbon monarchy.[36]

Gassicourt's little book outlines the insidious conspiracy that set off the French Revolution. It was a plot by Templar initiates and Masons that went back to the suppression of the Knights Templar and the execution of their last Grand Master, Jacques de Molay. While he was imprisoned, Molay instructed Templars to establish four Masonic lodges in Naples, Paris, Edinburgh and Stockholm as a covert way of maintaining the Templar order. These lodges were dedicated to exterminating the Bourbon dynasty and destroying the papacy. In order to achieve this goal, these Templar Masons allied themselves with the Jesuits, who were behind the assassination of Henry IV in 1610. The Comte de St Germain, a mysterious occult adventurer, and Alessandro Cagliostro were both initiates and agents of the Templar Masons. Various leaders of the French Revolution were also initiates of the Templar Masons such as the Comte de Mirabeau, Philippe Duc d'Orleans, Maximilian Robespierre and Georges Danton. According to Gassicourt there were only 108 Templar Masons. The vast majority of the other Masons were unaware of the Templar Masonic plot to exterminate the monarchy and destroy the Church. The purpose of Gassicourt's *Tomb* was to reveal the true cause of the Reign of Terror and prevent it from happening again. From this convoluted beginning the conspiracy theory of a Templar Masonic plot being the cause of the French Revolution spread and expanded.[37]

One of the great classics of conspiracy theory literature appeared soon after Gassicourt's book: Abbé Augustin Barruel's massive *Memoirs Illustrating the History of Jacobinism* (1797–8). He joined the Jesuits in 1756 when he was fifteen years old. In 1762 he began teaching at a Jesuit grammar school in Toulouse, but when France dissolved the Jesuit order in 1764, he went into exile. When the papacy's complete suppression of the Jesuits took place in 1773, Barruel returned to France and worked in the Church along with publishing various books on ecclesiastical matters. As an adherent of the Counter-Enlightenment and other conservative movements of the French clergy, he wrote or helped to publish attacks on the Enlightenment and the philosophes prior to the start of the French Revolution.[38]

When the French Revolution did break out Barruel opposed its anti-clerical policies, including the civil oath imposed on the clergy and the Civil Constitution of the Clergy of 1790. During this time he worked with Abbé Lefranc. In 1792 he fled into exile before he could be arrested for subversion. After settling in England, Barruel began to research and write his *Memoirs Illustrating the History of Jacobinism* to explain how a world-shattering event like the French Revolution and its horrific Reign of Terror came to occur.

The first two volumes appeared in 1797 and were followed by third and fourth volumes in 1798. Barruel asserted that there was a vast conspiracy against Church and state. It had been operating for many years as philosophes like Voltaire attacked Christianity and sought to bring it low. This revelation formed the content of the first volume of *Memoirs*. The Church was a major supporter of monarchical government, which many philosophes also disliked along with the accompanying aristocracy. Advocating liberty and equality for all people, the philosophes really meant the bringing down of kings and aristocrats. Barruel went on to declare that the allies of the philosophes in these anti-clerical and anti-monarchical attacks were the Masons. Their secret ceremonies promoted ideals of liberty and equality in their lodges. The second volume presented this Masonic aspect of the conspiracy. A third component of the conspiracy was the clandestine leadership of the Illuminati of Bavaria, who had gone underground and surreptitiously survived the earlier attempt to suppress them. The Illuminati were the leaders or unknown superiors who coordinated and directed the activities of the other conspirators. Applying the corrosive tenets of the Enlightenment's philosophes, the Illuminati plotted to destroy all religion and government. Barruel admitted that the great majority of Masons would never knowingly support such an agenda. He asserted, however, that the clandestine activities of the Illuminati leaders had kept the bulk of the Masons in ignorance of the true nature of the conspiracy's diabolical agenda. The third and fourth volumes of the *Memoirs* described the origins and organization of the Illuminati, along with the details of how they carried out their nefarious work.[39]

From the time Barruel's *Memoirs* first appeared, the book has proved popular in conservative and conspiracist circles. Despite being overly long and tedious, it still manages to enthral readers. A big attraction of the *Memoirs* is that it provides an all-embracing explanation for the bewildering and alarming success of the French Revolution.[40] Of course, it is an all-embracing explanation only if you did not bother to wonder why rational and civilized people like Voltaire, Diderot or even Adam Weishaupt would seek to destroy civilization.

In between the publication of the first two volumes of the *Memoirs* and the last two volumes in 1798, another classic text of conspiracy theory made its appearance – John Robison's *Proofs of a Conspiracy against All the Religions and Governments of Europe, carried on in the Secret Meetings of Free Masons, Illuminati, and Reading Societies*. Robison was a respected chemist and physicist who had a varied career in the navy, on diplomatic missions and as a professor at Glasgow and Edinburgh. Later in life he became interested in conspiracy theory.[41] His *Proofs of a Conspiracy* presents basically the same conclusions as Barruel's *Memoirs* but in a more concise though less well-documented form. Towards the end of the book Robison summarized his conclusions about the dire consequences of the philosophes', Masons' and Illuminati's abominable actions and plots. First, religion and morality were attacked. Then the conspiracy worked to destroy property, economic inequality and the social elite. Robison viewed the Illuminati as liars and hypocrites. He accused them of perverting women into being the equals and partners of men in these iniquitous designs. In addition, he pointed out that the secret society's strategy was to advance from frivolous criticism to wicked sedition. Furthermore, he argued that the ideals of the Declaration of the Rights of Man had degenerated into the Reign of Terror because those ideals were unsustainable. Like Barruel, Robison asserted that the Illuminati had infiltrated both schools and Masonic lodges to gain unknowing recruits and corrupt those institutions into sedition. From there he went on to criticize the liberal political theorists Joseph Priestley and Thomas Paine for supporting the French Revolution. On a hopeful note, Robison expressed the opinion that British society and Masonry were too level-headed to fall for the Illuminati's warped and dangerous ideals. In the second edition of *Proofs of a Conspiracy* published later in 1797, he added a postscript in which he praised Barruel's *Memoirs*. It was a sentiment that Barruel did not reciprocate, since he criticized the superficialities and errors of Robison's book.[42]

From the time that they first appeared, Barruel's and Robison's books attracted considerable attention and many readers. Both books rapidly sold thousands of copies. *Memoirs* was quickly translated from French into English by Sir Robert Clifford, a younger son of the Catholic Lord Hugh Clifford of Devonshire. The younger Clifford spent much time in France and probably even knew Barruel prior to his flight to exile in England in 1792. Given that Clifford's translation of the massive *Memoirs* appeared just shortly after the French version's publication, he had to have been working on it well before the *Memoirs* were published in French. Other translations in various European languages – German, Italian, Spanish, Portuguese and Dutch – followed in the next few years. Clifford's English translation also soon appeared in an American edition. Barruel produced an abridgement of his *Memoirs* in 1798, and other writers published excerpts and commentaries. Robison's *Proofs* experienced similar success with multiple editions along with translations into French, Dutch and German. Both books became foundational texts for future conspiracy theorists whether they were anti-Masonic, antisemitic, anti-Illuminist or New World Order fantasists.[43]

Barruel's *Memoirs* were an exhaustive study of the alleged triple conspiracy of the philosophes, the Masons and the Illuminati. In comparison, Robison's *Proofs* did not provide the same detail. In fact, he spent a fair amount of effort exonerating British Masonry from any role in causing the French Revolution or plotting a vile global conspiracy to promote harmful equality and liberty. Many readers, particularly British readers, were not convinced by Barruel's triple conspiracy or Robison's either. At the time, people observed that Masons suffered from the Reign of Terror at least as much as everyone else. Barruel's book was heavily documented, but its claims of sinister secret influences involved leaps of faith and ignored the manifest ills plaguing Old Regime France. For those who wanted to believe, Barruel's depiction of the conspiracy behind Jacobinism and the French Revolution connected everything in a chain of influences going back to the third-century Persian prophet Mani, founder of Manicheanism. As the historian Peter Partner has pointed out, 'In Barruel . . . everything connects; all thoughts are transmitted from one group and one historical period to another by magical contagion.' Barruel's contention about secret conspiracies causing the French Revolution could not stand up to the critical assessments of later historians. Instead, his true and lasting contribution was to enshrine the concept of conspiracies and conspiracy theories into political discourse and popular culture.[44]

The Legacy of Barruel

The books of the later conspiracist writers Nesta Webster and Una Pope-Hennessy née Birch bear out the continuing survival of Barruel's Illuminati conspiracy. Both women published books about conspiracy theories. Birch published *Secret Societies: Illuminati, Freemasons and the French Revolution* in 1911 at the start of her career as an author, during which she wrote mostly biographies. Her *Secret Societies* was actually four loosely related essays dealing with the Revolutionary and Napoleonic eras in France. Only the first essay dealt with the Illuminati's conspiracy. She believed it was true, but she argued that their goal was to make France a just and free society based on the ideals of the Enlightenment. In effect, she turned Barruel on his head. Nesta Webster, in her turn, took the Barruel line that there was an Illuminist conspiracy that sought to destroy government and religion. In 1910 Webster became convinced that she was the reincarnation of a female aristocrat who had lived through the French Revolution and its carnage. Based on this shaky foundation, she decided to start researching and writing about it. In 1919 she published *The French Revolution: A Study in Democracy*, which promoted Barruel's contention that the triple conspiracy of philosophes, Masons and the Illuminati ignited the French Revolution and had continued ever since to promote global conspiracy and revolution. After learning about 'The Protocols of the Elders of Zion', she took an antisemitic turn and added Jews to her list of secret conspirators in her *World Revolution: The Plot against Civilization* (1921). She continued with these conspiracy theories in her *Secret Societies and Subversive Movements* (1924). Her antisemitic and anti-communist opinions put her on the path to join the British fascist movement and become an admirer of Adolf Hitler (at least until the German–Soviet non-aggression pact of 1939). Both Birch's and Webster's books have remained readily available and continue to be cited by conspiracy theorists and antisemites.[45]

Conspiracies were endemic for many parts of Europe in the aftermath of Napoleon's defeat. The French Revolution had broken the old European order of domination by monarchy, aristocracy and the Church. Europe's conservative elites led by the Austrian statesman Klemens von Metternich worked hard to roll back the effects of the French Revolution and block further revolutionary activity with only partial and ultimately temporary success. Democratic liberalism and nationalism proved impossible to suppress. A series of revolutions occurred between 1815 and 1848, making it an era of secret societies and revolutionary plots. The Italian lands generated more than their fair share of secret societies like the Carbonari and revolutionary organizers such as Filippo Michele Buonarroti, but other European lands also experienced a proliferation of revolutionary activity. In many places, Masons played a part in the various plots and conspiracies.[46]

Many in the conservative elite believed that the attempted revolutions and conspiratorial secret societies were all a continuation of Barruel's great Masonic/Illuminati conspiracy of the unknown superiors who caused the French Revolution. In reality, the secret societies were a predictable response to the reactionary and oppressive policies of the conservative governments. They were not the unwitting pawns of unknown superiors of the Illuminati or some similar group. The changing nature of European society and its politics caused the decline and near disappearance of revolutionary secret societies after 1848 except in the Balkan lands and Russia. From that point supporters of liberalism and nationalism began to operate in the open. Nevertheless, the myth of a global conspiracy directed by the Illuminati or some other despicable group continued to hold its grip on the minds of the conservative elite. Into the 1870s the British politician and sometime prime minister Benjamin Disraeli continued to fret about secret societies. About the same time, Karl Marx was accused of being behind a vast conspiracy that became the rebellion of the Paris Commune of 1871. In fact, Marx was an opponent of insurrectionary secret societies. Beliefs in the conspiracy theory of secret societies and global plots not only survived, but evolved and expanded. The hidden masters or unknown superiors of the global conspiracies – the Masonic Illuminati – were joined by another group: the Jews.[47]

Antisemitism, Secret Societies and Conspiracy Theories

Jews have suffered from prejudice and animosity since the Hellenistic Era (323–31 BCE). The rise of Christianity and Islam resulted in the root religion of Judaism being dwarfed and dominated by its progeny. The Middle Ages and the early modern era saw Crusader pogroms; expulsions from England, France, Spain and Portugal; myths of Red Jews and blood libels. Then there were the restrictions placed on Jews such as prohibitions about land ownership and the requirement to live in segregated ghettos. With the coming of the Enlightenment and the growth of a global market economy, conditions for Jews began to improve.

It is important to remember that until the last quarter of the nineteenth century, being Jewish was a religious identification. From the 1870s onwards, however, to be Jewish increasingly became a racial identification. The significant difference was that baptism ended the convert's religious Judaism and integrated them into general Christian society. However, if Jewishness was a racial condition, Jews could never become part of Christian society. They would always be Jews. The man primarily responsible for this shift to a biological rather than a religious antisemitism was Wilhelm Marr. He was a German newspaperman who wrote *The Victory of Jewdom over Germandom Viewed from a Nonconfessional Standpoint* (1873), which successfully propagated the racial view of Jewishness using the recently coined term 'antisemitism'.[48]

Prior to Marr, there was a long tradition of blaming the misfortunes of Europe on Jewish plots and conspiracies. Those alleged Jewish outrages ranged from poisoning wells to kidnapping and ritually murdering Christian children, spreading plague, and serving as spies and saboteurs for the Mongols and other foreign invaders. These actions sought the destruction of Christian civilization. It was a small step from this view of the despised Jews to link them with the global conspiracy of the Masonic Illuminati who also wanted to destroy Christianity and civilization. Thus the myth of a Jewish world conspiracy quite naturally insinuated itself into the European popular culture of Masonic and Illuminist conspiracy theories. As historian Norman Cohn has put it so well, 'In the Middle Ages Jews had been seen as agents of Satan, devil worshippers, demons in human form. It is one of the achievements of the modern antisemitic movement that in the late nineteenth century, it was able to revive this archaic superstition.'[49]

'The Protocols of the Elders of Zion'

The most notorious and influential antisemitic document to identify the Jews as the leaders of global conspiracy was 'The Protocols of the Elders of Zion'. Although this pamphlet was first published in 1903, it did not become well known outside of Russia until the early 1920s. It also bears the dubious distinction of being a complete fabrication as well as being plagiarized from another fraudulent canard and several novels. There was a long line of tracts and books asserting the existence of the Jewish global conspiracy going back to the French Revolution. During the late 1860s European antisemitism began to really heat up and theories about global Jewish conspiracies proliferated. Jacob Brafman, a renegade Jewish Russian convert to Christianity, wrote a number of books, including *Local and Universal Jewish Brotherhoods* (1868) and *The Book of the Kahal* (1869), that criticized both local and international Jewish organizations for their oppression of ordinary Jews and their plots to promote Jewish global domination. Brafman's own Kahal (Qahal) had tried to dragoon him into the Russian army as a young man. Forced to run away, he became an embittered critic of the Jewish leadership and so provided seemingly inside information about sinister Jewish machinations that fuelled antisemitic conspiracy theories. Brafman's contemporary the French antisemite Roger Gougenot des Mousseaux published *Le Juif, le judaisme et la judaisation des peoples chretiens* in 1869, which accused Jews of being allies of the Masons in using the Enlightenment's ideals to bring on the French Revolution and continuing to seek world domination. Other promoters of the conspiracy theory of Jewish global domination were *Conquest of the World by the Jews* (1878) by Major Osman Bey (aka Frederick Millingen) and *The Talmud and the Jews* by Hippolytas Lutostansky, a Polish Roman Catholic priest who switched to Orthodox Christianity after being disciplined for scandalous behaviour. A very influential contributor to the theory of a Jewish world conspiracy was Hermann Goedsche, whose novel *Biarritz* (1868, written under the pseudonym Sir John Retcliffe) included the classic scene of a gathering of Jewish leaders at a cemetery in Prague. There they plotted how to achieve Jewish domination of the world after a speech by the chief rabbi that outlined their nefarious plans. The creators of the 'Protocols of the Elders of Zion' plagiarized *Biarritz*'s antisemitic scenes and presented them as historical fact. As bad as that might seem, it should be noted that Goedsche himself plagiarized from Maurice Joly's *Dialogue in Hell between Machiavelli and Montesquieu* (1864), Alexandre Dumas *père*'s novel *Joseph Balsamo* and Eugène Sue's seven-novel series *Le Mystères du people* (1849–56) to create his antisemitic storyline. So, the 'Protocols' are actually a plagiarized calumny of a plagiarized novel based on several other works of fiction.[50]

The origins of 'The Protocols of the Elders of Zion' are both murky and convoluted. What is not in dispute by any reasonable researcher and scholar, however, is that it is a completely fabricated document. It has been conclusively and incontrovertibly debunked many times from Lucien Wolf in 1920 to Michael Hagemeister in the present. Some authorities such as Norman Cohn place the beginning of the 'Protocols' in Paris during the years 1893–9. At that time the Russian secret police of the Tsarist era, the Okhrana, had agents in Paris who were keeping an eye on Russian revolutionaries in exile. Lead by Piotr Rachofsky, they also engaged in creating propaganda against revolutionaries, hostile foreign powers, modernizing Tsarist ministers like Sergei Witte and unpopular minorities like Jews. This activity included looking for publications like Joly's *Dialogue in Hell* and Goedsche's *Biarritz*. According to older scholarship, it was during these years that the 'Protocols' were composed. The 1890s were a time of intensifying persecution of Russian Jews and widespread pogroms. Eventually, the Russian religious writer Sergei Niles in 1905 published the 'Protocols' as part of a book about the impending arrival of the Antichrist.[51]

Newer scholarship of Cesare De Michelis and Michael Hagemeister, in contrast, places the composition of the 'Protocols' to the years 1902–3. They do not identify the author or authors of the 'Protocols', but consider the document to be a product of the increasingly unsettled state of Russia on the eve of the Revolution of 1905. Either way, the facts of the publication history of the 'Protocols' are that it languished in minor publications from the world of antisemitic and extreme right-wing Russians that attracted only very modest attention. The Tsarist government neither embraced the 'Protocols' nor did much to suppress or restrain it. That situation changed with the outbreak of the Russian Revolution.[52]

So, prior to the Russian Revolution, the 'Protocols' had been confined to Russia, where it was just one piece of antisemitic propaganda among many. The coming of the Russian Revolution gave the 'Protocols' a plausible utility. The secret Jewish cabal depicted were also the unknown superiors behind the revolution in Russia. The Bolsheviks were Jews, or so the propaganda of the counter-revolutionary White Russians would have the world believe. During the Civil War, White Russian forces distributed the 'Protocols' to the peasants in an attempt to harness antisemitism in their fight against the Bolshevik Reds. And when they lost the civil war and fled into exile in the West, they brought the 'Protocols' with them.[53]

By early 1919 White Russian exiles were handing out copies of the 'Protocols' at the Versailles Peace Conference and to various United States government officials, including members of the intelligence services of the army and the navy. Earlier in November 1918 the Tsarist officials Piotr Shabelsky-Bork and Fyodor Vineberg had fled to Germany with the German occupation forces who were evacuating the Ukraine. They apparently came into possession of a copy of Sergei Niles's book *The Great in the Small*, which included the 'Protocols'. They brought the 'Protocols' to the attention of the antisemitic German publisher Ludwig Müller von Hausen.[54] He had it translated into German as *Protokolle der Weisen von Zion*, which came out in January 1920 with a publication date of 1919. It was the first non-Russian version of the 'Protocols' and would go through 33 editions by 1933. The German translation was quickly joined by several other translations during 1920: English (one in England and two in the United States), French and Polish. Arabic and Italian translations followed in 1921. In Great Britain, the English translation was published by Eyre & Spottiswoode under the title *The Jewish Peril*. It was followed by a series of approving articles in the conservative *Morning Post*, which rhapsodized about the much needed exposure of the conspiratorial 'Formidable Sect': the Jews. Meanwhile in the United States, Henry Ford gave the 'Protocols' a big boost in publicity by publishing a series of antisemitic articles in his newspaper, the *Dearborn Independent*, from May through to October 1920. These would be collected and published as the infamous book *The International Jew: The World's Foremost Problem*. Half a million copies flooded the United States, promoted by a well-funded publicity campaign. The book was quickly translated into German, Russian and Spanish. Ford's backing and prestige gave credibility to the 'Protocols' and made it a global sensation. An intense negative reaction, however, also followed and the ensuing storm of condemnation forced Ford to repudiate his own antisemitic publication and the 'Protocols'. Ford pled ignorance about the nature of the 'Protocols' and *The International Jew* and claimed that his assistants had duped him. But despite Ford's backtracking, the damage was done, and the 'Protocols' and the myth of a Jewish world conspiracy became a central motif and fixture of conspiracy theories.[55]

What should have been devastating criticisms of the 'Protocols' soon appeared. In Britain, Peter Graves, a correspondent for *The Times* of London, published three articles on 16, 17 and 18 August 1921. These articles first exposed the 'Protocols' blatant plagiarism of Maurice Joly's *Dialogue in Hell*. Lucien Wolf followed with three articles in the *Manchester Guardian*, *The Spectator* and the *Daily Telegraph* debunking the Jewish global conspiracy and criticizing the *Morning Post*. These were quickly gathered together and expanded into a small book, *The Myth of the Jewish Menace in World Affairs*. It pointed out the illogic of the 'Protocols' and the *Morning Post*'s series of antisemitic articles. Wolf viewed the 'Protocols' as a manifestation of antisemitic and anti-British Germanic sentiments. He also pointed out the plagiarism of Hermann Goedsche's *Biarritz*. One particular absurdity that Wolf pointed out would have especially garnered the attention of his British readers. That was the attempt to link the British to the Jewish global conspiracy by declaring them also to be Jews, based on the quirky theories of British Israelism, which asserted that the British people were descendants of the lost tribes of Ephraim and Mannesah. None of these efforts put a dent in the antisemitic and conspiratorial convictions of the flagitious and indefatigable conspiracy theorist Nesta Webster. Her *Secret Societies and Subversive Movements* presented a disingenuous defence of the 'Protocols' by reaching an inconclusive appraisal of their authenticity.[56]

In the United States, the Jewish journalist and diplomat Herman Bernstein published *The History of a Lie: 'The Protocols of the Wise Men of Zion'* (1921), which covered the same ground as Wolf but in more detail. Bernstein would also bring lawsuits against Henry Ford's *International Jew*, which dragged on for years. Such efforts significantly blunted the impact of its fostering of antisemitism, as Ford's forced repudiation of the *International Jew* demonstrates.[57]

Similar efforts on continental Europe to combat the pernicious 'Protocols' failed. The post-war disruptions, the need for scapegoats to blame for problems and a persistent culture of antisemitism in Central and Eastern Europe were too great to be overcome by mere rational arguments. Norman Cohn has also pointed out the role and responsibility of the middle-class adherents of *völkisch* ideology. They proclaimed that Germans were the last remnant of an ancient Aryan super-race and therefore special in their own right. This belief meshed readily with the depiction in the 'Protocols' of a Jewish global conspiracy. It was a toxic combination. As a result, the Polish émigré and Jew Binjamin W. Segel and other German Jews discovered that combatting and debunking antisemitic falsehoods like the 'Protocols' had become a hopeless task after 1918. Segel's *Welt Krieg, Welt-Revolution, Welt-Verschworung, Welt-Oberrerierung* (World War, World Revolution, World Conspiracy, World Supreme Government,

1926) thoroughly debunked the 'Protocols' to no avail. At the same time Hitler and the Nazis were making it a foundation text of their ideology.[58]

Germany's relatively close location to Russia meant that Tsarist and White Russian exiles took refuge there. Many of these refugees were Baltic Germans, as was Alfred Rosenberg, the future Thulist and pioneer Nazi who would become the Nazi Party's ideologue. He helped to bring the 'Protocols' to the attention of Hitler and his fledgling party. In 1923 Rosenberg placed the 'Protocols' into an up-to-date context for the Nazi movement in *The Protocols of the Elders of Zion and Jewish World Policy*. All through the 1920s up to 1933, right-wing publishing companies like Theodore Fritsch's Hammer-Verlag were churning out copies of the 'Protocols' along with Ford's *International Jew* and other works supporting or echoing the 'Protocols'. The 'Protocols' even inspired assassinations of officials of the Weimar Republic – most notably that of Walther Rathenau, Germany's first Jewish foreign minister.[59]

The idea of a global Jewish conspiracy resonated with Hitler and the Nazis; it provided a simple explanation for all of Germany's woes. The 'Protocols' provided a justification for the Nazis' brutal suppression of all Germans who disagreed with them, their plans for wars of aggression and their attempt to exterminate the Jews during the Holocaust. Hitler discussed the 'Protocols' in *Mein Kampf*. Railing against the Jews as an evil race, not a religion, he praised the 'Protocols':

> To the extent the whole existence of this people [Jews] is based on a continuous lie is shown incomparably by the 'Protocols of the Wise Men of Zion', so infinitely hated by the Jews. They are based on a forgery, the *Frankfurter Zeitung* moans and screams once every week: the best proof that they are authentic. What many Jews may do unconsciously is here consciously exposed. And that is what matters ... For once this book has become the common property of a people, the Jewish menace may be considered broken.[60]

The Nazis worked hard to share the 'Protocols' with the world and so spread the gospel of antisemitism and Jewish global conspiracy. Its pride of place in Nazi propaganda did not exclude the promotion of other Nazi ideological classics – *Mein Kampf* and Rosenberg's *Myth of the Twentieth Century*. Furthermore, Hitler used the Jewish world conspiracy of the 'Protocols' to claim that any group or country which opposed him and his Third Reich was a tool of the Elders of Zion. At the same time, it has been suggested by Hannah Arendt that Hitler and the Nazis actually tried to copy the strategies and tactics for world domination described in the

'Protocols'. By 1939, as the outbreak of the Second World War loomed ever nearer, the 'Protocols' was enjoying its highest level of acceptance and greatest success.[61]

The Second World War ended with the total crushing of the Third Reich and the death of Hitler. Such a defeat did not end the career of the 'Protocols'. It was just too useful for anyone pushing a conspiracy theory. The Elders of Zion as unknown superiors can easily be transferred to other unpopular groups in addition to or instead of the Jews. They could be the Illuminati, the Trilateral Commission, alien infiltrators, communists or any group supposedly seeking world domination. Like the works of Barruel and others, the 'Protocols' has habituated many people to believe in conspiracies of world domination by some shadowy group, no matter how preposterous they might be. As the debunker Herman Bernstein observed and predicted back in 1921:

> And now cowardly anonymous writers are embellishing the 'protocols' adding new lies to the old ones, making accusations against the Jews that even Nilus-Lutostansky-Butmi dared not make in darkest Russia. Perhaps someday these new legends and absurd, malicious myths may evolve into a new and revised edition of the secret Jewish 'protocols.'[62]

He was right.

New World Orders

National sovereignty is a big issue for many people throughout the world. Even the slightest interference with a country's freedom to operate as it sees fit – no matter how reprehensible, irrational or insignificant the prohibited action or policy might be – raises the spectre of an inexorable march towards a global government or, as it is commonly known, the New World Order. Historically, resistance to some sort of world government is a relatively new phenomenon. The Roman empire was a world government in its day. Many people did not like being subjects of Rome, as periodic rebellions in the provinces demonstrated. Still, after the Roman empire fell in the West, the people of late antiquity and the Middle Ages looked back with nostalgia and longing on that imperial era. The medieval ideal was that there might be a restoration of the universal Church and a universal empire. That goal was the motivation behind the establishment of the Holy Roman Empire. Restoration of a universal empire was lauded as sacred even though various kings and popes did all they could to thwart its accomplishment. Still, the ideal of a universal empire persisted into the seventeenth century when the rise of absolutist nation states became the new normal. That new political system dominated the eighteenth century until the French Revolution swept it away.

The Revolutionary and Napoleonic era brought on the rise of nationalism, first in France and later in Spain, Germany, Italy and beyond. Of course, kings of the medieval and early modern eras had always been deeply concerned to preserve their sovereignty. With the rise of nationalism, however, sovereignty became a source of pride and comfort for all the citizens of the state. As the Industrial Revolution and the growth of economic prosperity and scientific knowledge progressed, national rivalries also intensified dangerously. Even before 1914, some leaders and thinkers began suggesting that supranational organizations ought to be established to reduce tensions, promote cooperation and be more efficient. After the carnage of the First World War, the creation of the League of Nations seemed to be an imperative. The League's failure and the further devastation of the Second World War led to the setting up of the United Nations to promote international peace and cooperation. Although these developments were seen by many as a sign of progress towards the assurance and continuation of a better and safer world, others saw them as part of a conspiracy to end human freedom.

Global conspiracy theories have been around for a long time. The French Revolution sparked fears of the Masons and Illuminati destroying Christianity and monarchy and setting up a world government on the ruins. By the middle years of the nineteenth century, it was the Jews who were the conspirators. After 1917 they were joined by the Bolsheviks. Ironically, the Nazis, who arose to combat the supposed Jewish and Bolshevik threats of global domination, would themselves seek to establish a world government under the Third Reich. Allied victory in the Second World War and the creation of the United Nations did not bring about a golden age of international cooperation. Instead, it brought the Cold War between the capitalist West and the communist East, which lasted for 45 years.

Western nations not only faced a military threat from Russia and its allies, but lived in dread of internal subversion by communist infiltrators and collaborators. The United States suffered the Red Scare. The Cold War environment of East versus West promoted an essentially Manichean good-versus-evil worldview. This way of thinking encouraged dualistic and simplistic explanations for political and social problems. As a result, the United States became a hothouse for the conspiracy theories and paranoid fantasies that commonly flourish in the dark corners of societies and sometimes even in the mainstream of the lives of nations. These conditions led to the appearance of the New World Order conspiracy with its vague, shape-shifting and fearsome master narrative of global domination by unknown superiors.

Prior to the Second World War, right-wing groups in Europe and the United States had tended to see communism and the Soviet Union as a greater threat than Hitler and the Third Reich. Nazi aggression leading to the Second World War changed that perception. Once Germany was defeated and Nazism destroyed, they quickly refocused on the threat of Stalin's Russia and communist expansion. In turn, Stalin and the Russians viewed the hardcore anti-communists as a threat. Such mutual suspicions and fears made an East/West conflict inevitable. It also further stoked the fears of conspiracists so that conspiracy theories abounded.[63]

Studies have shown that right-wing political beliefs and conspiracist thinking have an affinity for each other. People on the left also have their conspiracy theories, but left-wing conspiracy theories are far less numerous and almost always less extreme in their beliefs. Because the prevalence of conspiracy theories in the United States since 1945 has been so great and varied, the most concise way to depict them is an overview focusing on a few representative examples of how various conspiracy theories have changed and evolved. One of the leading groups promoting right-wing, anti-communist conspiracy theories was the John Birch Society.[64]

The John Birch Society was founded in Indianapolis, Indiana, in 1958 under the leadership of Robert W. Welch. Born in North Carolina, Welch was a child prodigy who graduated from high school at the age of twelve and from the University of North Carolina when he was seventeen. He also attended the United States Naval Academy and then went on to Harvard's law school, although without completing a degree from either institution. After Welch left Harvard, he claimed to have become disenchanted with academic life. Instead, he turned to making and selling confectionery. In partnership with his brother, he became successful and turned out to be adept at marketing. The Welch brothers' company developed Sugar Daddies and Junior Mints along with several other popular varieties of candy and sweets. By the time he retired in 1956, Welch had amassed a fortune. Over the years, he became more and more active in Republican Party politics and the campaign against communism.[65]

Soon after his retirement, Welch became so concerned about the threat of communist domination that he decided to found the John Birch Society. He named his new organization after an American missionary and serviceman who had been killed in China by a communist soldier ten days after the end of the Second World War on 25 August 1945. Some people, especially Birch's mother, Ethel, considered her son a martyr and later declared him to be the first American casualty of the impending Cold War. Superficially Birch made a perfect icon for Welch's anti-communist organization. Given the questionable reputation that the John Birch Society would soon develop, many people who knew Birch well questioned whether he would have been pleased with its use of his name. Among that group was the war hero James (Jimmy) Doolittle, who led the bombing raid on Tokyo in April 1942. Doolittle and his crew had to bail out over Japanese-occupied China, where Birch rescued them and brought them through enemy lines to safety. The two men became friends and as Doolittle later put it, 'He [Birch] had no way of knowing that the John Birch Society ... would be named after him ... I feel sure he would not have approved.'[66]

Among those involved at the beginning of the John Birch Society was the industrialist Fred Koch, father of David and Charles, the future funders of the Heritage Foundation and the Tea Party. David and Charles Koch would join the society but later left it to launch their own conservative enterprises.[67] The John Birch Society was not just anti-communist; it was against just about anything progressive, such as civil rights, women's rights, the Federal Reserve System, social welfare, immigration and anything that seemed to promote one world government, the United Nations and globalization. Communist infiltration of American institutions was seemingly ubiquitous, including the Parent–Teacher Association (PTA) and all branches of the United States government up to the highest levels, including the president. Welch wrote a book, *The Politician*, in 1956 (although it was not published until 1963) that basically accused President Dwight Eisenhower of being a Russian agent. It was all part of an immense communist conspiracy. *The Politician* caused mainstream Republicans and conservatives to reject Welch and the John Birch Society as irrationally radical. One of Welch's biggest detractors was a former friend, William F. Buckley Jr, an old-line conservative and the editor of the *National Review*. So the John Birch Society earned a dubious reputation as a preposterously anti-communist organization. Paranoia and conspiracies were high among its trademark imagery. That was the way Welch wanted it, and he ruled the John Birch Society despotically until near his death in 1985.[68]

Shortly after Welch died, the empire of the Soviet Union crumbled and its communist government fell. One might have thought that the John Birch Society would also have faded away with the end of the Cold War and the demise of the threat of communist world domination. Not so: for Welch, the John Birch Society was never just about the threat of

communist expansionism. For him, communism was just one manifestation of the secret global conspiracy that went back to ancient Greece but
had only come fully into its own with the Bavarian Illuminati. In other
words, the global conspiracy remained a dangerous threat – communists or
no communists. The John Birch Society's ability to shift the focus to ever
vaguer conspiracy theories is an example of how improvisational conspiracy theories can change and evolve. With the help of the cultic milieu, any
conspiracy theory can find plenty of resources to reinvent itself.[69]

The John Birch Society had a resurgence during the first decade of the
twenty-first century. Bircher ideology became a major intellectual foundation of the very conservative Tea Party wing of the Republican Party. The
conservative media commentator Glenn Beck became an avid promoter
of its literature and ideas and introduced them into the emerging Tea
Party. It was a prime example of conspiracist politics going mainstream.[70]

Milton William Cooper represents another variety of post-Second
World War conspiracism. He was born into a military family in Long
Beach, California, but information about Cooper's early life is sketchy,
other than that the family moved frequently due to the father's military
assignments. When he was nineteen in 1962, he joined the United States
Air Force, where he served through the Cuban Missile Crisis and the
assassination of President John F. Kennedy. After receiving an honourable discharge, he quickly joined the United States Navy in 1966. Cooper
requested a combat assignment and he arrived in Vietnam during the
last days of the Tet Offensive in 1968. When his tour of duty finished, he
went to work in naval intelligence under Admiral Bernard A. Clarey. His
position included significant security clearance, and later Cooper would
claim that he encountered all sorts of classified documents revealing dirty
secrets and nefarious activities on such topics as the Kennedy assassination. Cooper would later claim that it was at this point that he had his
epiphany regarding the existence of the one world government or the
New World Order.[71]

Shortly after the fall of Saigon in 1975, Cooper left the navy. He
and a naval friend tried to open a diving school but that did not prove
successful. Meanwhile, he experienced mental and physical health problems related to his military service. He also went through several wives,
enough that FBI records are unclear on just how many times he was married. By the mid-1980s he had got a job at a for-profit vocational college,
where he experienced success and advancement until the attorney general
for California shut down the school for defrauding its students. All the
while, Cooper spent his spare time researching New World Order-style
conspiracies. By 1988 he began to present aspects of his own conspiracy

theory, which would eventually be revealed in his book, *Behold a Pale Horse*, in 1991. Starting out by posting his ideas on early computer chat boards, he began radio broadcasting in 1989 and gained a cult following among conspiracists. By 1991 Cooper had written and compiled enough material to publish *Behold a Pale Horse*. Thirty years later, it remains a bestselling UFO book on Amazon.com, sometimes edging out Erich von Däniken for the position of top seller in that category. What makes that achievement all the more remarkable is that UFOs comprise only a small part of Cooper's book.[72]

Behold a Pale Horse is a curious book. Its cover depicts death on a pale horse, in keeping with the reference to the biblical book of Revelation in its title. The style of the cover art is Southwestern, as befits the book's publication in Arizona and Cooper's residence there. Otherwise the content is something of a data dump. There are seventeen chapters with seven appendices in the original 1991 edition. The appendices are largely reproductions of various documents with no text written by Cooper. Most of the chapters are interspersed with facsimiles of documents, photographs, charts, tables and maps. Many of the chapters are also simply reprinted documents, so that Chapter Three reprints a piece of mid-nineteenth-century nativist anti-Catholic propaganda, while Chapter Fifteen consists of the 'Protocols of the Wise Men [Elders] of Zion' (which has been eliminated from the 2019 edition). Some of the chapter titles clearly reveal Cooper's concerns: 'Goodbye U.S.A., Hello New World Order', 'Are the Sheep Ready to Shear?' and 'The Secret Government'. There are sections dealing with the U.S. military's connections to a satanic Church, UFOs and Area 51, alien implants and the U.S. government's involvement with AIDS and the drug trade. The book concludes with a chart listing the members of and the overlapping connections between the Council on Foreign Relations and the Trilateral Commission, both perennially considered fronts for the New World Order. *Behold a Pale Horse* is a farrago of conspiracy theories from Freemasons to Illuminati, the Rothschilds, the Council on Foreign Relations and alien infiltrators.[73]

Michael Barkun, a scholar of extremist cults and conspiracy theories, has pointed out that UFO beliefs have become part of the New World Order conspiracy. From the time of the flying saucer craze of the late 1940s and early 1950s, accusations of government conspiracies to suppress knowledge about extraterrestrial visitors have abounded. They were joined by tales of extraterrestrials experimenting on animals and humans. Supposedly, the United States government made secret alliances and treaties with the extraterrestrials, which have morphed into the government acquiescing to ghastly experiments being conducted by the alien visitors.

At that point it is a rather small step to believe that the extraterrestrials were the true unknown superiors behind the New World Order conspiracy. And that is exactly what Milton William Cooper did.[74] According to Cooper, mainstream films like *Close Encounters of the Third Kind* (1977) and *E.T. the Extra-Terrestrial* (1982) were based on real contact between humans and aliens during the early 1950s. In a conversation during 1991 with the French ufologist Jacques Vallée, Cooper asserted that 'there were four types of aliens . . . There were two kinds of Grays, including one race, not commonly seen that has a large nose. Then there are the Nordic types, tall blonde Aryans, and finally the Orange ones.' Just how he came to know this information is unclear. For the UFO community at large, Cooper's wild conspiracy theories were an embarrassment that threatened the credibility of the whole UFO movement. As for Cooper himself, he is never even clear as to whether the success of the aliens' New World Order conspiracy was ultimately bad or good for humans.[75]

After 1995 Cooper suddenly and drastically revised his conspiracy theory. Aliens were no longer the grand conspirators and unknown superiors of the New World Order. They were not even real. Instead, the human Illuminati were behind the New World Order all along. They simply created UFOs as part of a disinformation campaign to provide themselves with deniability if their own abominable plans ever started to come to light. Meanwhile, Cooper had been gravitating away from the UFO movement and towards the militia movement that flourished during the 1990s. As Barkun has pointed out, conspiracists like Cooper have been known to make such drastic changes in their theories when the drift of their improvisational theorizing has inadvertently created an invincible enemy such as aliens with super-technologies. To preserve hope for successful resistance, Cooper returned the New World Order plot to the hands of mere humans with their usual vulnerabilities.[76]

Whatever Cooper's opinions about the reality of UFOs and an alien New World Order conspiracy, like many conspiracy theories, his ideas are unfalsifiable. Any evidence that clearly refutes the theories of Cooper and other conspiracy theorists can be dismissed simply by claiming the evidence is a fabrication by a government or a New World Order cover-up. Hardcore believers in Cooper's conspiracy theories might be a small minority, but they are not without impact. The Oklahoma City bomber Timothy McVeigh listened regularly to Cooper's radio broadcasts, as did other anti-government activists. McVeigh came to visit Cooper in the summer of 1994, shortly before the bombing of the Alfred P. Murrah Federal Building. Little is known about their conversation. Cooper claimed not to know McVeigh and that their conversation was innocuous. Of course, he had a strong reason for making that claim, since the FBI, soon after the bombing, began asking him some uncomfortable questions. It is both telling and not coincidental that Cooper and his associates almost immediately started to contend that McVeigh was a government patsy and that the bombing was a false flag operation intended to discredit the anti-government and militia movements.[77]

Moving further into the world of the militia and anti-government movements, Cooper kept up his radio broadcasts and publications, including a newspaper, *Veritas*. He also engaged in the militia's paramilitary activities. All of this cost money, and some of his projects proved to be expensive failures. As a result, Cooper's financial difficulties caused him to cut corners, which resulted in federal indictments for bank fraud and tax evasion on 18 June 1998. Following his long-standing anti-government principles, Cooper rejected the charges as illegitimate and unconstitutional. He also promised armed resistance to any attempt to serve or to arrest him. Loath to risk the potential bad publicity of another deadly incident like Ruby Ridge or the Branch Davidians at Waco, federal law enforcement officials bided their time about confronting Cooper. Trouble, however, had a way of finding the obsessively suspicious Cooper. On 11 July 2001 Dr Scott Reynolds Hamblin drove his family to a hill near Cooper's residence to watch a distant lightning storm. Making only a brief stop, Hamblin took his family home and noticed a pickup truck was following him. Arriving at his house, Hamblin was confronted by the driver, who told him to stay off of his property and pointed a cocked pistol at his face. The driver was Milton William Cooper, who had a long history of running people off the hill near his home, although it was not his property. Hamblin, a respected local resident, filed a complaint with the sheriff. Initially, the sheriff's department took the FBI's advice and did not press the matter. The aggrieved Hamblin continued to demand justice. Finally, on 29 August 2001, the state of Arizona issued a warrant for Cooper's arrest on the felony charges of aggravated assault and reckless endangerment. The plan was to arrest Cooper on 11 September, but the possibility that Cooper had been tipped off caused a delay and the terror attack on the World Trade Center that same day further intervened. Cooper broadcast his radio show all that day, and the authorities were reluctant to arrest him while he was on air. So the sheriff's department looked for other opportunities for a low-profile arrest. It was not to be. On the evening of 5 November 2001 seventeen members of the Apache County Sheriff's Department attempted to lure Cooper out of his house. The plan went wrong and gunfire ensued. Cooper shot one deputy in the head while another deputy emptied his gun into Cooper. Miraculously, the wounded deputy lived, although he was left paralysed for life. Cooper did not survive.[78]

The death of Milton William Cooper did not mean the end of conspiracy theories, particularly those involving the New World Order. Cooper was not alone in the demon-haunted world of conspiracism; its name is truly legion. There were and remain plenty of proponents of conspiracy theories, and they generally tend to proselytize the unfalsifiable improvisational versions of conspiracy theories that are seemingly immortal and invincible to refutation.

Probably the most notorious and influential conspiracy theorist operating today is Alex Jones. He was born in Dallas, Texas. Later his family moved to Austin, where he played football in high school and graduated in 1993. After a brief stint at the local community college, he started a live call-in show on public-access television but switched to talk radio in 1996. The libertarian Ron Paul appeared on his show several times, and Jones's topics shifted towards conspiracism and anti-government subjects such as accusing the federal government of being behind the Oklahoma City bombing and the murder of the Branch Davidians at Waco. In 1999 he was the co-winner of a newspaper poll selecting the best Austin talk radio host award. That same year, his employer, KJFK-FM, fired him for refusing to broaden his range of topics away from the focus on conspiracy theories. Undeterred, Jones began to broadcast over the Internet from his home and by 2001 was syndicated on one hundred radio stations. By 2010 his show attracted 2 million listeners a week, and his website, InfoWars, was being accessed 10 million times a month. Along the way to this success, he accused President George W. Bush of being behind the 9/11 attacks on the World Trade Center, and verbally attacked the erstwhile tabloid talk show host and now frequent Fox News commentator Geraldo Rivera in 2007, among other shocking acts. Later he would engage in a nasty gun control debate with Piers Morgan in 2013 and plot to oust Ted Cruz of Texas from his senate seat for his opposition to Donald Trump.[79]

Jones's InfoWars website and radio show have become lucrative enterprises. In 2014 Jones testified in court that InfoWars generated an income of $20 million a year. In 2017 the German magazine *Der Spiegel* reported that two-thirds of Jones's income was produced from sales of the products offered on the InfoWars website.[80] The 'store' section on InfoWars is quite a bit different from those of websites like the John Birch Society. On the latter, the focus is on educating readers to the correct ideology and getting them organized politically to achieve concrete ends. Items for sale include books, pamphlets and DVDs that inform the readers about its ideology or support it. Some items are produced in-house; others are kindred works from similar groups or conspiracist classics like John Robison's *Proofs of a Conspiracy*.[81] The InfoWars website and its companion site – PrisonPlanet – are different. Both have an obvious focus on Alex Jones. You do not have to browse long to find his picture displayed: it is ubiquitous. The home page of InfoWars lists various videos and news stories that purport to be real news, as opposed to what appears in the mainstream media. Both of Jones's websites have a 'store' button to click on. It takes the visitor to the InfoWars' shop in both cases. The first thing visitors see is 'Bestsellers', which consist largely of health- and wellness-related products that are produced for InfoWars. Featured are items like Ultra2 (an enhanced vitamin B-12 for energy), Brain Force Plus (which claims to clear your mind and energize it), DNA Force Plus (for re-energizing the body and helping it to fight environmental toxins) and Super Male Vitality (more re-energizing to help a man, well, you know what they mean). Not to neglect his female audience, Jones also sells a Super Female Vitality. Clearly, Jones's followers have concerns about their energy and their performance both mentally and in the bedroom. Combatting the unknown superiors of the New World Order can be exhausting in several different ways, it would appear. Furthermore, InfoWars consumers are also worried about toxic elements in the environment, which is ironic given their opposition and general disdain for environmental problems and pollution. Another section is called 'Preparedness', which sells camping and food preparation equipment apparently to help one get through the coming apocalypse, and home security items for warding off home invasions by criminal gangs like the MS-13 or tyrannical government agencies such as the Bureau of Alcohol, Tobacco, and Firearms. A 'Media' section sells books and videos. Conspiracy theories including Illuminati materials, anti-government productions or publications, and UFO-related materials, including ancient aliens and other products of a pseudo-historical or pseudoscientific nature, are also presented. Finally, there is the section 'Gear', mostly apparel. T-shirts are on sale with such messages as 'Build the Wall', 'Californians Keep Out' printed over a Texas flag logo, and 'Alex Jones Did Nothing Wrong' (probably not something his ex-wife would care to wear) along with other items appealing to supporters of anti-immigrant and pro-gun policies or that engage in hero-worship of Donald Trump. Like Glenn Beck and Rush Limbaugh, Alex Jones has found a way to make conspiracism pay – big time.[82]

Jones is a classic example of improvisational conspiracy thinking. His radio show and InfoWars website propagate a wide and even bewildering

variety of conspiracy theories: for example, that vaccinations of children cause autism, that the mass shootings in schools like Sandy Hook
Elementary and the Stoneman Douglas High School were false flag
operations, as were the Oklahoma City bombing and the attack on the
World Trade Center, and that the government can control the weather
and even create and direct tornados and hurricanes. This list is just a
sample. At the bottom of all this diabolical activity and plotting is the
New World Order. It is a New World Order that is vague and fleeting
in its composition and agenda. The only certainties are that the New
World Order is up to no good and that it is plotting and conspiring
unceasingly. Every tragedy is twisted to serve the needs of the conspiracy theory. A perusal of the InfoWars website bears out the diversity,
ubiquity and incessant nature of the grand conspiracy of the New World
Order. And it is all conveniently unfalsifiable, at least as far as the minds
of the true believers go. At the same time, any thoughtful person should
take the time to imagine how they would feel if they were the parent
of a child killed during the massacres at Sandy Hook Elementary or
Stoneman Douglas High and have Jones call them crisis actors in a
false flag tragedy.[83]

There are many other conspiracists like Alex Jones, as Thomas Milan
Konda's recent book, *Conspiracies of Conspiracies: How Delusions Have
Overrun America* (2019), has surveyed and classified. Jones has many predecessors. The question is: will this irrational conspiracism turn out to be
a fad that burns itself out and goes into decline? One would like to think
so. Unfortunately, as Michael Barkun has observed, the growing overlap
of UFO theories with the conspiracies of the New World Order type has
created a synergy that has brought both groups much greater outreach
into segments of the general public. Assisted by the Internet, social media,
television shows like *Ancient Aliens* and talk radio, the mother of all cultic
milieus has come into being. As Konda has gloomily concluded:

> At present, conspiratorial thinking, its increasing de facto linkage to
> right-wing and authoritarian politics and the conspiracy-friendly
> imperatives of web-based communications have all combined in
> American politics to create a situation many people find extremely
> ominous. At the same time, no one wants to circumscribe free
> speech or have an authority designate which ideas are reasonable
> and which are conspiratorial nonsense. It may be comforting to
> think that the situation will resolve itself or that a shift in political
> beliefs will undo it. But the evidence suggests otherwise.[84]

It is hard to disagree with Konda's assessment.

> Do not call conspiracy all that this people calls conspiracy, and do not fear what they fear, nor be in dread.
>
> ISAIAH 8:12

FIVE

A Road to Perdition: Germans, Nazis and a Culture of the Supernatural

Clearly, nobody would have been a Nazi if rational belief in the Nazi promises had been a prerequisite.

PETER DRUCKER, 1939[1]

Every German has one foot in Atlantis, where he seeks a better fatherland.

HERMANN RAUSCHNING, 1940[2]

In 1936 Heinrich Himmler, the Reichsführer of the SS, instituted an annual commemoration. The ceremony took place at Quedlinburg Cathedral and celebrated the anniversary of the birth in 876 of Henry I of Saxony, also known as Henry the Fowler. Later that same year, on 2 July, Himmler would organize a memorial for the thousandth anniversary of Henry I's death in 936.[3] The annual commemoration of his death continued until 1944, an event that Himmler missed. It was reported that in the absence of the Reichsführer, the normally solemn affair involved unseemly amounts of alcohol. But perhaps Germany's deteriorating military situation at that time was to blame.

There was nothing remarkable about patriotic Germans of any era regarding Henry I as a national hero. He has been widely credited with revitalizing the Holy Roman Empire in Germany and with laying the foundations for the achievements of his highly successful son, Otto I the Great. Virtually all modern historians of medieval Germany would agree with that assessment. But Himmler had some rather more fantastical reasons for honouring Henry I.[4]

Himmler's interest in Henry I went well beyond his contributions towards making Germany the greatest European power during much of the High Middle Ages. As an ardent anti-Christian and anti-Catholic, Himmler depicted Henry I as a fellow anti-Christian German, who held the Church at arm's length and yearned to return to Germany's pre-Christian past and its old Nordic gods. Reviving German paganism was one of Himmler's goals, which he went on to attribute to Henry I as well. To promote this view of Henry I's historical significance, Himmler established a King Heinrich Memorial Institution to research the medieval king. It has even been suggested that Himmler might have considered himself to be the reincarnation of Henry I, although other scholars are sceptical of that claim.[5]

Heinrich Himmler was the foremost example of the aspect of Nazism that was fascinated by and provided support to fringe or pseudo-history, pseudo or border science, and a hotchpotch of esoteric or occult beliefs and practices. He was hardly alone in these beliefs. They were a fascination and even an obsession for many Germans that long pre-dated the rise of Nazism and the Third Reich. If an obsession with Henry I had been the extent of Himmler's and other Germans' eccentric beliefs, the history of the Third Reich might have been less bloody.

The *Völkisch* Milieu

Scholars have debated the role of fringe or border knowledge, the supernatural and the occult in Nazi Germany from the beginnings of the Nazi Party in the early 1920s to the present. Some dismiss the connection between Nazism and esoterism as insignificant, while others claim that fringe, supernatural or occult beliefs played a significant, although not the primary, role in driving the ideology, policies and actions of the Third Reich. One source of the disagreement is that some scholars confine their attention to the role of the occult while largely ignoring the influence and role of pseudoscience, pseudo-history and related beliefs in pre-1945 Germany. A further complication is that these forms of fringe or border knowledge are not clearly demarcated. Pseudo-history, pseudo-science, supernatural beliefs and occultic beliefs overlapped and were mixed together in what the historian Eric Kurlander refers to as the supernatural imaginary of German society and culture. The scholarly debate over the role of fringe knowledge, the supernatural and the occult is further complicated by the later proliferation of highly sensationalistic books and documentaries and ideas about Hitler, the Nazis and the weird fringe knowledge of that era. These sensationalist writers claim that the Nazi leadership believed supernatural and occult powers were real and that they could be harnessed by the Nazis to advance the Third Reich to world domination. Some of the sensationalist writers even seem themselves to believe that supernatural and occult powers and phenomena exist.

Going into the 1920s, Germany could claim a long and distinguished heritage of culture, science and rigorous scholarship that stretched back to the sixteenth century. Germans were a well-educated people and many of their universities were world-class institutions of advanced research. Between 1901 and 1932, Germans won eleven Nobel Prizes in physics and fourteen in chemistry. In comparison, French scientists won Nobel Prizes for physics and chemistry five times each during the same period, while British scientists won the Nobel Prize for physics four times and for chemistry five times. Scientists from the United States were even further behind, with only three Nobel Prizes in physics and two in chemistry. German scholarship in history, sociology, biblical criticism and other disciplines was highly respected. These are the German intellectual achievements that are admired and remembered rather than the surprisingly widespread acceptance of the supernatural and the occult.[6]

It would be easy to say that the Nazis and their fixation on the supernatural and the occult were just an aberration. But it would not be true. Nazis were not the only Germans fascinated by the border sciences and the study of the supernatural, the esoteric and the occult. A significant segment of German society was preoccupied with these same sensational and enthralling beliefs. It was not a recent attraction either. It pre-dated the great scholarly achievements of German culture. Late medieval Germany was the heartland of the particularly vicious mythology of the savage and warlike Red Jews who lurked in the murky East. They were waiting for the right time to strike and destroy Christendom with the assistance of the European Jews. By the first decades of the seventeenth century, Germany had spawned the Rosicrucians in what would become a growing mix of esoteric secret societies. Later, eighteenth-century Germany would evolve an elitist, aristocratic, conservative and deeply mystical form of Masonry exemplified by the Order of the Golden and Rosy Cross. It bore little resemblance to the staid rationality and egalitarianism of the original Scottish Freemasonry.[7]

Meanwhile the rationalism and materialism of the Enlightenment and the later science, industrialization and mass culture of the nineteenth century would steadily demystify human existence. It was a process that the great social scientist Max Weber would call the disenchantment of the world. Although these changes are generally portrayed as advances for human civilization, many people found them to be confusing, stressful and alienating. They resisted disenchantment and sought wonder, mystery, faith and the supernatural.

During the nineteenth century, the discomfort and alienation from modern rationalism and materialism increased. Urbanization and industrialization cut people off from traditional community and nature. Secularization undermined the assurances provided by religious faith. At the same time, increasing prosperity and the accompanying mass culture provided people with the means and opportunities to re-enchant their lives. Cheap newspapers, magazines and books provided yearning readers with access to fringe ideas about history, science, health, astrology, occultism and spiritualism. Discretionary income allowed people to engage the services of professional astrologers, fortune tellers and purveyors of fantastical cures and diets. Increased leisure time gave people opportunities to join societies of likeminded people and attend classes dealing with various and sundry fringe topics. These developments made it possible for supernatural, occult and fringe ideas about Atlantis, fad diets, strange cults, magic, conspiracies and astrology to reach new and wider audiences. In this way those offshoots of the new mass media performed much the same function in the nineteenth and early twentieth centuries that the Internet has done since the 1990s. It fosters and cultivates beliefs in the strangest conspiracies, UFOs, alien invasions and dubious diets and health practices. Germany was not unique in this regard. The rise of a reaction against the disenchantment of the world was present in all Western industrialized societies. Each national culture had its own version of fringe knowledge and beliefs. They were, however, broadly similar because they arose out of a general reaction against modernity with its industrialization, urbanization, rationalism, science and secularism. All of this went hand-in-hand with the so-called occult revival in the Western world that began during the Enlightenment and expanded during the nineteenth century and into the twentieth. The fact is, the occult never really died.[8]

This is not to say that Germany was not more ardent with its subculture of fringe knowledge and beliefs than other nations in its reaction to modernity. But it did not predestine Germany to the rise of Nazism and the horrors of the Third Reich. Unlike other Western industrial nations, Germany became an advanced industrial society before it became a unified nation. The creation of the German empire in 1871 resulted in an instantaneous world power and economic dynamo. This event gave Germans a lot to be proud of, but it also created rising expectations of even further greatness. These expectations went unfulfilled to a degree and so created a vague sense of discontent and disillusion in the years prior to 1914. Such feelings lead people to seek out mystery, wonder and a nostalgia for past glory that never really existed. Unexpected defeat in the First World War was followed by a harsh and unfair peace, political instability and economic hard times that helped make possible the rise of Nazism and greatly aggravated the existing antisemitism. It also increased the appeal of escapism into the realms of the supernatural, the occult, pseudoscience and a mythical past. Again, Germany was not unique. Southern and Eastern Europe all succumbed to fascist takeovers of the government, and there were rising levels of antisemitism in Eastern Europe.[9]

During the nineteenth century, Germans went through many of the same experiences as other Western countries. Romanticism, with its veneration of the Middle Ages, the sublime, the mysterious and the supernatural, was very influential in Germany. With all of medieval history along with the Norse mythology of Odin and Thor and the legends of Siegfried and the Nibelungs, German Romanticism had an abundance of material to work with. Like other Europeans, Germans continued to engage in antisemitism, but they were not alone in this prejudice. Other Western nations contained their own antisemitic elements, which were often far more venomous than the German variety. Germany, however, was the place where the term 'antisemitism' was first used. Wilhelm Marr, the little-known writer of the tract 'The Victory of Jewdom over Germandom Viewed from a Non-confessional Standpoint' (1873), invented the term. His work sparked an ominous shift from religious antisemitism to racial antisemitism. Jews were no longer a people who practised a defective religion and could be converted and thus redeemed. Instead, they were an evil race, distinct from other humans, that had threatened Christian society through the ages and were thus irredeemable. As such, Jews could be regarded as vermin or a disease that needed to be eradicated. When Marr wrote in the 1870s, the great majority of Germans neither held nor approved of such abhorrent beliefs. Going into the twentieth century, however, Germany and other European nations experienced a revitalization of antisemitism. It was exemplified by the appearance of 'The Protocols of the Elders of Zion' and other works of vicious antisemitic propaganda. These writings further transformed perceptions of Jews from being a religion to being a race in the biological sense and attributed to them a plot to take over the world.[10]

Germans also joined in the late nineteenth-century enthusiasm for social Darwinism and ideas of racial hygiene that swept Western nations. social Darwinism taught that the struggle for the survival of the fittest in the natural world also applied to human races, nations and social classes. The richest and most powerful race or nation or social class was clearly the most fit and therefore the most deserving to thrive. Ernst Haeckel was a prominent German zoologist who supported Darwinian evolutionary theory and did much to popularize it in Germany. He also promoted social Darwinism and its ideas of superior and inferior races and the struggle to survive among humans. Haeckel's ideas were very popular in Germany, and they influenced the thinking of Hitler and the Nazis, among others. Since Germany was a rich and powerful nation, particularly after unification in 1871, the Germans clearly belonged among the fittest category of humanity. The British, French, Americans and even the Russians felt the same way about themselves. They all desired to maintain their status, so ideas of racial hygiene arose that sought to keep the unfit, the disabled and the aberrant from dragging a successful and fit society down. Preventing disabled or deviant people from having children by forced sterilization was a goal of racial hygiene, whose supporters saw it as a cruel necessity. Germans also found Aryanism to be a highly attractive belief. Many considered themselves to be descendants of the Aryans, a supposedly ancient and superior white race. Racial hygiene and Aryanism would become central tenets of Nazi ideology that would culminate in the atrociously inhumane policies of euthanasia for people with perceived defects and disabilities and in the genocide of Jews, Gypsies and other unpopular groups. In fact, Nazism became so closely linked with Aryanism that the popular historical memory has lost sight of the fact that many of the Western elite also advocated Aryanism and its offshoot of social Darwinism.[11]

During the Enlightenment, many European scholars rebelled against Judeo-Christian views of the origins of humanity and civilization. Some argued that northern India was the true birthplace of civilization. About the same time, William Jones, a colonial administrator in British India, proposed the existence of a prehistoric language that was the ancestor of Sanskrit, Greek, Latin and other European languages. The German Romantic scholar Friedrich Schlegel enthusiastically adopted Jones's linguistic ideas but went on to connect race and language. In his *Language and Wisdom of the Indians* (1808), he presented the theory that after founding a peaceful and brilliant culture in the Himalaya, the speakers of the Sanskrit root language embarked on warlike migrations that resulted in the conquest of the Indian subcontinent and a westward journey to settle northern Europe. By 1818 he had also popularized the term 'Aryan', which in Sanskrit means 'noble', for the ancient root language and the people who spoke it. Schlegel's concept of this blonde and blue-eyed Aryan race gained acceptance in France, Britain, the United States and Germany. Theodore Roosevelt was an avid supporter of Aryanism. In Germany, Aryanism appealed to nationalism and pan-Germanism since it identified them as a superior race. Not surprisingly, later on the Nazis wholeheartedly incorporated Aryanism into their ideology.[12]

The nineteenth century was an era of rising nationalism, especially the Romantic nationalism that emerged during and shortly after the

Napoleonic wars. Romantic nationalism sought to base the legitimacy of nation states on the bonds of culture, language, traditions, ethnicity and race. Existing nation states, like France and Russia, tried to intensify their national identifies. People who did not have their own nation state hoped to become one. Pan-Germanism arose out of this nationalistic drive. It wanted to bring together all the German-speaking peoples into one great nation state that would unite those living in what is now Germany and Austria along with possibly the Dutch and Scandinavians. As it turned out, Italy and Germany were the two new nation states created during the nineteenth century. Both were created by violence. A series of insurrections and wars of independence culminated in the unification of Italy with Rome as its capital in 1871. The unification of Germany was the result of Prussian victories under the leadership of the Iron Chancellor Otto von Bismarck in the Austro-Prussian War of 1866 and the Franco-Prussian War of 1870–71. The resulting unified nation did not include Austrian Germans. They remained part of the multi-ethnic Austro-Hungarian empire. That outcome disappointed pan-Germans in Germany and particularly in Austria, and it would later be revisited by the Nazis.[13]

The *völkisch* movement is another manifestation of Romantic nationalism that also complemented pan-Germanism. The term *völkisch* comes from the German 'volk' (meaning 'people') and is the root for the English word 'folk'. There is no equivalent word in English, but 'ethno-nationalism' or 'racial nationalism' convey what it stood for, which was a form of nationalism based on ethnic or racial identity. It was also part of the revolt against the rationalism, scientific materialism and disenchantment of the world that characterized the modernism which dominated mainstream thought during the nineteenth and early twentieth centuries.[14] The *völkisch* movement was a widespread and influential phenomenon in German society from the end of the Napoleonic wars to the Third Reich. It was diverse to the point of being amorphous owing to its many interests and manifestations. Folklore, local history, prehistory, back to the land programmes, esoteric and occult interests, promotion of a national community, the revival of pagan traditions and customs, and an affinity for antisemitism were all part of the *völkisch* movement. So it is not surprising that the ideas of Aryanism found a congenial home in it.

All of these activities and interests encouraged Germans with an attachment to *völkisch* ideas to think of themselves as special, far more special than other peoples such as Slavs. *Völkisch* ideas were spread by writers of books and articles for magazines and newspapers that discussed romantic history or folklore. Novels appeared with *völkisch* themes and settings. A number of publishers actively supported these types of writings because they believed in them and because they were popular and sold well. Groups that promoted back to the land agrarianism or a love of nature supposedly based on a mystical link between people and their land also gave support to the *völkisch* movement. Particularly influential was the German youth movement known as the *Wandervogel* for its devotion to hiking the countryside. The *Wandervogel* also tended to be committed to Aryanism and *völkisch* ideology as well. Many teachers and professors in German schools and universities were adherents of *völkisch* ideas and gave encouragement to like-minded students. All of these groups agreed that German nationalism was special and needed revitalizing in the face of a prevailing non-German world and especially its subset, the threatening non-Aryan world. It was in this setting that various Aryanist or Ariosophic groups began to form prior to the First World War.[15]

Ariosophy and Origins

Ariosophy means 'wisdom of the Aryans'. The term was coined by the Austrian occultist Jörg Lanz von Liebenfels in 1915, although Ariosophic ideas had first appeared during the 1890s. It was a movement that arose out of the ferment of pan-Germanism, Aryanism, antisemitism, theosophy and *völkisch* nationalism during the 25 years prior to the beginning of the First World War in 1914. Many future Nazi leaders found Ariosophic ideas attractive and brought them into their ideology. To understand Ariosophy, it is important to look at the careers and ideas of Guido von List and Lanz von Liebenfels. Both men were Austrians and so were part of the same milieu of pan-Germanism, *völkisch*ness, antisemitism and occultism that confronted the young Hitler during his years in Vienna. Both List and Lanz von Liebenfels invented aristocratic lineages for themselves. It was part of their own personal efforts to be part of a German past and heritage that was pretty much a fantasy.[16]

Guido von List was born in Vienna. His parents were middle class and his father owned a prosperous leather goods business. Economically, List grew up secure, indulged and relatively carefree. Like many other Germans in the Austro-Hungarian empire, however, he felt anxious about rising Slavic nationalism and turned to pan-Germanism. Otherwise, he pursued the popular leisure activities of hiking, mountaineering and folklore studies with *völkisch* overtones.

In 1877 List's father died, which allowed the son to leave the family business to pursue a literary career as a journalist, essayist and novelist of *völkisch* subjects. Soon his writings made him well known in pan-German and *völkisch* circles in both Austria and Germany. From the mid-1890s his writings began to display antisemitic sentiments. In 1888 his first novel, *Carnuntum*, appeared. It had a German setting in the fourth century of late antiquity. Two more novels followed in 1894 and 1895, which also depicted a heroic German past. List next turned to writing plays with *völkisch* themes, which increased his celebrity in pan-German circles.

The biggest contribution of List to right-wing German supernatural beliefs was to be the first popular writer to combine *völkisch* ideology with occultism and theosophy. Along the way, List promoted the existence of an ancient German religion that he called Wotanism. Wotan, also known as Odin or Woden, was the chief god of the Scandinavian/Teutonic pantheon of gods. Those gods formed an important part of Teutonic mythology and folklore. Using the Prose and Poetic Eddas as his sources, List advanced Wotanism as a religion that provided and preserved secret knowledge about natural mysteries. Over time List added more esoteric details. By the 1890s he was claiming that a Wotanist priesthood with special and powerful knowledge had existed in pre-Christian German society. From that point, occult ideas became increasingly prominent in List's writings. By 1908 the Wotanist religion with its gnostic knowledge had become the centrepiece of his worldview. Another of List's claims was that ancient Germans had been ruled by the Armanen, who were the descendants and heirs of a god-like sun-king. The social and political hierarchy of ancient German society or *Armanenschaft* was based on how much of the ancient wisdom or gnosis that a person possessed. Those most highly initiated in this wisdom were the priest-kings who ruled the Germans. According to List's telling of it, ancient German society was a harmonious meritocracy of gnostic wisdom.[17]

List's Wotanist Eden encountered a serpent. Early Christian missionaries arrived and began making converts, including members of the elite and the kings. Once in a position of power, the Christian Church began to demonize Wotanism. Its efforts were aided by allies like the emperor Charlemagne, who launched a campaign of persecution and forced conversion among the remaining Wotanists. Defeated, the *Armanenschaft* went underground. Groups like the Templars, various Renaissance humanists, Kabbalists and Rosicrucians were all secretly part of the hidden *Armanenschaft*. One of these underground Armanist scholars was the great fifteenth- and early sixteenth-century Hebraist Johann Reuchlin, from whom List claimed to be reincarnated. No wonder Himmler was so drawn to Ariosophy; reincarnation is so much better than ancestry.com. List had no evidence for the existence of the ancient Wotanist society. Some ideas came to him in the form of visions or dreams that occurred during visits to sacred places like the Geiselberg hill fort. In other cases, his study and unorthodox interpretation of runes supposedly revealed hitherto unimagined truths to him. He claimed to see Wotanism everywhere in ancient ruins and supposed architectural designs and motifs used by the Armanist underground. Much the same flawed arguments are used by those who claim to see evidence of ancient aliens, medieval Chinese circumnavigators or Atlantean remnants scattered across the face of the Earth. List wanted the *Armanenschaft* to be restored and then, in turn, to revive the greatness of the German people.[18]

Beginning in 1902, occult concepts began to appear in List's writings about the ancient German past and Wotanism. Specifically, theosophical influences began to appear during 1903. This development is not surprising since the theosophy of Madame Helena Blavatsky played a big role in the modern German occult revival since the abortive start of a German Theosophical Society in 1884. Theosophy provided an antidote to the positivism of nineteenth-century science as well as a way to reconcile science with humanistic religious beliefs. Theosophy fitted nicely into List's efforts to merge Wotanism and *völkisch* ideas into a coherent ideology through somewhat methodologically dubious studies of folklore, archaeology and runes. Theosophy's elite of mahatmas possessing powerful secret wisdom meshed comfortably with List's concept of Armanen priest-kings. List also adopted Madame Blavatsky's evolutionary scheme of the seven root races of humanity. She taught that theosophy's wisdom had a long history stretching back into unknown ages while remaining hidden from most humans. That matched List's depiction of Wotanism as a very ancient system of knowledge that had been forced underground. At the same time, List only adopted certain theosophical teachings. He rejected its cyclical worldview. List was a millenarian with a linear view of history. For him, the future held a restoration of Wotanism's wisdom and power along with the final triumph of the good, great and wise German people. Theosophy appealed to many segments of German society, including some on the left and right, liberal and conservative. Each student of theosophy, like List, took from it those ideas that served their purposes.[19]

List considered himself to be a modern-day prophet. His prophecies would be fulfilled by the creation of a mighty pan-German empire. This empire would be ruled by an elite of Aryan Germans who would lead lives of luxury and privilege based on the labours of the lesser non-Aryan peoples, who would essentially be slaves. Strict racial segregation would be the rule so that the purity of the Aryans could be preserved. Patriarchy would also be the standard of Aryan society with male heads of households being the highest level of citizens. The historian Nicholas Goodrick-Clarke has pointed out that this vision of the perfect society was very much in line with the racial laws that the Nazis passed during the mid-1930s. List's racially pure Aryan elite also anticipated Himmler's plans to make his ss troopers into a racially pure elite that would populate the Earth with a master race. When the First World War broke out in 1914, List saw it as the catalyst that would bring about his pan-German empire. Although deeply disappointed by the outcome of the war, at the time of his death in 1919 List still maintained that by both mystic and earthly means, the triumph of the great pan-German empire was at hand.[20]

Another important Ariosophic thinker was Jörg Lanz von Liebenfels. A generation younger than List, he was also born into a Roman Catholic, middle-class family from Vienna. Like List, he also added the aristocratic particle 'von' to his name and with an equally weak claim to that distinction. In 1915 he coined the term 'Ariosophy' for the ideas that he, List and other like-minded people were promoting. In 1893 the young Lanz entered the Cistercian order as a novice. While visiting a Templar grave in 1894, he claimed to have experienced some sort of enlightenment concerning the Aryan and inferior races. Some years later, he had to leave the Cistercians owing to some issue involving 'carnal love'. None of this proved to be an obstacle to Lanz making a career as an occultist.[21]

Unlike List, Lanz's ideas about human history were not particularly *völkisch* or Teutonic. Instead, he advocated a vision of prehistory in which Aryan supermen living on the lost continents of Atlantis and Lemuria possessed telepathic and omniscient powers similar to the powers of Blavatsky's root races. The military religious orders of the Middle Ages carried on these powers. Lanz sought to recreate these powers in the present with the restoration of the Aryan warriors and sages. These ideas were cloaked in a Christian veneer in which the fall of man occurred when Eve mated with a demon. Their offspring was the origin of the inferior dark races. For Lanz, maintaining the racial purity of the Aryans was a matter of survival for the civilized and good segment of human society. He presented this worldview in his book *Theozoology* in 1893.

Lanz first met List in 1893 when he was just beginning his time with the Cistercians. List incorporated a number of Lanz's ideas into his own writings, such as the occult nature of the Templars and that the original homeland of the Aryans was the Arctic continent of Arktogãa. Both men held the millenarianist and apocalyptic worldview that a great war would result in an Aryan triumph over the inferior races. That victory would establish a racially pure paradise on Earth. Lanz believed that enforced racial segregation would ultimately allow the Aryan race to purify itself to the extent that it would regain its lost superpowers. It was crucial for him to provide his rather bizarre ideas with an air of scientific legitimacy. This desire led him to associate with the scientifically orientated Monist League.[22]

Lanz's continuing fascination with the Templars led him to construct a dubious genealogy that supplied him with a Templar ancestor (since the Templars were sworn to chastity, it was apparently an ancestor who was non-celibate and unchaste, like Lanz himself). In 1907 he founded (or, from his point of view, refounded) the Ordo Novi Templi (Order of the New Temple, ONT) and set up its headquarters at Werfenstein Castle in Austria. The group had multiple layers of membership based on Aryan ancestry and elaborate rituals and paraphernalia. After the defeat of Germany in 1918 and the chaos that ensued until 1923, the ONT gained a new relevance for pan-German nationalists. They sought to resist the foul forces of communism and democratic republicanism that they considered to be destroying their nation. Lanz's ideology also became more antisemitic as he came to see Jews and Masons as allies of Bolshevism. The Ariosophy and the ONT of Lanz combined science, religion, the occult and prejudice into a gnostic ideology. It was a perfect expression of the discontents and anxieties of Austrians and Germans in the years before and after the First World War. Never one to suffer competition, Hitler and the Nazis suppressed the ONT as soon as they came to power in 1933.[23]

It is important to remember that the Guido von List Society, a sort of fan club/secret society founded in 1908 to study's List's writing, and the ONT had small formal memberships, but there was a broader public that also found their *völkisch* and Ariosophic ideas plausible and attractive. Their ideas were spread through Germany by the articles and books of *völkisch* writers and rune enthusiasts who applied List's ideas to their own interpretations of runes. Theodor Frisch and other members of the List Society founded the Reichshammerbund (Reich Hammer Society) in 1912. Its purpose was to coordinate and to unify the various antisemitic organizations and bring them under their leadership. At the same time, Frisch and his associates founded the Germanenorden, which was a secret group consisting of the more prominent leaders of the Reichshammerbund. Although the Reichshammerbund worked and spent a significant portion of its resources on recruitment, its membership remained only a few hundred in 1913. Prior to the Great War, German society as a whole had little interest in mystical extremism.[24]

Despite being a secret society, the Germanenorden did a much better job of recruiting members than the Reichshammerbund. Its call for an Ariosophic revival and the creation of a pan-German Armanist empire (or Armanenreich) of racially pure Germans had a definite appeal to the

*völkisch*ly inclined. The idea of a secret antisemitic society also had a definite appeal. Many antisemitic Germans, as well as antisemites of other
nations, believed that Jews were engaged in a vast, secret conspiracy to
dominate German society or the whole world. So it was felt that that
the best way to resist this immense plot was through their own secret
societies. In addition, some German Masons were disillusioned by what
they saw as the degradation of Masonic principles by Jewish and foreign
influences. For them, the Germanenorden provided a secret alternative.
The advent of the First World War stunted the Germanenorden's membership growth, and its numbers declined as members joined the military.
After the armistice, it renewed efforts to increase membership. In the
chaos that gripped Germany during 1919–23, the Germanenordern also
inspired a number of murders and assassinations of Jews and supporters
of the Weimer Republic.[25]

In late 1916 the activities of the Germanenorden attracted the attention
and adherence of Rudolf von Sebottendorf, born Adam Alfred Rudolf
Glauer. Sebottendorf would play a significant but suppressed role in the
origins of the Nazi Party and its connections to the occult, fringe history
and pseudoscience that was Ariosophy. He was born in Prussian Silesia,
the son of a railway engineer. He did some wandering as a young man,
serving as a merchant seaman and working in Egypt and Turkey as an
engineer. Experiencing legal problems over forgery in Dresden, he returned
to Turkey and became an Ottoman citizen in 1911. Baron Heinrich von
Sebottendorf adopted him in Turkey, hence his use of the Sebottendorf
name. Later a German adoption took place, which was questioned, but
the Sebottendorf family actively supported it. He fought in the Turkish
army and was wounded during the First Balkan War (1912–13). In 1913
he returned to Germany using a Turkish passport. His Turkish citizenship and war wound kept him out of the German army during the First
World War. Prior to his return to Germany, Sebottendorf had shown
strong interest in secret societies and the occult. In 1901 he had joined
a Turkish Masonic lodge. He also became a Sufi of the Bektashi Order
after becoming a Muslim. By 1912 he began experimenting with numero-
logical meditations, but events would show that Sebottendorf was no mere
dreamy and dilettantish occultist.[26]

Soon after Sebottendorf had joined the Germanenorden in late
1916, Hermann Pohl, the leader of the occultist Walwater faction of the
Germanenorden, put him in charge of reviving the order's chapters in
Bavaria. There Sebottendorf proved to be an adept recruiter and organizer.
A reinvigorated Bavarian chapter was operating with high efficiency by
Christmas 1917. This success led Sebottendorf to set up headquarters at the

Hotel Vier Jahreszeiten (Four Seasons) in July 1918. The Germanenorden occupied five large club rooms that could accommodate three hundred attendees. The owners of the hotel were Germanenorden sympathizers, and allowed Sebottendorf and other members of the Germanenorden and later the Thule Society to use the servants' entrance to conceal their comings and goings. In order to conceal further its questionable right-wing and antisemitic activities from socialist opponents and officials of the Weimar Republic, the Germanenorden began calling itself the Thule Society. It purported to be a benign folklore studies society interested in the Eddas and Norse mythology. The name 'Thule' was derived from 'Ultima Thule', which was what the ancient Greek voyager Pytheas had called Iceland. It was the supposed refuge of ancient German Armanists fleeing the persecutions of the Christians. This Arctic connection also meshed nicely with Ariosophic interests in Atlantis and other lost continents derived from theosophy. In the Thule Society's case, the Ariosophic focus was on the lost continent of Hyperborea, the alleged homeland of the Aryans. Sebottendorf was an ardent promoter of the ideologies of List, Lanz von Liebenfels and other Ariosophists. As the historian David Luhrssen succinctly put it: 'Ariosophy was the argot of the Thule Society.'[27]

Beginning in the autumn of 1918 through to the spring of 1919, Germany descended into turmoil and violence as German Bolsheviks attempted to overthrow the Weimar Republic and establish a soviet republic. They actually did briefly establish a soviet government in Munich. There, however, Sebottendorf adroitly used the Thule Society to mount a successful counter-revolution. He was the right man in the right place at the right time, in several senses of the term 'right'. During July 1918 Sebottendorf took ownership of a weekly Munich newspaper, the *Münchener Beobachter und Sportblatt*. It was used to disseminate Thulist propaganda while posing as a benign sporting news sheet. The Thule headquarters at the Hotel Vier Jahreszeiten under Sebottendorf's leadership became a state within a state which fought the Bolsheviks covertly and overtly. It came to house an armoury and during November 1918 organized one of the first para-military and anti-Bolshevik Freikorps in Germany. Later Sebottendorf raised a second unit, the Freikorps Oberland, which would join Hitler in his failed Beer Hall Putsch of 1923. All sorts of damaging counter-revolutionary activities came out of the Hotel Vier Jahreszeiten without the Munich Bolsheviks realizing the source of their troubles. Finally, in late April 1919 they realized the nature of the threat and the need to crack down on the Thulists. A raid on the Thule headquarters resulted in the capture of only a few counter-revolutionaries thanks to warnings from spies in the Bolshevik organization. The Thulist prisoners were summarily executed at Luitpold Prison on 30 April. This ruthless act aroused the fury of the anti-Bolsheviks and energized them further. Reprisal massacres of Bolsheviks followed with the defeat of the Munich Soviet. Sebottendorf's leadership through this struggle brought him and the Thule Society into contact with future Nazi luminaries such as Ernst Röhm and Rudolf Hess. The Thule Society's victory and activities contributed greatly to making Munich a hothouse for *völkisch*, pan-German nationalism and Ariosophic fantasies conducive to the germination and growth of Nazism.[28]

Just when Sebottendorf's leadership had helped to secure the defeat of the Munich Bolsheviks, his personal fortunes began to crumble. Jewish businesses sued him, and his control of the Freikorps Oberland was taken away. Furthermore, there were accusations that he had impersonated an aristocrat and accepted Turkish citizenship to avoid conscription into the German army. Most damning, fellow Thulists held his negligence to be responsible for the capture and execution of the seven Thulists at Luitpold Prison; they also accused him of embezzling funds from the Thule Society during the Munich insurrection. By June 1919 he had resigned as master of the Thule Society. This development has blurred and obscured Sebottendorf's role as a bridge between the Ariosophy and the origins of the early Nazi Party.[29]

Nazi Origins and Ariosophy

Before and shortly after Sebottendorf's departure from the Thule Society and Germany for Switzerland, two tools came into being that assisted the rise of Hitler. On 5 January 1919 the Thule Society formed the German Workers' Party (Deutsche Arbeiterpartei or DAP) under the leadership of Anton Drexler with assistance from Dietrich Eckart, a poet and Thulist. The new party was to be nationalist and appeal to the common man; it was not particularly occultist. Meanwhile, Sebottendorf incorporated the *Münchener Beobachter* as the Franz Eher Verlag (publishing company) in the summer of 1919, and during March 1920 a group of Thulists took ownership.[30]

Initially, Drexler and his German Workers' Party struggled to attract members. They did, however, manage to draw the attention of the German army. In an unfortunate twist of fate, the soldier sent to spy on the group was Adolf Hitler. His army commanders ordered him to join the new party. Rather than viewing the DAP as a potentially subversive organization, he liked what he saw and heard about nationalism, antisemitism, anti-capitalism and anti-Marxism. Attending meetings, Hitler began to speak up and his oratorical skills proved impressive. They swiftly propelled him into a leadership position. His rise to power was also greatly assisted by Dietrich Eckart, who had been looking for a messianic leader for the party who would return Germany to greatness. Some considered him to have been the John the Baptist to Hitler's Jesus. In addition, he was a promoter of *völkisch* nationalism, antisemitism and supernaturalism, and had a great impact of Hitler's thinking and early Nazi ideology. On 24 January 1920 Hitler got the DAP's name changed to the National Socialist German Workers' Party (NSDAP), more commonly known as the Nazis. At this point, Drexler resigned as leader. Later in December, the Germany military commander in Bavaria used the Thulist Dietrich Eckhart to sell Sebottendorf's *Münchener Beobachter* to the Nazis. Eckart would be the editor and another Thulist and future Nazi, Alfred Rosenberg, would serve as his assistant. In November 1921 Hitler came to own the newspaper personally through the party. Eventually, the Thule Society and its membership were absorbed into the Nazi Party. The Thulists would bring with them the Ariosophic doctrines and concepts of Guido List and Lanz von Liebenfels that Sebottendorf had made a big part of the Thule Society's programme. As the historian Nicholas Goodrick-Clarke put it, 'Without this man [Sebottendorf] it is likely that both the Germanenorden and Ariosophy would have been condemned to oblivion.'[31]

Does this mean that Ariosophy, the occult, pseudo-history and pseudo-science played a crucial role in Hitler and the Nazis' rise to power? No, there were plenty of circumstances that contributed to Nazi success. Their *völkisch* nationalism, antisemitism, anti-Bolshevism and anti-capitalism attracted support from various segments of German society, which was badly divided, and the Weimar Republic had many enemies besides the Nazis. Communists, monarchists, the German army and other right-wing or conservative groups or parties all disliked it. Many Germans associated it with defeat, the so-called stab in the German army's back and the inequitable Treaty of Versailles. The onset of the Great Depression made the crisis of the Republic even worse, with both the Nazis and the communists creating chaos in the streets. For many in the German elite, the Nazis seemed the lesser of two evils and also easier to control when compared to the communists. It was an underestimation of the Nazis that would quickly be shown to be tragically mistaken after the Republic's president Paul von Hindenburg made Hitler the chancellor in 1933. There was nothing supernatural or occult about the fall of the Weimar Republic.[32]

The occult, the supernatural, pseudo-history and pseudoscience, however, did play a significant role in aspects of the culture and ideology of the Third Reich and its policies. Germany was an unhappy country that was in turmoil. Fear and hate were ever present. The Nazis played on the anti-Bolshevism, the anti-modernism and the antisemitism of many Germans. On the positive side, at least from a Nazi point of view, Hitler and his party were working to create the longed-for pan-German empire of many Germans. Those Germans were also told they were the *Herrenvolk* (master race) destined to rule the world. In other words, they were the true chosen people of human history. This pan-German empire would grow in population so it would need to grow geographically as well. This need for space was called *Lebensraum* (living space). Such a worldview legit-imized aggression and conquest that would result in the forced removal or extermination of the original inhabitants of lands needed by the Germans. Such a diabolically ambitious programme required a ruthless and efficient government. So the Nazis promoted an authoritarian government with a *Führer* or leader at the top whose judgement was not to be questioned. The unquestionability of the national leader was called the *Führerprinzip*.[33]

Some people will simply and easily accept a belief or ideology that flatters their ego or coddles their prejudices. It does not hurt, however, to bolster the credibility of abhorrent and weird ideas with something that looks like scientific, historical or religious evidence or support. That is where the occult, fringe or pseudo-history and border or pseudoscience came into play. During the Wilhelmine empire and Weimar Republic, many Germans believed and practised occult beliefs or some of the weird historical or scientific theories that were percolating.[34] Nazism and offbeat belief systems such as Ariosophy complemented each other symbiotically. Furthermore, the widespread credence given to bizarre and fantastical things helped to normalize the irrational beliefs of the Nazis. Finally, belief in occult and strange scientific ideas and a far-fetched past was a reaction against the scientific materialism and the disenchantment of the world that took all the fun, wonder and mystery out of life in the modern age. It was far more attractive to believe your ancestors were primordial hero-warriors with superpowers living it up on a lost continent than it was to believe they were primitive and bestial cavemen in animal skins barely surviving the Ice Age.

The Early Hitler and Fringe Knowledge

A big question is, did the Nazi leadership believe all this occult, supernatu-ral and border knowledge? The answer is clearly no. Many Germans had no use for the occult or fringe knowledge. Einstein considered the astrology that was so popular in Weimar Germany to be superstition and made no allowance for it even in social situations such as a dinner party in Berlin during 1927.[35] Some prominent Nazis felt the same way. Martin Bormann, Joseph Goebbels, Albert Speer and Hermann Goering were sceptics and cynics who scoffed at the occult. For these Nazis, their concern and goal was getting power, using it and keeping it, although in Goering's and Bormann's cases, plunder was an additional goal. Goebbels and Speer were highly educated while Bormann and Goering were anti-intellectuals of the thuggish type. None of them believed the myths of Nazism – not that Goebbels was above using the prophecies of Nostradamus for propaganda purposes.[36]

On the other hand, Heinrich Himmler, Rudolf Hess, Alfred Rosenberg and Richard Walther Darré all held some pseudoscientific or occult beliefs, and those beliefs significantly influenced their policies, as will be shown later. Hitler's mentor, the poet Dietrich Eckart, also appeared to hold occult and other weird beliefs. He was a member, or at least a close associate, of the Thule Society along with Hess and Rosenberg. His premature death in 1923, however, limited his impact on the Nazi Party's relations with fringe knowledge and the supernatural.[37] In their various stances on the occult, pseudoscience and pseudo-history, the upper level leadership of the Nazi Party was a microcosm of the macrocosm of their party and German society as a whole. That leaves another big question: where did Adolf Hitler stand on the occult and the supernatural?

Historians have debated and continue to debate Hitler's relationship with the occult and other forms of border knowledge. Early biographies emphasized his megalomaniac quest for power and viewed any connections to the occult or supernatural as insignificant distractions. Certainly, the occult and fringe knowledge were not the pre-eminent focus of Hitler's world of thought – rather it was the establishment of the thousand-year Reich and world domination that obsessed him. In broad strokes, Hitler believed the Germans as descendants of the Aryans were a people of destiny. In contrast, Jews were corrupters and evil. Mixing Aryans and Jews could only produce bad results, indeed diabolically catastrophic results. Aryan Germans were engaged in an existential struggle with Jews, and as their leader Hitler would lead them to victory. Like many fellow Germans, Hitler was not fond of the various Slavic peoples and other dark-skinned peoples beyond Europe. That said, he did not obsess over the details of this apocalyptic scenario, such as whether the Aryans had originated on the lost continents of Atlantis or Hyperborea or the Himalaya Mountains. Occasionally he lost patience with those who did, such as Himmler or Rosenberg.[38]

One thing that has muddied the waters of Hitler's relationship with the Ariosophists and the Thule Society was his efforts, along with members of his inner circle in the rising Nazi Party, to disassociate himself from these occult groups and their ideas. Part of this aversion stemmed from claims made by Sebottendorf and Lanz von Liebenfels about their being mentors and inspirations for Hitler. The problem with these claims was that they undercut the lone hero image of Hitler that he and the Nazi Party wanted to promote. The party wanted to portray Hitler as a messianic demigod who was in a class by himself and a self-made man in his powers and his ideas. Furthermore, the Nazis did not like competition for the loyalty and commitment of the masses.[39] They grudgingly tolerated organized religion, but they suppressed groups that they regarded as sectarian whether or not their beliefs were in step with those of the Nazi Party. Hence it was not just Masons and Jehovah's Witnesses who were suppressed; so were the Thule Society, the List Society, the ONT and other Ariosophist groups.

Lanz von Liebenfels in Vienna was quick to claim to have influenced Hitler's ideas after the Nazi movement in Germany gained political strength. In 1927 he wrote in *Ostara*: 'One shall remember that the swastika and fascist movements are basically the offspring of *Ostara*.' He hoped that Hitler would acknowledge how much Ariosophy had shaped his Nazi ideology. The problem was that Hitler denied any indebtedness or influence. That does not mean Hitler was being truthful. When the Nazis took power in Germany in 1933, Hitler promptly shut down Lanz's secret society, the ONT, in Germany. At that point, the cautious Lanz moved to the safety of Switzerland. When Germany annexed Austria in 1938, Hitler shut down *Ostara* and the ONT there as well. Not until 1946 was Lanz able to return to Vienna, where he revived the ONT, which still exists in Austria and Germany. As discussed in the following pages, Lanz claimed to have met and given the impoverished young Hitler some back issues of *Ostara*. The authenticity of this claim, along with the whole idea of Lanz significantly influencing Hitler and Nazi ideology, is the subject of debate among historians with no consensus emerging. The same situation applies to the question of whether Hitler and the Nazis even banned Lanz's writings.[40] But as Willy Ley, who became an exile and refugee from Nazism in January 1937, later put it in his 1947 essay 'Pseudoscience in Naziland', 'To my surprise no Party Group or Nazi community ever erected a state in honor of Dr. Jörg Lanz von Liebenfels.'[41]

Rudolf von Sebottendorf was another person who claimed an important role in the prehistory of Nazism for himself and the Thule Society. And he was also spurned. After Sebottendorf fell out with the Thule Society and the right wing in Munich, he moved to Switzerland and on to Turkey, all the while engaging in business and writing books on astrology and the occult. When the Nazis came to power in 1933, he returned to Munich where he attempted to revive the Thule Society. Within a few months, he also published *Bevor Hitler Kam: Urkundliches aus der Frühzeit der nationalsozialistischen Bewegung* (Before Hitler Came: Documentary Evidence from the Early Years of the Nazi Movement). In it he claimed that he, the Thule Society and other small groups were the foundation of Hitler's rise to power. Sebottendorf asserted: 'Thule members were the people to whom Hitler first turned and who first allied themselves to Hitler.'[42] It was a claim that many historians have found to be very plausible. Needless to say, Hitler and Nazi authorities did not view such claims with favour. They incarcerated Sebottendorf at the beginning of 1934 but quickly released him. He was allowed to go to Switzerland and from there made his way back to Turkey, where he worked for German intelligence in Istanbul. Unfortunately, the German embassy found his information to be generally useless. Faced with the impending defeat of Germany at the end of the war, Sebottendorf committed suicide by drowning in the Bosporus. In the assessment of Nicholas Goodrick-Clarke, 'Thus ended the life of the adventurer who introduced Ariosophy to the Nazi Party.' The early Nazis, however, were embarrassed by the Thule Society, and Hitler wanted any links between him and the Thulists suppressed. This suppression included the very evident connections of the early Nazis Rudolph Hess, Dietrich Eckart and Alfred Rosenberg. It was a process that left Sebottendorf a largely forgotten figure.[43] As a result, the extent of Hitler's occult connections has remained blurred and partially erased.

Under the circumstances, it is interesting to speculate about the fate of the poet and playwright Dietrich Eckart, an undoubted mentor of Hitler, if he had not died shortly after the Beer Hall Putsch in 1923. In the course of his mentoring, Eckart broadened Hitler's intellectual and ideological horizons including the occult, coached him on social etiquette and public speaking, introduced him to wealthy patrons, secured him financial support and promoted him as the German messiah. By the end of 1922, the once close relationship of Eckart and Hitler had cooled. Hitler was becoming arrogant and Eckart did not like it. As Eckhart complained to another Hitler associate, Ernst Hanfstaengl, in May 1923, Hitler exhibited a 'megalomania halfway between a Messiah complex and Neroism'. Despite their growing estrangement, Eckhart still joined Hitler in the Beer Hall Putsch the following November. Briefly imprisoned, he was released due to poor health, only to die of a heart attack at the age of 54 on 26 December. Years of drinking and drug use had brought on his premature death. Despite their differences, Hitler professed to remember Eckart fondly and saw that his memory was honoured within Nazi culture. But what if Eckart had lived on as a critic, rival and reminder of the Führer's occult Thulist connections? Would Eckart also have gone the way of Sebottendorf?[44]

Hitler lived in Vienna as an impoverished young man seeking an education and a career. Vienna was a hotbed of *völkisch* pan-Germanism that had spawned the Ariosophy of Guido List and Jörg Lanz von Liebenfels. According to Lanz, during 1909 Hitler visited the offices of *Ostara*, which focused on Aryanism and *völkisch* race theory along with some antisemitism, to buy back issues of the magazine. Taking note of the young man's manifest poverty, Lanz not only gave him the back issues but provided Hitler with the fare to take public transportation home. As a result of this encounter, Lanz would claim to be the man who gave Hitler his ideas, a claim that Hitler scholars consider to be greatly exaggerated.[45]

Hitler started attending DAP meetings on 12 September 1919, initially as a spy but soon after he became a convert and a committed member. At these meetings he would have encountered the *völkisch* and Ariosophic ideas of the Thulists. As far as Hitler was concerned, *völkisch* principles were the right road for Germany to follow. What he did not like was some Ariosophists' tendency to focus on arcane studies and discussions in their secret meetings rather than getting out in the streets, agitating and fighting to create a *völkisch* state. It was this sort of situation that prompted Hitler's critical remark about 'those wandering German folkish scholars' in *Mein Kampf*. Throughout *Mein Kampf* he reiterated again and again the need for action and not rambling, inconsequential discussions.[46]

The Führer's Love/Hate Relationship with Fringe Knowledge

Völkisch German scholars continued to occasionally irritate Hitler after he came to power. At the great Nazi Party rally at Nuremberg in September 1936, Hitler excoriated Ludwig Roselius, a rich coffee merchant and patron of modernist architecture, and Herman Wirth, the president of Himmler's prized *völkisch* research institute, the Ahnenerbe. As Hitler put it, 'We have nothing to do with those elements who only understand National Socialism in terms of hearsay and sagas and who therefore confuse it too easily with vague Nordic phrases and who are beginning their research based on motifs from some mythical Atlantean culture.' The Führer had come to find Wirth personally irritating, and Wirth's attacks on Christianity were considered premature by Hitler. Like many Nazis, Hitler was a lapsed Roman Catholic who had become fiercely antiChristian. He wanted to eliminate Christianity in German society, but he knew that the time was not ripe. Himmler was forced to demote Wirth.[47]

Two years later on 6 September 1938, in a speech given at the Culture Convention, Hitler attacked his inner circle members Himmler and Rosenberg on the same issue. Their efforts to establish Wotanism as a rival religion to Christianity threatened to antagonize the Third Reich's relations with the various German Church bodies. Hitler told his audience: 'National Socialism is not a cult movement; rather, it is a *völkisch* and political philosophy which grew out of considerations of an exclusively racist nature. This philosophy does not advocate mystic cults, but rather aims to cultivate and lead a *Volk* determined by its blood.' Hitler had small dinner parties during the Second World War at which he mind-numbingly ruminated on Nazi ideology and current events while members of his inner circle listened slavishly. Bormann and others dutifully took notes of their leader's words. On 11 April 1942 he denigrated Rosenberg's *Myth of the Twentieth Century* and stated it was not 'an expression of the official doctrine of the Party', adding, 'It is in any case written in too abstruse a style.' Yet, despite these seeming disparagements of occult and fringe ideas, Hitler valued those beliefs for himself, the Nazi Party and Germans in general. As the historian Eric Kurlander has put it, 'Whatever his reservations regarding "*völkisch* wandering scholars", Hitler recognized the power of the supernatural imaginary in appealing to his party colleagues and ordinary Germans.' As will be shown later, he let members of his inner circle such as Himmler and Rosenberg pursue their interests in fringe knowledge. They were allowed to develop policies and institutions within the Third Reich that consumed considerable resources.[48]

While Hitler was not as deeply committed to supernatural and fringe knowledge as Himmler and others, he still had his interests in magic, astrology and a variety of pseudosciences. The writings of Ernst Schertel attracted Hitler's attention and influenced him. Schertel was a sort of popular psychology and self-improvement writer whose works were tinged with occult and supernatural aspects. In particular, Hitler read and annotated Schertel's *Magie: Geschichte, Theorie, Praxis* (Magic: History, Theory, Practice, 1932) and used it to improve his public speaking, among other things. For Hitler, Schertel's 'magic' was practical, lending itself to self-improvement and mastery.[49] Hitler also shared an enthusiasm for astrology with his long-time right-hand man Rudolf Hess and other highly placed Nazis. One manifestation of Hitler's astrological interests was his close relationship with the celebrity psychic and astrologer Erik Jan Hanussen. Hanussen's real name was Hermann Steinschneider and he was a Moravian Jew. By 1930 he had developed a close relationship with leaders of the Nazi movement. His Jewishness was an open secret, but his supposed occult gifts meant that it was overlooked. Hanussen and Hitler had many meetings. Just prior to the election of 1932, he taught Hitler oratorical techniques of crowd control. A few months later, in February 1933, Hanussen went on to predict the infamous Reichstag fire. It is unclear whether it was a lucky guess or the result of insider information from his Nazi patrons. Unfortunately for Hanussen, he became a victim of his own success. His prediction of the Reichstag fire coupled with his closeness with leading Nazis cast suspicion on the party. He also knew too many prominent Nazis' secrets for their own comfort. His closeness with Hitler also aroused the jealousy of the Nazi inner circle, while his popularity with the German public presented potentially unwelcome complications to the party's leadership and authority. So, sometime during 24–5 March, Hanussen was murdered and secretly buried. His body was discovered in early April.[50]

The Hanussen murder did not lessen the popularity of astrology with Hitler and some of his inner circle. Rudolf Hess, second in line to succeed Hitler, remained a dedicated follower of astrology and other supernatural beliefs. Increasingly worried about his fading influence with Hitler and the perils of the planned war with Russia, Hess took action. Basing his decision on astrological advice and a supernaturally inspired dream, he flew to Scotland on 10 May 1941 to negotiate peace with the UK. It was a huge embarrassment to the Third Reich and a bitter personal betrayal for Hitler.[51]

The astrological aspects of Hess's flight brought on the Hess Action of May–June 1941, a crackdown on German astrologers. Despite being headed by the relentless and ruthless Reinhard Heydrich, this persecution of the occultists was short-lived and very restrained when compared with actions against other groups who aroused the ire of the Nazis. As Eric Kurlander has demonstrated, occult and supernatural beliefs were too popular with both the Nazi Party and the general German population to be eradicated. In addition, many Nazi leaders, including Hitler, believed in the occult and supernatural themselves; they only objected to fraudulent occultists. Otherwise, they simply wanted occultism and the supernatural under their control and serving their ideology and authority.[52]

Hitler had an ongoing interest in science, particularly if it promised the possibility of producing wonder weapons to defeat his enemies. Otherwise, his interest did not discriminate between mainstream science and border knowledge or pseudoscience. Race science obviously appealed to Hitler since it explained the basis for *völkisch* beliefs, Aryanism and antisemitism while seeming to justify them scientifically. The World Ice Theory or Glacial Cosmology of Hans Hörbiger also attracted Hitler's attention. In fact, it was the only fringe science to gain his wholehearted support. Hitler's zeal for Hörbiger's theory was not merely a personal quirk. The World Ice Theory had a significant following among the German public despite being resolutely opposed by mainstream German scientists. Hörbiger was an Austrian engineer who in 1894 invented a steel valve that greatly improved the operation of blast furnaces. It proved a lucrative invention. Meanwhile, hoping for equal success in cosmology, Hörbiger, with his co-author, amateur astronomer Philipp Fauth, published in 1913 *Wirbelstürme, Wetterstürze, Hagelkatastrophen und Marskanal-Verdoppelungen* (Tornadoes, Sudden Temperature Drops, Severe Hail Storms and the Doubling of Canals on Mars). The First World War initially blunted the book's impact, but after the war Hörbiger aggressively promoted his theory through public lectures and newspaper stories. Put simply, he claimed that the universe was full of water in the form of ice. The Milky Way consisted of blocks of ice while planets beyond the Earth were covered with ice, as was the Moon. Wandering celestial ice and ice build-ups had created various catastrophes in the Earth's past. Although astronomical observation and scientific experimentation did not support Hörbiger's assertions, many Germans passionately accepted them as scientific fact. World Ice Theory harmonized nicely with *völkisch* and Nazi ideology. It appealed to the *völkisch* and Ariosophic fascination with the Arctic. In addition, the catastrophism of World Ice Theory had the appearance of providing scientific proof for the destruction of lost continents like Atlantis or Hyperborea, the purported homelands of the primordial Aryan super-civilizations. Heinrich Himmler and other Nazis were great patrons of World Ice Theory. It certainly enjoyed Hitler's support even though he was not prone to the same level of ardour as Himmler. Discussions of Hörbiger's ideas took place during some of Hitler's dinner parties with his inner circle. On the night of 25–6 January 1942, Hitler proclaimed: 'I am well inclined to accept the cosmic theories of Hörbiger.' A few weeks later on 20–21 February, he would favourably compare Hörbiger to Copernicus in their advancement of scientific knowledge. He also congratulated himself and the Third Reich for encouraging such innovative scientific thinking. It was claimed that the proper application of World Ice Theory would make it possible to forecast weather for weeks, months and even years into the future. Thus the winter of 1941–2 was predicted to be a mild one. This incorrect forecast had calamitous and tragic consequences for the German army when it launched Operation Barbarossa, the invasion of Russia, in late June 1941. The winter that followed inflicted a brutal toll on the ill-prepared German troops.[53]

The fact is that Hitler had a wide-ranging interest in the occult, the supernatural, fringe history and pseudoscience. He did not pursue his interests with the passion or obsession of Himmler or Hess, but it was still more than a little abnormal for the leader of an important and educated nation to support such baseless beliefs and ideas.

Nazi Leaders on the Fringe

Other Nazi leaders were far more invested in the occult and supernatural knowledge than Hitler. Rudolf Hess was a decorated combat veteran of the First World War. After the war he attended the University of Munich during 1919. There he studied under Karl Haushofer, a proponent of *Lebensraum*. Hess would later introduce the concept to Hitler, and it became a significant tenet of Nazi ideology. Haushofer and Hess also shared a common interest in astrology. Hess had been a Thulist, but after hearing Hitler speak at a DAP meeting, he became a faithful and steadfast acolyte of the future Führer. Standing with Hitler during the Beer Hall Putsch, he was arrested and sentenced to prison with Hitler in the aftermath. While in prison, he helped Hitler to write *Mein Kampf*. Like Hitler, he practised vegetarianism and did not smoke or drink. From 1923 he served as Hitler's personal secretary. When the Nazis came to power in 1933, Hitler named him deputy Führer of the Nazi Party and minister without portfolio in the government of the Third Reich. Totally devoted to Hitler, Hess, unlike most other members of the Nazi inner circle, tried neither to build his own personal power base nor to enrich himself. Because of his self-effacing manner, his occult and supernatural beliefs had little or no impact on Nazi policies. He did employ many occultists in his chancellery and was a steadfast supporter of parapsychology, World Ice Theory and *Lebensraum*.[54]

When it came to promoting the occult, supernaturalism and fringe knowledge in the Nazi Party and the Third Reich, pride of place goes to Heinrich Himmler. Too young to join the army until near the end of the First World War, Himmler missed serving in combat. When the war ended, Himmler, like many other young Germans, struggled to make his way in the world. In August 1923 he joined the Nazi Party and participated in the Beer Hall Putsch, but managed to avoid arrest and was never charged or jailed. It was during 1923 and 1924 that he shifted from his conservative Catholic upbringing to being a devotee of occultism and Nordic mythology. His antisemitism also grew in virulence. Joining the *Schutzstaffel* (ss) in 1925, he found it a very small subunit of the Sturmabteilung (sa or Storm Troopers) with the job of protecting Hitler. With Hitler's backing, over the next few years Himmler became the head of the ss and transformed it into an independent, elite paramilitary unit and the instrument for creating a genetically pure racial elite of Aryan supermen. It was the embodiment of Ariosophic pseudoscientific and pseudo-historical ideas. All sorts of rules and policies were put into place to ensure that ss members married properly and lived cleanly. To make the ss more cohesive, all sorts of occult and supernatural indoctrinations, rituals and symbols were created. As Dieter Wisliceny, an ss captain, described it during his trial for war crimes, under Himmler 'the ss gradually turned into a new kind of religious sect.'[55]

In his efforts to transform the ss and Germany, Himmler was advised and assisted by the Ariosophist Karl Maria Wiligut. Wiligut has been labelled the Rasputin of Himmler, although he called himself Weisthor (Wise Thor). Born into an Austrian military family, he fought in the First World War and attained the rank of colonel before he retired in 1918. Engaging in all sorts of Ariosophic fantasies that went far beyond even the imaginations of List and Lanz von Liebenfels, his behaviour became erratic and he was involuntarily committed to a mental asylum in November 1924. Released in 1927, he took up Ariosophy again but left his family and moved to Munich. There he became an acclaimed runic scholar. Introduced to Himmler after the Nazi takeover in 1933, he joined the ss and developed a close and cordial friendship with Himmler, serving as a trusted advisor. Wiligut designed the death's head ring of the ss, and his suggestions gave its rituals and symbols a seemingly traditional *völkisch* and Ariosophic ambience. He also assisted with the selection of Wewelsburg Castle as the ss academy and advised on its decor. Both Himmler and Wiligut dreamed of supplanting Christianity in Germany with a revival of the old Germanic religion. However, the staff of the Ahnenerbe considered Wiligut to be a crackpot, and continually clashed with him over his bizarre ideas and suggestions for research he wanted performed. Despite their shared beliefs, in early 1939 Himmler distanced himself from Wiligut after Hitler's outburst of irritation towards occult obsessions. Wiligut's official retirement took place on 28 August 1939, but effectively he had been deprived of any authority the previous February. In addition, Himmler had learned that Wiligut had been declared mentally incompetent and committed. It would have been potentially a huge embarrassment if that information became public knowledge.[56]

In Himmler's ss, Hitler had a potent weapon against external and internal threats to his regime and a tool for carrying out his policies. Some have classified Himmler as a cynical opportunist merely seeking more and more power like Goebbels or Goering. According to the ss captain Dieter Wisliceny, 'The usual view of Himmler is that he was an ice-cold, cynical politician. This view is certainly wrong. In his whole attitude Himmler was a mystic, who embraced this world-view [of the ss] with religious fanaticism.' By providing the ss with a rich heritage of *völkisch* history, lore, rituals and trappings, Himmler hoped to solidify their loyalty and devotion to the Third Reich. Like all true Nazis, Himmler was fanatically committed to the racist ideologies of the Aryan master race, subhuman Slavs and other lesser races and the diabolical and verminous Jews. These beliefs were tied to *Lebensraum*, which required the removal of lesser races from lands needed for the expansion of Aryan Germans. In the case of the Jews, a policy of removal shifted to one of extermination known as the Final Solution. Himmler used his indoctrinated and obedient ss to assist in carrying out these policies.[57]

Himmler fancied himself as both a scholar and a promoter of Ariosophy, race science and other forms of fringe knowledge with a bearing on Nazi ideology and goals. In an effort to expand the occult, supernatural and fringe knowledge available to Nazis and other Germans, Himmler, along with Richard Walther Darré, created the research institute known as the Ahnenerbe in 1935. The term meant 'something inherited from the forefathers'. The new institute's mission was to make discoveries about the German past, meaning the *völkisch* or Ariosophic version of it, and to present its findings to the public through popular magazine articles, books, museum exhibitions, documentaries and scholarly conferences. During the time of its existence the Ahnenerbe sponsored archaeological and scientific expeditions to promising sites in Germany and Scandinavia. One expedition famously made its way to Tibet under the leadership of Ernst Schäfer during 1938 and 1939. Other expeditions travelled to Crimea and the Caucasus Mountains in search of ancient Gothic homelands and to provide an excuse to remove the current occupants and replace them with Germans in need of *Lebensraum*.

One of the quixotic quests of the Ahnenerbe was to perfect the techniques of physical anthropology for identifying Jews and Aryans. Race scientists like Bruno Beger failed to achieve success in that effort. They continually bumped up against the unmentionable reality that Jews were not a biological race and Aryans were an imaginary cultural construct, not a scientific classification. The negative results did not deter Ahnenerbe scientists from engaging in increasingly inhumane and grisly research, such as the skeleton collections of Bruno Beger at the University of Strasbourg and the Natzweiler concentration camp. Ahnenerbe scientists such as Sigmund Rascher and August Hirt engaged in horrific medical experiments on the inmates of Dachau and other concentration camps. Himmler's scientists even pursued fruitless research into creating a failed super-weapon called Thor's Hammer, which utilized electronic pulses.

Ahnenerbe also conducted research to provide proof and support for that perennial Nazi favourite – World Ice Theory.

If the Second World War had not broken out, Himmler would have sent Edmund Kiss, an architect and author of adventure and fantasy novels using Ariosophic themes, to explore the ancient city of Tiwanaku in Bolivia. According to the claims of an expatriate German, Arthur Posnansky, an ancient advanced civilization had thrived there thousands of years ago. If so, its existence appeared to bear out the idea that an ancient Aryan civilization had been destroyed by some cataclysm related to the World Ice Theory. With a planned team of twenty scholars, the expedition would have been the Ahnenerbe's largest. Other expeditions were devised to visit Iran, the Canary Islands and Iceland but were cancelled due to the war. If all of this sounds rather like an Indiana Jones film, it is because the plot of *Raiders of the Lost Ark* was based on the existence of these real-life futile fantasies of the Nazis. With Ahnenerbe employing 137 scholars and scientists and another 82 support staff by 1939, considerable resources were being invested into dubious research.[58]

Furthermore, the widespread dissemination of Ahnenerbe's findings to the German public and their use in formulating and conducting Nazi policies show that occult and supernatural beliefs were not without a significant impact on the Third Reich. Certainly, Himmler took his *völkisch/* Ariosophic beliefs and the Ahnenerbe's work very seriously. Recalling a six-hour train journey with Himmler in 1929, the Nazi official Albert Krebs found his company extremely tedious with his forced posturing and nit-picking commentary on other Nazis. But as Krebs put it, most of all, it was the 'stupid and endless prattle that I had to listen to' about occult and supernatural beliefs that related to Nazi ideology.[59] Krebs would not have been alone in thinking Himmler was a tedious bore. Fortunately for Himmler, he was a tedious bore cut from the same cloth as Hitler, another tedious bore, as a perusal of the notes of his table talk from 1941 to 1944 shows.

Lebensraum and 'Blood and Soil' were two aspects of Nazi ideology that justified wars of aggression and the forceable removal or eradication of Slavs and Jews from lands coveted for a pan-German empire. Both concepts had their roots in social Darwinist pseudoscience and the *völkisch* nationalism of the late nineteenth century. During the 1890s, the geographer Friedrich Ratzel proposed that human beings interacted with their geographical environment, which influenced social development. Healthy and successful societies needed sufficient space, and growing societies would need more and more land. In formulating this concept, Ratzel was influenced by the social Darwinism of the biologist Ernst Haeckel. His approach gained further support from the Swedish geographer Rudolf

Kjellén, which made it a tenet of the discipline of geopolitics in the early twentieth century. *Lebensraum* formed a part of Germany's military goals during the First World War. The high command anticipated adding large amounts of Poland and the Baltic states to the German empire. Defeat negated that plan, but defeat also convinced many Germans that a Eurasian empire for Germany was a necessity to match the British and French overseas empires and the American West. One of the post-war advocates of *Lebensraum* was Karl Haushofer, a professor of geography at the University of Munich and the teacher of Rudolf Hess during 1919. Hess, in turn, brought *Lebensraum* to the attention of Adolf Hitler, and it was incorporated into Nazi ideology with tragic consequences.

The social Darwinism and geographical determinism of the *Lebensraum* school of geopolitics is now viewed as pseudoscientific. In its day, however, the Darwinian idea of the struggle for existence and the survival of the fittest connected comfortably with the worldview of many members of the elites of Western industrial nations. The Nazis simply took *Lebensraum* to its more logical, inhumane conclusion. In so doing, they added the concept of Blood and Soil. During the nineteenth century, German *völkisch* romanticism glorified rural life and the German peasantry's deep connection to the land. Reacting against urbanization and industrialization, *völkisch* nationalists promoted rural life as healthier and sought to preserve and increase the numbers of sturdy and hardworking peasants, who formed the backbone of German society and made the best soldiers. The Artaman League promoted the back-to-the-land ideal to young Germans, including Richard Walther Darré and Himmler. Darré was an agricultural expert and found the concept of Blood and Soil very congenial. He popularized it in his writings and ultimately joined the Nazi Party in 1930. Blood and Soil asserted that there was a profound and mystical relationship between a people and the land they inhabited. For Darré, Germans were a special people and Germany was their special land. Darré's Blood and Soil meshed quite well with Himmler's desire to restore traditional German rural life. Like Himmler, Darré wanted to bring back ancient German religion and replace Christianity.[60]

In 1932 Himmler made Darré chief of the newly created Race and Settlement Main Office within the ss. Later, between 1932 and 1938 Himmler fell out with Darré, which resulted in Darré losing this position and as Reich Minister of Food and Agriculture. But *Lebensraum* and Blood and Soil remained embedded in Nazi ideology with its forcible removal of people from their homelands and the genocide that often followed. It was a powerfully tragic example of just how dangerous mystical pseudo-scientific theories could be.

The philologist Hans F. K. Günther lent a dubious academic support for Aryanism and *völkisch* beliefs about German racial superiority. The *völkisch* publisher Julius Lehmann had been seeking reputable German scholars to write books that demonstrated the superiority of Aryans or Nordic peoples. The only one willing to undertake the task was Günther, an obscure academic with mediocre credentials. His first book appeared in 1920. It was *Racial Typology of the German People*, a five-hundred-page tome that proved to be quite popular: it was in its sixteenth edition by 1933. Hitler had four of the editions in his personal library, all of them presented to him by Julius Lehmann. It was one of the books that Hitler read while he was in the Landsberg Prison after the Beer Hall Putsch. He also used it in writing *Mein Kampf*. According to Günther's *The Racial Elements of European History* (1927), five races inhabited Europe and the greatest of them was the Nordic. They were superior in terms of their physical, intellectual and moral traits. These traits were biological, not products of environment or culture.

Needless to say, Günther played to the prejudices and *völkisch* fantasies of many Germans, which contributed substantially to his book's popularity. Large sales made Günther rich and famous. In 1930 he was appointed to a chair of anthropology at the University of Jena through the connivance of local Nazis and over the objections of the faculty. Nazis considered him to be their foremost expert on racial questions, and he worked on racial policy with Richard Walther Darré. He joined the Nazi Party in 1932. From 1939 he held a chair at the University of Freiberg until his dismissal in 1945. Interned for three years, Günther remained unrepentant by both denying the Holocaust and continuing to advocate discredited views about eugenics and racial hygiene.[61] Martin Gardner, a pioneer historian of fringe or border knowledge, summed up Günther's work this way: 'The books of men like Günther stand as striking testaments to the ease with which a science can be perverted by strong emotional prejudices which a scientist derives not from his subject matter but from cultural forces surrounding him.'[62]

Nazi ideology was drawn from a hotchpotch of dubious sources, some of which were contradictory, preposterous or simply off-putting to many ordinary Germans. Trying to pull these often absurd elements into an organized and coherent system was further hampered by the anti-intellectual attitudes of various members of the Nazi elite such as Goering and Bormann. Some Nazis, however, did try to create a comprehensive philosophy and ideology for the party and the Third Reich. Alfred Rosenberg made the most significant attempt.

Rosenberg was an ethnic German born in what is now Estonia. He moved to Munich at the end of the First World War. There he became the protégé of Dietrich Eckart and wrote antisemitic and anti-Bolshevik articles for the *Völkischer Beobachter*. Rosenberg joined the German Workers' Party in January 1919, some months before Hitler. He may also have been a member of the Thule Society. After the death of Eckhart in 1923, Rosenberg became editor of the *Völkischer Beobachter*, now the Nazi Party's newspaper. While Hitler was in prison for the Beer Hall Putsch, he appointed Rosenberg to be head of the party. After Hitler resumed the leadership, Rosenberg continued his efforts to systematize and promote Nazi ideology.

Rosenberg brought out his magnum opus, *The Myth of the Twentieth Century: An Evaluation of the Spiritual-intellectual Confrontations of Our Age*, in 1930. The book, of course, furthered the ideas of Germans as the heirs of Aryan supermen, extreme nationalism and vicious antisemitism. It has been pointed out that Rosenberg, along with Hitler, were mythmakers. Rosenberg's 'myth' was the belief in blood, by which he meant the pure blood of race that forms the essential character of a people, their 'race-soul'. He maintained that primordial Aryans were a superior and advanced race that spread their cultural achievements around the world, including a sun cult. In the process of expansion, they engaged in race-mixing with inferior peoples, which led to their degeneration. They also faced competition from rival races with opposing characters or race-souls. Rosenberg traces this historical process from the lost continent of Atlantis to the present. His narrative is a mishmash of pseudo-historical speculations, fractured history, mystical leaps of faith, dubious science and anti-Christian or antisemitic distortions. Rosenberg even threw in that Jesus was an Aryan. In other words, the *Myth* owed a lot to Ariosophy.[63]

Prior to its publication, Rosenberg tried to get Hitler to read the manuscript and provide both feedback and his permission to publish. Apparently, Hitler never read the manuscript but still gave it his approval. When it came out Rosenberg faced strong criticism for seeming to advocate the replacement of Christianity in Germany with the revival of some sort of Nordic paganism. The fact is that the bitterly anti-Christian Hitler and other like-minded Nazis wanted to replace traditional Christianity with either a Nordicized Christianity or a Nazi version of old Germanic paganism. Rosenberg and Himmler definitely favoured the latter. It is also important to remember that Nazism was the only fascist movement that was anti-Christian and wanted to replace it with some sort of concocted nationalist pagan cult. What Hitler did not want was Rosenberg stirring up trouble with the churches and German Christians. As he stated over dinner with his inner circle on 11 April 1942, 'I must insist that Rosenberg's *Myth of the Twentieth Century* is not to be regarded as an expression of the official doctrine of the Party.' Rosenberg's *Myth* sold over a million copies and has been called, along with *Mein Kampf,* 'one of the two greatest unread bestsellers of the Third Reich'. Most purchases of both books were made to present evidence of loyalty to the Third Reich on one's bookshelves or coffee table. In addition, it is important to remember that Rosenberg was not writing to convert committed Christians to paganism. His intended readership was those people who were uncommitted and were looking for a new faith. Meanwhile, various members of Hitler's spiteful and mean-spirited inner circle took turns sniping at Rosenberg. Hermann Goering held Rosenberg's ideas in contempt. Goebbels had initially declared the *Myth* 'very good' in his diary, but Albert Speer reported that he mocked Rosenberg. He even referred to the *Myth* as an 'ideological belch'. Given that Goebbels was never one to let a rival or potential rival get one up on him, one wonders if the private diary might be nearer to his true feelings.[64]

Rosenberg's *Myth* was certainly quite close to Himmler's approach to Nazi ideology, but in many ways the two men were more rivals than allies. In 1934 Rosenberg became commissar for the Nazi Party's office for cultural policy and surveillance, also known as Amt Rosenberg, which included folklore and esoteric subjects. Its work overlapped with that of Himmler's Ahnenerbe. Besides the Amt Rosenberg, Hitler gave Rosenberg multiple responsibilities. He also headed the foreign policy office of the Nazi Party from 1933 to 1945 and later became Reich Minister for the Occupied Eastern Territories from 1941 to 1945. The latter office was an important responsibility in terms of the efforts to convince the local populations to support Germany against Stalin and the communist Russians. Its mission was severely compromised since the process of implementing *Lebensraum* had also begun, which meant the brutal relocation of local Slavs and replacing them with German settlers. Hitler could be critical of Rosenberg on occasion, but he clearly had confidence in him. As Hitler commented in a birthday letter that he wrote to Rosenberg on 11 January 1943, 'I still remember the day I met you in the house of Dietrich Eckhart. Since then you have become the first spiritual and intellectual co-builder of the party. One day history will record how much you did to clarify and stabilize the world-view foundations of the movement.' The historian Irving Hexham has convincingly argued that Hitler had great respect for Rosenberg's advice and ideas, which were widely disseminated throughout Germany.[65]

Historians and the Nazi Fringe

Hitler and the Nazi movement built a fearsome empire of brute power, genocide and devastating wars of aggression. In the end they were defeated and crushed at great cost and sacrifice to Europe and the world. The supernatural, the occult, fringe history and pseudoscience all played a role in the creation of the perverse ideology that supported Nazism. During the 1930s and through the course of the Second World War, it was recognized that a connection existed between Nazism and the supernatural. After the defeat of Germany in 1945 and through to the 1960s, scholars began to study the Nazis' beliefs and connections with the supernatural and border knowledge. At the same time, other scholars such as Alan Bullock emphasized the megalomania and cynical lust for power that motivated Hitler and other leading figures.[66] Both judgements of Hitler and Nazism were valid.

Meanwhile, the deviant and horrific nature of Nazism attracted the attention of sensationalists promoting weird theories, particularly its connection to the occult and supernatural. In 1960 two French writers, Louis Pauwels and Jacques Bergier, brought out a book that appeared in an English translation in 1964 as *The Morning of the Magicians*. It was a jumble of occult, pseudo-historical and pseudoscientific speculations about lost super-civilizations along with claims about ancient alien visitors and the creation of secret mutant superhumans that pre-dated Erich von Däniken. Hitler and the Nazis were supposedly involved in all these aberrant goings-on. *The Morning of the Magicians* became a cult classic for the counterculture, the New Age and conspiracists. It has remained an often dimly remembered ur-text for adherents of fringe history and the supernatural ever since. It also inspired others to develop their own dubious theories about Hitler, the Nazis and the occult. In these books, the occult and supernatural possess real power that Hitler and other Nazis were trying to harness for their own evil agenda – or the evil agenda of the shadowy, occult figures that were the powers behind Hitler and the Nazis and were using them to achieve their own diabolical goals.[67]

A good example of such occult history is Trevor Ravenscroft's *The Spear of Destiny* (1973), which speculates about the spear of Longinus that had pierced the side of Christ and had become a source of supernatural powers. Hitler, who was demonically possessed, became obsessed with acquiring the spear for his plan to conquer the world. Ravenscroft also claimed that various mysterious figures were directing Hitler, who was essentially their puppet. Apart from having to accept the existence of ancient artefacts possessing immense magical powers, readers also have to accept that some of Ravenscroft's research was acquired from the deceased occultist scholar Walter Stein through seances conducted by a medium. So, unless the reader shares Ravenscroft's beliefs in such supernatural sources, genuine historical knowledge about Hitler and the Nazis is not much advanced by *The Spear of Destiny.* The same can be said about other books of this type, which still continue to appear periodically with no end in sight. They are usually fun reads if one wants to experience a runaway imagination but they are not history.[68]

The solid historical research of Nicholas Goodrick-Clarke's *The Occult Roots of Nazism* (1985 and 1992) has shown that occult ideas and beliefs played a discernible and significant role in the genesis of the Nazi movement. He did not, however, look closely at the question of whether the occult continued to influence the Nazis after they came to power in 1933. More recently, scholars such as Corinna Treitel (in her *A Science for the Soul* in 2004) have argued that occultism and fascism were not intrinsically related. That is true. New Agers and occultists can be liberal, conservative or non-political. In Germany, during the first half of the twentieth century, Rudolf Steiner and his Anthroposophy were quite the opposite of fascism and Nazism. Treitel has shown clearly that German occultists sought to transform their beliefs and practices into a form of science. It was, however, a goal that many German scientists and intellectuals rejected, which Treitel glosses over. Moreover, she minimizes the role of occult and pseudoscientific beliefs in the formulation of Nazi policies. As she puts it, 'Himmler indubitably consulted occult practitioners, but there is nothing to suggest that the advice he received ever found its way into important political decisions.'[69] That statement ignores the influence of Karl Maria Wiligut, among others. It also puts the emphasis on the occult but ignores the very evident influence of pseudoscience, border science and fringe history in Nazi thinking.

In reaction to the arguments of Treitel and other like-minded scholars, in 2017 the historian Eric Kurlander published *Hitler's Monsters: A Supernatural History of the Third Reich.* It provides a detailed and heavily documented study of the role of supernatural thinking and beliefs among the Nazis and the society of Nazi Germany. Most importantly, he continues past 1933 the work of Goodrick-Clarke on the occult and Nazism. In addition, his definition of the supernatural encompasses pseudoscience, border science and fringe history as well as the occult.[70] This definition brings in everything from parapsychology to *völkisch* religion, as well as World Ice Theory, lost continents and occult studies.[71]

Nazi ideology offered an all-encompassing alternative to the rational materialism of the Enlightenment and modern science as well as the spiritual reassurance traditionally provided by Christianity. Kurlander points out:

> Based on this evidence, I argue that no mass political movement drew as consciously or consistently as the Nazis on what I call the 'supernatural imaginary' – occultism and 'border science', pagan, New Age and Eastern religions, folklore, mythology and many other supernatural doctrines – in order to attract a generation of German men and women seeking new forms of spirituality and novel explanations of the world that stood somewhere between scientific verifiability and the shopworn truths of traditional religion. Certainly no mass party made similar efforts, once in power, to police or parse, much less appropriate and institutionalize such doctrines, whether in the realm of science and religion, culture and social policy, or the drive toward war, empire and ethnic cleansing. Without understanding this relationship between Nazism and the supernatural, one cannot fully understand the history of the Third Reich.[72]

Pseudoscientific racial theories combined with apocalyptic, pagan and anti-biblical beliefs, distortions of Darwinism and the false history promoted by such fraudulent publications as 'The Protocols of the Elders of Zion' transformed and justified the Holocaust from being senseless mass murder to an existential struggle to save the Aryans and Germany from a millennia-old, diabolical Jewish plot. Racist anthropological theories and bogus research into prehistory merged with *völkisch* religion to create an image of the Germanic peoples as superhumans who needed to recapture their ancient legacy of greatness from, and at the expense of, what they considered were the inferior races. Mumbo jumbo about mystical bonds between the land and its inhabitants reinforced by a supposed need for ever more land to support the growing Aryan population provided the justification for wars of conquest and imperialism leading to genocide. All of it was further supported by the social Darwinistic concept of the struggle for the survival of the fittest.

Did the German people buy into this ideology with its occult, pseudo-scientific and fringe historical trappings? Some did, some did not. During 1934 a conversation took place in Berlin between the English journalist Sir Philip Gibbs and an unnamed French businessman. It offered Gibbs and us today some grim insights into German society at the beginning of the Nazi regime. Gibbs asked the Frenchman for his analysis of the situation in Germany. It turned out that the Frenchman had been closely

observing the situation for six months as well as reading the Nazi literature of Rosenberg and others. He concluded that 35 per cent of Germans
would die for Hitler, while the rest of the population were indifferent to
and unsupportive of Nazism or actively hated it. But the Nazis were in
firm control. Their ideology was about racism, tribalism and a revival of
Nordic paganism. As the Frenchman put it:

> That is the stuff they write and that's the stuff they are teaching to
> young minds in Germany. We do not take it seriously enough. In
> my judgment it is very serious. It's a challenge to European civil-
> ization and Christianity. We are apt to dismiss it and say it is just
> the ravings of a few lunatics. But it is a definite philosophy which
> is held by men who have the destiny of a nation in their hands.
> It is the education being given to the minds of the young people,
> plastic in the hands of those who would mould them. One cannot
> understand what has happened in Germany – the attack on the
> Jews and Catholics and the Protestant dogma – without taking
> all this into account. It is the mainspring of German energy. It is
> the reason why we cannot regard them as equals and partners in
> European progress.

Initially somewhat sceptical, Gibbs found that his stay in Berlin brought
him to the same conclusion.[73]

The Germans were not the only people drunk on the venomous brew
formed by false and hateful ideas. In the 1930s they just drank the deep-
est. The abomination of desolation that was the fate of Nazi Germany
and Europe from 1933 to 1945 is a frightening warning about what happens when nations and societies abandon standards of objective truth and
reason for fake news, pseudoscience, fringe history and perversions of
religion.[74] As the writer Christopher Hale put it powerfully and concisely:
'Myth is never harmless.'[75]

SIX

The Myth of Roswell

Naturally, it will always be impossible to prove there *never was* a flying saucer. Believers in the elusive platters are likely to be around for decades. But there is every reason now to expect that the saucer mania will go down in history as merely one more example of mass delusion.

MARTIN GARDNER, 1952

Martin Gardner was a true polymath. He was an expert on Lewis Carroll, a magician of some renown and a prolific writer on popular mathematics and science. One of his great accomplishments was creating and collecting mathematical games and puzzles. These were published in a number of books which remain in print thanks to Dover Publications. More relevant to the current subject, Gardner was one of the foremost debunkers of pseudoscientific claims during the second half of the twentieth century. His first book, *In the Name of Science: An Entertaining Survey of the High Priests and Cultists of Science, Past and Present*, appeared in 1952. It was updated with a new title, *Fads and Fallacies in the Name of Science*, in 1957. In this book, Gardner surveyed various pseudoscientific beliefs and groups ranging from flat Earth theorists to Lysenkoism, Charles Fort and his followers, lost continents, pyramidology, various medical fads and cults, food fads, Dianetics (the forerunner of Scientology) and antisemitism along with other forms of racism. *Fads and Fallacies* became and remains a classic of sceptical literature. After more than sixty years, it is still in print.[1] For good reason, too: much of its information remains relevant and it is a very good read. Gardner continued his battle with pseudoscience, and in 1976 helped to found the Committee for the Scientific Investigation of Claims of the Paranormal, now known as the Committee for Skeptical Inquiry (CSI).

When Gardner was writing the two editions of *Fads and Fallacies* during the 1950s, the United States and other parts of the world were swept by the outbreak of flying saucer mania that had begun in 1947 and became the modern Unidentified Flying Object (UFO) movement. Needless to say, Gardner included a chapter on flying saucers in both editions of his book. Early on Gardner noted that belief in flying saucers had become fodder for Theosophists and occultists. It is also clear that Gardner expected the flying saucer craze and the UFO movement ultimately to fade into relative obscurity and even extinction. That has not happened. Although the UFO movement has had its ups and downs, it has not disappeared. Instead, it has become a significant aspect of popular culture globally. At the centre of the UFO movement is the Roswell Incident of 1947 – an event that Gardner did not even bother to mention in *Fads and Fallacies*. How could that be? There is a reason for his neglect, as a close look at the origins of the myth of Roswell will reveal.

The Road to Roswell

Roswell is a small city of around 50,000 people located in the southeastern corner of New Mexico. The terrain of that area is arid and relatively flat. You can see for miles. Texas is about 90 miles to the east and over 100 miles to the south. In 1947 there was no interstate highway system. The nearest major highway was the fabled Route 66, which was located 100 miles to the north. Even today, there is no interstate highway that passes within a hundred miles of Roswell since I-40 in New Mexico follows much of the old Route 66. A potential visitor has to want to go there. Despite this inauspicious location, tourists do want to go there – some 200,000 visitors a year. Why? Because Roswell is the site of an alleged flying saucer crash that occurred in early July 1947. As such, it is the Mecca of the UFO movement, as sceptical authority Michael Shermer has dubbed it.[2]

I decided to drive to Roswell in September 2019. Starting from northern Alabama, it was a journey of about 1,300 miles. Most of it was on Interstates 65 and 20, but shortly after Sweetwater, Texas, the best route was to exit I-20 and head north on Highway 85. Travellers should beware that this route passes through a veritable forest of giant wind turbines with the cancer-causing noise that these satanic machines generate or at least some seem to think. Roswell is still 300 miles away. This region was the jumping-off point for the great cattle drives that followed the Chisum and Goodnight–Loving Trails. The seeming flatness of the land conceals the fact that the actual elevation is between 3,600 and 4,000 feet above sea level. It might sound like a long journey, but the average driving speed on this relatively empty road is 80 miles per hour. Travellers will know that Roswell is near when they cross the Pecos River, assuming they realize that small stream is actually a river. Soon after, telltale signs with images of little green men will start to appear, then buildings and finally Main Street in Roswell.

The intersection of Highway 380 (which is Second Street in Roswell) and Main Street is ground zero for ufology. The International UFO Museum and Research Center is just a block to the south. Various UFO-related businesses are scattered along the street both to the north and to the south. Even the lamp covers on the street lights are decorated like the classic grey alien heads. Three blocks to the north is the Roswell Visitors Center with its UFO decor, where the friendly staff will provide travellers with helpful brochures and even take your picture with a couple of grey aliens. Meanwhile back at the International UFO Museum, visitors of a certain age will recognize that the building was originally a movie theatre. The Plains opened in 1946 as a single-screen theatre with seating for 1,030 people. After closing during the 1970s, it was eventually repurposed at the International UFO Museum in 1996.[3]

The creation of the International UFO Museum at Roswell took place about 45 years after the alleged flying saucer crash in 1947 and over ten years after the resurrection of the Roswell Incident as a UFO event in 1980. Walter Haut was a young lieutenant at the Roswell Army Air Force base who handled public relations. He wrote the 8 July 1947 press release that announced the recovery of a crashed flying saucer near Roswell. While attending a UFO conference in Washington, DC, another attendee suggested to Haut that a UFO museum ought to be established in Roswell. Haut took the suggestion seriously and shared it with two others who were supposed witnesses to aspects of the Roswell Incident: Glenn Dennis and Max Littell. They also thought it was a good idea. So, in 1991 the three set up a small museum on the seventh floor of the Sunwest Bank Building on Main Street in Roswell. It was a bad location and in its first two years the museum only attracted 2,000 visitors. During 1992 the museum relocated to a storefront on Main Street, which gave it more visibility. Attendance picked up and by 1996 it was the biggest tourist attraction in Roswell, with over 106,000 people visiting the city just to see the UFO-related sites during the previous four years. Those tourists spent $16 million and generated almost $1 million in tax revenue.[4]

The first UFO festival in Roswell was scheduled for July 1996. About two months before that event was to occur, the UFO museum moved into the former Plains Theater. Needless to say, the thrust of the exhibits in the museum is to show that one or more flying saucers did crash near Roswell in July 1947. These purported crashes included the discovery of dead alien bodies, and even a live one or two as well, along with debris and wreckage.

In addition, the exhibits assert that the crashed saucers were extraterrestrial in origins and that aliens continue to visit the Earth. Furthermore, they claim that aliens have been visiting the Earth stretching back into time immemorial, as is suggested by Erich von Däniken and *Ancient Aliens*.

While the International UFO Museum has its focus on the Roswell Incident, its exhibits also present a host of other hypotheses or claims that form the myriad subsets of the UFO movement. A number of the exhibits were originally props and sets that were used in various television shows about Roswell and UFOs. Probably the most impressive is a three-dimensional diorama of a flying saucer landing in the desert. It was used in the series *Making Monsters* on the Travel Channel. Besides the flying saucer it includes flashing lights, fake smoke and sound effects with a group of grey aliens gathered around. The museum also has a well-stocked gift shop that, according to Dusty Huckabee, the director of Mainstreet Roswell, had sales of $1 million in 1996 alone. Needless to say, the 1997 UFO Festival was the zenith of Roswell's tourism since it marked the fiftieth anniversary of the alleged flying saucer crash. During the years following, the number of visitors to Roswell declined but remained respectable. The UFO Festival of 2019 experienced a significant increase in visitors with 14,000 attendees. The COVID-19 pandemic forced the cancellation of the 2020 festival but the 2021 festival equalled that of 2019. According to Jim Hill, the director of the International UFO Museum, some 220,000 people visit the museum in a normal year and generate $57 million for the Roswell economy. With the 2022 UFO Festival being the 75th anniversary of the alleged crash, the future of Roswell tourism looks healthy both during the festivals and throughout the year. Crashed flying saucers and dead aliens are good business.[5]

Roswell has suffered from the usual economic woes of small cities located in isolated rural areas. Unlike similar cities, popular culture has handed Roswell a ready-made UFO theme. The revival of the Roswell Incident as an important UFO event from 1980 onwards made Roswell a world-famous destination. By the early 1990s the myth of the Roswell flying saucer crash was becoming a central focus for the UFO movement. More and more books, magazine articles, documentaries, films and television series mentioned Roswell or focused on it. Local witnesses were coming forward. Over time closer investigations revealed their testimony was not probative or was of dubious reliability. The establishment of the International UFO Museum in 1991 was an aspect of this revival. Then in 1994 the TV movie *Roswell* starring Kyle MacLachlan and Martin Sheen appeared. It took the sensationalistic stance that there was a flying saucer crash and that the government was covering it up. In the process, it raised Roswell's name recognition even higher. Ironically, the film was shot in Arizona, not on location at Roswell, much to the chagrin of its community leaders.

All of these developments caused some of Roswell's civic and business leaders to start considering UFOs and the Roswell flying saucer crash as a viable theme for attracting tourists. The existence of the International UFO Museum provided a solid foundation. So, in 1996 Haut, Dennis and Littell, the owners of the museum, approached Huckabee about organizing a UFO festival. Huckabee and board member Stan Crosby liked the idea and took it to the full board for a vote. The other board members turned it down. They felt that an emphasis on UFOs would not reflect well on Roswell as a community. In addition, the topic of UFOs tended to offend some people's religious sensibilities. Undaunted, Huckabee and Crosby decided to go ahead with the festival idea on their own. Coincidentally, Crosby's wife, Deon, was on the museum's board. The first UFO festival was held on 4 July 1996 and attracted 1,000 attendees, almost all from out of town and out of state. Locals shunned the event. What caught local attention, however, was that hotels, restaurants and fuel stations all showed a significant increase in sales.

After experiencing the economic benefits that resulted from the first UFO festival, the organizers decided to hold a second festival in 1997, the fiftieth anniversary of the Roswell Incident. This time the community supported it. Various economic and business groups like Mainstreet Roswell and civic societies all got involved. Stan Crosby engaged in a highly successful effort on the Internet to promote the festival as Encounter 97. The New Mexico State Department of Tourism also provided substantial support. Besides publicizing Encounter 97 in its brochures, the Department of Tourism conducted workshops for local businesses to help maximize the economic impact of the event. They also promoted it to national and international media and provided foreign journalists with interpreters. They clearly wanted Roswell to become a permanent tourist attraction.[6] The event even made the cover of *Time* magazine for 23 June 1997.[7] As a result of this publicity, an estimated 48,000 people attended Encounter 97. In other words, during the festival Roswell's population doubled. Meanwhile, UFO-themed gift shops had been springing up around the International UFO Museum. Once empty storefronts now housed flourishing businesses. A push began for other businesses in the area to adopt UFO and alien themes, decor and motifs. The Dunkin' Donuts on Main Street currently boasts a statue of a 6-metre-tall (20 ft) green alien holding up a Dunkin' sign while a nearby McDonald's is UFO themed. Roswell had found its subject for successfully promoting tourism.

Not every Roswellian agreed with the focus on UFOs and crashed flying saucers. Some people felt that the theme cheapened the town's image by touting a fictional event (no, not all Roswellians are believers). Still, as Deon Crosby put it, when asked if she believed in UFOs, 'What do I believe? I believe in tourism.' Tourism meant money. With 200,000 tourists coming to Roswell each year and 85 per cent of them visiting the International UFO Museum, the UFO theme was clearly working very well indeed. It certainly worked for Walter Haut, who was driving around town in a very nice BMW sporting the vanity plate 'Mr. UFO'. Not to be outdone, Mrs Haut's car's licence plate proclaimed her 'Mrs. UFO'.[8]

At this point, one might be wondering, if the Roswell Incident happened in 1947, why did it take almost fifty years for the International UFO Museum and the UFO festival to come into being? That is an interesting and crucial question. Its answer tells a lot about the origin, nature and substance of the myth of Roswell and the UFO movement. From this point onwards, when the term 'the Roswell Incident' is used, it is referring to the official and historical story of the crash of a United States Air Force surveillance balloon. The term 'the myth of Roswell' refers to the story of the crash of an alien spacecraft or spacecrafts in its assorted versions.

The Roswell Incident: The Historical Version

To fully understand the Roswell Incident of 1947, it is crucial to be clear about its historical and geographical context. In 1947 the United States and the Western world were transitioning from the relative moral clarity of the Second World War and the euphoria of its victorious end to the murky and uncertain world of the Cold War. The United States had a monopoly on nuclear weapons, but it was only a matter of time before the Russians acquired the knowledge to make their own atomic bomb. Just as the Russians frantically scrambled to develop a nuclear weapon, the United States was desperate to find out when the Russians would be successful. It was a time before the development of U-2 spy planes and well before spy satellites could be launched into space. There were no eyes in the skies.[9]

New Mexico was the birthplace for weapons of the atomic age. Its isolation and desert wilderness made it an ideal place for carrying on secret weapons development and testing. Los Alamos became the location for Project Y, whose purpose was to design and construct an atomic bomb. The first detonation of an atomic bomb occurred at the Alamogordo Bombing and Gunnery Range on 16 July 1945. After the war ended, the Roswell Army Air Field became the home base for the 509th Bomb Wing, the world's first and, in 1947, only bomber unit to carry nuclear weapons.

At the same time, some of the efforts to monitor the progress of the Soviet Union's nuclear programme were also located in New Mexico. In 1946 New York University won a contract to create and fly high-altitude balloons carrying equipment capable of sensing the sound of a nuclear test in Russian territory. This operation was named Project Mogul and was based at Alamogordo. It was a highly classified operation. So, New Mexico was home to many very important and extremely secret military projects. Not only were neighbouring civilians unaware of them, the great majority of military personnel also knew nothing about all the top-secret activity.

It was in this context of Cold War secrecy and apprehension that the Roswell Incident took place. During the first week of June 1947, three Project Mogul balloon trains were released at Alamogordo. Wind and weather conditions were carefully recorded. One of the balloons was launched on 4 June with a B-17 bomber following its flight path. Later Alamogordo lost contact with the balloon. It probably came down in the vicinity of the Foster Ranch managed by William 'Mack' Brazel. On 14 June Brazel and his son were making their rounds of the ranch when they came upon debris from the crashed balloon. Weather balloons had previously come down on the Foster Ranch but this debris was different. Brazel would later describe finding rubber pieces, a tinfoil-like material and bits of balsawood sticks. There was nothing that caused him to give the debris much thought. Ten days later on 24 June, reports of Kenneth Arnold's encounter with flying discs over Washington state made the national news. Within a few days, press reports would quickly change Arnold's initial 'flying disc' description into what became the standard term – 'flying saucer'. Brazel returned to the debris site with his wife and daughter on 4 July. The sheep that were grazing in that area were spooked by the debris and refused to cross it to get drinking water. They came to clean up some of the debris so that the sheep would be able to reach their water supply.

Meanwhile, the flying disc or saucer mania that resulted from the Arnold sightings was sweeping the country. The modern UFO movement was born, and the United States was experiencing its first flying saucer flap. It is important to place this flap and the Roswell Incident into their proper historical and cultural context. In 1947 and for a year or two afterwards, when people spotted a flying saucer, they usually assumed it was some sort of secret experimental aircraft of the United States military. Alternatively, horror of horrors, it was a top secret, experimental aircraft belonging to the Russians. Nobody jumped to the conclusion that a flying saucer was an extraterrestrial spacecraft. The assumption that any flying saucer was from outer space would come later but not in 1947.

Back at the Foster Ranch, Brazel had to travel to the nearby town of Corona, where he learned about the Arnold flying disc encounter. That news got him thinking. What he concluded was that his unfamiliar debris might be part of some secret military project. Next, Brazel travelled to Roswell for business on 7 July. While he was there, he reported the crashed debris to George Wilcox, the sheriff of Chaves County (Roswell was the county seat). Brazel linked the debris to the recent Arnold flying disc sightings. Wilcox dutifully passed on Brazel's information to the Roswell Army Air Field administration. At that point, Lieutenant Colonel Jesse Marcel and Captain Sheridan Cavitt spoke with Brazel and then followed him out to the Foster Ranch. The three men visited the debris site and gathered up what remained. Brazel gave them what he and his family had collected. Marcel thought the debris might have been from a kite and estimated it weighed about 2 kilograms (5 lb). Marcel and Cavitt returned to the base that night.

The next day Lieutenant Walter Haut, the Roswell public relations officer, issued a press release claiming that the military had debris from a crashed flying saucer. The story immediately made the front page of the *Roswell Daily Record* for 8 July 1947. Wire services picked up the story, and it spread almost instantly across the country and overseas. Meanwhile, Marcel and the debris had been flown to Fort Worth for a meeting with the regional commander, General Roger Ramey. There Ramey and his staff identified the debris as a weather balloon. That evening a local radio station interviewed Ramey, and again he identified the debris as a weather balloon. He also had reporters come to his office to inspect the debris and take pictures. News that the initial identification of the debris had been mistaken again spread quickly across the United States and the world. The next day the *Roswell Daily Record* printed another front-page story correcting the previous day's report and stating that the debris came from a weather balloon.[10]

In this way the original Roswell flying saucer story came and went almost in the twinkling of an eye or perhaps of a UFO. Despite the dramatic initial claim of a flying saucer recovery, the burgeoning UFO movement forgot Roswell for thirty years. Martin Gardner had good grounds for not bothering to mention Roswell. The historian David Michael Jacobs, who sympathized with the UFO movement, also declined to mention the incident in his 1975 UFO *Controversy in America*. Ted Bloecher, an indefatigable compiler and evaluator of UFO sightings, considered the Roswell Incident to be a mistake and called Haut's press release a 'reckless statement'. Bloecher was writing in 1967, twenty years after the Roswell Incident, so he showed a high degree of prescience when he commented, 'There remains the possibility that some super-secret upper-atmosphere balloon experiment had crashed near Corona, which would have accounted for all the confusion and secrecy involved in its recovery.'That is exactly what the United States Air Force's *The Roswell Report: Fact versus Fiction in the New Mexico Desert* would reveal in 1995 when it admitted that the debris came from a Project Mogul surveillance balloon, hence the cover-up. The USAF would follow up with a second report, *The Roswell Report: Case Closed*, in 1997 which added additional details. It debunked the stories of alien bodies being recovered at the Roswell crash site on the Foster Ranch that had started to appear with the rise of the myth of Roswell after 1980.[11]

Meanwhile, it has been claimed that the Roswell community and the small army of alleged witnesses never forgot the Roswell Incident.[12] The evidence for that claim is both sparse and dubious. One wonders if the revival of the Roswell Incident and its transformation into the myth of Roswell had more to do with the UFO hunters' need for and search for a fresh UFO story to revitalize the flagging UFO movement of the 1970s. Ufologist investigators began poking and prodding Roswellians of a certain age with leading questions that might have awoken memories of events long gone by, or they might have sparked the merger of vague memories and suggestions into a confabulation about a non-event that grew and grew into a myth. That raises the question: were those memories reliable? Perhaps some Roswellians were overly eager to be part of the fame and the profits that came with being a celebrity witness. Certainly, as will be shown further on, most of the eyewitness testimony has turned out to be insubstantial or unreliable and has fallen apart. For now, it is time to look at the history of the modern UFO movement from its beginnings in 1947 to the emergence of the myth of Roswell as the major UFO narrative during the 1980s and 1990s.

The UFO Movement

Kenneth Arnold's encounter on 24 June 1947 with the flying discs in the skies of the Pacific Northwest while flying his own plane marked the beginning of the modern UFO movement. According to Ted Bloecher, there were 853 UFO sightings after the Arnold encounter until the end of 1947. It was the first of the UFO 'flaps' or 'waves'. Several more waves of UFO sightings followed in 1952, 1957, 1965–7 and 1973.[13] Initially, people assumed that the flying saucers were probably experimental aircraft built by the United States or the Russians. That changed fairly quickly with the appearance of the extraterrestrial hypothesis that the flying saucers came from outer space. It came to dominate discussions. After the 1952 wave of strange and unexplained objects in the skies, the USAF created the term Unidentified Flying Object (UFO). Many of the unexplained aerial objects were not saucer-shaped and often simply appeared as lights in the sky. In addition to being a more accurate description of the uncertainty and variety of the phenomenon, the term 'UFO' was thought to be less suggestive of the unexplained aerial phenomenon having to be a machine from another world. The flying saucer movement embraced the term as well. For it, however, the equation generally was UFO = flying saucer = extraterrestrial spacecraft.[14]

Very early in the modern UFO movement, the public began accusing the United States government, particularly the military, of covering up that UFOs were alien spaceships. In fact, military officials did have concerns about UFOs and wanted to dampen down the UFO mania. First, they feared a panic about alien invaders like the one sparked by Orson Welles's radio broadcast of a dramatization of H. G. Wells's *War of the Worlds* in 1938. Second, the Air Force viewed UFOs as a potentially dangerous distraction. Attention to UFOs could undermine preparedness for a Russian surprise attack. Furthermore, a UFO incident might be mistaken for a Russian attack and inadvertently trigger a nuclear war.[15] Public criticisms about cover-ups and its own concerns caused the Air Force to conduct various investigations of UFOs. Starting in 1948, Project Sign concluded that some UFO sighting might be physical aircraft of unknown origin. It was replaced by Project Grudge by early 1949, which in turn became Project Blue Book towards the end of 1951. Project Blue Book remained in operation until 1969. The astronomer J. Allen Hynek was a consultant for all three projects. Starting out as a UFO sceptic, by 1969 Hynek had transformed into a believer that UFOs were real and not just quirky natural phenomena. Hynek had become disillusioned by the Air Force's unscientific handling of UFO investigations and its covert agenda of conducting a public relations campaign to discredit belief in UFOs and cool the public's interest and enthusiasm about them.

In 1966 the USAF sought to put to rest permanently any questions about UFOs by commissioning a scientific study. It contracted with the University of Colorado to produce that study, and the respected physicist Edward U. Condon was made the project's director. Once the so-called Condon committee began meeting, the divisions between sceptics and proponents of the UFO phenomenon erupted into public view. Critics accused Condon and others on the committee of having started with a predetermined conclusion that UFOs were not physical phenomena and so were not worthy of study. Certainly, that is what the massive Condon Report of 1969 finally concluded. Those conclusions did gravely undercut public support for the UFO movement, which declined almost to extinction during the 1970s. The conclusion also gave the Air Force a justification for ending Project Blue Book and getting the government out of the burden of UFO investigations, at least public ones.

If the government was weary of dealing with the pesky UFO movement, the movement itself suffered from internal problems. The original core mission of the UFO movement was to investigate UFO sightings. To be successful, this goal required the serious, systematic and hopefully scientific investigation of the many sightings. A prominent leader of this scientific approach to UFO investigations was Donald Keyhoe. He was an unrelenting opponent of both government cover-ups and the sensationalist branch of the UFO movement. He was also hard to get along with and a poor manager. J. Allen Hynek took over Keyhoe's informal leadership position during the late 1960s. Along the way various civilian organizations for the study of UFOs in the United States and around the world arose and often fell. One of the oldest was the Aerial Phenomenon Research Organization (APRO), founded by the pioneering ufologists Coral and Jim Lorenzen in 1952. Faced by the Condon Report's seeming discrediting of ufology, competition from other UFO groups and internal schisms (ufologists can be quarrelsome), APRO went into decline and became inactive by 1988. Another early group was the National Investigations Committee on Aerial Phenomena (NICAP) that formed in 1956. Donald Keyhoe was the combative director of NICAP from 1957 to 1969. Plagued by mismanagement and infighting, NICAP also declined after the Condon Report and ceased operation in 1980.[16]

As some UFO organizations died, new ones were born. The Mutual UFO Network (MUFON) came into independent existence in 1969. It had started out as the Midwest UFO Network under the umbrella of APRO but seceded and is still active. In 1973 J. Allen Hynek organized the Center for UFO Studies (CUFOS), which is also still in operation. These groups, along with similar organizations, great and small, dedicated to studying UFOs empirically and scientifically, can be found in the United States and throughout the world. Not all ufologists and UFO groups, however, take this sober and scientific approach.

The UFO movement is not monolithic. There are many hypotheses and opinions, all with people who are fiercely invested in them. Factions exist and schisms occur periodically. As the historian of late nineteenth-century UFO sightings, Daniel Cohen, has vividly described it:

The world of ufologists is riddled with intrigue and passion. It is a world in which charges like 'blind' and 'stupid' are the nice things you say about your enemies and sometimes the nice things you say about your friends. Somewhat nastier epithets are 'money-grubbing charlatan' and 'McCarthyite book-burner,' 'Agent provocateur,' 'CIA flack,' and hints that one is the agent of some sinister ultraterrestrial force are not uncommonly heard. Vendettas can be fiercer between people who agree with one another than they are between believers and skeptics. Anyone who has spent any time in the maelstrom of ufological politics will know that I am not exaggerating.[17]

People involved in the debates about Roswell are no exception.

Sensationalistic claims about UFOs tended to grab the headlines, such as the highly publicized tales of the 'contactees' that flourished during the 1950s. Contactees were people who claimed to have met aliens from flying saucers and interacted with them. The first and the most famous was George Adamski. Born in Poland in 1891, his family emigrated to the United States when he was two. During the 1930s he developed an interest in Eastern occultism, but by the early 1940s his focus shifted to aliens visiting the Earth. Then on 20 November 1952 he experienced telepathic communication and physical contact with Venusians, in particular one named Orthon. During this encounter, he claimed to have witnessed along with six other people a large formation of 184 spacecraft passing overhead. The Venusians even took him for a ride on one of their spaceships. Adamski dubbed his alien visitors 'Space Brothers'. They were tall, blonde and good-looking humans who wanted to warn humanity about the dangers of nuclear war and to teach humanity to live peacefully. It was a tale that bore a definite similarity to the plot of the film *The Day the Earth Stood Still* (1951), which had come out the previous year. The teachings of the Space Brothers echoed the ideas of the Eastern occultism that Adamski had previously espoused. Adamski went on to write several books about his experiences, gave talks and created several organizations, all of which provided him with a nice income until his death. Close examination revealed that Adamski's contact stories were full of holes and contradictions. Evidence accumulated that he was engaged in a cynical confidence scheme. Still, Adamski had created the basic framework of 'contactee' narratives: that aliens were attractive humans, they wanted to warn people on Earth about nuclear dangers, they kept a low profile to avoid creating a panic and they came in peace and love.[18]

Other contactees followed. One of the more interesting was Truman Bethurum. He claimed that on 28 July 1952, while working in the Nevada desert, eight small men took him to their spaceship to meet their leader.

The leader was a beautiful brunette woman named Aura Rhanes. The aliens came from a planet named Clarion that was in an orbit that always kept it behind the sun, which was why humans did not know it existed. Like the Space Brothers, Clarionites visited the Earth to warn us about the dangers of nuclear war and the need to change our dangerous and aggressive ways. Bethurum's story provoked a lot of scepticism and accusations of being a hoax, even from the UFO community. His shaky account did not prevent him from attracting a large and profitable following. Just as Adamski's story appears to have been modelled on a Hollywood film, Bethurum's may have inspired an early UFO cult.[19]

The UFO cult of the Seekers was the creation of Dorothy Martin, a housewife from Oak Park, Illinois. She had long been interested in occult ideas and experiences. In 1954 she claimed that aliens calling themselves the Elder Brothers and the Guardians had contacted her through automatic writing. Automatic writing is the phenomenon of a person unconsciously writing out psychic messages from a paranormal entity. One of them, named Sanada, even claimed to have been Jesus Christ in a previous life. Furthermore, the Guardians claimed to be from the planet Clarion. Martin never claimed to have seen a spaceship. Based on this narrative of alien contact, she attracted a small but devoted following. Her automatic writing began to contain a prophecy that an impending catastrophic flood would destroy Chicago and devastate the planet in late December. The existence of the Seekers came to the attention of the social psychologist Leon Festinger of the University of Minnesota and several other researchers. Interested in studying the phenomenon, they managed to infiltrate the Seekers with some of their graduate students. Their plan was to observe closely how the Seekers would react when the promised catastrophe failed to occur. And it did fail to occur. The resulting study, *When Prophecy Fails*, described how Martin (called Mrs Keech in the study) and her followers weathered the crisis of faith that ensued. They claimed that the Guardians had informed them that the Seekers' prayers had held off the flood and saved Chicago. Festinger's research became the foundation for the concept of cognitive dissonance. Like other contactees, Martin's alien mentors came in peace and wanted to save humanity.[20] With the end of the 1950s the contactee era faded, but new forms of wild speculation and hoaxing appeared to fill the gap and vex the believers seeking genuine proof and explanations about the reality of UFOs and the UFO sceptics as well.[21]

The next prominent phenomenon of the UFO movement was the abductees. Abductees are people who claim that aliens kidnapped them and took them aboard the spacecraft, where their captors carried out examinations and experiments on them and sometimes flew with them into outer space for some period of time before returning them. Most abductees reported losses of time and had little or no conscious memory of their abduction experience. Hypnosis has been used to recover memories – a decidedly dubious methodology.[22]

The famous ur-story of the abductee phenomenon occurred on 19 September 1961 in the New Hampshire countryside. There Barney and Betty Hill were travelling home when they encountered a pancake-shaped flying object that blocked their route. They were taken aboard the alien craft by its occupants and examined. Allowed to return to their automobile, they had a second episode with the spacecraft that resulted in their having no memory of 35 miles of their journey. Their experience left them with feelings of anxiety, and they reported their UFO encounter to the Pease Air Force base on 21 September. The Air Force tentatively identified the spacecraft as actually being from the planet Jupiter but later changed their explanation to atmospheric conditions being the cause of the strange sighting. Later that year the Hills started talking to the ufologists from NICAP about their experience. Eventually in early 1963, the Hills sought help through hypnosis. Under hypnosis Betty started describing her extra-terrestrial abductors as the now classic grey aliens, a significant change in her original story. Professionals examining the results of the hypnotically derived testimony of the Hills found it to be very tainted.

Other abduction stories followed, but the volume of reports remained small and did not start to increase dramatically until the mid-1980s. The best known and most influential abduction was that of Whitley Strieber in 1985. Strieber was the author of horror thrillers. He claimed that during the night of 26 December grey aliens levitated him out of his room in the family's upstate New York cabin in the woods and on to their spaceship. There they engaged in various intrusive examinations of which Strieber had only mixed-up recollections until he underwent regression hypnosis. The doctor who performed the hypnosis also diagnosed Strieber with a form of epilepsy that causes hallucinations. Notwithstanding that diagnosis, Strieber wrote an account of his abduction, *Communion*, in 1987 which became a bestseller. He followed it up with four more accounts of his encounters with aliens. Lately he has appeared on episodes of *Ancient Aliens*.

Accounts of alien abductions took over the UFO movement during the 1980s and 1990s even though scientists view them as cases of imagined or implanted memories or sleep paralysis. *The X-Files* (1993–2002; revived 2016 and 2018) turned into an extremely popular television series with a story arc based on alien abductions, government cover-ups and conspiracies involving alien infiltration that is interspersed with episodes dealing with monsters or monstrous phenomena. Other alien-related phenomena included mysterious crop circles and the mutilation of cattle and horses. The mutilations and abductions gave rise to theories that aliens were harvesting DNA or something from humans and animals for nefarious purposes. Some claim that the aliens were creating a hybrid alien-human race that would take over the Earth and enslave the rest of humanity. It has even been suggested that some governments (including the United States) might be part of a vast conspiracy to assist the alien infiltration: a plot straight out of *The X-Files*, although it is unclear whether art is imitating life or life is imitating art.[23]

Parallel to the tales of the contactees and the abductees, the myth of ancient alien visitors emerged as another offshoot of the UFO movement. Erich von Däniken's *Chariots of the Gods* appeared in German in 1968 with an English translation in 1969. The book became an international bestseller. The ideas in *Chariots of the Gods* were hardly new. Jason Colavito has traced the concept of extraterrestrials visiting the Earth during prehistory and ancient times back to the horror writer H. P. Lovecraft. During the late 1910s until his death in 1937, Lovecraft was a very prolific writer of short stories based on horror themes. Enigmatic and rather nasty aliens appear in a number of his stories. By the end of the 1940s, interest in Lovecraft had faded in the United States and did not revive until the 1960s. In France, on the other hand, Lovecraft became a popular author and a subject of literary study along with, inexplicably, Jerry Lewis and the perennial French fascination with Edgar Allan Poe. As a result, in France Lovecraft's stories inspired some definitely fringe books about the distant past. In 1960 Louis Pauwels and Jacques Bergier brought out their *Morning of the Magicians* in French and English. The book covered a wide range of highly speculative conjectures about human history. Among those speculations was the existence of ancient super-civilizations and ancient astronauts using the same so-called evidence that von Däniken would use a few years later in his book. Another French author, Robert Charroux, would add his take on ancient extraterrestrials in his *One Hundred Thousand Years of Man's Unknown History*, which appeared in French in 1963 and English in 1970. It also postulated the existence of an ancient super-civilization that had its origin in a migration from Venus, again using the same evidence that von Däniken would cite in his book.[24]

Another writer of ancient alien books that pre-dated von Däniken was W. Raymond Drake. As an ardent follower of Charles Fort, Drake ploughed through all sorts of libraries and archives seeking evidence that extraterrestrials had brought a super-civilization to Earth in the distant past. The civilization degenerated and, in the process, lost its advanced technological knowledge. Drake's first book, *Gods or Spacemen?*, appeared in 1964, four years before the German edition of *Chariots of the Gods*. In 1968 Drake published his second book, *Gods and Spacemen in the Ancient East*, but the British edition of *Chariots of the Gods* appeared soon after in 1969, to be followed by the American edition in 1970. Von Däniken's book took off and its sales quickly dwarfed those of Drake's. During the 1970s Drake published another eight books on ancient astronauts compared to von Däniken's five, but von Däniken's sold far more copies. Although Drake preceded von Däniken, his books were consigned to the periphery of the ancient astronaut craze along with von Däniken's many imitators. Any modest success of these rivals was largely a function of the reading public's insatiable appetite for ancient astronaut books. In fact, Zecharia Sitchin with his 'Earth Chronicles' series (seven volumes from 1976 to 2007) was von Däniken's only serious rival for primacy in the world of the ancient alien phenomenon. He claimed that the Earth has been visited by inhabitants of Nibiru, a mysterious planet with a very eccentric orbit. His ancient setting for alien civilizations and colonies was Mesopotamia.[25]

The Origin and Evolution of the Myth of Roswell

The decade of the 1970s was a time of disarray and decline for the UFO movement in the aftermath of the Condon Report. Believers in UFOs had hoped that new sightings of UFOs, theories that UFOs were behind the mysterious disappearances of ships and airlines, stories that astronauts had observed alien spaceships, and that finally the United States government would officially reveal that UFOs were alien spacecraft visiting the Earth would prove UFOs were real and from outer space. None of these things came to pass. Instead, hoax after hoax was exposed. The Bermuda Triangle and the tales of astronaut sightings turned out to be erroneous, while the government refused to announce that any extraterrestrial visitation had occurred. The public was losing interest in UFOs in light of thirty years of investigations failing to produce any reliable physical evidence that they exist. It was in this milieu that the myth of Roswell was born.[26]

If any single person deserves credit for the creation of the myth of Roswell, it would be Stanton Friedman. Certainly, the International UFO Museum at Roswell would agree. They have a very laudatory exhibit expressing gratitude to Friedman and his work at the front of the museum near the entrance. Some might even call it a shrine. Friedman studied nuclear physics at the University of Chicago where he earned his Bachelor of Science degree (1955) and Master of Science degree (1956). After graduation he worked in industry as a nuclear physicist from 1956 to 1970. When he was laid off in 1971, he became a UFO investigator: giving lectures, appearing on radio and television shows, consulting and writing articles. On 21 February 1978 he visited Baton Rouge, Louisiana, to lecture on UFOS and make an appearance on a local television show. While he was at the television station, someone working there told him of a friend who claimed to have helped recover a crashed flying saucer. That friend turned out to be Jesse Marcel from the Roswell Incident of 1947. Friedman called Marcel to enquire about his flying saucer experiences. What he learned was disappointing. Marcel could not remember what year his encounter took place; nor did he possess any contemporary documentation or artefacts. Still, Friedman suggested that Marcel participate in a Chicago-based talk show about crashed UFOS. It took place on 7 April 1978 with Leonard Stringfield, a well-known ufologist specializing in crashed UFOS. Stringfield took notes as Marcel told his story and included it in a paper he gave at the MUFON conference.[27]

Meanwhile, Friedman was also writing articles about UFOS for the *National Enquirer*. In early 1979 the production company Group I International approached Friedman about working on a documentary film, *UFOS are Real* (in video release the title was *Flying Saucers are Real*). Friedman appeared extensively as a talking head during the course of the film. In May 1979 he and a film crew travelled to Houma, Louisiana, where they spent one day interviewing Marcel. *UFOS are Real* was released in November 1979. It used a style of presentation similar to the TV series *In Search of . . .* hosted by Leonard Nimoy that had been broadcasting since 1977. Marcel appeared briefly. He claimed that the news reporters who viewed the crash debris from Roswell in General Roger Ramey's office saw only a little of the real debris and nothing that was important like the parts with strange hieroglyphs on them. Marcel stated that Ramey had ordered him to be quiet, so he never actually spoke to the reporters. This claim is flatly contradicted by the account of the meeting at Ramey's office by J. Bond Johnson in the 9 July 1947 issue of the *Fort Worth Morning-Star-Telegram*. Johnson quoted Marcel in his news story, which included the detail that Marcel was from Houma, which no one else at the Fort Worth Army Air base meeting would have known. Critics of the myth of Roswell, such as Philip J. Klass, have noted that Marcel's story expanded and changed the more he told it, calling the reliability of his testimony into question.[28]

Friedman wanted to write a book on his discoveries about Roswell, but he lacked good contacts with any publishers. In 1979 the idea that an alien spacecraft had crashed near Roswell in 1947 was considered to be a thoroughly debunked tale even by most mainstream ufologists. Many people in the UFO movement would never have heard of the Roswell

Incident. From a publisher's point of view, a book by a relatively unknown author that claimed a flying saucer crashed at Roswell, New Mexico, in 1947 was not a promising venture. Fortunately for Friedman, he met an old friend, William L. Moore, at a lecture in Minneapolis. When he told of his research with Roswell witnesses, Moore proved to be interested and agreed to work on the project. A classic solution for getting a publisher interested is to attract a well-known author to join the project. Moore knew such an author. He had just co-authored *The Philadelphia Experiment: Project Invisibility* that was published in 1979. His co-author was Charles Berlitz, who was well known as a result of his books about Atlantis and the Bermuda Triangle. Berlitz also possessed close contacts with a number of publishers. He agreed to work with Moore. It was a combination that would help to secure a favourable contract from a major publisher. In Great Britain, Berlitz presented Granada Publishing with a four-page outline for the book and came away with a £50,000 advance, which would have been equivalent to about $100,000, a substantial amount for that era. The American publisher was Grosset & Dunlap. The book was titled *The Roswell Incident* and appeared in 1980. It quickly came out in a mass-market paperback along with translations into French and German. The book sold well despite receiving telling criticisms from both sceptics and traditional ufologists who complained of inaccuracies and sensationalism. Friedman's name did not appear as an author. He did receive part of Moore's share of the royalties, but a full admission by Moore and Berlitz of his contributions and role in the creation of *The Roswell Incident* failed to make it into the published book. Moore and Berlitz mentioned Friedman in the book's acknowledgements – along with several dozen other people. The use of some of his interviews was mentioned parenthetically a few times in the book. It was a meagre recognition of Friedman's role. Then again, how much Berlitz actually contributed to the writing of the book is a murky question. When criticisms arose, Moore was quick to blame Berlitz for errors and overwrought tales. Despite adverse reactions, *The Roswell Incident* provided the myth of Roswell with a foundation that others would build on and embellish in the following years.[29]

In the same year that *The Roswell Incident* was published, the television series *In Search of . . .* aired an episode titled 'UFO Cover-ups' on 20 September which included a segment with Jesse Marcel. He was even flown to Roswell so that his interview could be done on location. Marcel told of Brazel taking him to the crash site, which was large and full of debris. He picked up as much debris as he could and took it back to the Roswell Army Air Force base. From there he flew with the debris to Fort Worth and a meeting with General Ramey, who pronounced the debris to be the remains of a weather balloon. He also told Marcel to remain silent in the presence of reporters. Years later, Marcel would state that the debris was not of the Earth. At no point in his account does Marcel claim to have seen or heard anything about a crashed flying saucer, dead aliens or alternative crash sites.[30]

According to Berlitz and Moore's *Roswell Incident*, on 2 July 1947 a flying saucer was struck by lightning near Roswell. It scattered some debris on the Foster Ranch managed by Mack Brazel but managed to fly another hundred miles to the Plains of San Augustin where it crashed. There on 3 July the soil conservationist Grady Barnett came upon the wreckage as did a group of archaeologists. They were soon run off by the arrival of military personnel. That same day Mack Brazel discovered the strange debris on his ranch. Later, on 5 July, Brazel visited the town of Corona where he learned about the wave of flying saucer sightings. Thinking he may have found a flying saucer, he reported it to Sheriff Wilcox in Roswell. Wilcox passed the information on to the Roswell Army Air Force base, which brought in Jesse Marcel. Brazel took him to the ranch where they picked up hard and unbreakable debris that had hieroglyphs on it. Marcel took the debris back to the base, and on 8 July Haut composed a press release claiming that the base had discovered a crashed flying saucer. It is suggested that the press release was an attempt to distract from the wrecked flying saucer at the Plains of San Augustin. General Ramey promptly repudiated the press release with his weather balloon identification which both the media and the public accepted. In this way, the United States military avoided a panic over an alien invasion while allowing it to exploit the recovered alien technology for weapons development. From that point the Roswell Incident languished seemingly debunked and largely forgotten for thirty years.[31]

Seven years after the publication of *The Roswell Incident*, a second version of the myth of Roswell appeared with Stanton Friedman, William Moore and Jaime Shandera's release of the Majestic 12 or MJ-12 papers. These papers purported to be a 1952 memo prepared for the incoming president Dwight Eisenhower that discussed UFOs and the efforts of a group of government and military officials to manage the situation. This new version claimed that a flying saucer malfunctioned and exploded over Brazel's ranch on 2 July 1947. The military began a clean-up on 7 July, when they discovered alien bodies 2 miles east of the debris field. Although the spacecraft's propulsion system was destroyed, the wreckage and bodies were sent to several locations for scientific study.[32]

Four years later, in 1991, the UFO investigators Kevin D. Randle and Donald R. Schmitt brought out UFO *Crash at Roswell*. In their version, the flying saucer experienced a malfunction on 2 July that forced it to land on the ranch managed by Mack Brazel. Attempting to continue, the flying saucer tried to take off, faltered and struck the ground leaving a 45-metre-long (150 ft) gash and a trail of debris before becoming airborne. Still malfunctioning, the alien craft crashed a few miles away. Brazel found the debris on 3 July and the military was called in on 6 July. Aerial reconnaissance on 8 July sighted the wrecked flying saucer jammed against a cliff 2 miles away along with a few alien bodies scattered around. There Grady Barnett and the archaeologists stumbled on to the wreckage shortly before the military arrived. The military expelled the civilians from the site and threatened them if they ever talked about what they had seen. Meanwhile the army removed the wreckage and bodies to the Roswell Army Air Field's hospital where a civilian saw the bodies. That same day the military put out its press release. The next day Brazel gave an interview to the *Roswell Daily Record* in which he presented an untruthful story he was coerced to give by the military. At the same time, General Ramey repudiated the press release and promoted the weather balloon story. Fake debris was shown to the press and so began a government cover-up that had lasted until this day.[33]

Jesse Marcel became something of a Roswell celebrity thanks to his appearances in documentaries and tabloid interviews, and he no longer even lived there. Friedman and Moore continued their quest to find more witnesses. The attention given to Marcel also apparently jogged the memories of other people living in Roswell. New witnesses came forward. Other ufologists, like the writing team of Randle and Schmitt, also joined the search for more witnesses. Eventually, Randle and Schmitt would claim to have over three hundred witnesses, some of whom wished to remain anonymous. It was an impressive number but a closer look at the list by another ufologist, Karl Pflock, revealed some problems. Only 41 of the witnesses were present at Roswell in 1947 and able to give a first- or second-hand account. Of these, only 23 were in a position to have seen any sort of physical evidence or debris from the crash at the Foster Ranch. Even more telling, only seven claimed that the debris they saw had any strange qualities that might indicate it was extraterrestrial. Such doubts, however, only appeared later.[34]

Media attention increased the fame of Roswell and its myth. On September 1989 the television series *Unsolved Mysteries*, hosted by the grave Robert Stack, broadcasted an episode titled 'Roswell'. Stack began the show by stating something strange happened at Roswell in 1947. From there it proceeded to the standard Roswell narrative of Mack Brazel's and Jesse Marcel's encounters with crash debris. Although Jesse Marcel died in 1986, his son Jesse Jr, who was eleven years old in 1947, was brought in to talk about the unearthly debris. From there the documentary moved on to the alleged Socorro flying saucer crash that occurred on the same day as the Roswell crash. It was discovered by the soil conservation officer Grady 'Barney' Barnett and a band of wandering and anonymous archaeology students. This crash included alien bodies. Barnett died in 1969 so his story only came to light because he told it to his friend Vern Maltais. Next the MJ-12 document was discussed with its seeming corroboration of a flying saucer crash and dead aliens. Unfortunately, the MJ-12 document had been thoroughly debunked, but diehard ufologists refused to let it die. The documentary went back and forth between the official military version of the Roswell Incident and the UFO crash version put forward by supposedly reliable witnesses. Millions viewed this show, which introduced a more complex version of the myth of the Roswell UFO crash. Many more got to see it when it was rerun on 24 January 1990.[35]

The myth of Roswell got another boost when the Showtime cable network aired the docudrama *Roswell* on 31 July 1994 (it was alternatively titled *Roswell: The UFO Cover-up*). The script was based on Randle and Schmitt's *UFO Crash at Roswell*. The plot of the film focuses on the experiences of Jesse Marcel. It portrays Marcel as believing that the crash was an extraterrestrial craft from the start. Of course, the historical record shows that is simply not true about either Marcel or people in general. In 1947 the standard position on flying saucers and UFOs was that they were very much of earthly origins, being either American or Russian experimental aircraft. Sheridan Cavitt's name is changed to Sherman Carter in the film. He is portrayed as a mysterious and somewhat spooky intelligence officer from the Pentagon who is engaged in the cover-up and obstructs Marcel's search for the truth. The film depicts the presentation of the crash debris in General Ramey's office as a substitute of the otherworldly artefacts with balloon debris. Marcel's career is ruined by the Roswell Incident as he is labelled as an unsound officer who jumped to a fantastical and groundless conclusion about a crashed alien spacecraft.[36]

As the film continues, Mack Brazel is portrayed as knowing the truth but being intimidated and bought off to aid the cover-up. It also reveals that aerial reconnaissance did discover a crashed flying saucer a bit crumpled up against a cliff with dead alien bodies scattered about. It goes on to incorporate Glenn Dennis's testimony about seeing flying saucer wreckage and dead alien bodies at the Roswell Army Air Field. There is an appearance of the nurse Naomi Self (renamed Janet Foss), who participated in the alien autopsy. Of course, one of the aliens is alive but badly injured and is taken to Area 51. It is a classic grey alien with a big head and eyes. There at Area 51, James Forrestal, a real historical person depicted in the film, goes to view the alien with other government officials. The dying alien communicates telepathically with Forrestal and informs him that more aliens of a different species are coming. Back in Roswell, a mysterious figure named Townshend (played by Martin Sheen) informs Marcel that the Roswell crash is just the tip of the iceberg of contact with aliens. There have been other landings, the aliens might be from a different universe, and they have been altering the biological evolution of humans. It is also revealed that Forrestal was working on a diary of his alien encounter. Before he is able to do anything about it, he is admitted to Bethesda Hospital where he commits suicide. A vague insinuation is made that there is more to that story. On that note the film ends with Marcel and his family revisiting the barren crash site. The film says that since Marcel's death in 1986, some 350 witnesses have been found to talk about the Roswell UFO crash, even though the government is no longer investigating the possibility of extraterrestrial life. Given the large numbers of people depicted clearing both crash sites and dealing with alien bodies and flying saucer wreckage on the Roswell Army Air Field, one would actually expect there to be many more witnesses. Time would also show that despite the film *Roswell*'s claim to be based on a true story, almost all that it presented had fallen apart as a result of the debunking of the late 1990s, as will be shown in the following pages.

Some weeks later on 18 September 1994, *Unsolved Mysteries* updated the Roswell myth when it aired a segment on the Roswell crash and Area 51 connection. Glenn Dennis, a recent co-founder and co-owner of the International UFO Museum in Roswell, tells his story about flying saucer wreckage and dead aliens. He is the basis for the character of the mortician portrayed in the *Roswell* film who got a call from the military about child-sized coffins. He also visited the base, saw the strange wreckage, met the nurse involved in the alien autopsy, got kicked off the base and afterwards met with the nurse who drew a picture of the aliens for him. As will be shown later, Glenn Dennis's testimony is contradictory and highly suspect. At this point the show turned to Area 51. It discussed speculations that wrecked alien technology was being reverse-engineered to be used by the United States military for the development of better aircraft. The show then concluded by saying it is clear that aliens from an advanced technological civilization are curious and are exploring the Earth.[37]

The myth of Roswell is protean. It changes and evolves according to circumstances. New versions of the Roswell story continued to appear before and after the television movie *Roswell* was being prepared and aired. In 1992 Friedman and his new co-author Don Berliner brought out *Crash at Corona: The United States Military Retrieval and Cover-up of a UFO*. The big difference from previous books is that Friedman and Berliner added a second crashed flying saucer. One saucer crashed near Brazel's ranch leaving four dead aliens, but now a second spacecraft about the same time crashed on the Plains of San Augustin about 150 miles away. This was the Grady Barnett crash. Apparently, it was very bad day for flying saucers.[38]

Friedman and Berliner's insertion of a second saucer crash created a schism in the UFO movement. Some supported it; others preferred the version in Randle and Schmitt's *UFO Crash at Roswell*. Overall, most people in the movement supported Randle and Schmitt. However, the UFO movement is fractious, and their book also suffered a lot of telling criticism. In response, they brought out *The Truth about the UFO Crash at Roswell* in 1994. They continued to reject the Plains of Augustin crash, but in the process, they add a new crash site. Once again, a flying saucer malfunctions and lands on the Brazel ranch on 4 July. When it tries to take off again, it comes back to Earth and ploughs a 500-foot-long gash in the ground and leaves some debris. The saucer manages to become airborne but instead of crashing a couple of miles away, it manages to fly 35 miles north of Roswell where it crashes and creates a whole new debris site. Radar at the White Sands base picks up the UFO so military personnel quickly arrive at the site to find a badly damaged spacecraft and four dead aliens with one still alive. Civilian witnesses are chased away after being warned to keep quiet about what they saw. The next day, on 5 July, Mack Brazel discovers the first landing site and debris and reports it to Sheriff Wilcox, who brings in the military.[39]

The same year a new player entered the controversies over the myth of Roswell: Karl T. Pflock. He worked for the CIA from 1966 to 1972 and served as a deputy assistant secretary for defence during the Reagan administration. In 1992 he became a professional UFO investigator and brought out his *Roswell in Perspective* for the Fund for UFO Research in 1994. In this report Pflock asserted that most UFO sightings were really Project Mogul balloons, making him the first person to thrust that highly sensitive, secret programme into UFO and Roswell controversies. He also rejected the authenticity of the MJ-12 report and the testimony of key witnesses used by the Berlitz and Moore and the Friedman and Berliner books. Furthermore, he argued that much of the evidence presented by Randle and Schmitt in their first book was also unreliable. He suggested that a downed Mogul balloon was the source for most of the debris found by Mack Brazel, although a malfunctioning alien spacecraft may have collided with the Mogul balloon. In this scenario, three dead aliens and flying saucer wreckage were mixed in with the Mogul balloon debris. The Roswell Army Air Field commander Colonel William Blanchard had Lieutenant Walter Haut prepare the fateful press release about the recovery of the crashed flying saucer. But Blanchard did not know about the dead aliens. So, both the Strategic Air Command and Project Mogul created stories to cover up the alien contact and the top-secret project. Although professing to be a pro-ufologist, Pflock's report began the process of discrediting the myth of Roswell.[40]

One of the stranger books to appear in the evolution of the myth of Roswell was published in 1997. It was Philip J. Corso's *The Day after Roswell*, which was timed to coincide with the fiftieth anniversary of the Roswell Incident. Corso served in the United States Army from 1942 to 1963, during which time he rose to the rank of lieutenant colonel. He served in army intelligence during the Second World War and dealt with prisoner of war affairs during the Korean War. From 1961 to 1963 he worked as chief of Foreign Technology under Lieutenant General Arthur Trudeau in the division of Army Research and Development in the Pentagon.

The Day after Roswell makes some astounding claims. Corso was nowhere near Roswell at the time of the alleged flying saucer incident, but he claimed it would have a big impact on his career. In July 1947 he was stationed at Fort Riley and saw trucks conveying mysterious materials to the Wright Army Air Field (now Wright-Patterson Air Force Base) while he was on guard duty. He did a bit of snooping in the trucks' cargo and discovered they were carrying the wreck of some spacecraft. He also saw a dead alien body. This cargo was from the flying saucer crash that had occurred at Roswell. It would not be Corso's last Roswell encounter.[41]

Corso appears to have been a protégé of General Trudeau, and in 1961 the general hired him to head up the Foreign Technology desk at the Pentagon. After arriving to assume his duties, Trudeau told him about the artefacts and wreckage that the military had acquired from the Roswell crash. Everyone realized these materials were important, but until Trudeau took charge no one had tried to reverse engineer them into useful technology. Trudeau assigned Corso the task of getting the Roswell materials into the hand of the research and development divisions of the proper defence contractors. Corso learned from Wernher von Braun and Willy Ley that Nazi Germany had somehow also acquired alien technology that they used to create some of their wonder weapons. According to Corso, control of the alien technology was in the hands of a secret group that sounds a lot like the Majestic-12.[42]

From that point, Corso's account becomes even more incredible. Ufologists had claimed for some years that the government was studying the alien wreckage from Roswell and other UFO crashes. Corso provides the details of how night-vision goggles, fibre optics, lasers, integrated circuits, irradiated food, particle beams and electromagnetic propulsion systems, among other things, were all the fruits of knowledge gleaned from alien technology. Supposedly, much of this technological progress was due to the stewardship of Corso and Trudeau. But not all, as Corso humbly admits that it was thanks to General Trudeau sharing some of the Roswell technology with Bell Labs and Motorola in 1947 that led to the development of transistors.[43]

Needless to say, the military was very interested in acquiring alien technology from crashed flying saucers. To facilitate that enterprise, it established two secret projects. One was Project Moon Dust, which created teams to rapidly and quietly recover crashed alien craft. Clearly, the aliens had a lot of trouble with malfunctioning or poorly piloted flying saucers. The other programme was Project Blue Fly, which provided the transportation to get the alien wreckage safely and secretly to Wright-Patterson Air Force Base where it could be studied.[44]

Not only did Corso and Trudeau anonymously orchestrate a technological revolution in the United States during the second half of the twentieth century, but they played a role in saving humanity from invasion and conquest by some malevolent alien invaders. According to his account, it would appear that Corso was one of the only loyal Americans working in the Pentagon in 1961. Apparently, President Kennedy's cabinet included people who were dupes of or actual secret agents for the Soviet Union. The CIA was infiltrated by the KGB and ineffective as well. Even back in 1947, the base at Alamogordo, which developed the atomic bomb, contained some Russian spies – which was true. In Corso's version, those Russian spies also informed Stalin about the Roswell flying saucer crash and recovery. That information made Stalin very unhappy, and he wanted in on the harvest of the alien technology. These circumstances meant that Corso and Trudeau had to be careful to whom they gave access to the Roswell artefacts, lest they fall into the wrong hands.[45]

Far more startling, Corso went on to claim that after 1947 the Cold War became a cover story for the real conflict: the secret war with the alien invaders. This assertion would seemingly explain General Douglas MacArthur's cryptic comments at that time about possible invasion from outer space. Despite being disgruntled about not having their own supply of alien technology, Stalin and subsequent Soviet leaders recognized the dire threat posed by an alien invasion and covertly supported the United States in the struggle. Throughout the struggle, there were chronic anxieties among the American military that the Russians might make a separate treaty with the aliens. Foot-dragging and political and bureaucratic inertia plagued the efforts of Corso and others engaged in the covert war with the aliens. Finally, the American effort was galvanized by President Ronald Reagan. His Strategic Defense Initiative (SDI, also known as Star Wars) was publicly an anti-missile defence system that would protect the United States from attacks by Soviet intercontinental ballistic missiles carrying nuclear warheads. In reality, or rather in Corso's reality, Star Wars was actually a missile defence system based on alien technology that thwarted alien invaders. Reagan and the Soviet leader Mikhail Gorbachev had reached a secret agreement in which Star Wars would protect both Russia and the United States and presumably the rest of the world. Corso maintained that the anti-UFO weapons, which included particle beams, forestalled the impending invasion from outer space. And that was a very good thing, since he asserted that the aliens had evil intentions. In Corso's assessment, the United States military possessed weapons that are far better and more powerful than the weapons used against the alien invaders in the film *Independence Day*. That should be a relief to all humanity, since we cannot always count on Jeff Goldblum inserting a computer virus into an alien computer network or Randy Quaid destroying an alien battleship in a suicide attack. Someday the true story of this secret war with the aliens will come out, or so Corso said. Over twenty years later, that war still remains a secret except for Corso's revelations.[46]

The Day after Roswell sold very well at the time, some 250,000 copies, and continues to remain in print in multiple editions. Corso's contentions were rejected by both sceptics and mainstream ufologists. The relentless and meticulous researcher Philip Klass did a line-by-line examination of *The Day after Roswell* that revealed many factual errors and inconsistencies. Stanton Friedman and William L. Moore both went so far as to call the book pure fiction, which given the circumstances is not an outrageous statement. Another ufologist, the retired United States Army colonel John B. Alexander, takes a more sympathetic view of Corso, describing him as 'a consummate gentleman and basically a great guy'. Alexander actually met with Corso prior to the publication of *The Day after Roswell*. On 9 September 1994, after the book was published, he sent Corso a long letter containing a list of 92 factual errors and queries about Corso's sources. Furthermore, Alexander stated to Corso, 'This is not a complete list.' Attempting to look deep into Corso's claims, no evidence could be found to confirm that alien technology played a crucial role in American weapons development or that a secret war with aliens had occurred or was continuing. On the other hand, when interviewed, prominent people – who should have been in the know – did not support or contradict Corso's sensational contentions. Karl Pflock, the ufologist with a strong sceptical streak, reached the same conclusions as Klass and Friedman.

On first meeting him in 1994, Pflock came away with the impression that Corso was a 'blowhard'. One of Corso's claims to credibility was that the conservative senator Strom Thurmond wrote a foreword for *The Day after Roswell*. The problem was that Thurmond thought he was writing a foreword for a memoir about Corso's military and government career. When Thurmond found out that the book was about UFOS, he sent an irate demand to the publisher calling for his foreword to be removed from any future printings. It was not an episode that reflects well on Corso's integrity. Another supposed friend that Corso claimed was J. Edgar Hoover, the longtime director of the Federal Bureau of Investigation. In Corso's FBI file, however, Hoover wrote, 'Corso is a rat.'[47]

The Empiricists Strike Back: Roswell Debunked

From its very beginning, the UFO movement and the myth of Roswell have been vexed by hoaxers, charlatans, the delusions of overzealous true believers, schisms among ufologists and over-reliance on witnesses of shaky credibility. In October 1947 there were the Maury Island sightings of flying saucers by two men claiming to be harbour patrol. They turned out to be barely solvent salvagers of floating timber, who admitted the hoax when interrogated by Army Air Force intelligence officers. Another hoax started out as a prank. The editor of the *Aztec Independent Review* wrote a joking story about a flying saucer crash at Aztec, New Mexico. Unfortunately, the story was picked up by more than a hundred newspapers who published it as a true account. The ufologist Frank Scully used the Aztec story in his book *Behind the Flying Saucers* (1950). In fact, Scully was being duped by a couple of conmen – Silas M. Newton and Leo A. Gebauer – as revealed by the journalist J. P. Cahn in an article published in the September 1952 issue of *True*. It turned out that Newton and Gebauer had been defrauding a lot of people. Charges were brought against them in Denver and they were convicted. Scully refused to accept that he had been fooled, but the incident rendered crashed flying saucer stories toxic within the embarrassed UFO movement for 25 years. Most of the stories told about alien encounters by the so-called contactees, like George Adamski, also savoured of either delusion or outright deception.[48]

The myth of Roswell suffered from similar problems, including faulty memories. The books of Berlitz and Moore, Randle and Schmitt, Friedman and Berliner and Corso created the myth of Roswell and made it a national sensation. Part of their success can be attributed to their being based on seemingly reliable witnesses, but were they reliable? UFO sceptics and debunkers had their doubts and began to look closely at the testimony of the witnesses and other forms of evidence. Between 1986 and 1990 the veteran UFO debunker Philip J. Klass published four articles in *Skeptical Inquirer* that thoroughly debunked the MJ-12 documents as forgeries. These Majestic documents purported to show that at the highest level of government the existence of UFOs, crashed flying saucers and dead aliens was known and being hidden from the public. Furthermore, the Majestic 12 was a super-secret commission that oversaw UFO-related affairs. The problem was that the whole story was based on forged or grossly misinterpreted documents. Of course, true believers rejected or ignored Klass's research.[49]

A new history of the UFO movement appeared in 1994: *Watch the Skies! A Chronicle of the Flying Saucer Myth* by Curtis Peebles, an aerospace history contractor at NASA's Dryden Flight Research Center. It traces the evolution of concepts about UFOs and alien visitors as they have developed over time. Reports of what UFOs and alien spacecraft looked like have progressively changed, with many variations. There has also been a wide diversity of aliens ranging from bug-eyed monsters to beautiful blonde Aryan-type humans. For now, however, the image of the alien has stabilized on the short, grey humanoid with a big head and big eyes. The problem is that the image of aliens has tended to parallel how fictional aliens have been depicted in comic books, science fiction stories, films and television. Again, it appears life, or more accurately modern myth, was imitating art, or rather popular culture. Peebles's genealogical approach to the lore of ufology called into question the plausibility of the myth of Roswell just as the fame of that myth was reaching its zenith.[50]

One of the first studies to raise serious doubts about a UFO crashing at Roswell was Karl T. Pflock's preliminary report, *Roswell in Perspective*, in 1994. It suggested that what really crashed at Roswell was actually a Project Mogul balloon. His suggestion was soon bolstered by the publication in 1995 of the United States Air Force's *The Roswell Report: Fact versus Fiction in the New Mexico Desert*. It thoroughly documented Project Mogul and its connections to UFO sightings and crashes. Many UFO sightings were really people seeing Project Mogul balloons high up in the sky. The problem was that in 1947 Project Mogul balloons were a highly secret means for spying on the Russian nuclear weapons programme. Naturally, the government wanted to conceal the existence of the programme and avoid any attention to crashed Mogul balloons. At that level, ufologists were correct: there had been a government cover-up at Roswell. It just was not the cover-up of a crashed flying saucer. The revelation of Project Mogul also put a new light on the testimony of the 41 people who had seen the Roswell debris and the scrambling around by the personnel of the Roswell Army Air Field in early July 1947. What they saw was the military trying to keep Project Mogul secret. This explanation was simple and plausible. It fit very well with what the witnesses has been reporting. Later debunking books would continue to make the same telling argument.[51]

The year 1997 saw the publication of two more well-researched and lucidly written books that critically analysed the credibility of the myth of Roswell. One was UFO *Crash at Roswell: The Genesis of a Modern Myth* by Benson Saler, Charles A. Ziegler and Charles B. Moore, which for the most part took an anthropological approach. As the title indicates, Saler and Ziegler consider the story of Roswell and a flying saucer to be a myth. The term 'myth' has many definitions or meanings, so it is important to understand how Saler and Ziegler define it. For them, in the context of Roswell, myth is 'a story that many people say they believe: a story about an alien ship that crashed'. They identify the myth of Roswell as 'a story of folk narrative . . . that is not treated as factual in the annals of our society, but is avowedly believed to be true by many of its members . . . and that deals with transcendental issues'. As Saler and Ziegler point out, some myths like Roswell's are not conventionally religious, but they 'deal with transcendental issues related to the human condition . . . that is perhaps most aptly expressed by poetic imagery'. The myth of Roswell reassures us that we are not alone in the universe and that life has meaning. This aspect of the myth of Roswell explains why so many people want to believe it. This latter reassurance is further reinforced by the *Ancient Aliens* myth that extraterrestrial visitors have been influencing human evolution and history for untold thousands of years.[52]

Utilizing the concept of the myth of Roswell as a folk narrative, Saler and Ziegler analyse the testimony of the Roswell witnesses. They view them and the Roswell authors as storytellers or traditors (a term in folklore studies for a person who conveys a group's traditions or beliefs effectively). The witnesses are oral traditors who tell their stories to others. Roswell authors are literary traditors who perform the function of putting together all the Roswell stories into a logical and coherent narrative in written form. Both types of traditors operate on some mixture of psychological and economic rewards. Witnesses' rewards are usually psychological: that is, the pleasure of telling their story to avid listeners. UFO writers' rewards tend to be more financial. Many people have made money writing about UFOs, including the myth of Roswell, through book royalties and paid appearances on television or radio. Some UFO writers have turned it into a profession, occasionally a quite lucrative one. The problem is that there is a natural tendency for the witnesses to embellish their stories. It is particularly true when the witness is testifying about events thirty or more years in the past. If the memory is incomplete, witnesses tend to fill in the gaps to make it complete. There is also a tendency to make a story more interesting so that it will attract more appreciative listeners. It also might attract a tabloid newspaper, radio or television interview which could involve paid travel or a fee. For the literary traditors, being increasingly sensationalistic also attracts more attention which leads to more television appearances or book sales. Some of these embellishments would be largely unconscious, but in some cases they could be a conscious deception. Examples of these sorts of embellishment will be looked at in more detail when the cases of Glenn Dennis, Frank Kaufman, Gerald F. Anderson and Jim Ragsdale are examined. Meanwhile, the myth of Roswell functions as both folk narrative and myth. It gives its audience what they want: to know their place in the universe, to know that there is purpose and meaning to existence and to be entertained. The empirical truth of the myth of Roswell is not an important consideration to those who want to believe.[53]

UFO *Crash at Roswell* also contains a chapter by Charles B. Moore, 'The Early New York University Balloon Flights', along with two appendices. Moore was in charge of the Project Mogul balloons at the Alamogordo Army Air Field during 1947. He believes it was one of his balloons that crashed on Mack Brazel's ranch in 1947 and that provided the circumstantial foundation for the initial appearance of the myth of Roswell in 1978–80. Moore provides some compelling circumstantial evidence for his claim, unless you are a ufologist who dismisses all evidence debunking the myth of Roswell as just another part of the government's cover-up.

Other debunking books appeared in 1997. The tenacious Philip J. Klass brought out *The Real Roswell Crashed-Saucer Coverup*, which turned the ufologists' persistent accusation of government cover-up on its head. He proceeded to demonstrate over and over how ufologists leave out pertinent facts and evidence that would weaken or even demolish the myth of Roswell. In addition, they continue to use Roswell tales that have been thoroughly debunked. In the same year, another UFO sceptic, Kal K. Korff, published a very similar book: *The Roswell UFO Crash: What They Don't Want You to Know*. An updated edition of Korff's book was published by Dell as a mass-market paperback in 2000. It included an extensive critique of Corso's *The Day after Roswell*.[54]

Then in 2001 the renegade ufologist Karl T. Pflock followed up *Roswell in Perspective* with yet another more complete debunking of the Roswell evidence with *Roswell: Inconvenient Facts and the Will to Believe*. In the following year, Pflock published a zany history of the UFO movement and his role in it: *Shockingly Close to the Truth! Confessions of a Grave-Robbing Ufologist*. It was co-authored with James W. Moseley and again it expresses a high level of scepticism about whether the Roswell crash ever occurred.[55]

Needless to say, all three of these sceptical authors have been and remain the targets of derision by believers in UFOs and the myth of Roswell. Klass has been pejoratively dubbed a 'pseudosceptic' for alleged distortions and deceptions in his own use of evidence. Korff has even inspired a blogspot, 'Kalvin Korff is an idiot.'[56] Pflock occupies an uneasy position. He believed that UFOs are extraterrestrials visiting the Earth. At one time, he also believed that the myth of Roswell was a true event. A detailed examination of the evidence, however, changed his mind largely due to the crumbling and final collapse of the credibility of Glenn Dennis. As a result, he is respected in some segments of the UFO movement but not others, including adherents of the myth of Roswell.

The discovery and appearance of a growing number of alleged eye-witnesses to a cover-up was the biggest reason for the Roswell Incident being boosted from a forgotten episode of miscommunication into a myth that became a cornerstone of the UFO movement. The ufologist Stanton Friedman was at the forefront of this process that gave the myth of Roswell apparent credibility. He pioneered the quest for Roswell witnesses. As more and more witnesses emerged during the 1980s, they vied to have the most compelling and most telegenic story in order to get a documentary inter-view. With all this testimony, contradictions and incompatibilities soon appeared among the eyewitnesses' accounts and even within the accounts that individual eyewitnesses have provided at various times. Things were asserted as facts that conflicted with times and locations provided by exist-ing public records. As a result, sceptics like Klass, Korff and Pflock among others began to focus on the flaws in the eyewitnesses' stories.

One of the witness accounts that attracted considerable scrutiny was that of Gerald F. Anderson. After watching the *Unsolved Mysteries* epi-sode dealing with Roswell in 1989 and 1990, he came forward with the claim that he and his family were visiting the Plains of San Augustin at the time of the UFO crash that allegedly took place there. They saw the crashed spaceship, dead aliens and one live one, Grady Barnett and the group of archaeologists. It was stunning confirmation of Friedman's account of the Roswell flying saucer crash. Now Anderson was only five at the time, and unfortunately by the time he came forward everyone else in his family was dead and so were unable to confirm his story (or deny it). To bolster Anderson's story, his alleged cousin Vallejean Anderson, a Catholic nun, sent Stanton Friedman several pages from 1947 in the diary kept by Anderson's Uncle Ted. These pages discussed the crash. The problem was that the ink on the supposed pages of the diary was not in use before 1972. In response, Gerald Anderson claimed the pages were not from the original diary but had been copied by hand by Uncle Ted. Once again, chronology raised its ugly, debunking head: Uncle Ted died in 1965. Another problem was that Anderson had never mentioned his UFO encounter to anyone else prior to his coming forward in 1990. This reticence included his ex-wife and his employer, the sheriff of Taney County, Missouri.[57]

Glenn Dennis is a far more important witness to the events at Roswell. Now one of the owners of the International UFO Museum, in 1947 he was in his early twenties and worked as a mortuary technician at the Ballard Funeral Home in Roswell. During the late 1980s, Walter Haut, the author of the Roswell flying saucer press release and a resident of Roswell, heard about Dennis's UFO story. He suggested that Friedman talk to Dennis, which took place in early August 1989. Dennis claimed that at the time of the Roswell crash, he had used the Ballard hearse to transport an injured soldier to the Roswell Army Air Field's hospital. On the base, he observed ambulances full of wreckage and military police swarming around. Inside the hospital he encountered a nurse he was acquainted with, who asked him what he was doing there. She warned him that he was going to get himself killed. At that point military police intervened, ordered him out of the hospital and off the base, and even followed him back to the funeral home. Later he met the nurse for lunch and drinks at the base officer's club. There she told him about two doctors who had commandeered her to assist in the autopsy of an alien. She drew a picture of the alien and swore him to secrecy. Soon after, she was transferred from Roswell to England. When he tried to write her, his letter was returned, marked 'deceased'. Later he heard that she had died in a plane accident.

As time went by Dennis altered his story, adding some details and backtracking on others. Initially, he claimed that the nurse's drawings had disappeared. Later he admitted that he had given the pictures to the UFO researchers Kevin Randle and Donald Schmitt to use in their book, *UFO Crash at Roswell*. All supposed efforts by Randle and Schmitt to locate the nurse failed. In fact, they claimed that no information about any nurses serving at Roswell could be found. This circumstance only added to the suspicion of a government cover-up swirling around the Roswell Incident. Dennis added the claim that the nurse had become a nun and had died. He also added the detail that he had seen three dead aliens. All of these juicy details catapulted Dennis into the status of a Roswell celebrity witness for documentaries, TV and radio appearances and interviews. In 1994 he declared he had experienced a 'blinding flash of recall'. He now remembered that a call he had received from the Roswell base inquiring about child-sized coffins had occurred on 7 July, which in turn dated his lunch meeting with the nurse to 8 July.

The problem for Dennis was that the more detail he added to his story, the more facts there were to check. In 1995 the freelance writer Paul McCarthy proposed a sympathetic article about Roswell to *Omni* magazine. *Omni* was interested but insisted that he examine the claims about the missing nurses. McCarthy feared the search would be fruitless since Randle and Schmitt claimed they had searched in vain for several years. Instead, when McCarthy got started, he quickly tracked down the nurses in three days through telephone inquiries to the appropriate records repositories. At that point, McCarthy contacted Randle and Schmitt about his locating the nurses. Randle was chagrined while Schmitt was elusive, dodging calls and directing McCarthy to unhelpful research assistants. In the article that followed, 'The Missing Nurses of Roswell', McCarthy stated that Randle and Schmitt's evidence was either insufficient or fabricated. Putting it bluntly, he wrote, 'They have been caught with their pants down.' This embarrassing revelation created a crack in Randle and Schmitt's writing partnership that would ultimately break down completely, as will be discussed later.[58]

The revelations about the missing nurses of Roswell not being missing also put a spotlight back on Glenn Dennis's nurse story. He had confidentially named her to Stanton Friedman during an interview on 5 August 1989. Later he provided her name to Randle and Schmitt and then to Karl Pflock. The nurse's name was Naomi Self or later Naomi Maria Selff. The problem was that no nurse named Self or Selff appears in the military personnel records and the surviving Roswell nurses could not remember her, Dennis or any hubbub at the hospital over aliens during 1947. When pressed further, Dennis admitted he had not provided the nurse's real name to anyone since he had promised to keep her identity secret until she died. Since he did not know if she was alive or not, he was obliged to keep his word and, in the process, provided a great example of a Catch-22. There were other evasions and changes in Dennis's story as well. All in all, grave doubts arose about Dennis's veracity with both Randle and Pflock, former supporters. Of course, Klass and Korff never gave his story much credence in the first place. Another piece of eyewitness testimony was decisively discredited.[59]

Frank J. Kaufman is another crucial witness whose testimony supported the myth of Roswell. His first appearance as a witness occurred in 1991 in Randle and Schmitt's first book, UFO *Crash at Roswell*. There all he provided was hearsay testimony about the Roswell crash. In Randle and Schmitt's second book, *The Truth about Roswell*, he was given the pseudonym Steve McKenzie and claimed to have seen a live alien being walked into the base hospital for Roswell. He also claimed to be tracking UFOS on radar at the White Sands base. In addition, he confirmed that calls had been made to the Ballard Funeral Home that seemingly confirmed Dennis's account, although some details of the two men's stories contradicted each other. Kaufman also claimed to have been a member of a nine-man recovery team sent to the flying saucer crash site. All of this is more than a little odd since Kaufman was working on the Roswell base as a civilian. He also refused to have his diary and other corroborating documents forensically tested. It was a set of tales that only a true believer could swallow, and Klass, Korff and Pflock were not biting.[60]

Jim Ragsdale was another witness who was discovered later and interviewed by Randle and Schmitt on 26 January 1993. According to Ragsdale, he and his girlfriend Trudy Truelove were parked in the country north of Roswell in early July. While they were enjoying each other's company, there was a crash nearby which caused them to leave the scene. The next morning, however, they returned and found the wreckage of a spacecraft and several dead aliens. Soon after, a military recovery team arrived which prompted the couple to depart once again. This crash site was about 35 miles north of Roswell. By the time Ragsdale came forward in 1993, Trudy Truelove had died and was not available to back up his account. While he was not sure about the date of the crash, he was certain that it was during the Fourth of July weekend. In 1947, the Fourth fell on a Friday. Ragsdale's timely appearance supported Glenn Dennis's testimony. It also introduced a new crash site many miles east of the original crash site on Mack Brazel's ranch. This new information allowed Randle to assert that what happened at the new Ragsdale crash site was a real flying saucer crash while the Brazel crash site was simply the downed remains of a weather balloon or Project Mogul balloon.[61]

Like other witnesses, Ragsdale's story also began to shift and expand. On 16 October 1994, Randle announced at a UFO meeting in Pensacola that Ragsdale had changed his story significantly. In the new version, Ragsdale changed the location of his crash site to 55 miles west of Roswell. Another new detail was Ragsdale's claim that he had tried to remove one of the dead aliens' helmet and saw his black eyes. He also described the aliens' appearance somewhat differently from that in previous accounts. Furthermore, Ragsdale claimed that he and Truelove had picked up several sacks full of debris from the wreck, but they had inexplicably gone missing over the intervening years. Ragsdale's shifting or shifty account prompted Randle to accuse him of changing his story as a result of a financial partnership with officials of the International UFO Museum that had been reached on 10 September. In the agreement, the new crash location would be named 'The Jim Ragsdale Impact Site', and Ragsdale would receive 25 per cent of the gross income generated by promotion of the site. Presumably there would be tours of the site and entrance fees. There would also be a booklet, 'The Jim Ragsdale Story', a video and T-shirts sold at the museum's gift shop. Max Littell, Walter Haut and Glenn Dennis in early 1994 had attempted to buy the land on which the first Ragsdale crash site was located. Its owner, Hub Corn, refused to sell. He would later allow tourists to visit Ragsdale's original crash site for a charge of $15. It was at this point that Randle lost faith in the trustworthiness of Ragsdale's claims.[62]

The year 1995 was a bad one for Donald R. Schmitt, one of the leading ufologists investigating the Roswell crash and co-author with Kevin D. Randle of UFO Crash at Roswell (1991) and The Truth about the UFO Crash at Roswell (1994). Schmitt's calling as a ufologist began with an interest in government cover-ups involving the Kennedy assassination. From there he moved on to UFOs and the related cover-ups. This interest led to his involvement with the Center for UFO Studies that J. Allen Hynek helped to found in 1973.[63] Schmitt claimed to have worked with Hynek but apparently not enough to warrant a mention in a recent biography of Hynek.[64] When The Roswell Incident appeared in 1980 and the promise of more eyewitness testimony loomed, CUFOS became interested. They sent Schmitt to investigate in 1988 and he asked Randle to join him. Their own books on Roswell were the eventual fruits of this collaboration. Both books sold well and came out in mass-market paperback editions. UFO sceptics did not find the books persuasive since they were based on so much problematic and vague witness testimony. Some fellow ufologists also disliked the books because Randle and Schmitt's narrative conflicted with their own version of the myth of Roswell.[65]

Success brought journalistic attention to Randle and Schmitt which proved to be a double-edged sword, at least for Schmitt. In June 1993, the freelance writer Gillian Sender wrote a very complimentary article about Schmitt for the Shepherd Express, a weekly Milwaukee newspaper. It was a local-boy-makes-good sort of story, as Schmitt lived in Hubertus, a small town near Milwaukee. About the time that The Truth about the UFO Crash at Roswell came out, Sender decided to do a second article about Schmitt for the monthly Milwaukee Magazine. The article 'Out of this World' appeared February 1995 issue. In the course of researching the story, Sender discovered some disturbing facts. In 1990 Schmitt had made claims to having a bachelor's degree from Concordia College and a masters from the University of Wisconsin at Milwaukee. He also claimed to have attended Marquette University and to be working on a PhD in criminal justice at Concordia College. Records showed these claims about his degrees and education to be false. Concordia College did not even offer a PhD in criminal justice. After examining the Randle and Schmitt books, Sender observed that the documentation was vague and had to rely on the reader's confidence in the scrupulousness and trustworthiness of the two authors. When asked to provide more information about his documentation, Schmitt declined to return phone calls. It was becoming clear that Schmitt's research lacked integrity. Initially, Randle was quick to defend Schmitt. The next issue of the *Milwaukee Magazine*, however, contained more bad news. It published an anonymous letter stating that Schmitt worked as a full-time mail carrier in Hartford, Wisconsin. That alone would have been no great revelation. Many ufologists have day jobs to pay the bills, and being a mail carrier is an honourable occupation. The problem lay in the fact that Schmitt claimed to be a medical illustrator but no evidence of this career was forthcoming. Schmitt had also made claims about having worked undercover for the Drug Enforcement Administration along with other clandestine employment that bolstered his credentials to investigate UFOs. When confronted, he denied being a postman. Subsequent revelations confirmed that he was, in fact, a postal worker, much to Randle's discomfiture. At that point, Randle repudiated Schmitt. Soon after that Schmitt resigned as director of special investigations for CUFOS. Unabashed, Schmitt spread a rumour that Randle was actually a government agent working to keep the truth about Roswell from coming out: a common tactic of desperate ufologists.[66]

Schmitt's troubles were not over. The revelations about Glenn Dennis's fraudulent claims about Roswell and the missing nurses were becoming public. Paul McCarthy's article, 'The Missing Nurses of Roswell', in the autumn 1995 issue of *Omni* revealed that Schmitt's research techniques were shoddy and inept at best and were likely disingenuous as well. The appearance of the *Omni* article caused Randle to write an open 'To Whom It May Concern' letter to the ufological community on 10 September 1995. Randle distanced himself from Schmitt in no uncertain terms. He stated, 'Let me now point out that I do not believe anything that Schmitt says and neither should you . . . I am not sure he understands the truth.' That said, not all of the problems with the soundness of the two Randle and Schmitt books were solely connected to Schmitt's fraudulent research or the growing problems with the witness testimony. Less than two weeks after Randle's open letter appeared, Robert Todd, another UFO sceptic, mocked Randle's attempt to place all the blame on Schmitt in an online essay, 'Randle Dumps – And Dumps – on – Schmitt', dated 22 September

1995. Thus ended a ufological partnership and started Randle's growing doubts about the myth of Roswell. On the other hand, Schmitt emerged unashamed and unapologetic, and he continues to publish books with a new co-author, Thomas Carey.[67]

Roswell documentaries continued to proliferate with most being long on sensationalism and short on reliable evidence. An exception was the television series *History's Mysteries*, which aired an episode, 'Roswell: Secrets Unveiled', in 1999. The series used a format in which rival interpretations of a mystery were given a chance to make their case to the viewers. In 'Roswell: Secrets Unveiled', it was the ufologists insisting a flying saucer crash with dead alien bodies had been covered up by the government versus the sceptics who asserted that a Project Mogul balloon had crashed. In spite of the thorough debunking, Glenn Dennis's story about Nurse Self and the alien autopsy was presented as fact. In response, sceptics suggested that Dennis's story was a confabulation arising out of some military airplane crashes that occurred in the region around Roswell. Nothing was mentioned about Dennis's shifting versions of his story or the missing nurse problem that had come to light. The documentary closed on a sceptical note. Michael Shermer, the editor of *Skeptic* magazine, observed that the case of the myth of Roswell 'will never be closed, the mystery is more compelling than the solution.' He also mentioned that there is a profit motive for keeping the myth alive. The city of Roswell benefits greatly from the tourism that the myth generates. Shermer considers Roswell to be an example of mass hysteria and urban legend that will rank among the top ten myths of the second half of the twentieth century. In fact, it continues to rank high in the twenty-first century as well.[68]

Michael Shermer and the people at *Skeptic* continue to apply critical thinking to the UFO phenomenon including the myth of Roswell. The first issue of *Skeptic* for 2003 focused on UFOs and had a hard-hitting essay by B. D. 'Duke' Gildenberg which drew on his experience working with Charles Moore on Project Mogul. He explained how the real Roswell crash was a Mogul balloon not a flying saucer manned by extraterrestrials. From there he discussed the emergence of the myth of Roswell from the late 1970s to the first few years of the twenty-first century. After the discovery of Jesse Marcel in the late 1970s, the ufologist Stanton Friedman and others began a quest for more and more witnesses. It has been pointed out, however, by the sceptic Kal Korff that Jesse Marcel had never considered an extraterrestrial explanation for the Roswell crash until ufologists suggested it to him while they were interviewing him. From that point onwards, the witness testimony morphed into wilder and wilder accounts. Gildenberg paid special attention to the flaws of Glenn Dennis's testimony. At the same time, he also pointed out the very evident ambiguities that arise when elderly informants are interviewed about events that took place forty or more years in the past. He went on to reiterate Philip Klass's revelations of how ufologists engage in their own cover-up when they suppress evidence that is contrary to the myth of Roswell. Inconvenient facts are not allowed to get in the way of a good story. Most telling is the fact that Gildenberg was writing some 55 years after the crash at Roswell. In the intervening time, not a shred of supposedly reliable witness testimony has withstood critical scrutiny nor has one piece of physical evidence of a UFO been found. What is more remarkable is that no physical evidence has been recovered despite the alleged multiple flying saucer crashes by aliens advanced enough to engage in successful interstellar travel. That point has been made by many sceptics who study UFO crashes. As Gildenberg concludes, 'Roswell is the world's most famous, most exhaustively investigated and most thoroughly debunked UFO claim. It's far past time for ufologists to admit it and move on.'[69]

Roswell Abides, Dude

Of course, the myth of Roswell is not moving on. The mid- to late 1990s may have been the myth's zenith, but since then it has remained a very healthy component of popular culture and the UFO movement. Roswell is still visited by significant numbers of UFO tourists and the International UFO Museum has plenty of visitors. The popular culture of science fiction in the form of magazine stories, books, films and television series has been an ally of the UFO movement from its very beginning.[70] H. G. Wells's classic *War of the Worlds* first appeared as a magazine serialization in 1897, fifty years before the Roswell incident, and in book form a year later. It introduced the public not only to the idea of extraterrestrial spacecraft visiting the Earth, but to the concept of an alien invasion. People clearly found the concept compelling and plausible since Orson Welles's adaptation of the novel set off a major panic when it was broadcast over the radio in 1938. The beginning of the UFO movement in 1947 quickly spawned flying saucer films – some classics, some classless. Two of the classics – *The Thing from Another World* (1951) and *The Day the Earth Stood Still* (1951) – were based on science fiction stories: respectively, a novella, 'Who Goes There?', by John W. Campbell from 1938 and a short story, 'Farewell to the Master', by Harry Bates from 1940. Both these stories pre-date the UFO movement and demonstrate that the idea of aliens visiting the Earth had been quite imaginable prior to 1947.[71]

Science fiction quickly embraced the myth of Roswell. The popular television series *The X-Files* depicted various aspects of UFO phenomena and speculations in its plots from abductions to cattle mutilations to alien infiltration. Some episodes included references, both passing and detailed, to Roswell. The made for TV movie *Roswell* that appeared on Showtime during 1994 helped to increase the myth of Roswell's public name recognition, as did the very popular theatrical film *Independence Day* (1996). Stanton Friedman readily acknowledged the important role of *The X-Files* and *Independence Day* in thrusting the myth of Roswell into the mainstream.[72] Television documentaries about UFOs periodically brought Roswell back into the public eye. The History Channel's *UFO Files* aired 41 episodes from 2004 to 2007, of which ten were about Roswell or used Roswell in the episode's title, such as 'Chinese Roswell' or 'Brazil's Roswell'. In 1998 the first of the *Roswell High* series of young adult novels appeared and continued to appear – two alien survivors are adopted by local humans and get to experience the very alien world of an American high school. The books were quickly adapted into a television series called *Roswell*. It ran for three seasons from 1999 to 2002 on the WB channel for seasons one and two and on UPN for the third season. The CW channel revived the series in 2019 as *Roswell, New Mexico*. The characters from *Roswell* are now twenty- or thirty-somethings. The premise apparently works for someone since the series has been renewed for a second and third season as of January 2020.

A more powerful support for the myth of Roswell and the UFO movement in general is provided by the ostensible documentary series *Ancient Aliens*. The History Channel debuted the series on 8 March 2009. That episode has been called either a special or a pilot. Whichever it was, *Ancient Aliens* struck a chord with the twenty-first-century zeitgeist, and the History Channel ordered a season of five episodes of 90 minutes each. After the first season, individual episodes were shortened to 45 minutes while the number of episodes in each season was increased to between eight and fifteen. The show's fifteenth season began in early 2020. The Roswell crash still gets an occasional mention, and on 20 February 2020 a 'Relics of Roswell' aired.

In 2011 a new and unique version of the myth of Roswell appeared with the publication of Annie Jacobsen's *Area 51: An Uncensored History of America's Top Secret Military Base*.[73] Jacobsen, an investigative journalist, asserts that there were two flying saucer crashes at Roswell in July 1947, but they were not extraterrestrial in origin. As has been pointed out earlier, in 1947 it was generally assumed that flying saucers or UFOs were either secret U.S. experimental aircraft or secret Soviet experimental aircraft. According to Jacobsen, the crashed flying saucers at Roswell came from Russia. How that was possible is an enigma since no known aircraft in 1947 was capable of making the long flight from the Soviet Union to the United States and back again, or vice versa. Jacobsen contends the flying saucers or disc aircraft were either captured Nazi wonder weapons or were Russian copies based on the innovations and designs created by the brothers Walter and Reimar Horten, both top German aviation scientists. Neither the United States nor the Russian military managed to capture the Hortens. The Russians did manage to seize the Hortens' research materials and prototypes. The fiendishly crafty Stalin decided to use his flying saucer technology to create a panic in the United States. He wanted to spark an alarm similar to the one caused by Orson Welles's radio broadcast of *War of the Worlds* in 1938; indeed, he hoped that the new wave of hysteria would be nationwide and so intense that it would cripple U.S. air defences. To add to the shock, the flying saucers would be carrying some freakish 'alien' passengers.

As the Second World War ended, the diabolical Nazi medical scientist Dr Josef Mengele at Auschwitz was looking for a way to come out of the debacle of the Third Reich safely and hopefully prosperously. He contacted Stalin about continuing his experiments on humans for the Soviet Union. What caught Stalin's attention was Mengele's experiments that created deformed children. These experiments had produced victims with oversized heads and big eyes on small, stunted bodies; in other words, the experimental subjects looked quite a bit like the classic grey aliens. The proposed partnership between Stalin and Mengele never came to fruition but Stalin got his aliens. In 1947 the wretched children were packed into two flying saucers and were flown to the United States. There they ended up crashing in the vicinity of Roswell, New Mexico. The plan had been for the flying saucers to land, not crash, and have the 'aliens' emerge and frighten the Americans. Hysterical false sightings of flying saucers and calls to the authorities by tens of thousands of panic-stricken Americans would overwhelm the ability of the air defence system to respond. Instead, the U.S. military immediately repudiated initial newspaper reports about flying saucers with their story about weather balloons. As a result, any potential public frenzy was suppressed. The dead bodies of the deformed children and the wreckage of the flying saucers were clandestinely shipped to the Wright-Patterson base at Akron, Ohio. Four years later, the wreckage and bodies were transferred to Area 51. The U.S. military were well aware that the flying saucers were Soviet equipment since there was Russian labelling on them and that the deformed children were not extraterrestrial. So why did President Truman and the military not reveal to the world Stalin's depraved abuse of the deformed children? According to Jacobsen, it was because the Atomic Energy Commission was itself engaged in similar inhumane and illegal experiments on humans that actually continued into the 1980s.

What does Jacobsen present as evidence for her version of the alleged flying saucer crashes at Roswell? Her account is based on interviews with a long-retired engineer who worked for the company EG&G Special Projects Group, which was a contractor working for the government at Area 51. The engineer is not named by Jacobsen, and he supposedly told her that he had only revealed a small portion of the strange and terrible secrets of Area 51. Just to what extent Jacobsen relied on anonymous informants in the writing of her book is left somewhat vague, but it is clearly more than one person.

There are various aspects of Jacobsen's account of the Roswell incident that strain credulity. First, there clearly had to be a lot of people involved in the cover-up at the time and during the subsequent years. That said, only this anonymous engineer let a small amount about the horrors of Area 51 get out. Cover-ups and conspiracies just are not that successful at keeping secrets. Second, if Stalin had possessed Nazi flying saucers with remarkable flying ranges, why was this military technology not exploited any further? Jacobsen states that the people studying the wreckage of the flying saucers were particularly intrigued by the propulsion systems. The U.S. military and its contractors apparently never mastered or incorporated that technology into our aircraft. Were they unable to replicate or reverse-engineer the technology? That seems unlikely since the Germans invented it and the Russians were supposedly able to deploy the flying saucers. American technological expertise was at least as good as the USSR's. The fact is that Stalin did not have any flying saucers to send to Roswell. Jacobsen's account has been and remains thoroughly rejected by mainstream scientists and scholars along with other Area 51 retirees. It has been suggested that her anonymous informant may have been having a little fun and took advantage of her desire for a sensational story. What Jacobsen's Roswell story definitely shows is that 64 years after the incident, it is still possible to add another brick to the edifice of the myth of Roswell.[74]

At the beginning of 2019, the History Channel premiered a new historical drama series: *Project Blue Book*. The main protagonist is the actual historical figure J. Allen Hynek. His investigative partner and co-protagonist is Captain Michael Quinn, loosely based on the first director of Project Blue Book, Captain Edward J. Ruppelt. Each episode dramatizes a UFO incident from the late 1940s and early 1950s, and it is at least implied that an extraterrestrial spacecraft was involved. It has been pointed out that the episodes are full of factual inaccuracies and unwarranted speculations. Hynek is portrayed as a believer in UFOs almost from the start. In fact, Hynek was a sceptic until the mid- to late 1960s. Although the first season skipped Roswell, during January 2020 the second season presented a two-part episode focusing on the myth of Roswell. It is set shortly after the 20 January 1952 UFO flap over Washington, DC. The Project Blue Book investigators are sent to Roswell to put to rest the lingering story of a flying saucer crash. Of course, the military wants to cover up the truth. Along the way, characters based on Mack Brazel along with the thoroughly debunked Glenn Dennis and Jim Ragsdale make appearances. Needless to say, this whole two-part episode depicts a completely fictitious event as real while presenting Roswell tourism with some wonderful free advertising.

So where does the myth of Roswell stand over seventy years from the event and forty years from the emergence of the myth? One of its biggest original promoters, Kevin D. Randle, has been shaken and disillusioned by the thorough demolition of the major eyewitness testimony about the Roswell crash. The revelations about his trusted co-author Donald R. Schmitt's sloppy and possibly dishonest research have only added to Randle's woes and doubts. Like Karl Pflock, he continues to believe in and to write about UFOs, but his faith in the authenticity of the Roswell flying saucer crash has just about come to an end. Writing in 2016, Randle ambivalently or equivocally confessed:

I find myself drifting toward those who reject the extraterrestrial. At one time I was sure [about the truth of the Roswell flying saucer crash] but that was when we had all the robust testimony, much of which is now thoroughly discredited. I have hope that we'll find an answer and it might be extraterrestrial, but in today's world we just can't provide it.[75]

An unabashed and unrepentant Donald R. Schmitt has written nine books about Roswell and Area 51 since the revelations about his false claims about the research that he did (or actually did not) do. Seven of those books were co-authored with Thomas Carey, another ufologist. In Schmitt's *Cover-up at Roswell* (2017), he attempts to revive the claim that the memo held by General Roger Ramey in photographs taken during his 8 July 1947 press conference provides evidence of a cover-up. Supposedly, a digital blow-up of the text of the memo in Ramey's hand proves there was an effort to suppress the truth about the crash. Unfortunately, Schmitt's evidence of a cover-up is not convincing, since the photographic images of the memo do not provide a readable text. Interpretations of the memo in the photographs are all so much wishful thinking.[76]

Schmitt's books are not alone. Other Roswell books continue to appear. In 2017 Steven M. Greer published *Unacknowledged: An Exposé of the World's Greatest Secret* with an accompanying documentary. The book claimed that in 1947 three alien spacecraft were shot down near the Roswell Army Air Field. Other alien encounters have followed and, predictably, it is all being covered up by various governments.[77] D. W. Pasulka's *American Cosmic: UFOs, Religion, Technology* (2019) is written by a scholar of religion and published by a prestigious press. It devotes a fair amount of space to discussing Roswell and even gives an account of some fieldwork she conducted there. If this information gets a potential reader's hopes up, prepare to be disappointed. Yes, Pasulka visited Roswell in the company of two scientists who wish to remain anonymous. They are part of the so-called 'invisible college' of scholars who believe in UFOs and the preternatural or supernatural phenomena associated with them. Members of the invisible college keep these beliefs to themselves to avoid mockery and professional ostracism. So Pasulka labels her companions 'James' and 'Tyler' and proceeds to assure her readers that these men are amazing geniuses. Tyler is their guide at Roswell. Blindfolding Pasulka and James, he takes them to the site of a UFO crash from 1947 but it is not the Roswell event. The United States government recovered this particular spacecraft and cleared the crash site of debris. In case they missed some of it, they sowed the area with tin cans to confound people searching the area with metal detectors. Tyler, however, has supplied his companions with special metal detectors. Within a couple of hours James locates an artefact from the crash. Both James and Tyler identify it as otherworldly, absent any actual scientific testing. Remember, though, these guys are geniuses. Returning to civilization, James and Tyler keep the artefact and study it but do not share it with other scholars. So, all a reader of *American Cosmic* is asked to do is take several things on faith. First, accept that despite having the technology to conquer interstellar travel, alien spacecraft tend to crash a lot. (Thank goodness the starship *Enterprise* was better built and better piloted.) Second, somehow a crash site known to the government and cleared by it has actually managed to remain largely secret for over seventy years. Third, despite the government's cleaning of the site and the scattering of all those tin cans, James still manages to find artefacts from the crash. It is almost as if some unknown force or entity precipitated the artefact to give James a thrill.

Under the imprimatur of Oxford University Press, Pasulka has resurrected the style of witness testimony used by the ufologists to create the myth of Roswell during the 1980s and 1990s. She is not alone either, as a work by literary essayist James Gallant shows. Scientists and sceptics have always accepted that there are anomalies that are not explainable by science at this time. Eventually, however, the anomalies will be explained empirically and rationally. The new style of explaining UFOs shies away from claiming they are physical alien spacecraft that can be tested scientifically. Instead, UFOs are pronounced to be anomalies or manifestations caused by inter-dimensional visitors or time-travellers. Such preternatural or supernatural explanations of anomalies have the virtue of being unfalsifiable since they cannot be subjected to scientific testing. Pasulka and other like-minded people assert that these anomalies basically should just be accepted on faith. With a cultic milieu like that for support, it is no wonder that the myth of Roswell will never die.[78]

Why should Roswell ever die – or the UFO movement, for that matter? They are just harmless quirks of popular culture. Besides, many people take comfort in believing we are not alone in the universe and in some cases have even turned UFO beliefs into a religion. People watch *Ancient Aliens* because it is entertaining. It provides a lot of good chuckles for sceptics as they view the intellectual acrobatics that the talking heads use to bolster scientifically and historically absurd hypotheses about the past. Visiting the International UFO Museum at Roswell is a similar and equally fun experience. The exhibits provide information about the myth of Roswell in a museum setting. That information just happens to be thoroughly cherry-picked. Be that as it may, what harm is being done when some people believe in little grey men are visiting the Earth? It is sort of like asking what harm is being done by people who believe the Earth is flat. If you look at the situation just from that angle, the UFO movement and the myth of Roswell are largely harmless.

The problem is that the myth of Roswell and other UFO beliefs fall into the category of what the political scientist Thomas Milan Konda calls a conspiracy by cover-up. Such a conspiracy attracts new believers through a two-step process. First, there are some people who are temperamentally inclined to believe that the official explanation of some event or phenomenon is always a cover-up. Second, such people will then gravitate to a widely believed conspiracy theory. So, in the case of the myth of Roswell, they rejected the crashed balloon explanation and went with the cover-up of a flying saucer crash or crashes.[79] Now, when it comes to Roswell, there is no doubt that there was a cover-up. In fact, there is a choice between two cover-ups: it was the crash of either a balloon or a flying saucer. The United States government has long admitted to the first one, while the proof for the second is virtually non-existent. No matter, in conspiracy-theory thinking the lack of proof is simply more evidence of a cover-up by those in authority.

The UFO movement and its subset – the myth of Roswell – are phenomena that can be found throughout the world, particularly in relatively tolerant Western-style democracies, such as the United States and the United Kingdom. The political scientist Michael Barkun has pointed out that the level of popular belief in UFOs has been very stable over the last seventy years. More importantly, the level of belief is 'extraordinarily high', numbering in the 'tens of millions of believers' in the United States. The intensity with which people hold UFO beliefs varies greatly from a mild interest to a fanatical commitment.[80] Gallup conducted a poll about UFO beliefs in June 2019. It found that 68 per cent of Americans feel that the U.S. government knows 'more about UFOs than it is telling us', which is down from 71 per cent in 1996 when the last Gallup poll to ask about UFOs was conducted. Gallup decided to conduct the new poll because of recent news coverage of UFO videos released by the military along with the growing Storm Area 51 movement. It conducted a second poll in August 2019 that asked if people thought UFOs were alien spacecraft. A total of 33 per cent of those polled answered yes. The UFO movement is hardly a fringe movement in terms of its general popularity.[81]

During its early history, the UFO movement in the United States was largely apolitical. It just wanted the government to tell the truth about UFOs or rather what ufologists thought was the truth. That situation changed during the late 1980s. Some believers in UFOs began to add in the conspiracy of the New World Order. For some ufologists, the government was not just lying about UFOs and Roswell, it was lying about everything. Worse than that, they believed that a secret elite in the government was in league with alien visitors to enslave the human race or to replace it with an alien-human hybrid race. World government would be the end result. In other words, the alien conspiracy story arc of *The X-Files* was reality not fiction! Obviously, only a small portion of the UFO movement accepted the hybridized UFO conspiracy theory, but those who did included the hitherto respectable historian of the UFO movement David Michael Jacobs and the seemingly paranoid conspiracist Milton William Cooper.[82] Cooper would later shift to the former Scientologist Jim Keith's version of the UFO/New World Order conspiracy theory. In his *Saucers of the Illuminati* (1999), Keith contended that UFOs were not spacecraft from other planets. Instead, they were the products of Illuminati magic and were intended to divert the public's attention from the New World Order conspiracy of the Illuminati.[83]

With its millions of followers, the UFO movement had always been a semi-mainstream part of popular culture; its many books were published by prominent publishing houses, and it enjoyed frequent coverage by newspapers, magazines and television documentaries and regular appearances in science fiction novels, television shows and films. The New World Order conspiracy theories never received such attention. They were a much more disreputable form of stigmatized knowledge in comparison to the UFO movement.

When the overlap between UFO beliefs and New World Order beliefs appeared, it created a bridge for the New World Order conspiracy theories to assume a higher profile in popular culture and the media. In turn, this development further deepened many people's distrust of everything the government did or said, not just concerning UFOs. Obviously, the UFO movement and the New World Order conspiracy theories did not solely create distrust in the U.S. government. They did, however, contribute to it. In normal times, such beliefs are simply background noise in the life of the nation. During a crisis, such beliefs are a hindrance and a danger. Just look the denial of the seriousness of the coronavirus pandemic of 2020 and the myriad conspiracy theories that claimed the pandemic was a hoax.[84] Pity a nation when a significant minority of its citizens believes their own democratically elected government and their free press and media are mendacious and malevolent and instead prefer to live in an alternative reality where facts do not matter.

CONCLUSION

The most costly of all follies is to believe passionately in the palpably
not true. It is the chief occupation of mankind.

H. L. MENCKEN[1]

The modern myths, pseudo-history, pseudoscience and conspiracy
theories that comprise junk knowledge have deep roots in human
history. The preceding chapters demonstrate that in several different settings. This junk knowledge also has a vigorous persistence. Its
influence ebbs and flows but never completely goes away. The cultic milieu
allows junk knowledge to regenerate and to morph into new forms. In
our age of information technology, the opportunity has arisen to turn that
technology into a source of misinformation and disinformation. Some
persons and groups have seized the opportunity with gusto.

The most outstanding recent example of junk knowledge is the QAnon
phenomenon. Q, the anonymous prophet of the QAnon movement, first
appeared on the 4chan message board on 28 October 2017. It appears that
Q's first post was a response inspired by a typically cryptic comment made by
Donald Trump about a coming storm during an interview on 5 October. He
declined, also typically, to elaborate but he was definitely not talking about
the weather. In his post, Q predicted that Hillary Clinton would be arrested
on 30 October and that event would be accompanied by massive riots. To
add verisimilitude to that post and to subsequent posts as well, Q implied
that he was involved in intelligence work or was a military official who had
access to very sensitive information. Q's prediction never came to pass, but
his posts continued to make other predictions or declarations and came to
be called Qdrops by their readers. There have been thousands of them. Q has
since moved to 8kun, and there is no sign that his posts are coming to a halt.
Rather, they have spread to numerous social media sites. Several Internet
conspiracy theorists began promoting Q shortly after the first posts appeared

and attracted a rapidly growing following. This phenomenon became known as QAnon, which is a combination of Q and anonymous.[2]

Prediction after prediction appeared and prediction after prediction failed to come to pass. These failures have had no impact on the credibility and popularity of Q. Q's posts give their readers a sense of possessing special knowledge. The posts imply that a big change is coming, although the details are vague to non-existent. Readers of Q's posts are exhorted to 'enjoy the show' and 'trust the plan', along with being assured that 'Nothing can stop what is coming.' Q and QAnon are very pro-Trump, which makes the phenomenon attractive to him and his more fervent supporters. QAnon promotes a worldview of Deep State and global conspiracy, but it assures its readers that these nefarious forces will ultimately be defeated because Trump is in control of things. In the end, as Q declared on one post, 'GOD WINS.' QAnon posts contain many religious references of a Christian nature, although references to Christ's teachings and the Gospel message are largely absent. This religious rhetoric only increases QAnon's attraction for certain Evangelical Christians. Fox News has also done its part to bring QAnon favourably to the public's attention. However, in 2020 social media companies started to crack down hard on websites spreading blatantly false information.[3] To a great degree it was too late; the social damage had already been done.

The QAnon movement, like Trump, rejects traditionally legitimate sources of news and information as fundamentally false or fake. Q admonishes his readers to 'do your own research', which is not a bad piece of advice in general terms. Unfortunately, followers of QAnon restrict their research to undocumented Facebook material that is riddled with factual errors and falsehoods. Despite Q's predictions failing to come true, his followers deny that is really the case. Furthermore, QAnon followers make some very wild claims. One such set of claims says that John F. Kennedy Jr, who died in a plane crash in 1999, was actually assassinated. A related claim is that he is still alive and is a Trump supporter and might even be Q. Some even claim that Trump is Q. When they are asked what evidence exists for believing such wild claims, they are not bothered by the lack of any. Why should they be bothered, when they are already blithely ignoring the fact that the claims mutually contradict each other? Instead, they respond, 'Is there evidence not to [believe]?' In other words, they feel they are under no obligation to provide evidence that any of the preposterous claims are true or to be logically consistent. Instead, the burden is placed on sceptics to prove a negative.

Then there is the most horrific conspiracy theory of them all: the elite of the Deep State are not just plotting to maintain or to increase their domination of humanity; they are predatory paedophiles. This despicable elite of the wealthy, politically powerful and liberal Hollywood types are all behind the abduction and sexual abuse of children. Even more ghastly, this sinister elite is harvesting the substance adrenochrome from the children's bodies. Apparently, the consumption of adrenochrome allows this depraved cannibalistic/vampiric elite to maintain their youthful appearance. Did Q watch *Jupiter Ascending*, by any chance? The problem is that some people take this categorical nonsense seriously. As a result, it creates a situation where a deadly disaster can occur. A salutary example is the near disaster involving the Pizzagate conspiracy. On 4 December 2016 a sadly deluded and heavily armed conservative from North Carolina attempted the rescue of abducted children who were supposedly being held prisoner at the popular Comet Ping Pong pizzeria in Washington, DC. It turned out there were no captive children. Although shots were fired, mercifully no one was killed and the canard of the child sex ring was thoroughly debunked and discredited – but not for long. In 2020 QAnon took up the idea of a paedophile ring that went viral throughout the world and has not yet been consigned to oblivion. Support for QAnon within the Evangelical Christian movement has become a problem for that segment of American society. Many regard QAnon as a genuine Christian phenomenon, but many others regard it as antithetical to Christian teaching both theologically and morally. In particular, it makes the Evangelical right look bad, especially to the youth of those churches who are appalled by the hypocrisy.[4]

It only takes a brief perusal of the 4chan and 8kun message boards to notice that they contain a lot of rather risqué and kinky material. Other items on these boards are just plain indecipherable or incomprehensible unless the reader is a cognoscenti of that sort of thing. Despite the irrational, unsavoury and mendacious nature of QAnon, or perhaps because of it, QAnon predictably continues to attract the attention of people like Sean Hannity of Fox News and Alex Jones of InfoWars. Some 35 former or current candidates for the United States Congress have espoused QAnon. One of these is Laura Loomer, the losing candidate for a congressional seat in Florida. She is an unabashed Islamophobe with no inhibitions. She has been banned from all major social media outlets, along with assorted businesses. A rather frenetic appearance on Alex Jones's InfoWars provides a telling glimpse of Loomer's personality. Her concerns focused on how the banning of her baseless conspiracy theories and agitation was undermining her income. Another example is the aspiring politician Jo Rae Perkins, who in 2020 unsuccessfully ran for the United States Senate in Oregon. She is against wearing masks to prevent the spread of COVID-19. Some of her opposition to masks might stem from her belief that the pandemic is a hoax whose goal is to bring down Donald Trump. Apparently, it never crosses her mind that COVID-19 is a worldwide phenomenon which would in turn make it a hoax of immense proportions. As a QAnon supporter, she is a proponent of Q's 'do your own research' maxim. The problem is that her information repository is QAnon materials. In that world of thought, everything is evaluated on the bedrock belief that cannibalistic paedophile elite figures are engaged in a secret but epic struggle with Trump and military intelligence, who want to expose their vile deeds and arrest them for their crimes. She claims to read a lot but if all she reads is compiled by QAnon, any conclusions she draws are highly dubious. Perkins is a staunch believer in Q's predictions. When asked how she explains the arrest of Hillary Clinton failing to take place, her reply is a question: 'Do you know, beyond a shadow of a doubt, are you 100 per cent sure that she was never arrested?' That is an obfuscation that is both disingenuous and obtuse. The burden is on Q and Perkins to provide proof that such an outlandish claim is actually true. This is what is meant when it is said that hell is the absence of reason.[5]

While Perkins and most of the QAnon candidates failed to win their elections, two did. The two successful candidates were Lauren Boebert and Marjorie Taylor Greene, both Republicans. Boebert won in the third congressional district of Colorado, which sprawls across most of the western half of the state. It is deep in the Rocky Mountains and is very sparsely populated. Boebert and her husband own the Shooters Grill in Rifle, Colorado, where she encourages the waitresses to openly carry guns. One assumes that this practice has a dampening effect on customer complaints about the quality of the service, but otherwise it is hard to determine what good purpose is being served. Predictably, during the COVID-19 pandemic, Boebert defied stay-at-home orders concerning restaurants. Her refusal to comply was hardly her first run-in with the law. Marjorie Taylor Greene, who inherited her father's construction company, also totes a gun and is a more outspoken advocate of the QAnon conspiracy theory and other far-right views. Shortly after their elections to the House of Representatives, both enquired about being able to carry arms in the Capitol building. Why they asked is unclear, since carrying guns there has always been allowed. Hopefully they are not planning a confrontation with Alexandria Ocasio-Cortez and the rest of the progressive Squad. At any rate, one can almost certainly be assured that they will have plenty of attention-getting moments while in office.[6]

Once Boebert and Greene were sworn in as members of the House of Representatives, both proceeded to make news. Boebert flamboyantly flashed her guns and ostentatiously accepted a red, white and blue pistol from a biker gang. More ominously, it was reported that Boebert had conducted a tour or tours of the Capitol building. These tours took place in the days immediately before an insurrectionary mob of thousands stormed the United States Capitol Building and forced the members of Congress to flee to secure havens on 6 January 2021, which will be discussed further in the following pages. It was alleged that the tour group included people who were also involved in the insurrection. Some even suggested that the tour was a reconnaissance mission for the insurrectionists. In response, Boebert denied the allegation and claimed she was merely showing round her relatives. That said, Boebert won her seat narrowly with 51 per cent of the vote and it has been predicted that her QAnon ideology may not wear well with her constituents over time. Whatever the case might be, Boebert was quickly eclipsed by the antics of her fellow congresswoman and QAnon adherent Marjorie Taylor Greene during and after the events of 6 January.[7]

Marjorie Taylor Greene, an outspoken supporter of conspiracy theories, especially of the QAnon variety, is making history as possibly the most controversial freshman Congressperson in the history of the House of Representatives. An ardent Trump supporter, she claims he actually won the presidential election of 2020. She also supports the standard Republican cultural positions on gun rights and abortion. In her case, she had also been espousing some non-standard, extremist positions over the past few years. She had claimed that the 9/11 terrorist attacks were a false flag operation, as were the mass shootings at the Sandy Hook and Parkland schools. Two years before her election, she was calling for violence against various prominent Democratic politicians, which included suggestions about assassination and execution for treason. Besides having long-held anti-Muslim and anti-vaxxer beliefs, during the COVID-19 pandemic she became a vehement opponent of protective masks and lockdowns. Prior to QAnon's appearance, she believed in the Pizzagate paedophilia ring and connected immigrants to the white genocide conspiracy theory, which claimed that immigration was part of a plot to bring about the extinction of the white population of Europe and North America. Lately she asserted that space lasers run by Jewish bankers had caused the catastrophic wildfires in California. This claim begs the question, who caused the Australian wildfires? Was it kangaroos allied with grey aliens or koalas collaborating with the North Koreans?[8]

In addition to all these beliefs, especially QAnon, she maintains she is a staunch Evangelical Christian, which would seem to indicate that her preacher is not well versed in the biblical warnings about the dangers of false teachers and antichrists. She and Lauren Boebert are bellwethers of the dangers and degradations that threaten a democratic society when baseless conspiracy theories have gone mainstream. On 6 January 2021 that potential danger manifested itself in the most concrete way with the storming of the Capitol by pro-Trump insurrectionists. While the mob of insurrectionists rampaged through the Capitol, members of the House of Representatives were sheltering. Greene sat with a group of Republicans who refused to wear masks to protect against the spread of COVID-19. That dubious act was to become relatively insignificant as other current and past actions of Greene began to pepper the political news.[9]

As more and more troubling information about Greene's views became public, calls for her expulsion from the House of Representatives began. That action requires a two-thirds vote of the members. Then it was announced that she had been assigned to the prestigious House budget and education committees. As a result, there were calls for Greene to be stripped of her committee assignments. That action only required a majority vote by the House of Representatives. Few Republicans, however, dared to criticize her openly. On 3 February the House minority leader Kevin McCarthy called a closed meeting of the Republican caucus. Finding a solution for the Greene controversy was one of the reasons why the meeting had been called. At the meeting Greene apologized for her behaviour and received a standing ovation from some of those present. Others in the room questioned just how much of an apology it really was. Otherwise, McCarthy declined to strip her of either of her committee assignments. That action, or inaction, opened the way for the Democratic majority to vote to strip her of both committee assignments. The vote on 4 February was 230 to 199, with eleven Republicans joining the Democrats. In the days that followed, Greene showed herself to be neither chastened by the experience nor contrite. Anyone who thinks Greene will fade into oblivion is probably going to be disappointed. She is a personification of the conspiracy theory culture gone mainstream.[10]

Republican Party voters and Donald Trump have projected the QAnon movement into the mainstream of American politics. Like Trump, some Republican politicians have embraced QAnon along with other far-right beliefs and far-fetched conspiracy theories since doing so provides them with a reliable base of enthusiastic supporters. The downside is that while this choice helps politicians to get elected, it cripples their ability to legislate since it makes bipartisan cooperation and compromise significantly more difficult. It has also been plausibly suggested that QAnon is one of the reasons for the inaccuracy of polling before the 2020 election. QAnon believers tended to dodge answering pollsters and even may have misled them by not being truthful in their answers.[11]

Legitimate social causes have also found themselves hijacked by QAnon. Save the Children and other anti-human-trafficking groups have experienced QAnon supporters using their name or inserting QAnon themes into their websites and social media pages. The good name of these humanitarian groups is being exploited to legitimize the QAnon claims that a secret elite is eating missing and kidnapped children to stay young. Such unsavoury actions force the legitimate groups to waste time and resources debunking and removing the offending QAnon materials. It is a clever but insidious strategy on the part of QAnon to try to camou-flage themselves by association with a respectable and unassailable cause. These actions hurt the legitimate humanitarian groups because it blurs their non-partisan position and threatens their broad-based support by sullying their reputation.[12]

While the QAnon movement was initially disheartened by Donald Trump's defeat in the presidential election of 2020, baseless conspiracy theories about the election being stolen from Trump quickly mitigated any cognitive dissonance among the true believers. QAnon adherents have played a significant but not necessarily effective or rational role in Trump's efforts to overturn the election results. The sometime Trump team lawyer Sidney Powell was a high-profile example of a QAnon adherent. At the same time QAnon has helped to exacerbate the civil war within the Republican Party over whether to accept the results of the 2020 election or support Trump's, QAnon's and other far-righters' efforts to set aside the election results.

On 6 January 2021 years of unfounded conspiracy theories and months of baseless claims by Trump and others that he could only lose the presi-dential election if it were rigged against him, or, if he lost, then the election was stolen from him because he actually won it by a landslide, finally bore their poisoned fruit. On the day that Congress met to approve the Electoral College's results, a crowd of somewhere between 8,000 and 20,000 Trump supporters gathered near the Capitol building. Many of them were there with the intention of preventing Congress from approv-ing the results of the 2020 election. Trump spoke to his supporters and urged them on, as did his personal lawyer Rudy Giuliani and Alabama congressman Mo Brooks. The American people and the world watched on live TV as thousands of angry Trump supporters stormed the Capitol and overwhelmed the badly outnumbered Capitol police. Senators and Representatives were taken to refuges while at least eight hundred mem-bers of the insurrectionist mob careened through the Capitol, engaging in acts of theft and vandalism while continuing to attack the Capitol police. They also called for the hanging of Vice President Mike Pence for not illegally supporting Trump's attempt to subvert the election. The desecration of the Capitol lasted for several hours until more law enforcement and National Guard units arrived. That night the shaken but unbowed Congress reconvened and completed the task of accepting the Electoral College votes. Incredibly some Republican senators and representatives still voted against accepting the votes of some states but they were a minority. The insurrectionist mob had failed to attain its goal of overthrowing the election of 2020 and keeping Trump as president.[13]

The storming of the Capitol shook the democratic republic of the United States to its roots but it survived. It was, however, yet another wake-up call for Americans and all nations with democratically elected governments regarding the dangers posed by conspiracy theories, right-wing extremism, white supremacists and antisemites. The danger was magnified by the ease with which false and hateful ideas could be spread by the Internet and social media. A defeated president desperate to hold on to office had used social media to spread the big lies that he had actually won the election and that the victory was being stolen from him. It was a baseless conspiracy theory without credible evidence to support it.[14]

The storming of the Capitol is being intensively investigated and almost every day brings new revelations. Arrests of rioters by law enforcement are proceeding. Undoubtedly these investigations will go on, not just for months, but more probably for years. Scholars will write many books describing and analysing this event. In the aftermath of the insurrection, new conspiracy theories have emerged. Some claimed that it was the left-wing anti-fascist movement Antifa, a continuing target of right-wing deflections, who were really responsible for that attack on the Capitol. FBI intelligence, however, reported that there was no evidence indicating Antifa participation. In addition, it has been pointed out that Antifa involvement would have been irrational action against their own political interests. Why would they want to spark the storming of the Capitol to stop Congress from certifying the election of their preferred candidate in favour of keeping a president they despise? Another claim is that the insurrection was one more false flag operation by leftists to discredit Trump. Again, there is no evidence to support this claim. It also begs the question, to what end was a false flag operation intended? Trump was defeated; what more was needed? It also means that Trump, Giuliani and others who addressed the crowd were participating in that false flag operation. In fact, outrage over Trump's dubious and reckless actions during the weeks leading up to and on 6 January, the day of the insurrection, quickly led the House of Representatives to impeach him for incitement to insurrection. The impeachment vote took place on 13 January. It was an unprecedented second impeachment of a United States president. A month later, he was acquitted by the Senate trial on 13 February. Those voting to convict Trump failed to reach the required two-thirds majority in a vote of 57 to 43. Too many other people voted to acquit and so declined to support the rule of law and the Constitution. In the aftermath, an unabashed Trump has continued to promote his baseless conspiracy theories.[15]

Two weeks later Joe Biden was inaugurated as president of the United States on 20 January. The ceremonies took place almost without incident, since security had been significantly strengthened with the presence of thousands of National Guard troops. It was also an event that traumatized many QAnon adherents. According to the QAnon worldview, Trump was their saviour and with the help of military intelligence, he would ultimately triumph over the paedophile elite. This belief had intensified after the presidential election of 2020. Trump and his followers claimed a landslide victory but a vast conspiracy had stolen the election. This shadowy conspiracy was called the Kraken, after the mythological sea monster. Since Trump, however, supposedly had everything under control, QAnon believers were expecting him to launch the Storm, in which he and his supporters would strike. Mass arrests and even executions would follow and Trump would remain president. Apparently, the Joint Chiefs of Staff controlling the United States military never got the memo. Inauguration Day came, Biden was sworn in as president, and Trump skulked and sulked his way out of Washington.[16]

Incredibly, many people believed this prophecy of Q that a Trump triumph would happen. When it didn't occur, the worldview of many QAnon supporters was shaken to the core. Initial speculation among commentators was that QAnon was in a state of collapse. Various QAnon believers recanted publicly and remorsefully admitted that they had been duped, naive and foolish, and were regretful and embarrassed. Despite the severe cognitive dissonance, however, new prophecies quickly appeared that allowed QAnon beliefs to persist. Fundamentally, it is a repeat of the failure and recovery of cultic prophecy described in Leon Festinger's classic 1956 study *When Prophecy Fails*. Just as Mrs Keech and some of her Seekers group in Oak Park, Illinois, recovered when her prophecy about the end of the world failed by concocting an explanation they could live with, so has QAnon. In the case of QAnon, they moved the date of the next Trump triumphal comeback to 4 March. And, of course, when that prophecy inevitably fails, another prophecy will appear and continue to appear. QAnon's prophecies have never come to pass since they first appeared in 2017 but that has not bothered the true believers. They find a perfect fantasy preferable to an imperfect reality.[17]

It has not been a pretty picture for the United States or the rational members of the traditional and true Republican Party. Even worse, QAnon is not an exclusively American phenomenon. It has developed followings in the United Kingdom, Germany and other European nations. Social media outlets such as Facebook and Twitter began cracking down on the posting of blatantly false material beginning in mid-2020. It was, however, too late. By that time, the Pandora's box of falsehood and delusion had disgorged its poison with predictable results.[18]

The historian Norman Cohn pointed out long ago that societies experiencing rapid and profound change often fall victim to malign forms of junk knowledge and conspiracy theories. People fear the large-scale shifts and changes that are roiling their societies. That unhealthy reaction is a quest to preserve the old and familiar and stave off the threatening change.[19] In the first decades of the twenty-first century, much of the developed world is going through wrenching changes and dislocations due to globalization. Hence the appeal of questionable conspiracy theories and freakish fantasies. One hopes that ultimately people who have embraced Q and other prophets of deceitful fantasies will come to realize that junk knowledge and conspiracy theories are just not working for them. On the other hand, perhaps the cultic milieu will just conglomerate some new form of junk knowledge that will replace QAnon with something less pernicious. Or will it be something even more nasty and pathological?

References

Introduction

1 J. M. Roberts, *The Mythology of the Secret Societies* [1972](London, 2008), p. 15.
2 Saul Bellow, *To Jerusalem and Back: A Personal Account* (New York, 1976), p. 127.
3 Daniel Pipes, *Conspiracy: How the Paranoid Style Flourishes and Where It Comes From* (New York, 1997), pp. 11–12, 23 and 118–19; Alex Johnson, 'Lyndon LaRouche, Bizarre Political Theorist and Perennial Presidential Candidate, Dies at 96', www.nbcnews.com, 13 February 2019; Jesse Walker, 'Lyndon LaRouche: The Conspiracists Who Earned a Following', *Politico*, www.politico.com, 29 December 2019; and 'Views of Lyndon LaRouche and the LaRouche Movement', www.en.wikipedia.org, accessed 5 October 2020, see especially the section 'The "British" Conspiracy'.
4 David Icke, *The Biggest Secret* (Derby, 1999), passim. David G. Robertson, *UFOs, Conspiracy Theories and the New Age: Millennial Conspiracism* (London, 2017); its Chapter Five, '"Problem-Reaction-Solution": David Icke and the Reptilian Hypothesis', provides a good, concise biography of Icke as well as an excellent summary of his ideas, as does Michael Barkun, *A Culture of Conspiracy: Apocalyptic Visions in Contemporary America*, 2nd edn (Berkeley, CA, 2013), pp. 69 and 104–10. See also Tyson Lewis and Richard Kahn, 'The Reptoid Hypothesis: Utopian and Dystopian Representational Motifs in David Icke's Alien Conspiracy Theory', *Utopian Studies*, XVI/1 (2005), pp. 45–74; David G. Robertson, 'David Icke's Reptilian Thesis and the Development of New Age Theodicy', *International Journal for the Study of New Religions*, V/1 (2013), pp. 27–47; and Marcus Lowth, 'What Should We Make of Claims of Shapeshifting Reptilian Aliens Ruling the Earth?', *UFO Insight*, www.ufoinsight.com, 16 October 2016, updated 18 July 2020.
5 Ambrose Evans-Pritchard, 'U.S. Cult Is Source of Theories', *Electronic Telegraph*, www.telegraph.co.uk, 3 December 1996; Icke, *Biggest Secret*, pp. 32, 407 and 411–69; and Marcus Lowth, 'The Death of Diana – Accident? Assassination? Or Ritual Sacrifice?', *UFO Insight*, www.ufoinsight.com, 16 October 2016, updated 17 July 2020.
6 Robertson, 'David Icke's Reptilian Thesis', p. 35.
7 Ibid., pp. 36–7; Robertson, *UFOs, Conspiracy Theories*, pp. 156–7; and Barkun, *Culture of Conspiracy*, p. 107.
8 Barkun, *Culture of Conspiracy*, pp. 183–92.
9 Ibid., pp. 184–5; Jim Geraghty, 'Obama Could Debunk Some Rumors by Releasing his Birth Certificate', *National Review*, www.nationalreview.com, 9 June 2008; Jim Geraghty, 'A Few Other Possibilities on Barack Obama's

Birth Certificate', *National Review*, www.nationalreview.com, 10 June 2008; and Jim Geraghty, 'Obama's Certification of Live Birth Found and Posted at Daily Kos', *National Review*, www.nationalreview.com, 12 June 2008.

10 Barkun, *Culture of Conspiracy*, pp. 184–5; Robert Farley, 'Was Hillary Clinton the Original "Birther"?', www.factcheck.com, 2 July 2015; and Ben Smith and Byron, 'Birtherism: Where It All Began', *Politico*, www.politico.com, 22 April 2011, updated 24 April 2011.

11 Chuck Todd, *The Stranger: Barack Obama in the White House* (New York, 2014), p. 254, and Michael D'Antonio, *Never Enough: Donald Trump and the Pursuit of Success* (New York, 2015), pp. 284–8 and 330.

12 Todd, *Stranger*, p. 254 and Jerome R. Corsi, *Where's the Birth Certificate? The Case that Barack Obama Is Not Eligible to Be President* (Washington, DC, 2011), which was a bestseller although one has to wonder how many purchasers read it. It is an example of 'death by footnote' scholarship. The reader is barraged by an overload of evidence which is hard to evaluate in terms of credibility and/or relevance.

13 Todd, *Stranger*, pp. 253–4; D'Antonio, *Never Enough*, pp. 284, 290, 325 and 330; Mark Sumner, 'Newsweek Claims Birtherism Article about Kamala Harris Isn't about Race – It's Absolutely about Race', www.dailykos.com, 13 August 2020; and 'Trump Stokes "Birther" Conspiracy Theory about Kamala Harris', www.bbc.com, 14 August 2020. These last two articles are merely a small sampling of stories discussing and deriding birtherism concerning Kamala Harris. I picked the BBC News report because it was not a source from the U.S. mainstream media.

14 Ryan Prior, 'Meet the Guy behind the "Area 51" Page: He's Terrified of What He's Created', www.cnn.com, 18 July 2019; David Montero, 'Storm Area 51 Creator: I sparked a Movement while I Was Bored at 2 a.m.', *Los Angeles Times*, www.latimes.com, 12 September 2019; 'Storm Area 51', www. en.wikipedia.org, accessed 5 October 2020 (this is a very well-sourced article); and Sophie Lewis, 'Oklahoma Animal Shelter Encourages Area 51 Fans to "Storm Our Shelter"', www.cbsnews.com, 20 July 2019.

15 E. J. Dickson, 'Coronavirus is Spreading – And So Are the Hoaxes and Conspiracy Theories Around It', *Rolling Stone*, www.rollingstone.com, 18 March 2020; Max Fisher, 'Why Coronavirus Conspiracy Theories Flourish. And Why It Matters', www.nytimes.com, 8 April 2020; Katherine Schaeffer, 'A Look at the Americans Who Believed There Is Some Truth to the Conspiracy Theory that COVID-19 Was Planned', Pew Research Center, *Facts and News in the Numbers*, www.pewresearch.org, 20 July 2020; and Megan Marples, 'Pandemic Denial: Why Some People Can't Accept Covid-19's Realities', www.cnn.com, 16 August 2020.

16 West Palm Beach County Commissioners Meeting, 23 June 2002, at www. bing.com/videos. The comments about not wearing underwear start at 2 hours and 30 minutes. The comments of the woman in the red T-shirt occur after 1 hour and 24 minutes. There are numerous shorter videos excerpting these comments. For the interview by the local television station WPTV with the woman in the red T-shirt, see www.wptv.com. There is a small video of interviews with anti-maskers done after the meeting that is available further down the page. The interview with the woman in the red T-shirt begins at 8:08 minutes with the comments about the New World Order at 8:36 and the comments about the government's plan to kill over 95 per cent of the population at 9:58.

17 Caroline Warnock, 'America's Frontline Doctors Summit COVID-19 Video Called "False Information"', www.heavy.com, 28 July 2020; Caroline Warnock, 'Watch: Dr. Stella Immanuel COVID-19 Hydroxychloroquine "Cure"' Video', www.heavy.com, 29 July 2020; and Will Sommer, 'Trump's New Favorite COVID Doctor Believes in Alien DNA, Demon Sperm, and Hydroxychloroquine', www.thedailybeast.com, 28 July 2020.

18 Mark Potok, 'Carnage in Charleston', *Intelligence Report* of the Southern Poverty Law Center, www.splcenter.org, 27 October 2015; Joel A. Brown, 'Dylann Roof, the Radicalization of the Alt-Right, and Ritualized Racial Violence', *Sightings* of the Divinity School of the University of Chicago, www.divinity.uchicago.edu, 12 January 2017; and J. M. Berger, 'How Terrorists Recruit Online (and How to Stop it)', *Brookings* (9 November 2015), accessed 17 March 2021.

19 W.E.B. Du Bois, 'The Propaganda of History' [1935], in *Writings* (New York, 1986), p. 1029.

20 Mark Twain, *The Innocents Abroad* [1869] (New York, 1984), p. 24.

1 Thinking about Pseudoscience, Pseudo-History, Modern Myths and Conspiracy Theories

1 Charles Fort, *Book of the Damned: The Collected Works of Charles Fort* (New York, 2008), p. 3.

2 Nicoli Nattrass, 'Understanding the Origins and Prevalence of AIDS Conspiracy Beliefs in the United States and South Africa', *Sociology of Health and Illness*, XXXV/1 (2013), pp. 113–29; Jesselyn Cook, 'A Toxic "Infodemic": The Viral Spread of COVID-19 Conspiracy Theories', www.huffpost.com, 8 April 2020; and Ben Collins, '"What are we doing this for?": Doctors Are Fed Up with Conspiracies Ravaging ERS', www.nbcnews.com, 6 May 2020. These references are just a tiny sample. Of course, in certain circles they are all fake news.

3 Susan Jacoby, *The Age of American Unreason* (New York, 2008), pp. 210–41.

4 Glyn Daniel, *Myth or Legend?* (New York, 1968), pp. 14–15.

5 Robert Segal, *Myth: A Very Short Introduction* (New York, 2015), pp. 3–5.

6 Eric Kurlander, *Hitler's Monsters: A Supernatural History of the Third Reich* (New Haven, CT, and London, 2017), pp. xiv–xv.

7 David Aaronovitch, *Voodoo Histories: The Role of Conspiracy Theory in Shaping Modern History* (New York, 2010), p. 6.

8 Kathryn S. Olmsted, *Real Enemies: Conspiracy Theories and American Democracy, World War I to 9/11* (Oxford, 2009), pp. 3–5 and 236–8.

9 Michael Barkun, *A Culture of Conspiracy: Apocalyptic Visions of Contemporary America*, 2nd edn (Berkeley, CA, 2013), pp. 6–7; Thomas Milan Konda, *Conspiracies of Conspiracies: How Delusions Have Overrun America* (Chicago, IL, 2019), p. 6; Massimo Pigliucci, *Nonsense on Stilts: How to Tell Science from Bunk*, 2nd edn (Chicago, IL, 2018), pp. 2–3 and 14–15; and Anna Merlan, *Republic of Lies: American Conspiracy Theorists and their Surprising Rise to Power* (New York, 2019), p. 14.

10 Olmsted, *Real Enemies*, p. 6.

11 Milton William Cooper, *Behold a Pale Horse* (Sedona, AZ, 1991).

12 Michael Shermer, *The Believing Brain: From Ghosts and Gods to Politics and Conspiracies – How We Construct Beliefs and Reinforce Them as Truths* (New York, 2011), pp. 208–9 and 225; 'Too Many Minions Spoil the Plot', www.ox.ac.uk, 26 January 2016; and D. R. Grimes, 'On the Viability of Conspiratorial Beliefs', *PLOS ONE*, XI/1 (2016): e0147905, www.journals.plos.org.

13 Shermer, *Believing Brain*, pp. 208–9 and 225.

14 Barkun, *Culture of Conspiracy*, pp. 3–4, and Aaronovitch, *Voodoo Histories*, pp. 354–5.

15 Barkun, *Culture of Conspiracy*, pp. 5–6, and Olmsted, *Real Enemies*, pp. 192–3 and 200.

16 Barkun, *Culture of Conspiracy*, pp. 18–23.

17 Richard Hofstadter, 'The Paranoid Style in American Politics' [1964], in *Richard Hofstadter*, ed. Sean Wilentz, Library of America, vol. cccxxx (New York, 2020), pp. 532–3.

18 Barkun, *Culture of Conspiracy*, pp. 6–7.

19 Ibid., pp. 26–7.

20 James Webb, *The Occult Underground* [1974] (LaSalle, IL, 1990), pp. 191–2, emphasis in quote is Webb's, and ibid., 193–234 passim, for a historical over-view of this rejected knowledge, and Barkun, *Culture of Conspiracy*, pp. 23–4. See also James Webb, *The Occult Establishment* [1976] (LaSalle, IL, 1998), p. 15.

21 Barkun, *Culture of Conspiracy*, pp. 27–9.

22 Colin Campbell, 'The Cult, the Cultic Milieu and Secularization', in *A Sociological Yearbook of Religion in Britain: 5*, ed. Michael Hill (London, 1972), pp. 119–36. My discussion of the cultic milieu is based on this article. It is reprinted in Jeffrey S. Kaplan and Heléne Lööw, eds, *The Cultic Milieu: Oppositional Subcultures in the Age of Globalization* (Walnut Creek, CA, 2002), and includes other essays using the concept of the cultic milieu.

23 Colin Campbell, 'The Cultic Milieu Revisited' (2012), pp. 18–37 passim, www. researchgate.net, accessed 5 October 2020.

24 For the reaction against the Enlightenment and disenchantment, see John V. Fleming, *The Dark Side of the Enlightenment: Wizards, Alchemists and Spiritual Seekers in the Age of Reason* (New York, 2013); Paul Kléber Monod, *Solomon's Secret Arts: The Occult in the Age of Enlightenment* (New Haven, CT, and London, 2013); Theodore Ziolkowski, *Lure of the Arcane: The Literature of Cult and Conspiracy* (Baltimore, MD, 2013); Alex Owen, *The Place of Enchantment: British Occultism and the Culture of the Modern* (Chicago, IL, 2004); and Corinna Treitel, *A Science for the Soul: Occultism and the Genesis of the German Modern* (Baltimore, MD, 2004).

25 Barkun, *Culture of Conspiracy*, pp. 25–6.

26 Roger M. McCoy, *Ending in Ice: The Revolutionary Idea and Tragic Expedition of Alfred Wegener* (Princeton, NJ, 2006), is a good concise biography of Wegener and the history of the theories of continental drift and plate tectonics. Besides showing how advances in scientific tests and instruments helped prove Wegener had been on the right track, the same advances proved that Charles Hapgood's crustal displacement and pole shift theories were wrong.

27 A notable exception to the fortress mentality is the field of alternative Egyptology. During the 1990s, it was dominated by a clique of scholars that included Graham Hancock and Robert Bauval. They were cogently criticized by Lynn Picknett and Clive Prince, *The Stargate Conspiracy: Revealing the Truth Behind Extraterrestrial Contact, Military Intelligence and the Mysteries of Ancient Egypt* (New York, 1999), and Ian Lawton and Chris Ogilvie-Herald, *Giza: The Truth – The People, Politics and History Behind the World's Most Famous Archaeological Site* (London, 1999). For an overview of this episode, see Ronald H. Fritze, *Egyptomania: A History of Fascination, Obsession and Fantasy* (London, 2016), pp. 297–9.

28 Ronald H. Fritze, *Invented Knowledge: False History, Fake Science and Pseudo-Religions* (London, 2009), pp. 34–9.

29 Tom Nichols, *The Death of Expertise: The Campaign against Established Knowledge and Why It Matters* (New York, 2017), and Michiko Kakutani, *The Death of Truth: Notes on Falsehood in the Age of Trump* (New York, 2019). See also Merlan, *Republic of Lies*.

30 Garrett G. Fagan, 'Diagnosing Archaeology', in *Archaeological Fantasies: How Pseudoarchaeology Misrepresents the Past and Misleads the Public*, ed. Garrett G. Fagan (London, 2006), pp. 36–7.

31 Shermer, *Believing Brain*, pp. 212–13, 327 and 338–43; Pigliucci, *Nonsense on Stilts*, p. 93; and Donald R. Prothero and Timothy D. Callahan, *UFOs, Chemtrails, and Aliens* (Bloomington, IN, 2017), p. 401.

32 David Hume, *An Enquiry Concerning Human Understanding*, in *Locke, Berkeley, Hume*, Great Books of the Western World, vol. XXXV (Chicago, IL, 1952), p. 489b, and Prothero and Callahan, *UFOs*, pp. 401–2.

33 Edward Bulwer-Lytton, *The Coming Race* [1871], ed. David Seed (Middletown, CT, 2005); Barkun, *Culture of Conspiracy*, pp. 29–33; 'Vril' and 'Vril Society', in John Michael Greer, *The Element Encyclopedia of Secret Societies and Hidden History* (New York, 2006); and Nicholas Goodrick-Clarke, *Black Sun: Aryan Cults, Esoteric Nazism and the Politics of Identity* (New York, 2003), pp. 112–13, 164–8 and 294–5.

2 Why Do People Believe Strange Things?

1 H. L. Mencken, 'Homo Neanderthalensis', *Baltimore Evening Sun*, 29 June 1925. Internet Archive, Full Text Coverage of the Scopes Trial, www.archive.org, accessed 5 October 2020.

2 James Webb, *The Occult Underground* [1974] (La Salle, IL, 1988), p. 11.

3 Michael Shermer, *The Believing Brain: From Ghosts and Gods to Politics and Conspiracies – How We Construct Beliefs and Reinforce Them as Truths* (New York, 2011), p. 5.

4 Robert Todd Carroll, 'Ley Lines', in *The Skeptics Dictionary: A Collection of Strange Beliefs, Amusing Deceptions, and Dangerous Delusions* (Hoboken, NJ, 2003), and 'Ley Lines', www.en.wikipedia.org, accessed 5 October 2020.

5 Michael D. Gordin, *The Pseudoscience Wars: Immanuel Velikovsky and the Birth of the Modern Fringe* (Chicago, IL, 2013), is a detailed account of the controversies associated with Velikovsky. For a more concise account, see Ronald H. Fritze, *Invented Knowledge: False History, Fake Science and Pseudo-Religions* (London, 2009), pp. 169–93.

6 Anna Merlan, *Republic of Spies: American Conspiracy Theorists and their Surprising Rise to Power* (New York, 2019), pp. 24–5; Rob Brotherton, *Suspicious Minds: Why We Believe Conspiracy Theories* (New York, 2015), pp. 224–39; and Shermer, *Believing Brain*, pp. 257 and 259–76.

7 Brotherton, *Suspicious Minds*, pp. 224–6, and Shermer, *Believing Brain*, pp. 258–76.

8 'Cognitive Dissonance', at www.psychologytoday.com, provides a brief overview of the concept, accessed 17 March 2021 and Leon Festinger, Henry W. Riecken and Stanley Schachter, *When Prophecy Fails: A Social and Psychological Study of a Modern Group that Predicted the Destruction of the World* [1956] (Mansfield Centre, CT, 2009).

9 Jesselyn Cook, 'A Toxic "Infodemic": The Viral Spread of COVID-19 Conspiracy

Theories', www.huffpost.com, 7 April 2020; 'Why Coronavirus Conspiracy Theories Flourish. And Why It Matters', *New York Times*, www.psychologicalscience.org, 17 April 2020; Ben Collins, 'Coronavirus Conspiracy Theories Are Frustrating ER Doctors', www.nbcnews.com, 6 May 2020; Jesselyn Cook, 'How Coronavirus Turbocharged QAnon Conspiracy Theories', www.huffpost.co.uk, 29 April 2020; and Jesselyn Cook, 'QAnon's Coronavirus Fueled Boom Is a Warning of What's to Come', www.huffpost.co.uk, 29 April 2020. These stories are just a small sampling of the news coverage.

10 Allison He, 'The Dunning-Kruger Effect: Why Incompetence Begets Confidence', www.nytimes.com, 7 May 2020; Bobby Azarian, 'The Dunning-Kruger Effect May Help Explain Trump's Support: A New Study Suggests Some People Grossly Overestimate their Political Knowledge', www.psychologytoday.com, 22 August 2018; 'The Dunning-Kruger Effect', www.psychologytoday.com, accessed 5 October 2020; and Ian G. Anson, 'Partisanship, Political Knowledge, and the Dunning-Kruger Effect', *Political Psychology*, XXXIX/5 (October 2018), pp. 1172–92.

11 'Narcissism' in Find a Therapist, www.psychologytoday.com, accessed 5 October 2020; 'Narcissistic Personality Disorder', www.mayoclinic.org, accessed 5 October 2020; and 'Narcissism', www.en.wikipedia.org, accessed 5 October 2020, provide a comprehensive overview of the topic.

12 Danielle Levesque, 'Narcissism and Low Self-Esteem Predict Conspiracy Beliefs' at Mental Health, www.psypost.org, accessed 5 October 2020; Ryan O'Hare, 'Believe in Conspiracy Theories: You're Probably a Narcissist; People Who Doubt the Moon Landings Are More Likely to Be Selfish and Attention-Seeking', www.dailymail.co.uk, 8 March 2016; John M. Grohol, 'The Psychology of Conspiracy Theories: Why do People Believe Them?', www.psychcentral.com, 5 October 2017; Viren Swami et al., 'Conspiracist Ideation in Britain and Austria: Evidence of a Monological Belief System and Associations between Individual Psychological Differences and Real-World and Fictitious Conspiracy Theories', *British Journal of Psychology*, CII/3 (August 2011), pp. 443–63; Aleksandra Cichocka, Marta Marchlewska and Agnieszka Golec de Zavala, 'Does Self-Love or Self-Hate Predict Conspiracy Beliefs? Narcissism, Self-Esteem, and the Endorsement of Conspiracy Theories', *Social Psychological and Personality Science*, www.researchgate.net, November 2015; Agnieszka Golec de Zavala and Christopher M. Federico, 'Collective Narcissism and the Growth of Conspiracy Thinking over the Course of the 2016 United States Presidential Election: A Longitudinal Analysis', *European Journal of Social Psychology*, XLVIII/7 (December 2018), pp. 1011–18; Evita March and Jordan Springer, 'Belief in Conspiracy Theories: The Predictive Role of Schizotypy, Machiavellianism, and Primary Psychopathy', *PLOS ONE*, XIV/12 (December 2019), pp. 1–10; and Anthony Lantian et al., '"I Know Things They Don't Know!": The Role of Need for Uniqueness in Belief in Conspiracy Theories', *Social Psychology*, XLVIII (2017), pp. 160–73.

13 Brotherton, *Suspicious Minds*, pp. 109–12, and Shermer, *Believing Brain*, pp. 77–84. For a brief description of the concept of locus of control, see Richard B. Joelson, 'Locus of Control: How Do We Determine our Successes and Failures?', www.psychologytoday.com, 2 August 2017. For a more detailed explanation, see 'Locus of Control', www.en.wikipedia.org, accessed 5 October 2020.

14 Jan-Willem van Prooijen and Michele Acker, 'The Influence of Control on Belief in Conspiracy Theories: Conceptual and Applied Extensions', *Applied Cognitive Psychology*, XXIX (2015), pp. 753–61; Jan-Willem van Prooijen and

Karen M. Douglas, 'Conspiracy Theories as Part of History: The Role of Societal Crisis Situations', *Memory Studies*, x/3 (2017), pp. 323–33; Ilan Shrira, 'Paranoia and the Roots of Conspiracy Theories', www.psychologytoday.com, 11 September 2008; James Lake, 'Locus of Control and COVID-19', www.psychologytoday.com, 5 April 2020; 'Conspiracy Beliefs Linked with Search for Certainty and Social Connection', www.psychologicalscience.org, 2 August 2018; and 'Psychological Science and COVID-19: Conspiracy Theories', www.psychologicalscience.org, 27 May 2020.

15 Francis Wheen, *How Mumbo Jumbo Conquered the World: A Short History of Modern Delusions* (London, 2004), p. 193; David Aaronovitch, *Voodoo Histories: The Role of the Conspiracy Theory in Shaping Modern History* (New York, 2010), p. 240, and Merlan, *Republic of Lies*, p. 9.

16 Aaronovitch, *Voodoo Histories*, p. 238.

17 David Ludden, 'Why Do People Believe in Conspiracy Theories?', www.psychologytoday.com, 6 January 2018.

18 Aaronovitch, *Voodoo Histories*, pp. 238–9.

19 Andrew Hartman, *A War for the Soul of America: A History of the Culture Wars* (Chicago, IL, 2015), provides an excellent survey.

20 Aaronovitch, *Voodoo Histories*, pp. 346 and 349, and Wheen, *Mumbo Jumbo*, p. 115. Both Aaronovitch's and Wheen's quotes were written in the context of their separate criticisms of Jodi Dean's postmodern study of the American UFO movement, *Aliens in America: Conspiracy Cultures from Outerspace to Cyberspace* (Ithaca, NY, 1998). Their assessments were right on target. For an account of Martin Bernal and his *Black Athena* controversy, see Fritze, *Invented Knowledge*, pp. 221–55.

21 Aaronovitch, *Voodoo Histories*, p. 348. See Tom Nichols, *The Death of Expertise: The Campaign against Established Knowledge and Why It Matters* (New York, 2017), for an in-depth analysis of the problem.

22 Kathryn S. Olmsted, *Real Enemies: Conspiracy Theories and American Democracy, World War I to 9/11* (Oxford, 2009), pp. 234–5 and 238–9.

23 Jenny Rice, *Awful Archives: Conspiracy Theory, Rhetoric, and Acts of Evidence* (Columbus, OH, 2020), pp. 173–9, and Merlan, *Republic of Lies*, pp. 245–6, discuss studies showing the difficulty of changing the opinions of conspiracy theorists.

24 Josephine Harvey, 'Leaked Video Shows Alex Jones Ranting That He's So "F**king" Sick of Trump', huffpost.com, 3 February 2021.

25 Herbert V. Prochnow and Herbert V. Prochnow Jr, *A Treasury of Humorous Quotations for Speakers, Writers, and Home Reference* (New York, 1969), p. 295.

26 Craig A. Anderson, 'Belief Perseverance', in *Encyclopedia of Social Psychology*, ed. F. F. Baumeister et al. (Thousand Oaks, CA, 2007), pp. 109–10; Craig Silverman, 'The Backfire Effect: More on the Press's Inability to Debunk Bad Information', *Columbia Journalism Review*, www.archives.cjr.org, 17 June 2011; and Cari Romm, 'Vaccine Myth-Busting Can Backfire', *The Atlantic*, www.theatlantic.com, 12 December 2014. I would like to thank my colleague Dr Susan Owen of the Psychology Department for suggesting that I look at belief perseverance.

27 Merlan, *Republic of Lies*, p. 116.

28 Ibid., pp. 244–7.

29 *Helen*, in Euripides II, *The Complete Greek Tragedies*, vol. VI, ed. David Grene and Richmond Lattimore (New York, n.d.), p. 73, l. 1615.

3 The Many Journeys of the Ten Lost Tribes of Israel

1 William H. Stiebing Jr, *Ancient Near Eastern History and Culture*, 2nd edn (New York, 2009), pp. 234–8, and for a concise overview of the Assyrians, see Karen Radner, *Ancient Assyria: A Very Short Introduction* (Oxford, 2015).

2 Stiebing, *Ancient Near Eastern History*, pp. 275–6, and Mark Van De Mieroop, *A History of the Ancient Near East ca. 3000–323 BC*, 2nd edn (Oxford, 2007), p. 248.

3 Van De Mieroop, *Ancient Near East*, p. 251; A. K. Grayson, 'Assyria: Tiglath-Pileser III to Sargon II (744–705 BC)', in *The Cambridge Ancient History*, 2nd edn, vol. III, pt 2: *The Assyrian and Babylonian Empires and Other States of the Near East from the Eighth to the Sixth Centuries BC*, ed. J. Boardman et al. (Cambridge, 1992), pp. 77–8; and T. C. Mitchell, 'Israel and Judah from the Coming of Assyrian Domination until the Fall of Samaria and the Struggle for Independence in Judah (c. 750–700 BC)', in *The Cambridge Ancient History*, vol. III, pt 2, pp. 323–7 and 334–7.

4 Mitchell, 'Israel and Judah', pp. 337–9, and Grayson, 'Assyria', pp. 85–6.

5 Eric H. Cline, *From Eden to Exile: Unraveling Mysteries of the Bible* (Washington, DC, 2007), pp. 158–65; Israel Finkelstein and Neil Asher Silberman, *The Bible Unearthed: Archaeology's New Vision of Ancient Israel and the Origins of its Sacred Texts* (New York, 2002), pp. 214–25; Van De Mieroop, *Ancient Near East*, p. 251; Grayson, 'Assyria', pp. 85–6; Mitchell, 'Israel and Judah', pp. 339 and 341; and Zvi Ben-Dor Benite, *The Ten Lost Tribes: A World History* (Oxford, 2009), pp. 32–5. Ben-Dor Benite is particularly insistent that Sargon II, not Shalmaneser, conquered Samaria although the consensus of archaeologists and historians of the ancient Near East says otherwise.

6 Van De Mieroop, *Ancient Near East*, pp. 232–3; Cline, *Eden to Exile*, pp. 171–2; Mitchell, 'Israel and Judah', p. 326; and Finkelstein and Silberman, *Bible Unearthed*, pp. 217–22. Long before, Allen H. Godbey discussed the issue of just how limited the deportation of the Ten Tribes actually was in *The Lost Tribes a Myth: Suggestions towards Rewriting Hebrew History* (Durham, NC, 1930).

7 Stiebing, *Ancient Near Eastern History*, pp. 304–9.

8 Ibid., pp. 335–40.

9 For concise and authoritative overviews, see 'Apocalypse and Apocalypticism', 'Eschatology', 'Messiah' and 'Messianic Movements in Judaism', in *The Anchor Bible Dictionary*, ed. David Noel Freedman, 6 vols (New York, 1992), along with the entries for 'Apocalypse', 'Eschatology' and 'Messiah', in *The Oxford Dictionary of the Jewish Religion*, ed. R. J. Zwi Werblowsky and Geoffrey Wigoder (Oxford, 1997).

10 A. Neubauer, 'Where are the Ten Tribes?: 1. Bible, Talmud and Midrashic Literature', *Jewish Quarterly Review*, I/1 (October 1888), pp. 14–28, surveys the biblical and Second Temple era writings which reveal nothing about the Ten Tribes being lost; Josephus, *Antiquities of the Jews* in *The Works of Flavius Josephus*, trans. William Whiston (Green Forest, AK, 2008), bk 12, ch. 2, pp. 287–92 and 'Septuagint', in *The Anchor Bible Dictionary*.

11 Josephus, *Antiquities of the Jews*, bk 11, ch. 5, p. 274. So Josephus still located the Ten Tribes basically where the Assyrians had put them according to the Old Testament accounts.

12 Josephus, trans. H. St J. Thackeray, Ralph Marcus and Louis Feldman, 10 vols (Cambridge, MA, and London, 1926–65). For the Samaritan prophet, see

vol. ix: *Jewish Antiquities*, books 18 and 19, trans. Louis H. Feldman (Cambridge, MA, and London, 1965), book 18, ch. 4, pp. 61–5; for the Theudas, see vol. x: *Jewish Antiquities*, book 20, trans. Louis H. Feldman (Cambridge, MA, and London, 1965), book 20, ch. 5, pp. 53–5; for the Egyptian prophet, see ibid., ch. 8, pp. 91–3 and Flavius Josephus, *The Jewish War*, trans. G. A. Williams (Baltimore, MD, 1959), p. 135; and for Simon bar Giora see ibid., pp. 338–42 and 348.

13 Emil Schürer, *A History of the Jewish People in the Time of Jesus Christ* [1910] (Peabody, MA, 2010), Division I, vol. II, pp. 287–321; Eusebius, *The History of the Church from Christ to Constantine*, ed. Andre Louth (London, 1989), bk 4, ch. 6, pp. 107–8; Yohanan Aharoni and Michael Avi-Yonah, *The Macmillan Bible Atlas* (New York, 1968), pp. 164–5; Richard Marks, *The Image of Bar Kokhba in Traditional Jewish Literature: False Messiah and National Hero* (University Park, PA, 1994); Peter Shafer, ed., *The Bar Kokhba War Reconsidered: New Perspectives on the Second Jewish Revolt against Rome* (Tubingen, 2003); and Yigael Yadin, *Bar-Kokhba: The Rediscovery of the Legendary Hero of the Second Jewish Revolt against Rome* (New York, 1971).

14 Louis Ginzberg, *The Legends of the Jews*, 6 vols [1913] (Baltimore, MD, 1998), vol. iv, p. 317, vol. v, p. iii, and vol. vi, pp. 407–9; Josephus, *Jewish War*, p. 347; Pliny, *Natural History*, bk 31, ch. 14.

15 Ginzberg, *Legends of the Jews*, vol. vi, pp. 407–9; 'Sambatyon', in *Oxford Dictionary of the Jewish Religion*; and Neubauer, 'Where are the Ten Tribes?', p. 20.

16 Francis Soyer, *Antisemitic Conspiracy Theories in the Early Modern Iberian World: Narratives of Fear and Hatred* (London, 2019).

17 Elkan Nathan Adler, ed., *Jewish Travellers in the Middle Ages: 19 Firsthand Accounts* [1930] (New York, 1987), pp. 6–15.

18 Ibid., pp. 15–21; A. Neubauer, 'Where are the Ten Tribes?: II. Eldad the Danite', *Jewish Quarterly Review*, I/2 (January 1889), pp. 95–114; and Pamela Barmash, 'At the Nexus of History and Memory: The Ten Lost Tribes', *AJS Review*, xxix/2 (2005), pp. 207 and 232–6.

19 Adler, *Jewish Travellers*, pp. 5 and 31–2; Neubauer, 'Where are the Ten Tribes?: II', pp. 98, 106 and 108–10; David J. Wasserstein, 'Eldad ha-Dani and Prester John', in *Prester John, the Mongols and the Ten Lost Tribes*, ed. Charles F. Beckingham and Bernard Hamilton (Aldershot, 1996), pp. 213–36; Tudor Parfitt, *The Lost Tribes of Israel: The History of a Myth* (London, 2003), pp. 9–11; and Ben-Dor Benite, *The Ten Lost Tribes*, pp. 90–92.

20 Adler, *Jewish Travellers*, pp. 52–4, 153 and 238; A. Neubauer, 'Where are the Ten Tribes?: III. Early Translators of the Bible and Commentators', *Jewish Quarterly Review*, I/3 (April 1889), pp. 188–92 and 195–6; Parfitt, *Lost Tribes*, pp. 11–12; and David Kaufmann, 'A Rumour about the Ten Tribes in Pope Martin v's Time', *Jewish Quarterly Review*, IV/3 (April 1892), pp. 503–6.

21 Adler, *Jewish Travellers*, pp. 251–328; 'David Reuveni' and 'Shelomoh Molkho', in *Oxford Dictionary of the Jewish Religion*; Moti Benmelech, 'History, Politics and Messianism: David Ha-Reuveni's Origin and Mission', *AJS Review*, xxxv/1 (April 2011, pp. 35–41; Bailey W. Diffie and George D. Winius, *Foundations of the Portuguese Empire, 1414–1580* (Minneapolis, MN, 1977), pp. 263–8; Parfitt, *Lost Tribes*, pp. 231–3; Ben-Dor Benite, *Ten Lost Tribes*, pp. 115–29; and Andrew Colin Gow, *The Red Jews: Antisemitism in an Apocalyptic Age, 1200–1600* (Leiden, 1995), pp. 144–8.

22 A. Neubauer, 'Where are the Ten Tribes?: IV. Concluded', *Jewish Quarterly Review*, I/4 (July 1889), pp. 408–23; A. Z. Aescoly, 'David Reubeni in the Light

of History', *Jewish Quarterly Review*, XXVIII/I (July 1937), pp. 3–20 passim; Benmelech, 'David Ha-Reuveni's Origin and Mission', p. 58.

23 Aescoly, 'David Reubeni in the Light of History', p. 35, and Benmelech, 'David Ha-Reuveni's Origin and Mission', pp. 35–6.

24 Benmelech, 'David Ha-Reuveni's Origin and Mission', pp. 49–53 and 60; Aescoly, 'David Reubeni in the Light of History', p. 36; Parfitt, *Lost Tribes*, pp. 231–2; and 'Avraham ben Eliezer Ha-Levi', in *Oxford Dictionary of the Jewish Religion*.

25 W. Bousset, *The Antichrist Legend: A Chapter in Christian and Jewish Folklore* [1899] (Atlanta, GA, 1999), pp. 215–17, and Romans 11:26–7.

26 Andrew Runni Anderson, *Alexander's Gate, Gog and Magog and the Inclosed Nations* (Cambridge, MA, 1932), pp. 44–51 and 63–72; Norman Cohn, *The Pursuit of the Millennium: Revolutionary Millenarians and Mystical Anarchists of the Middle Ages* [1957] (New York, 1970), pp. 28–9 and 77–9; and Gow, *The Red Jews*, pp. 23, 25, 37, 42–5 and 99.

27 Heiko Oberman, 'The Stubborn Jews: Timing the Escalation of Anti-semitism in Late Medieval Europe', in *The Impact of the Reformation* (Grand Rapids, MI, 1994), pp. 127 and 132–4; Hans Eberhard Mayer, *The Crusades*, 2nd edn (Oxford, 1988), pp. 40–41 and 97; Steven Runciman, *The First Crusade and the Foundation of the Kingdom of Jerusalem*, vol. I of *A History of the Crusades* [1951] (London, 1994), pp. 111–17; and Robert Bonfil, 'Aliens Within: The Jews and Antijudaism', in *Handbook of European History, 1400–1600: Late Middle Ages, Renaissance and Reformation*, ed. Thomas A. Brady, Heiko A. Oberman and James D. Tracy, 2 vols (Grand Rapids, MI, 1994), vol. I, pp. 263–76.

28 For a concise account of the concept of Prester John, see 'Prester John and his Kingdom', in Ronald H. Fritze, *Travel Legend and Lore: An Encyclopedia* (Santa Barbara, CA, 1998), pp. 291–7 (additional works about Prester John are listed in the entry's accompanying bibliography); Matthew Paris, *English History: From the Year 1235 to 1273*, 3 vols (London, 1889), vol. I, pp. 131–2, 312–14 and 356–8; Antonia Gransden, 'Matthew Paris', in *Great Historians from Antiquity to 1800*, ed. Lucian Boia (New York, 1989), pp. 119–21, provides a concise biography of Paris; *The Travels of Sir John Mandeville*, trans. and intro. C.W.R.D. Moseley (Harmondsworth, 1983), pp. 165–6; and Gow, *Red Jews*, especially Chapter Four, 'The Red Jews in their Native Habitat'.

29 Gow, *Red Jews*, pp. 2–3, 65, 177 and 180–81; Oberman, 'Stubborn Jews', pp. 130–33 and 136–40; Bonfil, 'Aliens Within', vol. I, pp. 263–71.

30 Gow, *Red Jews*, pp. 80, 143–50, 155–9 and 172, and 'Eschatology', in *Dictionary of Luther and the Lutheran Traditions*, ed. Timothy J. Wengert (Grand Rapids, MI, 2017), pp. 230–31.

31 Francesca Lardicci, ed., *A Synoptic Edition of the Log of Columbus's First Voyage* (Turnhout, 1999), pp. 195 and 199.

32 Lee Eldridge Huddleston, *Origins of the American Indians: European Concepts, 1492–1729* (Austin, TX, 1967), pp. 4 and 33.

33 Ibid., pp. 34–5.

34 Diego Durán, *History of the Indies of New Spain*, trans. and ed. Doris Heyden (Norman, OK, 1994), pp. 4–5.

35 Huddleston, *Origins*, pp. 33–47.

36 José de Acosta, *Natural and Moral History of the Indies*, ed. Jane E. Mangan et al. (Durham, NC, 2002), p. 70; Bernabé Cobo, *History of the Inca Empire* (Austin, TX, 1979), pp. 48–53.

37 Richard Popkin, 'Jewish–Christian Relations in the Sixteenth and Seventeenth Centuries: The Conception of the Messiah', *Jewish History*, VI/1–2 (1992), pp. 163–77 passim; Christopher Hill, 'Till the Conversion of the Jews', in *Millenarianism and Messianism in English Literature and Thought, 1650–1800*, ed. Richard H. Popkin (Leiden, 1988), pp. 13–17.

38 Popkin, 'Jewish–Christian Relations', passim; Gershom Scholem, *Sabbatai Sevi: The Mystical Messiah, 1626–1676* (Princeton, NJ, 1975, originally published in Hebrew 1957), pp. 1–102.

39 Ernestine G. E. Van Der Wall, 'Petrus Serrarius and Menasseh Ben Israel: Christian Millenarianism and Jewish Messianism in Seventeenth-Century Amsterdam', in *Menasseh Ben Israel and His World*, ed. Yosef Kaplan, Henry Mélchoulan and Richard H. Popkin (Leiden, 1989), pp. 162–90; Hill, 'Till the Conversion of the Jews', p. 14.

40 Menasseh ben Israel, 'The Relation of Antonio Montezinos', in *The Hope of Israel*, ed. and intro. Henry Méchoulan and Gérard Nahon [1987] (Liverpool, 2004), pp. 105–6; George Weiner, 'America's Jewish Braves', *Mankind*, IX/9 (October 1974), pp. 58–9; and Ronnie Perelis, '"These Indians Are Jews!" Lost Tribes, Crypto-Jews and Jewish Self-Fashioning in Antonio de Montezinos's *Relación* of 1644', in *Atlantic Diasporas: Jews, Conversos and Crypto-Jews in the Age of Mercantilism, 1500–1800* (Baltimore, MD, 2009), pp. 195–211.

41 Ben Israel, 'Relation of Montezinos', pp. 106–11.

42 Richard W. Cogley, 'The Ancestry of the American Indians: Thomas Thorowgood's *Iewes in America* (1650) and *Jews in America* (1660)', *English Literary Renaissance*, XXXIV/2 (March 2005), pp. 304–9; Richard W. Cogley, 'John Eliot and the Origins of the American Indians', *Early American Literature*, XXI (1986–7), pp. 215–16; Thomas Thorowgood, *Iewes in America; or, Probabilities that the Americans are of that Race* (London, 1650), sig. D4 and pp. 5–6; and Thomas Thorowgood, *Jews in America; or, Probabilities, that those Indians are Judaical, made more probable by some Additionals to the former Conjectures* (London, 1660), pp. 26–7.

43 Cogley, 'Ancestry of American Indians', pp. 308–10; Edward Winslow, 'The Glorious Progress of the Gospel amongst the Indians in New England . . .', in *The Eliot Tracts: With Letters from John Eliot to Thomas Thorowgood and Richard Baxter*, ed. and intro. Michael P. Clark (Westport, CT, 2003), pp. 144–67; Albert M. Hyamson, 'The Lost Tribes and the Influence of the Search for Them on the Return of the Jews to England', *Jewish Quarterly Review*, XV/4 (July 1903), pp. 660–64; and Michael Hoberman, *New Israel/ New England: Jews and Puritans in Early America* (Amherst, MA, 2011), pp. 14–16.

44 Ben Israel, *Hope of Israel*, pp. 88–9, 101, 112, 144–5, 159 and 161–4.

45 Méchoulan, 'Introduction', in Ben Israel, *Hope of Israel*, pp. 56–60; David S. Katz, *Philo-Semitism and the Readmission of the Jews to England, 1603–1655* (Oxford, 1982), pp. 158–231 passim; and Huddleston, *Origins*, pp. 131–4.

46 Cogley, 'John Eliot and the Origins', pp. 216–17; John Eliot, 'The Learned Conjectures of Reverend Mr. John Eliot touching the Americans, of new and notable consideration, written to Mr. Thorowgood', in *The Eliot Tracts*, pp. 416–22.

47 Hamon L'Estrange, 'To the Reader', in *Americans no Iewes; or, Improbabilities that the Americans are of that race* (London, 1652), unpaginated section and p. 12 (Edward Brerewood was the author of *Enquiries Touching the Diversities of Languages and Religions* [London, 1614], which also advocated the Tartar origin

theory of the Native Americans); Hyamson, 'The Lost Tribes', pp. 665–8; and
Richard Cogley, '"Some Other Kinde of Being and Condition": The Contro-
versy in Mid-Seventeenth-Century England over the Peopling of Ancient
America', *Journal of the History of Ideas*, LXVIII/1 (January 2007), pp. 35–56.

48 Scholem, *Sabbatai Sevi*, pp. 88–93.

49 Ibid., pp. 8–21 and 417–33.

50 Ibid., pp. 103–325 passim. For Scholem's diagnosis of manic-depressive psychosis, see pp. 126–34.

51 Brandon Marriot, 'Who Sacked Mecca? The Life of a Rumour (1665–
1666)', chap. 3 of *Transnational Networks and Cross-Religious Exchange in the
Seventeenth-Century Mediterranean and Atlantic Worlds: Sabbatai Sevi and the
Lost Tribes of Israel*, and Scholem, *Sabbatai Sevi*, pp. 288–9, 332–54, 549, 555,
557–8, 649, 657.

52 Scholem, *Sabbatai Sevi*, pp. 433–60 and 668–86; Samuel Pepys, *The Concise
Pepys* (Ware, 1997), p. 379; and 'Dönmeh', in *Oxford Dictionary of the Jewish
Religion*.

53 John Ogliby, *America: Being an Accurate Description of the New World* (London,
1670 [actually 1671], pp. 27–9 and 39–43; 'A Letter from William Penn ... to the
Committee of the Free Society of Traders ... in London containing a general
description of the said Province ...' (1683), in William Penn, *The Selected Works
of William Penn*, 3 vols, 4th edn (London, 1825), vol. III, pp. 232–3; Gabriel
Thomas, *An Historical and Geographical Account of the Province and Country of
Pensilvania; and of West-New-Jersey in America* (London, 1698), pp. 1–2; and
Daniel Gookin, *Historical Collections of the Indians in New England* (Boston,
MA, 1792), pp. 4–7.

54 James Adair, *The History of the American Indians*, ed. and intro. Kathryn E.
Holland Braund (Tuscaloosa, AL, 2005); Thomas Jefferson, *Writings* (New
York, 1984), pp. 1261–2, letter of Thomas Jefferson to John Adams, 11 June
1812; Charles Hudson, 'James Adair as Anthropologist', *Ethnohistory*, XXIV/4
(Autumn 1977), pp. 311–28; and Richard H. Popkin, 'The Rise and Fall of the
Jewish Indian Theory', in *Menasseh Ben Israel and His World*, pp. 71–2.

55 Kathryn E. Holland Braund, 'James Adair: His Life and *History*', in Adair,
History of the American Indians, pp. 38–9 and 51; Elias Boudinot, *Star in the
West* (Trenton, NJ, 1816), pp. iii, vi, 26–7 and 74; Popkin, 'Jewish Indian Theory',
p. 73; and Ronald Fritze, 'Hebrews in Ancient America', in *Legend and Lore of
the Americas before 1492* (Santa Barbara, CA, 1993), p. 116; Ethan Smith, *View
of the Hebrews; or, The Tribes of Israel in America*, 2nd edn (Poultney, NJ, 1825),
Dan Vogel, *Indian Origins and the Book of Mormon: Religious Solutions from
Columbus to Joseph Smith* (Salt Lake City, UT, 1986), pp. 98–9, n. 90; Robert
Silverberg, *The Mound Builders of Ancient America: The Archaeology of a Myth*
(Greenwich, CT, 1968), p. 94; 'View of the Hebrews', Wikipedia, www.en.
wikipedia.org, accessed 18 March 2021; and *Travels and Adventures of the Rev.
Joseph Wolff*, D.D., LL.D. (London, 1861), p. 518.

56 Popkin, 'Jewish Indian Theory', pp. 73–6, and Silverberg, *The Mound Builders
of Ancient America*, pp. 6–7 and 57–8.

57 Joseph Wolff, *Researches and Missionary Labours among the Jews, Mohammedans
and Other Sects*, 2nd edn (London, 1835), pp. 2, 49, 159, 164, 168–9, 194–6, 423–5
and 529, and *Travels and Adventures of the Rev. Joseph* Wolff (1860), pp. 290,
295, 328–35, 355–8 and 364–5.

58 David and Charles Livingstone, *Narrative of an Expedition to the Zambesi
and its Tributaries ... 1858–1864* (New York, 1866), pp. 83–4, and J.P.R. Wallis,

ed., *The Zambezi Expedition of David Livingstone, 1858–1863* (London, 1956), pp. 135–6.

59 Edgar Rice Burroughs, *Tarzan and the Lost Empire* [1929] (New York, n.d.), p. 8, and *Tarzan and the City of God* (New York, 1933), p. 12.

60 Godbey, *The Lost Tribes a Myth*, pp. 4 and 7.

61 John Sadler, *Rights of the Kingdom; or, Customs of our Ancestours* (London, 1649); Gerrard Winstanley, 'A Declaration to the Powers of England (The True Levellers Standard Advanced)', in *The Complete Works of Gerrard Winstanley*, ed. Thomas N. Corns, Ann Hughes and David Loewenstein, 2 vols (Oxford, 2009), vol. II, pp. 1–31; Claire Jowitt, 'Radical Identities? Native Americans, Jews and the English Commonwealth', *Seventeenth Century*, x/1 (Spring 1995), pp. 104–5; Amy H. Sturgis, 'Prophecies and Politics: Millenarians, Rabbis and the Jewish Indian Theory', *Seventeenth Century*, XIV/1 (Spring 1999), pp. 16–17; and Ronald H. Fritze, *Invented Knowledge: False History, Fake Science and Pseudo-Religions* (London, 2009), p. 11.

62 Fritze, *Invented Knowledge*, pp. 111–13; for more detailed biographical studies of Brothers, see Cecil Roth, *The Nephew of the Almighty: An Experimental Account of the Life and Aftermath of Richard Brothers, R.N.* (London, 1933), and Deborah Madden, *The Paddington Prophet: Richard Brothers's Journey to Jerusalem* (Manchester, 2010).

63 This paragraph and those following that discuss British Israelism and Christian Identity are a condensation of Fritze, *Invented Knowledge*, pp. 113–34.

64 Neubauer, 'Where are the Ten Tribes?: IV.', p. 423; Elliott Horowitz, ''A Jew of the Old Type: Neubauer as Cataloguer, Critic and Necrologist', *Jewish Quarterly Review*, c/4 (Autumn 2010), pp. 649–56; and F. W. Phillips, *Proofs for the Welsh that the British are the Lost Tribes of Israel: The Abrahamic Covenant* (Bangor, 1880).

65 In addition to the material in Fritze, *Invented Knowledge*, pp. 113–34, see also Nicholas Goodrick-Clarke, *Black Sun: Aryan Cults, Esoteric Nazism and the Politics of Identity* (New York, 2002), pp. 235–6.

66 Parfitt, *Lost Tribes*, pp. 123–31, 168–73, 176–92, 207–12 and 222–5; Tudor Parfitt, *Black Jews in Africa and the Americas* (Cambridge, MA, 2013), pp. 53–5, 129–32 and 149–69; and Edith Bruder, *The Black Jews of Africa: History, Religion, Identity* (Oxford, 2008), pp. 118–23, 130–32 and 153–8.

4 Templars, Secret Societies and Conspiracy Theories

1 Umberto Eco, 'Foreword', in Barbara Frale, *The Templars: The Secret History Revealed* (New York, 2004), pp. xii–xiii.

2 Nesta H. Webster, *Secret Societies and Subversive Movements* [1924] (Escondido, CA, 2000), p. xi.

3 Malcolm Barber, *The New Knighthood: A History of the Order of the Temple* (Cambridge, 1995), p. 314; Malcolm Barber, *The Trial of the Templars* (London, 2003), pp. 283–5; Frale, *The Templars*, pp. 196–8; and Michael Haag, *The Templars: The History and the Myth* (New York, 2009), pp. 236–7.

4 Barber, *New Knighthood*, pp. 314–20, and Haag, *The Templars*, pp. 260–67. For more sensationalistic approaches, see S. J. Hodge, *Secrets of the Knights Templar: The Hidden History of the World's Most Powerful Order* (New York, 2013), pp. 175–6, and especially Graeme Davis, *Knights Templar: A Secret History* (Oxford, 2013), pp. 34–6. Both books are heavily illustrated, with some of the illustrations in Davis being highly imaginative. There is an English translation

of Gassicourt, *The Tomb of James Molai; or, the Secret of the Conspirators* (Boston, MA, 1797). Its translator was an unnamed 'Gentleman of Boston'.

5 John V. Fleming, *The Dark Side of the Enlightenment: Wizards, Alchemists and Spiritual Seekers in the Age of Reason* (New York, 2013), pp. 108–9; Theodore Ziolkowski, *Lure of the Arcane: The Literature of Cult and Conspiracy* (Baltimore, MD, 2013), pp. 5–6; and Paul Kléber, *Solomon's Secret Art: The Occult in the Age of Enlightenment* (New Haven, CT, and London, 2013), p. 227.

6 R. E. Witt, *Isis in the Ancient World* (Baltimore, 1971), passim; Apuleius, *The Golden Ass* (Bloomington, IN, 1962), 'Book the Eleventh' with quotes at pp. 238 and 242; Ivor J. Davidson, *A Public Faith: From Constantine to the Medieval World, A.D. 312–600* (Grand Rapids, MI, 2005), pp. 250 and 262; Eric Hornung, *Secret Lore of Egypt: Its Impact on the West* (Ithaca, NY, 2001), p. 14.

7 Ronald H. Fritze, *Egyptomania: A History of Fascination, Obsession and Fantasy* (London, 2016), pp. 102 and 104–6.

8 Ziolkowski, *Lure of the Arcane*, p. 6.

9 Ibid., pp. 5–6, and David V. Barrett, *A Brief History of Secret Societies* (London, 2007), pp. xxi, 1 and 71.

10 Ziolkowski, *Lure of the Arcane*, p. 8.

11 David Underdown, *Royalist Conspiracy in England, 1649–1660* [1960] (Hamden, CT, 1971).

12 Caroline Hibbard, *Charles I and the Popish Plot* (Chapel Hill, NC, 1983), and John Kenyon, *The Popish Plot* [1972] (Harmondsworth, 1974).

13 Christopher McIntosh, *Rosicrucians: The History, Mythology, and Rituals of an Esoteric Order* (San Francisco, CA, 1997), p. 7, and Fritze, *Egyptomania*, p. 133. For the place of the occult sciences in Renaissance and early modern scholarship, see Wayne Shumaker, *The Occult Sciences in the Renaissance: A Study of Intellectual Patterns* (Berkeley, CA, 1972); Allen G. Debus, *Man and Nature in the Renaissance* (New York, 2004); and Anthony Aveni, *Behind the Crystal Ball: Magic, Science and the Occult from Antiquity through the New Age* (Boulder, CO, 2002).

14 Frances A. Yates, *The Rosicrucian Enlightenment* [1972] (New York, 1996), pp. 41 and 235.

15 This paragraph and the following one are based on ibid. For the history of Rosicrucianism after the early seventeenth century, see Arthur Edward Waite, *The Brotherhood of the Rosy Cross* [1924] (New York, 1993).

16 Allen G. Debus, *Man and Nature in the Renaissance* (Cambridge, 1978), pp. 11–12.

17 Ziolkowski, *Lure of the Arcane*, p. 61.

18 McIntosh, *Rosicrucians*, pp. 17–18.

19 Yates, *Rosicrucian Enlightenment*, for her translation of the *Fama* see pp. 242 and 250.

20 Barrett, *Secret Societies*, pp. 91 and 93–4; Fleming, *Dark Side of the Enlightenment*, pp. 117–18 and 129–30; McIntosh, *Rosicrucians*, pp. xix, 21, 27, 29 and 31; and Ziolkowski, *Lure of the Arcane*, pp. 47, 49–52, 55 and 60.

21 Barrett, *Secret Societies*, p. 94.

22 McIntosh, *Rosicrucians*, pp. 32–4 and 51.

23 Barrett, *Secret Societies*, p. 95; Fleming, *Dark Side of the Enlightenment*, p. 62; Monod, *Solomon's Secret Arts*, pp. 38–9; McIntosh, *Rosicrucians*, pp. 40–42 and 44; and Yates, *Rosicrucian Enlightenment*, pp. 179–80.

24 Jasper Ridley, *The Freemasons: A History of the World's Most Powerful Secret Society* (New York, 2001), pp. 17–18 and 22–3; Jay Kinney, *The Masonic Myth: Unlocking the Truth About the Symbols, the Secret Rites and the History of*

Freemasonry (New York, 2009), pp. 18–25; McIntosh, *Rosicrucians*, p. 64; Barrett, *Secret Societies*, p. 109; and Ziolkowski, *Lure of the Arcane*, p. 66. For a detailed account of the beginnings of Masonry, see David Stevenson, *The Origins of Freemasonry: Scotland's Century, 1590–1710* (Cambridge, 2015).

25 Fleming, *Dark Side of the Enlightenment*, pp. 144 and 163–4; Monod, *Solomon's Secret Arts*, p. 180; Ziolkowski, *Lure of the Arcane*, pp. 65–6; Peter Partner, *The Knights Templar and their Myth* [1981] (Rochester, VT, 1990), pp. 101–2; Kinney, *The Masonic Myth*; and Ridley, *The Freemasons*.

26 Albert Gallatin Mackey, *The History of Freemasonry: Its Legendary Origins* [1898] (Mineola, NY, 2008), is an overview of most of the Freemason origin legends. For a more modern account of Freemasonry's legendary origins, see Laurence Gardner, *The Shadow of Solomon: The Lost Secret of the Freemasons Revealed* (San Francisco, CA, 2007).

27 Fleming, *Dark Side of the Enlightenment*, pp. 116–17; Haag, *Templars*, pp. 270–72; Hodge, *Secrets of the Knights Templar*, pp. 192–3; Davis, *Knights Templar*, pp. 48–53, which includes a lavish colour illustration depicting Indians attacking a Templar settlement in the process of building a Templar round church. There many books dealing with supposed Templar exploration and settlement of the Americas, such as Andrew Sinclair's *The Sword and the Grail: Of the Grail and the Templars and a True Discovery of America* (New York, 1992), which was one of the first Templars in America books in recent times. Other examples are Robert Lomas, *Turning the Templar Key: The Secret Legacy of the Knights Templar and the Origins of Freemasonry* (Beverly, MA, 2007); Ruggero Marino, *Christopher Columbus, the Last Templar* (Rochester, VT, 2005); and Tim Wallace-Murphy and Marilyn Hopkins, *Templars in America: From the Crusades to the New World* (New York, 2006).

28 Partner, *Knights Templar Myth*, pp. 98, 103–6 and 108; Barrett, *Secret Societies*, pp. 112 and 116; and J. M. Roberts, *The Mythology of the Secret Societies* [1972] (London, 2008), pp. 109–10.

29 Partner, *Knights Templar Myth*, pp. 110 and 112–13, and Roberts, *Mythology of the Secret Societies*, pp. 15 and 114.

30 Barrett, *Secret Societies*, pp. 113–15; Partner, *Knights Templar Myth*, pp. 116–17, 121 and 130; Roberts, *Mythology of the Secret Societies*, pp. 53 and 121; and McIntosh, *Rosicrucians*, pp. 63 and 65.

31 Barrett, *Secret Societies*, p. xviii; Monod, *Solomon's Secret Arts*, pp. 303–4; and Roberts, *Mythology of the Secret Societies*, pp. 100–104, 131, 159 and 179.

32 Jonathan I. Israel, *Democratic Enlightenment: Philosophy, Revolution and Human Rights, 1750–1790* (Oxford, 2012), pp. 702, 748, 750–51 and 828–41; John Michael Greer, *The Element Encyclopedia of Secret Societies* (New York, 2006), pp. 96–102; Barrett, *Secret Societies*, p. 100; Fleming, *Dark Side of the Enlightenment*, p. 62; Partner, *Knights Templar Myth*, p. 125; and Roberts, *Mythology of the Secret Societies*, p. 133.

33 Monod, *Solomon's Secret Arts*, p. 321; Robert, *Mythology of the Secret Societies*, pp. 131, 136, 145–7, 149 and 188; Partner, *Knights Templar Myth*, pp. 126–7; and Israel, *Democratic Enlightenment*, pp. 702 and 828–41.

34 Darren M. McMahon, *Enemies of the Enlightenment: The French Counter-Enlightenment and the Making of Modernity* (Oxford, 2012), pp. 68–9 and 113; Graeme Garrard, *Counter-Enlightenment from the Eighteenth Century to the Present* (London, 2006), pp. 36–42; and Edmund Burke to Abbé Barruel, 1 May 1797, in *The Correspondence of Edmund Burke*, ed. R. B. McDowell (Cambridge and Chicago, IL, 1970), vol. IX, pp. 319–20.

35 Roberts, *Mythology of the Secret Societies*, pp. 182–92.

36 Jean Flahaut, *Charles-Louis Cadet de Gassicourt, 1769–1821: Bâtard royal, pharmacien de l'Empereur* (Paris, 2001).

37 Charles-Louis Cadet de Gassicourt, *Tomb of James Molai* (Boston, MA, 1797), pp. 5, 7, 11–14 and 17 (*Tomb* is a small book of 22 pages in English translation), and Partner, *Knights Templar Myth*, pp. 130–32.

38 Roberts, *Mythology of the Secret Societies*, pp. 199–201; McMahon, *Enemies of the Enlightenment*, pp. 27–8 and 41–2; Garrard, 'Counter-Enlightenment and Counter Revolution', in *Counter-Enlightenment*, pp. 42–8; and Amos Hofman, 'The Origins of the Theory of the Philosophe Conspiracy', *French History*, 11 (June 1998), pp. 152–72.

39 For an edition of Barruel in modern type and in one complete volume of 846 pages, see A. Barruel, *Illustrating the History of Jacobinism*, intro. Stanley L. Jaki (Fraser, MI, 1995). It was published by Rear-View Books for the American Society on Economics and Society. Neither entity has a website. Jaki's introduction takes a very conservative Roman Catholic viewpoint and takes Barruel's thesis seriously.

40 Roberts, *Mythology of the Secret Societies*, p. 199, and Partner, *Knights Templar Myth*, p. 131.

41 'John Robison', in *Oxford Dictionary of National Biography*, 60 vols (Oxford, 2004).

42 John Robison, *Proofs of a Conspiracy against All the Religions and Governments of Europe, carried on in the Secret Meetings of Free Masons, Illuminati, and Reading Societies* (1797), pp. 157–96. Information on the last page of the book indicates that this version was published by CreateSpace (a self-publishing service) in 2019. There are several other CreateSpace reprints. The John Birch Society brought out a reprint of *Proofs of Conspiracy* in 1967, and it is still on sale on its website, www.jbs.org.

43 Stanley Jaki, 'Introduction', in Barruel, *Memoirs*, pp. xvii–xviii, and Roberts, *Mythology of the Secret Societies*, pp. 203–4.

44 Partner, *Knights Templar Myth*, pp. 131 and 133; Roberts, *Mythology of the Secret Societies*, pp. 203–4 and 217; and Amos Hofman, 'Opinions, Illusion and the Illusion of Opinion: Barruel's Theory of Conspiracy', *Eighteenth-Century Studies*, XXVII (Fall 1993), pp. 27–60, esp. 59–60. For a Masonic critique, see W. K. Firminger, 'The Romances of Robison and Barruel', *Ars Quatour Coronatum*, 1 (1940), pp. 31–69.

45 Una Birch, *Secret Societies: Illuminati, Freemasons, and the French Revolution* [1911] (Lake Worth, FL, 2007); Webster, *Secret Societies and Subversive Movements*; 'Nesta Helen Webster', in *Oxford Dictionary of National Biography*. The reprint of Una Birch's book includes some brief biographical information. More detailed accounts about Nesta Webster can be found in Richard Griffiths, *Fellow Travellers of the Right: British Enthusiasts for Nazi Germany 1933–1939* [1980] (London, 2010); Richard M. Gilman, *Behind World Revolution: The Strange Career of Nesta H. Webster* (Ann Arbor, MI, 1982); Markku Ruotsila, 'Mrs. Webster's Religion: Conspiracist Extremism on the Christian Far Right', *Patterns of Prejudice*, XXXIX/2 (2004), pp. 109–26; and Martha F. Lee, 'Nesta Webster: The Voice of Conspiracy', *Journal of Women's History*, XVII/3 (2005), pp. 81–104.

46 [Jakob Levi Bartholdy], *Memoirs of the Secret Societies of the South of Italy, particularly the Carbonari* (London, 1821).

47 Roberts, *Mythology of the Secret Societies*, pp. 18–23, 262 and 314–60; Ziolkowski, *Lure of the Arcane*, pp. 99–101; Richard Evans, *The Pursuit of Power: Europe*

1815–1914 (New York, 2016), pp. 27, 32, 37–9, 44–5, 75, 81–3, 173, 213, 266 and 271–2; and Elizabeth L. Eisenstein, *The First Professional Revolutionist: Filippo Michele Buonarroti, 1761–1837* (Cambridge, MA, 1959).

48 Evans, *Pursuit of Power*, p. 78; 'Wilhelm Marr (1819–1904)', https://jewish-virtuallibrary.org, accessed 19 March 2021. The English translation of Marr's book is at www.kevinmcdonald.net; and Moshe Zimmermann, *Wilhelm Marr: The Patriarch of Anti-Semitism* (Oxford, 1986).

49 Norman Cohn, *Warrant for Genocide: The Myth of the Jewish World Conspiracy and the Protocols of the Elders of Zion* [1967] (London, 1996), pp. 26–8, 46 and 48, and Norman Cohn, *The Pursuit of the Millennium: Revolutionary Mille-narians and Mystical Anarchists of the Middle Ages* [1957] (New York, 1970), pp. 78–9 and 285.

50 Cohn, *Warrant*, pp. 44–9, and Umberto Eco, *Serendipities* (New York, 1998), pp. 13–16.

51 Cohn, *Warrant*, pp. 113 and 116–18, and Walter Laqueur, 'The Many Lives of "The Protocols of the Elders of Zion"', *Mosaic: Advancing Jewish Thought* (4 December 2017), unpaginated, https://mosaicmagazine.com. This essay is a fine summary of the state of scholarship on the 'Protocols'.

52 Laqueur, 'Many Lives', passim; Cesare G. De Michelis, *The Non-Existent Manuscript: A Study of the Protocols of the Sages of Zion* (1998, revd and expanded English trans., Lincoln, NE, 2004); Michael Hagemeister, 'The Protocols of the Elders of Zion: Between History and Fiction', *New German Critique*, XXXV/103 (Winter 2008), pp. 83–95; Michael Hagemeister, 'Sergei Nilus and the Apocalyptical Reading of *The Protocols of the Elders of Zion*', in *The Para-noid Apocalypse: A Hundred Year Retrospective on the Protocols of the Elders of Zion*, ed. Richard Landers and Steven T. Katz (New York, 2012), pp. 79–91; and Richard S. Levy, 'Setting the Record Straight regarding *The Protocols of the Elders of Zion*: A Fool's Errand?', *Nexus 2: Essays in German Jewish Studies* (Martlesham, 2013), pp. 43–62.

53 Cohn, *Warrant*, pp. 126, 132–4 and 139.

54 Ibid., pp. 139–42.

55 Ibid., pp. 139, 174 and 177–8; George L. Mosse, *The Crisis of German Ideology: Intellectual Origins of the Protocols of the Elders of Zion* (Lincoln, NE, 1995), pp. 25–7. Benjamin W. Segel, *A Lie and a Libel: The History of the Protocols of the Elders of Zion*, trans. and ed. Richard S. Levy (Lincoln, NE, 1996), pp. 24–7. This book is a translation and an abridgement of a book Segal published in Germany during 1925 with a detailed chronology of the history of the 'Protocols' and a substantial introduction by Richard S. Levy.

56 Lucien Wolf, *The Myth of the Jewish Menace in World Affairs* (New York, 1921), p. 9; Ziolkowski, *Lure of the Arcane*, p. 165; and Webster, *Secret Societies*, pp. 408–14.

57 Herman Bernstein, *The History of a Lie: 'The Protocols of the Wise Men of Zion'* (New York, 1921).

58 Cohn, *Warrant*, pp. 190–98, and Segel, *A Lie and a Libel*, pp. 12–14 and 20–29.

59 Cohn, *Warrant*, pp. 152–3, 155–62 and 187, and Ziolkowski, *Lure of the Arcane*, p. 164.

60 Adolf Hitler, *Mein Kampf* (New York, 1941), pp. 307–8.

61 Cohn, *Warrant*, pp. xiv, 197–8, 212, 214 and 268; Hannah Arendt, *The Origins of Totalitarianism* [1951] (London, 2017); and Ziolkowski, *Lure of the Arcane*, p. 164.

62 Bernstein, *The History of a Lie*, p. 83.

63 Robert J. McMahon, *The Cold War: A Very Short Introduction* (Oxford, 2003), p. 118; Alan Brinkley, 'The Illusion of Unity in Cold War Culture', in *Rethinking Cold War*, ed. Peter J. Kuznick and James Gilbert (Washington, DC, 2001), pp. 62–3; and Stephen J. Whitfield, *The Culture of the Cold War*, 2nd edn (Baltimore, MD, 1996), especially Chapters One and Two.

64 Thomas Milan Konda, *Conspiracies of Conspiracies: How Delusions Have Overrun America* (Chicago, IL, 2019), p. 231; Tom Jensen, 'Democrats and Republicans Differ on Conspiracy Theory Beliefs', www.publicpolicypolling.com, 2 April 2013; 'The Conspiratorial Mindset in an Age of Transition' (executive summary), Political Capitol Research Consulting Institute, www.deconspirator.com, 20 December 2013; and Steven Rosenfeld, 'Study: How Breitbart Media's Disinformation Created the Paranoid Fact-Averse Nation that Elected Trump', www.alternet.org, 20 July 2017.

65 Jonathan Houghton, 'Welch, Robert Henry Winborne, Jr.', in *Dictionary of North Carolina Biography*, ed. William S. Powell, 6 vols (Chapel Hill, NC, 1979–96), also available at www.ncpedia.org; Sharon D. Rudy, 'Welch, Robert', in *American National Biography*, ed. John A. Garraty and Mark C. Carnes, 24 vols (Oxford, 1999); and Terry Lautz, *John Birch: A Life* (New York, 2016), pp. 219–20.

66 Lautz, *John Birch*, pp. 255–7, and James H. 'Jimmy' Doolittle with Carroll V. Glines, *I Could Never Be So Lucky: An Autobiography* (New York, 1991), p. 279.

67 Christopher Towler, 'The John Birch Society Is Still Influencing American Politics, 60 Years after its Founding', www.theconversation.com, 6 December 2018.

68 Lautz, *John Birch*, pp. 234–48. Although Lautz's book is a biography, its last five chapters out of sixteen discuss the reputation and use of John Birch's name after his death. It also provides a concise history of the John Birch Society up to Robert Welch's death in 1985. Also see Sean Wilentz 'Confounding Fathers: The Tea Party's Cold War Roots', www.newyorker.com, 11 October 2010. This article contains a brief overview of the John Birch Society's history.

69 Konda, *Conspiracies of Conspiracies*, pp. 157, 278 and 281.

70 Wilentz, 'Confounding Fathers', is a good account of the John Birch Society's return to prominence in right-wing American politics with the help of Glenn Beck.

71 Mark Jacobson, *Pale Horse Rider: William Cooper and the Fall of Trust in America* (New York, 2019), pp. 44–9; William Cooper, *Behold a Pale Horse* (Flagstaff, AZ, 1991), pp. 315–30, provides facsimiles of military records documenting Cooper's service in the navy but not the air force. The introduction to *Behold a Pale Horse* is a brief autobiography of Cooper.

72 Jacobson, *Pale Horse Rider*, pp. 50–61, and Michael Barkun, *A Culture of Conspiracy: Apocalyptic Visions in Contemporary America*, 2nd edn (Berkeley, CA, 2013), p. 60, made the same observation in 2013.

73 Cooper, *Behold a Pale Horse*, passim. The revised edition, eliminating the chapter printing the 'Protocols of the Wise Men of Zion', was published in 2019 by Cooper's original publisher, Light Technology, now located at Flagstaff, Arizona. Cooper wrote as William Cooper, not using his first name, Milton. In social situations he went by Bill. See also Barkun, *Culture of Conspiracy*, p. 60, and Konda, *Conspiracies of Conspiracies*, p. 209.

74 Curtis Peebles, *Watch the Skies! A Chronicle of the Flying Saucer Myth* (Washington, DC, 1994), passim but esp. pp. 256–82; Barkun, *Culture of Conspiracy*, pp. 62–3, 85 and 90–92; and Cooper, *Behold a Pale Horse*, p. 382, where he

provides a facsimile of the title of the first American edition of John Robison's conspiracist classic, *Proofs of Conspiracy*.

75 Barkun, *Culture of Conspiracy*, pp. 30, 143, 220; Peebles, *Watch the Skies!*, p. 276; and Jerome Clark, 'Conspiracy Theories', in UFOS *and Popular Culture: An Encyclopedia of Contemporary Myth* (Santa Barbara, CA, 2000), pp. 84–5.

76 Peebles, *Watch the Skies!*, p. 279; Barkun, *Culture of Conspiracy*, pp. 36, 61, 96 and 226. According to Jacobson's *Pale Horse Rider*, pp. 103–5, Cooper had decided that aliens and UFOS were a government hoax prior to the publication of *Behold a Pale Horse*. Given Cooper's seeming ability to maintain contradictory beliefs simultaneously, it is often difficult to determine what he actually thought.

77 Barkun, *Culture of Conspiracy*, pp. xi and 70, and Jacobson, *Pale Horse Rider*, pp. 248–62.

78 Jacobson, *Pale Horse Rider*, pp. 310–13, 317–19 and 328–32.

79 'Alex Jones', www.en.wikipedia.org, accessed 19 March 2021. This article is copiously sourced.

80 Elizabeth Williamson and Emily Steel, 'Conspiracy Theories Made Alex Jones Rich. They May Bring Him Down', www.nytimes.com, 7 September 2018, and Veit Medick, 'Donald Trump's Propagandist', www.spiegel.de, 28 February 2017.

81 See the website of the John Birch Society at www.jbs.org.

82 For InfoWars, see www.infowars.com along with PrisonPlanet at www.prisonplanet.com and NewsWars at www.newswars.com.

83 Konda, *Conspiracies of Conspiracies*, pp. 294–5, 307, 310 and 329, and www.infowars.com.

84 Konda, *Conspiracies of Conspiracies*, p. 330.

5 A Road to Perdition: Germans, Nazis and a Culture of the Supernatural

1 Quoted by Irving Hexham, 'Inventing "Paganists": A Close Reading of Richard Steigmann-Gall's *The Holy Reich*', *Journal of Contemporary History*, XLII (January 2007), pp. 76–7.

2 Hermann Rauschning, *Gespräche mit Hitler* [1940] (Zurich, 2005), p. 208, which reads, 'Jeder Deutsche steht mit einem Fuss in jenem bekannten Lande Atlantis, in dem er middestens einen recht stattlichen Erbhof sein eigen nennt.' I have used Eric Kurlander's translation in 'The Nazi Magicians' Controversy: Enlightenment, "Border Science," and Occultism in the Third Reich', *Central European History*, XLVIII (2015), p. 500. This passage does not appear in the English translations of his book.

3 Peter Longerich, *Heinrich Himmler* (Oxford, 2012), pp. 272–3.

4 Chris Wickham, *The Inheritance of Rome: A History of Europe from 400 to 1000* (New York, 2009), pp. 430–35, for a brief historical overview, and Madelyn Bergen Dick, 'Henry I of Saxony', in *Who's Who in the Middle Ages*, ed. Richard K. Emmerson (London, 2006), pp. 454–5.

5 Peter Padfield, *Himmler* (New York, 1990), p. 249, and Christopher Hale, *Himmler's Crusade: The Nazi Expedition to Find the Origins of the Aryan Race* (Edison, NJ, 2003), p. 85.

6 Monica Black and Eric Kurlander, eds, *Revisiting the 'Nazi Occult': Histories, Realities, Legacies* (Rochester, NY, 2015), in which see Black and Kurlander, 'Introduction', pp. 2 and 8, and Peter Staudenmaier, 'Esoteric Alternatives in Imperial Germany: Science, Spirit and the Modern Occult Revival', pp. 24, 31

and 34–5; Eric Kurlander, *Hitler's Monsters: A Supernatural History of the Third Reich* (New Haven, CT, and London, 2017), pp. xv–xvi, 14–22 and 298–300; Corinna Treitel, *A Science for the Soul: Occultism and the Genesis of the German Modern* (Baltimore, MD, 2004), pp. 18, 27 and 66; and Nicholas Goodrick-Clarke, *The Occult Roots of Nazism: Secret Aryan Cults and their Influence on Nazi Ideology; The Ariosophists of Austria and Germany, 1890–1935* [1985] (New York, 1992), pp. 1 and 204. Goodrick-Clarke's Appendix, 'The Modern Mythology of Nazi Occultism', pp. 217–25, provides a survey and debunking of the sensationalistic literature of the Nazi occult up to 1992.

7 For the history of German occultism in the nineteenth and twentieth centuries, see Treitel, *Science for the Soul*. For the Red Jews, Rosicrucians and German Freemasonry, see Andrew Gow, *The Red Jews: Anti-Semitism in an Apocalyptic Age, 1200–1600* (Leiden, 1994); Christopher McIntosh, *The Rosicrucians: The History, Mythology and Rituals of an Esoteric Order*, 3rd edn (San Francisco, 1997); and David V. Barrett, *A Brief History of Secret Societies* (London, 2007).

8 Theodore Ziolkowski, *Lure of the Arcane: The Literature of Cult and Conspiracy* (Baltimore, MD, 2013), p. 133, and Paul Kléber Monod, *Solomon's Secret Arts: The Occult in the Age of Enlightenment* (New Haven, CT, and London, 2013), pp. 227 and 263. For studies of the occult revival in Britain and Germany, see Alex Owen, *The Place of Enchantment: British Occultism and the Culture of the Modern* (Chicago, IL, 2004), and Treitel, *Science for the Soul*.

9 Richard J. Evans, *The Coming of the Third Reich* (New York, 2003), pp. xxiv–xxviii, 2, 17, 20–21, 102, 111, 118 and 120–25; Kurlander, *Hitler's Monsters*, pp. xviii and 63; and Ian Kershaw, *To Hell and Back: Europe, 1914–1949* (New York, 2015), pp. 241–6.

10 Evans, *Coming*, pp. 27–31, and Norman Cohn, *Warrant for Genocide: The Myth of the Jewish World Conspiracy and the Protocols of the Elders of Zion* [1967] (London, 1996).

11 Evans, *Coming*, pp. 37–9; Goodrick-Clarke, *Occult Roots*, p. 13; Hale, *Himmler's Crusade*, p. 102; Frank Spencer, 'Rassenhygiene and Rassenkunde' [Racial Hygiene and Race Lore], and John V. Day, 'Aryanism', in *History of Physical Anthropology: An Encyclopedia*, ed. Frank Spencer, 2 vols (New York, 1997); and Leon Poliakov, *The Aryan Myth: A History of Racist and Nationalist Ideas in Europe* (New York, 1974), who takes the topic from prehistory into the nineteenth century. For the American experience with scientific racism and social Darwinism, see Richard Hofstadter, *Social Darwinism in American Thought* [1944] (Boston, MA, 1992), and Susan Jacoby, *The Age of American Unreason* (New York, 2008), pp. 61–81.

12 Poliakov, *Ayran Myth*, pp. 183–214, and Heather Pringle, *The Master Plan: Himmler's Scholars and the Holocaust* (New York, 2006), pp. 28–34.

13 George L. Mosse, *The Nationalization of the Masses: Political Symbolism and Mass Movements in Germany from the Napoleonic Wars through the Third Reich* (New York, 1975), surveys the various tactics and techniques used to create and strengthen German nationalism.

14 George L. Mosse, 'The Mystical Origins of National Socialism', *Journal of the History of Ideas*, XXII/1 (January–March 1961), pp. 87 and 96; George L. Mosse, *The Crisis of German Ideology: Intellectual Origins of the Third Reich* (New York, 1964), pp. 4–5; Kurlander, *Hitler's Monsters*, pp. 11 and 32; and Goodrick-Clarke, *Occult Roots*, p. 5.

15 Richard J. Evans, *Coming*, p. 48; Kurlander, *Hitler's Monsters*, pp. 11 and 32; Goodrick-Clarke, *Occult Roots*, pp. 98–9; Mosse, 'Mystical Origins', pp. 87, 94

and 96; and for a detailed analysis of the history of the *völkisch* movement, see Mosse, *Crisis of German Ideology*.

16 Goodrick-Clarke, *Occult Roots*, pp. 2–3 and 5.

17 Ibid., pp. 33, 49 and 56–7; Mosse, 'Mystical Origins', p. 89; and Treitel, *Science for the Soul*, p. 104.

18 Goodrick-Clarke, *Occult Roots*, pp. 50, 63, 66–70 and 77.

19 Mosse, 'Mystical Origins', pp. 81 and 84–5; Treitel, *Science for the Soul*, pp. 83–4 and 102; Goodrick-Clarke, *Occult Roots*, pp. 15, 18, 22–3, 29–31, 55, 65 and 79–80; Hale, *Himmler's Crusade*, pp. 26 and 30. For an example of List's writings in English there is *The Secret of the Runes*, ed., intro. and trans. Stephen E. Flowers [1908] (Rochester, VT, 1988). Flowers's extensive introduction provides biographical material and places List's work into a broader context.

20 Goodrick-Clarke, *Occult Roots*, pp. 63–4, 77–9, 81–3 and 88–9.

21 Ibid., pp. 90–92; Treitel, *Science for the Soul*, p. 104; and David Luhrssen, *Hammer of the Gods: The Thule Society and the Birth of Nazism* (Washington, DC, 2012), p. 37.

22 Goodrick-Clark, *Occult Roots*, pp. 55, 95, 98 and 101–2.

23 Ibid., pp. 90, 92, 106–14 and 122.

24 Ibid., pp. 45–6, 51, 62, 64 and 126–7, and Luhrssen, *Hammer of the Gods*, pp. 65–6. Frisch published the German translation of Henry Ford's *International Jew* in 1921, which went through 21 printings between 1921 and 1922.

25 Goodrick-Clarke, *Occult Roots*, pp. 127–8, 130 and 132–3.

26 Luhrssen, *Hammer of the Gods*, pp. 43 and 69, and Goodrick-Clarke, *Occult Roots*, pp. 133–5, 138 and 140–42.

27 Evans, *Coming*, pp. 159–60; Kurlander, *Hitler's Monsters*, pp. 34–41; Goodrick-Clarke, *Occult Origins*, pp. 133–4, 144–5 and 149; Luhrssen, *Hammer of the Gods*, pp. 61–2 and 74–5.

28 Evans, *Coming*, pp. 159–60; Luhrssen, *Hammer of the Gods*, pp. 76–7, 107–8, 113, 120, 133–8 and 147; Goodrick-Clarke, *Occult Roots*, pp. 144–7 and 149; and Kurlander, *Hitler's Monsters*, pp. 42–6.

29 Luhrssen, *Hammer of the Gods*, pp. 189–90.

30 Ibid., pp. 76–8.

31 Goodrick-Clarke, *Occult Roots*, pp. 133–4; Kurlander, *Hitler's Monsters*, pp. 34–41 and 50–56; and Luhrssen, *Hammer of the Gods*, pp. 155–6, 173–4 and 191–2.

32 For an excellent detailed account of these events, see Evans, *Coming*, pp. 232–308.

33 Besides Evans, *Coming*, see also Mosse, *Crisis of German Ideology*; and Kurlander, *Hitler's Monsters*. Both discuss in detail the types of pseudoscientific and pseudohistorical ideas held by many Germans, particularly the Nazis.

34 Treitel, *Science for the Soul*, provides a fine history of the occult in Wilhelmine and Weimar Germany.

35 Walter Isaacson, *Einstein: His Life and Universe* (New York, 2007), pp. 384–5.

36 Kurlander, *Hitler's Monsters*, pp. 384–5.

37 Ian Kershaw, *Hitler, 1889–1936: Hubris* (New York, 1999), pp. 138 and 154–5; Volker Ullrich, *Hitler: Ascent, 1889–1939* (New York, 2016), pp. 86, 105–7 and 126; Luhrssen, *Hammer of the Gods*, pp. 78, 155–6 and 173–4; Kurlander, *Hitler's Monsters*, pp. 50–56; and Evans, *Coming*, pp. 178–9.

38 Kurlander, *Hitler's Monsters*, pp. 46–9 and 56–7.

39 Goodrick-Clarke, *Occult Roots*, pp. 197–98, and Luhrssen, *Hammer of the Gods*, pp. 36 and 152–3.

40 Kurlander, *Hitler's Monsters*, p. 138; Luhrssen, *Hammer of the Gods*, pp. 42 and 152–3; Goodrick-Clarke, *Occult Roots*, pp. 97 and 197–8; Kershaw, *Hitler: Hubris*, pp. 49–52, 63 and 621, nn. 199, 201 and 203; and Ullrich, *Hitler: Ascent*, p. 44.

41 Willy Ley, 'Pseudoscience in Naziland', *Astounding Science Fiction*, XXXIX/3 (1947), pp. 90–98, and www.alpenfestung.com, accessed 20 March 2021.

42 Quote from Luhrssen, *Hammer of the Gods*, p. 149.

43 Goodrick-Clarke, *Occult Roots*, pp. 146 and 151–2, and Luhrssen, *Hammer of the Gods*, pp. xxi and 149–50.

44 Kershaw, *Hitler: Hubris*, pp. 155, 158 and 183, and Ullrich, *Hitler: Ascent*, pp. 105–7 and 126.

45 Goodrick-Clarke, *Occult Roots*, pp. 29, 194–5 and 198. Lanz told this story to the historian Wilfried Daim in 1951. For scepticism about Lanz's influence on Hitler, see Kershaw, *Hitler: Hubris*, pp. 50–52, and Ullrich, *Hitler: Ascent*, p. 44.

46 Goodrick-Clarke, *Occult Roots*, pp. 150–51, 196–9 and 201–3; Adolf Hitler, *Mein Kampf* (New York, 1941), p. 498. The more accessible Adolf Hitler, *Mein Kampf*, trans. Ralph Manheim (Boston, MA, 1973), p. 360, reads: 'those *deutschvölkisch* wandering scholars'. For Hitler's commitment to *völkisch* ideology in *Mein Kampf*, 1941 edition, see especially vol. I, ch. 12, 'The First Period of Development of the National Socialist German Workers' Party', and vol. II, ch. 4, 'Personality and the Concept of the Folkish State'.

47 Pringle, *Master Plan*, pp. 91–2. Quote is on p. 92.

48 Max Domarus, *Hitler's Speeches and Proclamations, 1932–1945*, vol. II: *The Years 1935 to 1938* (Wauconda, IL, 1992), pp. 1145–7; *Hitler's Secret Conversations, 1941–1944*, trans. N. Cameron and R. H Stevens, intro. H. R. Trevor-Roper (New York, 1972), p. 342 (Rosenberg was occasionally a guest at these dinners but was not present on this occasion); Kurlander, *Hitler's Monsters*, pp. 58–9, 168 and 182; Luhrssen, *Hammer*, pp. 164–5.

49 Kurlander, *Hitler's Monsters*, pp. 64–74, and Timothy W. Ryback, *Hitler's Private Library: The Books that Shaped his Life* (London, 2009), pp. 114n, 146, 147, 157 and 158–61.

50 Kurlander, *Hitler's Monsters*, pp. 89–94, 100, 105 and 133. See also Mel Gordon, *Hanussen: Hitler's Jewish Clairvoyant* (Los Angeles, CA, 2001), and Arthur J. Magida, *The Nazi Séance: The Strange Story of the Jewish Psychic in Hitler's Circle* (New York, 2011).

51 Kurlander, *Hitler's Monsters*, pp. 118–30. Richard J. Evans, *The Hitler Conspiracies* (New York, 2020), ch. 4, "Why did Rudolf Hess fly to Britain?" discusses the various theories about Hess's flight to Britain.

52 Ibid., pp. 100–106 and 110–20, and Kurlander, 'The Nazi Magicians' Controversy', pp. 503, 505–7, 512–15 and 519–21. Treitel, *Science for the Soul*, pp. 211 and 223–5, asserts that Nazis were hostile to the occult, but the evidence provided by Kurlander refutes her claim.

53 Kurlander, *Hitler's Monsters*, pp. xi, 30–31, 150–61 and 228; Eric Kurlander, 'Hitler's Supernatural Sciences: Astrology, Anthroposophy and World Ice Theory in the Third Reich', in *Revisiting the 'Nazi Occult'*, p. 145; *Hitler's Secret Conversations*, pp. 324–5 and 249–50. For a concise and amusing description of World Ice Theory, see Ley, 'Pseudoscience in Naziland'. This essay was originally published by the magazine *Astounding Science Fiction* in 1947. For a good book-length study, there is Robert Bowen, *Universal Ice: Science and Ideology in the Nazi State* (London, 1993).

54 Evans, *Coming*, pp. 176–7 and 196, and Kurlander, *Hitler's Monsters*, pp. 12, 28, 53, 37, 138–9, 152 and 267.

55 Two excellent biographies of Himmler are Peter Padfield, *Himmler* (New York, 1990), and Peter Longerich, *Heinrich Himmler* (Oxford, 2012), especially his Chapter Ten, 'Ideology and Religious Cult'. Quote from Wisliceny in Cohn, *Warrant for Genocide*, p. 209.

56 Goodrick-Clarke, *Occult Roots*, pp. 177 and 179–91, and Pringle, *Master Plan*, pp. 46–9.

57 Evans, *Coming*, pp. 226–30, and Richard H. Evans, *The Third Reich in Power* (New York, 2005), pp. 50–55. For more detail on Himmler's involvement, see Longerich, *Heinrich Himmler*, and Padfield, *Himmler*. Wisliceny quote from Cohn, *Warrant for Genocide*, p. 199.

58 Pringle, *Master Plan*, passim, is the source for much of this paragraph. Hale, *Himmler's Crusade*, while focused on the Schäfer expedition to Tibet, contains considerable background on Himmler and the Ahnenerbe. For a concise assessment of Ahnenerbe, see Kurlander, *Hitler's Monsters*, pp. 154–5. Arthur Posnansky, *Tihuanacu: The Cradle of American Man* (New York, 1945–57), is an English translation.

59 Longerich, *Heinrich Himmler*, p. 138, Padfield, *Himmler*, p. 93, and Hale, *Himmler's Crusade*, p. 85.

60 Evans, *Third Reich in Power*, p. 421; Kurlander, *Hitler's Monsters*, p. 233; Pringle, *Master Plan*, pp. 39, 41 and 137–44; Hale, *Himmler's Crusade*, pp. 82 and 91; and Treitel, *Science for the Soul*, p. 213.

61 Pringle, *Master Plan*, pp. 333–6; Hale, *Himmler's Crusade*, pp. 103–6; Ryback, *Hitler's Private Library*, pp. 69, 110 and 111; and Christopher M. Hutton, *Race and the Third Reich: Linguistics, Racial Anthropology and Genetics in the Dialectic of the Volk* (Cambridge, 2005), pp. 35–63 passim, 105, 108, 110, 113 and 221. Günther's *The Racial Elements of European History* has been available in English translation since 1927. Several reprints have appeared in the past two decades.

62 Martin Gardner, *Fads and Fallacies in the Name of Science* (New York, 1957), p. 153.

63 Kurlander, *Hitler's Monsters*, p. 190; Luhrssen, *Hammer of the Gods*, p. 164; and Gardner, *Fads and Fallacies*, p. 155. An English translation of *The Myth of the Twentieth Century* is available from Ostara Publications, a white supremacist site that reprints various books that support their ideology. My advice is to try inter-library loan or buy a used copy.

64 Evans, *Third Reich in Power*, pp. 249–52 and 256–8; *Hitler's Secret Conversations*, p. 342; Manfred Gailus, 'A Strange Obsession with Nazi Christianity: A Critical Comment on Richard Steigmann-Gall's *The Holy Reich*', *Journal of Contemporary History*, XLII (January 2007), pp. 166–72, 183, 186 and 194; Hexham, 'Inventing "Paganists"', pp. 65–8 and 75.

65 Kurlander, *Hitler's Monsters*, pp. 200–201; Luhrssen, *Hammer of the Gods*, pp. 162–3 and 166–7; and Hexham, 'Inventing Paganists', pp. 72–3, quote on p. 72.

66 Lewis Spence, *Occult Causes of the War* (London, 1940); Mosse, *Crisis of German Ideology*; and Alan Bullock, *Hitler: A Study in Tyranny* (New York, 1962).

67 Louis Pauwels and Jacques Bergier, *The Morning of the Magicians* (New York, 1964); Trevor Ravenscroft, *The Spear of Destiny: The Occult Power Behind the Spear Which Pierced the Side of Christ* (San Francisco, CA, 1973); Peter Levenda, *Unholy Alliance: A History of Nazi Involvement with the Occult* (New York, 1995, 2nd edn 2002); William Henry, *One Foot in Atlantis: The Secret Occult History of World War II and its Impact on New Age Politics* (Anchorage, AL, 1998); and

Paul Roland, *The Nazis and the Occult: The Dark Forces Unleashed by the Third Reich* (Edison, NJ, 2007), are just a sampling of the lurid and outlandish genre of writings and documentaries about Hitler, Nazis and the occult. Jason Colavito, *The Cult of the Alien Gods: H. P. Lovecraft and Extraterrestrial Pop Culture* (Amherst, NY, 2005), does an excellent job of demonstrating the contribution of Pauwels and Bergier to popularizing pseudo-history in popular culture.

68 Ken Anderson, *Hitler and the Occult* (Amherst, NY, 1995), thoroughly debunks Trevor Ravenscroft's claims about the 'Spear of Destiny' and Nazi attempts to utilize its occult powers. See also Keith Fitzpatrick-Matthews, '"The Spear of Destiny": Hitler, the Hapsburgs and the Holy Grail', at the Bad Archaeology website, https://badarchaeology.wordpress.com, accessed 6 October 2020.

69 Treitel, *Science for the Soul*, pp. 216 and 240.

70 Kurlander, *Hitler's Monsters*, pp. xi, xiv and xv.

71 Ibid., pp. 22–32.

72 Ibid., p. xi.

73 Philip Gibbs, *European Journey* (New York, 1934), pp. 243–6, quote on p. 245, and Julia Boyd, *Travellers in the Third Reich: The Rise of Fascism through the Eyes of Everyday People* (London, 2018), pp. 138–9.

74 Philipp Stelzel, *History after Hitler: A Transatlantic Enterprise* (Philadelphia, PA, 2019), describes the struggles of German historians after 1945 to come to grips with the Nazi era.

75 Hale, *Himmler's Crusade*, p. 31.

6 The Myth of Roswell

1 Martin Gardner, *In the Name of Science: An Entertaining Survey of the High Priests and Cultists of Science, Past and Present* (New York, 1952), and Martin Gardner, *Fads and Fallacies in the Name of Science* (New York, 1957), p. 60. The pagination is the same for both books, except that the 1957 edition added an 'Appendix and Notes' section that comprises pp. 325–55.

2 'Roswell Secrets Unveiled', History Channel, *History's Mysteries*, season 2, episode 12, 1999.

3 See www.cinematreasures.org, accessed 21 March.

4 David Noack, 'Unidentified Flying Newspaper', *Editor and Publisher* (8 August 1997), p. 29.

5 Joyce Ogle, 'Organizers Expect Possible Record Crowds for UFO Festival', *Roswell Daily Record* (26 June 2021), at www.rdrnews.com, and communication from Jim Hill. The rest of this section is based on William P. Barrett, 'Unidentified Flying Dollars', *Forbes* (18 July 1996), pp. 49–53; Toby Smith, *Little Grey Men: Roswell and the Rise of Popular Culture* (Albuquerque, NM, 2000); Thomas W. Paradis, 'The Political Economy of Theme Development in Small Urban Places: The Case of Roswell, New Mexico', *Tourism Geographies*, IV/I (2002), pp. 22–43; 'Aliens Must Have Come from NYC', *Forbes* (23 July 2007), p. 34; Eileen R. Meehan, 'Tourism, Development, and Media', *Society* (2008), pp. 338–41; and Andrew Stuttaford, 'Letter from Roswell: Among the Ufologists', *New Criterion* (March 2018), pp. 28–32.

6 Paradis, 'The Political Economy of Theme Development', pp. 31–2.

7 Leon Jaroff and James Willwerth, 'Did Aliens Really Land?', *Time*, CXLIX/25 (23 June 1997), and Lily Rothman, 'How the Roswell UFO Theory Got Started', www.time.com, 7 July 2015.

8 Jaroff and Willwerth, 'Did Aliens Really Land?'; Paradis, 'The Political Economy of Theme Development', p. 38; and Smith, *Little Grey Men*, p. 56.

9 This section is based on the following accounts: David Michael Jacobs, *The UFO Controversy in America* (Bloomington, IN, 1975), which is a well-researched book that is sympathetic to the UFO movement; Curtis Peebles, *Watch the Skies!: A Chronicle of the Flying Saucer Myth* (Washington, DC, 1994); Benton Saler, Charles A. Ziegler and Charles B. Moore, *UFO Crash at Roswell: The Genesis of a Modern Myth* (Washington, DC, 1997); B. D. 'Duke' Gildenberg, 'A Roswell Requiem', *Skeptic*, X/1 (2003), pp. 60–73; and Donald R. Prothero and Timothy D. Callahan, *UFOs, Chemtrails and Aliens: What Science Says* (Bloomington, IN, 2017).

10 The *Roswell Daily Record* sells facsimiles of the front pages for 8 and 9 July 1947.

11 Gardner, *Fads and Fallacies*, pp. 55–68 and 329–31; Ted Bloecher, *Report on the UFO Wave of 1947* [1967] (2005), section 1, p. 13; Philip J. Klass, *The Real Roswell Crashed-Saucer Coverup* (Amherst, NY, 1997), p. 22; United States Air Force, *The Roswell Report: Fact versus Fiction in the New Mexico Desert* (Washington, DC, 1995); Jacobs, *UFO Controversy in America*, passim; and James McAndrews, *The Roswell Report: Case Closed* [1997] (New York, 2013), passim.

12 Smith, *Little Grey Men*, pp. 7–8.

13 Bloecher, *UFO Wave of 1947*, passim, and Peebles, *Watch the Skies!*, p. 286.

14 Saler, Ziegler and Moore, *UFO Crash at Roswell*, pp. ix and 6–7.

15 According to historian Roger Launius, 'The U.S. Air Force considered the UFO phenomenon significant enough to begin in December 1947 a project to investigate occurrences, especially with a view to learn if "some foreign nation had a form of propulsion possibly nuclear, which is outside our domestic knowledge"' (Lt. Gen. Nathan F. Twining, Commander Air Material Command, to Commanding General, Army Air Forces, 'Flying Discs', 23 September 1947, reprinted in Edward U. Condon, *Final Report of the Scientific Study of Unidentified Flying Objects* (New York, 1969), p. 895; the letter setting up the study is Maj. Gen. L. C. Craigie to Commanding General Wright Field, 'Flying Discs', 30 December 1947, in Condon, *Final Report*, pp. 896–7). Although the researchers recognized the possibility that the UFOs might be extraterrestrial, few thought it was probable and they emphasized more earthly explanations. For instance, the Scientific Advisory Panel of the Central Intelligence Agency considered in January 1953 the UFO issue in the United States. After a lengthy discussion, members of the panel 'concluded that reasonable explanations could be suggested for most sightings'. Moreover, concerning one of the central questions this body had about UFOs, it 'concluded unanimously that there was no evidence of a direct threat to national security in the objects sighted' ('Report of Meetings of Scientific Advisory Panel on Unidentified Flying Objects Convened by Office of Scientific Intelligence, CIA, January 14–18, 1953', copy in 'NACA-UFO, 1948–1958', NASA Historical Reference Collection).

A report released by the Air Force in 1957 reached similar conclusions: 'First, there is no evidence that the "unknowns" were inimical or hostile; second, there is no evidence that these "unknowns" were interplanetary space ships; third, there is no evidence that these "unknowns" represented technological developments or principles outside the range of our present day scientific knowledge; fourth, there is no evidence that these "unknowns" were a threat to the security of the country; and finally there was no physical evidence or material evidence, not even a minute fragment, of a so-called "flying saucer" was ever found' ('Air Force's 10 Year Study of Unidentified Flying Objects', Department of Defense, Office of Public Information, News Release No. 1083-58, 5 November 1957, copy in 'NACA-UFO, 1948–1958', NASA Historical Reference Collection). I thank Dr Launius for graciously providing this information.

16 In *The X-Files*, the eccentric ufologist character, Max Fenig, wears a NICAP hat in the episodes 'Fallen Angel' in season 1 and 'Tempus Fugit' and 'Max' in season 4. They first aired respectively on 19 November 1993, 16 March 1997 and 23 March 1997, long after the demise of NICAP.

17 Daniel Cohen, *The Great Airship Mystery: A UFO of the 1890s* (New York, 1981), p. xi. Anyone who has ever attended an AlienCon or other meeting dealing with fringe knowledge will have observed that professional rivalries between the proponents of various pseudo-historical or pseudoscientific ideas come out when the cameras are not running, but when the cameras are on they close ranks against mainstream scholars.

18 Peebles, *Watch the Skies!*, pp. 93–9, and Ryan T. O'Leary, 'George Adamski', in *UFOs and Popular Culture: An Encyclopedia of Contemporary Myth*, ed. James R. Lewis (Santa Barbara, CA, 2000).

19 Peebles, *Watch the Skies!*, p. 99; Jacobs, *UFO Controversy*, pp. 111–12; and 'Bethurum Contact Claims', in *The UFO Encyclopedia*, 3rd edn, ed. Jerome Clark (Detroit, MI, 2018).

20 Prothero and Callahan, *UFOs*, pp. 287–8; 'Martin Contact Claims', in *The UFO Encyclopedia*; Leon Festinger, Henry W. Rieken and Stanley Schachter, *When Prophecy Fails: A Social and Psychological Study of a Modern Group that Predicted the Destruction of the World* [1956] (Mansfield Center, CT, 2009); Whet Moser, 'Apocalypse Oak Park: Dorothy Martin, the Chicagoan Who Predicted the End of the World and Inspired the Theory of Cognitive Dissonance', *Chicago Magazine*, www.chicagomag.com, 20 May 2011; and Julie Beck, 'The Christmas the Aliens Didn't Come: What a Failed Doomsday Prophecy Taught Psychologists about the Nature of Belief', *Atlantic*, 18 December 2015, www.theatlantic.com. Timothy Jenkins, *Of Flying Saucers and Social Scientists: A Re-Reading of 'When Prophecy Fails' and of Cognitive Dissonance* (New York, 2013), raised some questions about Festinger's methodology and conclusions but failed to undermine the results.

21 The contactee movement may have faded but it did not disappear. Anthony Brooke, who died in 2011 at 98 and was a descendant of Sir James Brooke (who became the Rajah of Sarawak and an heir apparent of the line of White Rajahs), was a believer in visitations by aliens in flying saucers that would bring peace and prosperity to the Earth. See Philip Eade, *Sylvia, Queen of the Headhunters: An Eccentric Englishwoman and her Lost Kingdom* (New York, 2007), pp. 305–6.

22 This section is based on Peebles, *Watch the Skies!*, pp. 225–41, and Prothero and Callahan, *UFOs*, pp. 170–206.

23 Peebles, *Watch the Skies!*, pp. 215–24, and Prothero and Callahan, *UFOs*, pp. 95–9. For an example of someone who believes that alien-human hybrids are infiltrating human society, see David Michael Jacobs, *The Threat* (New York, 1998). Another example of an academic gone wild?

24 Jason Colavito, *The Cult of the Alien Gods: H. P. Lovecraft and Extraterrestrial Pop Culture* (Amherst, NY, 2005). For a brief overview of the von Däniken phenomenon, see Ronald Fritze, *Invented Knowledge: False History, Fake Science and Pseudo-Religions* (London, 2009), pp. 201–10.

25 'W. Raymond Drake', in *The Encyclopedia of Extraterrestrial Encounters: A Definitive A–Z Guide to All Things Alien* (New York, 2001), and for Sitchin, see Fritze, *Invented Knowledge*, pp. 210–14.

26 Pebbles, *Watch the Skies!*, pp. 196–213; Charles A. Ziegler, 'Analysis of the Roswell Myth', in Saler, Ziegler and Moore, *UFO Crash at Roswell*, pp. 66–7.

27 Klass, *Real Roswell*, pp. 24–5.

28 Ibid., pp. 25–7. *UFOs are Real* is available in Amazon Prime under the video title *Flying Saucers are Real*.

29 Stanton T. Friedman and William L. Moore, 'The Roswell Incident: Beginning of the Cosmic Watergate', in *The Hidden Evidence: 1981 MUFON UFO Symposium Proceedings* (Seguin, TX, 1981), pp. 136–7, and Charles A. Ziegler, 'Analysis of the Roswell Myth', in Saler, Ziegler and Moore, *UFO Crash at Roswell*, p. 63; Robert Alan Goldberg, *Enemies Within: The Culture of Conspiracy in Modern America* (New Haven, CT, and London, 2001), pp. 195–6 and 283 n. 14; and Charles Berlitz and William L. Moore, *The Roswell Incident* (New York, 1980), pp. 42, 62, 73, 98 and 154.

30 'UFO Cover-ups', *In Search of . . .*, season 5, episode 1.

31 Berlitz and Moore, *Roswell Incident*, pp. 53–103.

32 Charles Ziegler, 'Mythogenesis', in Saler, Ziegler and Moore, *UFO Crash at Roswell*, pp. 18–19.

33 Kevin D. Randle and Donald R. Schmitt, *UFO Crash at Roswell* (New York, 1991), and Ziegler, 'Mythogenesis', pp. 19–21.

34 Randle and Schmitt, *UFO Crash at Roswell*, pp. 272–81, and Karl T. Pflock, *Roswell in Perspective* (Washington, DC, 1994), pp. 175–7.

35 'Roswell', *Unsolved Mysteries: The UFO Files*, season 2, episode 1, www.imdb.org.

36 See *Roswell* (1994) at www.imdb.com. The description of the plot in this paragraph and the next is mine.

37 'Mysteries of Alien Beings', *Unsolved Mysteries*, season 6, episode 32. See www.imdb.com.

38 Stanton T. Friedman and Don Berliner, *Crash at Corona: The United States Military Retrieval and Cover-Up of a UFO* (New York, 1992), and Ziegler, 'Mythogenesis', pp. 21–4.

39 Kevin D. Randle and Donald R. Schmitt, *The Truth about the UFO Crash at Roswell* (New York, 1994), and Ziegler, 'Mythogenesis', pp. 24–6.

40 Pflock, *Roswell in Perspective*, passim but especially pp. 113–17, and Ziegler, 'Mythogenesis', p. 26–9.

41 Philip J. Corso and William J. Birnes, *The Day after Roswell* (New York, 1997), pp. 31–6.

42 Ibid., pp. 60–69 and 79–82. Ley fled Germany in January 1935, which would have been very early in the Nazi regime.

43 Corso and Birnes, *Day after Roswell*, pp. 125–6, 144, 173, and Chapters 13, 15 and 16.

44 Ibid., p. 288.

45 Ibid., pp. 40, 51–2 and 70.

46 Ibid., Chapters 9–11, 14, 16 and 17. See especially pp. 134–5, 157, 284–5 and 291–5. Like many pro-UFO books, *The Day after Roswell* does not have some of the usual items found in books. It lacks an index and even a table of contents, which makes taking detailed notes essential. There are, of course, no notes or bibliography.

47 Prothero and Callahan, *UFOs*, p. 71; John B. Alexander, *UFOs: Myths, Conspiracies and Realities* (New York, 2011), pp. 40–50 and 289–98. The latter pages are a transcript of Alexander's 9 September 1994 letter with queries to Corso;

Karl T. Pflock, *Roswell: Inconvenient Facts and the Will to Believe* (Amherst, NY, 2001), pp. 203–8, with the Hoover quote on p. 208; Goldberg, *Enemies Within*, pp. 226–7.

48 Jacobs, UFO *Controversy*, pp. 38, 58–9 and 108–31; Peebles, *Watch the Skies!*, pp. 12–15, 47–50, 67–71 and 93–108; and Mikael Rothstein, 'Contactees', in UFOs *and Popular Culture*, pp. 86–91.

49 The four articles are 'Crash of the Crashed Saucer Claim' (1986); 'The MJ-12 Crashed Saucer Documents' (1987–8); 'The MJ-12 Papers: Part 2' (1989); and the 'New Evidence of MJ-12 Hoax' (1990); they can be found on the website for *Skeptical Inquirer* and are all reprinted in Kendrick Frazier, ed., *The Hundredth Monkey and Other Paradigms of the Paranormal: A Skeptical Inquirer Collection* (Buffalo, NY, 1991), pp. 327–52. *The X-Files* during its sixth season had a two-part episode, 'Dreamland', in which Mulder and Scully have an encounter at Area 51 with a Majestic agent, the slacker and philanderer Morris Fletcher, which aired on 29 November and 6 December 1998. It sends up Majestic and its Men in Black as just another federal bureaucracy and a not particularly effective one.

50 Peebles, *Watch the Skies!*, passim but especially pp. 245–54, and Prothero and Callahan, UFOs, pp. 138, 171 and 180–81.

51 Pflock, *Roswell in Perspective*, and Air Force, *Roswell Report*.

52 Saler, Ziegler and Moore, UFO *Crash at Roswell*, pp. 1, 34 and 62.

53 Ibid., Chapters 2, 4 and 5, especially pp. 32–44, 52–7 and 60.

54 Klass, *Real Roswell*; and Kal K. Korff, *The Roswell* UFO *Crash: What They Don't Want You to Know* (Amherst, NY, 1997).

55 Karl T. Pflock, *Roswell: Inconvenient Facts and the Will to Believe* (Amherst, NY, 2001), and Karl T. Pflock and James W. Moseley, *Shockingly Close to the Truth! Confessions of a Grave-Robbing Ufologist* (Amherst, NY, 2002).

56 See www.kalisanidiot.blogspot.com, accessed 21 March 2021.

57 Klass, *Real Roswell*, pp. 71–82; Korff, *Roswell* UFO *Crash*, pp. 78–81; and Pflock, *Roswell: Inconvenient Facts*, pp. 118–20.

58 Paul McCarthy, 'The Missing Nurses of Roswell', *Omni* (Autumn 1995), available at the Roswell Files website, www.roswellfiles.com.

59 Klass, *Real Roswell*, pp. 151–9 and 187–96; Korff, *Roswell* UFO *Crash*, pp. 86–91; and Pflock, *Roswell: Inconvenient Facts*, pp. 127–42.

60 Klass, *Real Roswell*, pp. 105–9 and 197–203; Korff, *Roswell* UFO *Crash*, pp. 95–8; and Pflock, *Roswell: Inconvenient Facts*, pp. 67–84.

61 Klass, *Real Roswell*, pp. 97–101, and Randle and Schmitt, *Truth about* UFO *Crash at Roswell*, pp. 3–4, 8–10, 13, 173 and 196–7.

62 Klass, *Real Roswell*, pp. 144–50; Korff, *Roswell* UFO *Crash*, pp. 99–100; Pflock, *Roswell: Inconvenient Facts*, pp. 51–7, 59–60 and 171–2, with Ragsdale's two affidavits on 27 January 1993 and 15 April 1993 reproduced on pp. 272–4. See also Kevin D. Randle, *The Randle Report:* UFOs *in the '90s* (New York, 1997), pp. 163–77 and 207–8.

63 It was later renamed the J. Allen Hynek Center for UFO Studies after his death in 1986.

64 Mark O. Connell, *The Close Encounters Man: How One Man Made the World Believe in* UFOs (New York, 2017).

65 'Kevin Randle and Donald Schmitt', www.roswellfiles.com, accessed 21 March 2021, and Kevin D. Randle, *The Roswell Encyclopedia* (New York, 2000), pp. 307–8 and 346–7.

66 Klass, *Real Roswell*, pp. 151–4; Pflock, *Roswell*, pp. 179–80; 'Kevin Randle and Donald Schmitt'; and Randle, *Roswell Encyclopedia*, pp. 309–10 and 347–50.

67 Klass, *Real Roswell*, pp. 154–9; Pflock, *Roswell*, pp. 131–2 and 181; Randle, *Roswell Encyclopedia*, pp. 350–51; McCarthy, 'Missing Nurses of Roswell', and Robert G. Todd, 'Randle Dumps – And Dumps – on – Schmitt', *Cowflop Alert* (22 September 1995), at www.roswellfiles.com.

68 'Roswell: Secrets Unveiled', *History's Mysteries* (1999).

69 Gildenberg, 'Roswell Requiem', pp. 60–73, and Pflock, *Roswell: Inconvenient Facts*, p. 179.

70 Prothero and Callahan, *UFOs*, pp. 311.

71 Peter Biskind, *Seeing is Believing: How Hollywood Taught Us to Stop Worrying and Love the Fifties* (New York, 1983), and Patrick Luanio, *Them or Us: Archetypal Interpretations of Fifties Alien Invasion Films* (Bloomington, IN, 1987), provide the historical and cultural context for the UFO movies. On the other hand, Bruce Rux, *Hollywood vs. the Aliens: The Motion Picture Industry's Participation in UFO Disinformation* (Berkeley, CA, 1997), suggests that the motion picture industry has been assisting with the government's cover-up of UFOs.

72 See Goldberg, *Enemies Within*, p. 215, for Friedman.

73 This and the following paragraphs are based on Annie Jacobsen, *Area 51: An Uncensored History of America's Top Secret Military Base* (New York, 2011), pp. 15–18, 36–7, 39–44, 268, 370–74 and 380.

74 Dave Gilson, 'Area 51 and Roswell: The Craziest Theory Yet', *Mother Jones*, www.motherjones.com, 10 May 2011; Lee Speigel, 'Area 51 Personnel Feel "Betrayed" by Annie Jacobsen's Soviet–Nazi UFO Connection', *Weird News* (6 July 2011, updated 6 December 2017), www.huffpost.com; Alexander, *UFOs*, p. 276; and Prothero and Callahan, *UFOs*, pp. 58–9.

75 Kevin D. Randle, *Roswell in the 21st Century* (Naples, FL, 2016), pp. 228–47, with quote from p. 247. This book shows little to no evidence of having been copy-edited or proofread. The evolution of Randle's ideas can be traced from his 1997 *Randle Report*, *Alien Mysteries: Conspiracies and Cover-Ups* (Detroit, MI, 2013), and *The Government UFO Files: The Conspiracy of Cover-Up* (Detroit, MI, 2014), to *Roswell in the 21st Century*.

76 Donald R. Schmitt and Thomas Carey, *Cover-Up at Roswell: Exposing the 70-Year Conspiracy to Suppress the Truth* (Wayne, NJ, 2017), pp. 133–47, and Pflock, *Roswell: Inconvenient Facts*, pp. 208–10.

77 Steven M. Greer, *Unacknowledged: An Exposé of the World's Greatest Secret* (Afton, VA, 2017). The documentary is available on Amazon Prime.

78 D. W. Pasulka, *American Cosmic: UFOs, Religions, Technology* (New York, 2019), pp. 18–21, 47–50 and 73–7, and James Gallant, 'The Humiliating UFOs', *Raritan*, XXX/4 (Spring 2011), pp. 66–91.

79 Thomas Milan Konda, *Conspiracies of Conspiracies: How Delusions Have Overrun America* (Chicago, IL, 2019), pp. 202 and 207.

80 Michael Barkun, *A Culture of Conspiracy: Apocalyptic Visions in Contemporary America*, 2nd edn (Berkeley, CA, 2013), p. 82.

81 Lydia Saad, 'Americans Sceptical of UFOs, but Say Government Knows More', https://news.gallup.com (6 September 2019), and Anne Merlan, 'Here's Why Gallup Polled Americans about UFOs for the First Time in Decades', www.vice.com, 25 February 2020. Of course, those who make a living promoting fringe knowledge and conspiracies put their spins on the poll's results; see, for example, Tim Binnall, 'New Gallup Poll Finds 68% of Americans Believe There Is a UFO Cover-Up', www.coasttocoastam.com, 6 September 2019, and Jazz Shaw, 'Why Did Gallup Poll Americans about their Beliefs about UFOs?', https://hotair.com, 25 September 2020.

82 For a good critique of David Michael Jacobs's alien abduction theory, see David Brewer, 'The Bizarre World of Doctor David Jacobs: An Interview and Review', *UFO Trail,* at https://ufotrail.blogspot.com, 26 and 29 April and 3 May 2013. The three posts include critiques of Jacobs's research from other scholars along with comments by readers. Back when I had no idea that Jacobs existed, I was corresponding with a historian friend on the faculty at Temple University about pseudo-history and pseudo-historians. He was a colleague of Jacobs's and mentioned the abduction theory: 'He [Jacobs] already had tenure before he announced these views. They destroyed his academic career. He never made full professor' (personal communication, 17 June 2013).

83 Barkun, *Culture of Conspiracy,* pp. xii–xiii, 81 and 83–4, for this paragraph and the two that follow.

84 Max Fisher, 'Why Coronavirus Conspiracy Theories Flourish and Why It Matters', *New York Times,* 9 April 2020, Section A, p. 10, www.nytimes.com, and E. J. Dickson, 'Coronavirus is Spreading – And So Are the Hoaxes and Conspiracy Theories around It', www.rollingstone.com, 18 March 2020.

Conclusion

1 H. L. Mencken, *A Mencken Chrestomathy* [1949] (New York, 1982), p. 616.

2 Adrienne LaFrance, 'The Prophecies of Q', www.theatlantic.com, June 2020; Mike McIntire and Kevin Roose, 'What Happens When QAnon Seeps from the Web to the Offline World', www.nytimes.com, 14 July 2020; Kevin Roose, 'Think QAnon is on the Fringe? So Was the Tea Party', www.nytimes.com, 13 August 2020; and Jane Coaston, 'QAnon, the Scarily Popular Pro-Trump Conspiracy Theory, Explained', www.vox.com, 20 August 2020.

3 Rick Wilson, 'Blame Fox News for the Rise of QAnon', www.thedailybeast.com, 14 August 2020, and Ben Collins and Brandy Zadrozny, 'QAnon Groups Hit by Facebook Crack Down', www.nbcnews.com, 19 August 2020.

4 James Emery White, 'What is QAnon?', www.crosswalk.com, 27 August 2020, and Katelyn Beaty, 'QAnon: The Alternative Religion That's Coming to your Church', www.religionnews.com, 17 August 2020.

5 Joshua Ceballos, 'Here's a List of All the Horrible Shit Laura Loomer Has Said and Done', www.miaminewtimes.com, 24 August 2020; 'Laura Loomer LOSES IT on the Alex Jones Show after Getting Banned from Facebook', www.youtube.com; and Sara Sidner, 'The U.S. Senate Candidate Who Took a QAnon Pledge', www.cnn.com, 22 August 2020.

6 Luke O'Brien, 'Most QAnon Candidates Lost Their Races But 2 Are Heading to Congress', www.huffpost.com, 5 November 2020; Esther Wang, 'Meet the Republican New Guard – The Far Right, QAnon-Fueled Answer to the Squad', www.theslot.jezebel.com, 30 October 2020; Esther Wang, 'The QAnon Congresswomen Who've Threatened the Squad with Physical Violence, Want to Carry Guns at the Capitol', www.msn.com, 24 November 2020; and Justin Wingerter, 'Congressional Candidate Lauren Boebert Has a History of Minor Arrests, Court No-Shows', www.denverpost.com, 13 October 2020.

7 James Anderson and Nicholas Riccardi, 'A Fluke or the Future? Boebert Shakes Up Colorado', Associated Press, www.apnews.com, 6 February 2021; Roger Sollenberger, 'Biker Group gave Rep. Lauren Boebert a Glock with Congressioanal Seal – Likely an Illegal Gift', www.salon.com, 25 January 2021; and Andrea Salcedo, 'GOP Rep. Lauren Boebert Gave a Tour to "Large"

Group Before the Riots, Democratic Lawmaker Says', www.washingtonpost. com, 19 January 2021.

8 Rachel E. Greenspan, 'Rep. Marjorie Taylor Greene's History of Spreading Bizarre Conspiracy Theories from Space Lasers to Frazzledrip', Business Insider, www.businessinsider.com.au, 5 February 2021; Reed Richardson, 'QAnon GOP Rep. Marjorie Taylor Greene Supported Calls to Assassinate Dems, Proposed Executing Pelosi for Treason', Mediaite, www.mediaite.com, 26 January 2021; 'Marjorie Taylor Greene', www.wikipedia.org which is good for up-to-date biographical information is used in this and the following paragraphs. Her official site can be found at www.greene.house.gov. Also see, 'Marjorie Taylor Greene: 5 Fast Facts You Need to Know', www.heavycom. This site was posted before Greene's election to Congress. If it were updated there would undoubtedly more 'Fast Facts' that people want to know.

9 Amanda Terkel, 'At least 9 GOP Lawmakers Refused to Wear Masks During Capitol Lockdown', HuffPost, www.huffpost.com, 12 January 2021.

10 John Kenneth White, 'In Marjorie Taylor Greene, A Glimpse of the Future', The Hill, www.msn.com, 5 February 2021.

11 Matthew Rosenberg, 'How Republican Voters Took QAnon Mainstream', www.nytimes.com, 10 November 2020; Will Somer, 'The GOP's QAnon Faction Is Waging War on Republicans', www.thedailybeast.com, 5 December 2020; and Cade Metz, 'Study Considers a Link between QAnon and Polling Errors', www.nytimes.com, 6 November 2020.

12 Kevin Rose, 'QAnon Followers Are Hijacking the #SaveTheChildren Movement', www. nytimes.com, 12 August 2020.

13 '2021 Storming of the United States Capitol', www.wikipedia.com, accessed May 2021, and George Petras, Janet Loehrke, Ramon Padilla, Javier Zarracina and Jennifer Borresen, 'Timeline: How the Storming of the U.S. Capitol Unfolded on Jan. 6', *USA Today*, www.usatoday.com, 9 February 2021.

14 Reality Check team, 'Capitol Riots: Who Broke Into the Building?', Reality Check Team, BBC, www.bbc.com/news, 7 January 2021, and Kathryn Kranhold, 'Social Media in 2020: A Year of Misinformation and Disinformation', *Wall Street Journal*, www.wsj.com, 11 December 2020.

15 Tammy Beer, 'FBI: No Evidence Antifa Involved in Capitol Chaos', *Forbes*, www.forbes.com, 8 January 2021; 'No, FBI Didn't Confirm Antifa Activists Breached Capitol', *PolitiFact* (8 June 2021), www.politifact.com, with a list of sources; Aleszu Bajak and Javier Zarracina, 'How the Antifa Conspiracy Theory Traveled from the Fringe to the Floor of Congress', *USA Today*, www. usatoday.com, 13 January 2021; Mike Adams, 'Breaking: After the Staged "Storming" False Flag Event, Congress to Reconvene Tonight and Finish Its Final Act of Betrayal Against America, Under the Cloak of Darkness', www. falseflag.news, 6 January 2021; and 'No, the Storming of the Capitol Wasn't a False Flag', *PolitiFact*, www.politifact.com, 7 January 2021.

16 Jim Vorel, 'An Epic Timeline of QAnon Delusions from Election Day to Inauguration Day', *Paste,* www.pastemagazine.com, 20 January 2021, provides a useful guide to shifting QAnon prophecies and posts that appeared during the weeks from 3 November 2020 to 20 January 2021. My wife and I had our own encounter with QAnon ideas on the night of 15 January. Our neighbour, who lives townhouses down from us, is a registered nurse and is a friend, good neighbour and seemingly normal. I was down in the basement moving between study and den as the spirit moved me. I came upstairs to discover my wife having a conversation with her on speakerphone. Our neighbour was

warning her to get the cars filled up with gasoline and stock up on groceries
and bottled water the next day, which was a Saturday, because after that it
might be too late. Apparently, the electricity was going to be off for a while
and the phones and Internet would be down as well. Stores would be closed.
This event would occur on the following Sunday, Monday or Tuesday before
the scheduled inauguration on Wednesday, 20 January. The end result would
be that Trump would remain president when the dust settled in a few days.
She did not call it the Storm, but to all intents and purposes she was describing the Storm. It was unclear what her sources of information were, but she
claimed that her son, who worked in some company located in the Huntsville,
Alabama, research park or for the Redstone Arsenal, had confirmed it and
his employer had offered shelter in their offices. This conversation took about
an hour and I wish my wife had recorded it. Our neighbour also claimed
that all the people further down the street believed it too. A few might have
been believers, but I suspect that most simply made non-committal noises
that were taken to be agreement. Every morning my wife and I got up and
commented that the power was still on. And by 20 January, as we all now
know, Q's record of failed prophecy remained unbroken.

17 David Klepper, 'Checked By Reality, Some Qanon Supporters Seek a Way
Out', Associated Press, www.ap.org, 29 January 2021. There are interviews
of former QAnon supporters recanting the conspiracy and explaining why
they first believed and why they stopped. Posts and interviews by Ashley
Vanderbilt are particularly informative. QAnon has ripped apart families as
well: see Jane Lytvynenko, 'Friends and Family Members of QAnon Believers
Are Going Through A "Surreal Goddamn Nightmare"', BuzzFeed News,
www.buzzfeednews.com, 18 September 2020; www.buzzreednews.com; Leon
Festinger, Henry W. Riecken and Stanley Schachter, *When Prophecy Fails: A
Social and Psychological Study of a Modern Group that Predicted the Destruction
of the World* [1956] (Mansfield Center, CT, 2009) and Ewan Palmer, 'Why
QAnon Followers Think Donald Trump Will Be Sworn Back in as President
on March 4', *Newsweek,* www.newsweek.com, 8 February 2021.

18 Will Sommer, 'QAnon Lost and Confused After Trump's Election Show-
ing', www.thedailybeast.com, 7 November 2020; Tom Porter, 'An Attorney
Leading Trump's Attempt to Subvert the Election is a Longtime QAnon
Supporter', www.businessinsider.com.au, 20 November 2020; Manu Raju and
Sam Fossum, 'Trump Praised QAnon During Meeting About Keeping the
Senate', www.msn.com, 3 December 2020; Ben Collins and Brandy Zadrozny,
'QAnon Group Hit by Facebook Crack Down', www.nbcnews.com, 19 August
2020; Shayan Sardarizadeh, 'What's Behind the Rise of QAnon in the UK?'
www.bbc.com, 19 October 2020; and Katrin Bennhold, 'QAnon is Thriving in
Germany: The Extreme Right is Delighted', *New York Times,* www.nytimes.
com, 11 October 2020.

19 Norman Cohn, *The Pursuit of the Millennium: Revolutionary Millenarians and
Mystical Anarchists of the Middle Ages* [1957] (New York, 1970), pp. 281–6.

Select Bibliography

Adair, James, *The History of the American Indians*, ed. and intro. Kathryn E. Holland Braund (Tuscaloosa, AL, 2005)

Barber, Malcolm, *The New Knighthood: A History of the Order of the Temple* (Cambridge, 1994)

Barkun, Michael, *A Culture of Conspiracy: Apocalyptic Visions in Contemporary America*, 2nd edn (Berkeley, CA, 2013)

Barruel, Augustin, *Memoirs Illustrating the History of Jacobinism*, intro. Stanley L. Jaki [1798] (Fraser, MI, 1995)

Ben-Dor Benite, Zvi, *The Ten Lost Tribes: A World History* (Oxford, 2009)

Ben Israel, Menasseh, *The Hope of Israel*, ed. and intro. Henry Méchoulan and Gérard Nahon [1987] (Liverpool, 2004)

Clark, Jerome, *The UFO Encyclopedia: The Phenomenon from the Beginning*, 3rd edn (Detroit, MI, 2018)

Cohn, Norman, *Warrant for Genocide: The Myth of the Jewish World Conspiracy and the 'Protocols of the Elders of Zion'* [1967] (London, 1996)

Colavito, Jason, *The Cult of the Alien Gods: H. P. Lovecraft and Extraterrestrial Pop Culture* (Amherst, NY, 2005)

Denzler, Brenda, *The Lure of the Edge: Scientific Passions, Religious Beliefs, and the Pursuit of UFOs* (Los Angeles, CA, 2001)

Festinger, Leon, Henry W. Riecken and Stanley Schachter, *When Prophecy Fails: A Social and Psychological Study of a Modern Group that Predicted the Destruction of the World* [1956] (Mansfield Center, CT, 2009)

Frale, Barbara, *The Templars: The Secret History Revealed* (New York, 2009)

Gardner, Martin, *Fads and Fallacies in the Name of Science* (New York, 1957)

Godbey, Allen H., *The Lost Tribes a Myth – Suggestions towards Rewriting Hebrew History* (Durham, NC, 1930)

Goodrick-Clarke, Nicholas, *The Occult Roots of Nazism: Secret Aryan Cults and their Influence on Nazi Ideology; The Ariosophists of Austria and Germany, 1890–1933* [1985] (New York, 1992)

Haag, Michael, *The Templars: The History and the Myth* (New York, 2009)

Hale, Christopher, *Himmler's Crusade: The Nazi Expeditions to Find the Origins of the Aryan Race* [2003] (Edison, NJ, 2006)

Jacobs, David Michael, *The UFO Controversy in America* (Bloomington, IN, 1975)

Jacoby, Susan, *The Age of American Unreason* (New York, 2008)

Konda, Thomas Milan, *Conspiracies of Conspiracies: How Delusions Have Overrun America* (Chicago, IL, 2019)

Kurlander, Eric, *Hitler's Monsters: A Supernatural History of the Third Reich* (New Haven, CT, and London, 2017)

McIntosh, Christopher, *The Rosicrucians: The History, Mythology, and Rituals of an Esoteric Order* (San Francisco, CA, 1998)

Mosse, George L., *The Crisis of German Ideology: Intellectual Origins of the Third Reich* (New York, 1964)

Nichols, Tom, *The Death of Expertise: The Campaign against Established Knowledge and Why It Matters* (New York, 2017)

Olmsted, Kathryn S., *Real Enemies: Conspiracy Theories and American Democracy, World War I to 9/11* (Oxford, 2009)

Parfitt, Tudor, *The Lost Tribes of Israel: The History of a Myth* (London, 2003)

Partner, Peter, *The Knights Templar and Their Myth* [1987] (Rochester, NY, 1990)

Peebles, Curtis, *Watch the Skies! A Chronicle of the Flying Saucer Myth* (Washington, DC, 1994)

Pigliucci, Massimo, *Nonsense on Stilts: How to Tell Science from Bunk*, 2nd edn (Chicago, IL, 2018)

Pringle, Heather, *The Master Plan: Himmler's Scholars and the Holocaust* (New York, 2006)

Prothero, Donald R., and Timothy D. Callahan, *UFOs, Chemtrails, and Aliens: What Science Says* (Bloomington, IN, 2017)

Roberts, J. M., *The Mythology of the Secret Societies* [1972] (London, 2008)

Robertson, David G., *UFOs, Conspiracy Theories and the New Age: Millennial Conspiracism* (London, 2017)

Saler, Benson, Charles A. Ziegler and Charles B. Moore, *UFO Crash at Roswell: The Genesis of a Modern Myth* (Washington, DC, 1997)

Scholem, Gershom, *Sabbatai Sevi: The Mystical Messiah, 1626–1676* (Princeton, NJ, 1973)

Shermer, Michael, *The Believing Brain: From Ghosts and Gods to Politics and Conspiracies – How We Construct Beliefs and Reinforce Them as Truths* (New York, 2011)

Treital, Corinna, *A Science for the Soul: Occultism and the Genesis of the German Modern* (Baltimore, MD, 2004)

Webb, James, *The Occult Establishment* [1976] (LaSalle, IL, 1988)

—, *The Occult Underground* [1974] (LaSalle, IL, 1990)

Yates, Frances A., *The Rosicrucian Enlightenment* [1972] (New York, 1996)

Ziolkowski, Theodore, *Lure of the Arcane: The Literature of Cult and Conspiracy* (Baltimore, MD, 2013)

Acknowledgements

I began this book in 2016, months before the presidential election in the United States. A lot has changed since then, and the subject of junk knowledge in all its forms is even more relevant. Along the way to completing this book, I received considerable help from friends, colleagues, fellow scholars and students. The staff of the Kares Library of Athens State University have been a tremendous help. A succession of inter-library loan librarians have supplied me with crucial books and articles, often of an esoteric nature. Thank you, Judy Stinnett (retired), Robbie King (retired) and Bethany Bruno. Mary Aquila has provided valuable reference assistance, as has Amber Skantz. Robert Burkhardt, the retired director of the library, has been a good sounding board, and I have enjoyed our book-buying and -selling excursions to Nashville. Lisa Mitten (now retired) and Fatima Mohie-Eldin at *Choice*, knowing my interests, have sent me many books to review that have also proved useful for my research. For that, I am very grateful. Various people have read all or parts of the manuscript and provided much appreciated assistance, advice and suggestions. William Smith, a former student, carefully and heroically read the whole manuscript. Another former student, Haylee Newton, read chapters until her move to Arizona for a teaching job in the midst of the pandemic made her life very busy, but she is doing great. My longtime friends from Clare Hall in Cambridge, Dr Peter Minshall and Dr Lorna Minshall, read almost the whole manuscript with constructively critical eyes. Lorna, in particular, corrected errors and infelicities in my German and Latin translations. Dr Roger Launius, retired from the Smithsonian and an old friend and classmate at Louisiana State University, brought his expertise in the history and pseudo-history of aerospace programmes and made extremely helpful comments and suggestion on the chapter 'The Myth of Roswell'. Dr David Castle, a political scientist and a friend and colleague from my time at Lamar University, also read and commented. My friend and colleague Dr Susan Owen of the psychology department at Athens State University read a number of chapters and most crucially provided an expert critique of my descriptions and discussions of the evolutionary, cognitive and social psychology behind why people believe strange and somewhat preposterous things.

Michael Leaman, the publisher of Reaktion Books, is always supportive and also patient with an author who has missed yet another deadline. Alex Ciobonu and Martha Jay have been great to work with in getting the book ready to make its appearance.

Professor Jeremy Black continues to be a supportive friend and the generous facilitator of the work of other scholars. Finally, I want to express to express my love and gratitude to my wife, Twylia, for once more enduring the writing of another book. She is patient and tolerant of the time I spend on research and writing. We share a love of travel, particularly travel to England. She is the best travelling companion I could hope for – adventurous, tireless, flexible and uncomplaining. And when this pandemic ends or at least moderates, we are going to resume our explorations and adventures.

Index